THE FIVE PERCENTERS

THE FIVE PERCENTERS

Michael Muhammad Knight

ONEWORLD

OXFORD

A Oneworld Book

First published by Oneworld Publications 2007
First published in paperback 2009

Copyright © Michael Muhammad Knight 2007

ISBN 978–1–85168–615–5

Typeset by Jayvee, Trivandrum, India
Cover design by Transmission
Printed and bound in the United States
of America by Thomson-Shore Inc.

Oneworld Publications
185 Banbury Road
Oxford OX2 7AR
England
www.oneworld-publications.com

Contents

Acknowledgements

This work would not have been possible without the trust and cooperation of the Nation of Gods and Earths. At every parliament I encountered Five Percenters that helped my understanding; though I did not catch every person's name, and there would be too many to list here, I value the kindness, respect and hospitality shown to me by this community as a whole. In particular I must extend peace to Allah B, Born Justice Allah, Um Allah, Abu Shahid, First Born ABG, Gykee Mathematics Allah, Beloved Allah, Ja'mella God Allah, Infinite Al'Jaa'Maar-U-Allah, I Majestic Allah, C'BS ALife Allah, Sha-King Cehum Allah, Jura Shaheed Allah, Supreme Understanding Allah, Prince A Cuba, the ciphers of New York, Pittsburgh, Buffalo and Milwaukee, and Gods in the Injustice (New York State Department of Corrections).

After the completion of this book, I was saddened to learn of the passing of First Born Al-Jamel. A beloved elder of the community, Al-Jamel, was kind, thoughtful and generous with his knowledge. Rest in peace.

Peace to Azreal for his teaching, friendship and name; to Intelligent Tarref Allah, for providing my introduction to the Nation; to Allah Supreme God for his extensive time and correspondence. Deep gratitude is also extended to the NGE's video archivist, Rasheen Universal Allah, and Cee Allah at the Allah School in Mecca for their help and generosity. Peace to Akbar Muhammad, international representative for the Honorable Minister Louis Farrakhan, for his assistance.

Peace to the RZA, Raekwon and Sadat X for taking the time to share their perspectives. It was my pleasure and honor to see excerpts from this work included with Lord Jamar's 5% Album; peace and appreciation to Jamar, Chuck Wilson and Jesse Stone at Babygrande Records.

I am deeply grateful to Barry Gottehrer, who not only shared his memories but also provided his personal archive relating to the Gods and Earths. Ted Swedenburg also supplied his collection of NGE materials and court documents. For their time, assistance, advice and encouragement I thank Willieen Jowers, Sid Davidoff, Omar Abdul-Malik, Muhammed Al-Ahari El, Paul Greenhouse, Thomas Cowles, Omid Safi, Yusuf Nuruddin, Anne Campbell, Karl Evanzz, Asra Nomani and Mary Burke at New York.

Much appreciation for Novin Doostdar, Michael Harpley, Kate Smith,

Michael Phillips and everyone at Oneworld Publications. Peace to Basim Usmani for the title "Burning Mosque." Salams and thanks to Aminah McCloud, who reviewed this manuscript.

There is not space here to allow a proper display of gratitude for Laury Silvers, who shared her expertise, read the manuscript at various stages of its development and offered tireless friendship when I could talk about nothing but Five Percenters.

Finally, love and appreciation to my mother, who has put up with too much to not have every book dedicated to her.

List of Plates

Plate 1. Allah "building" at first Universal Parliament. Mount Morris Park, April 30, 1967. From left to right: far left, holding folded jacket under left arm: Ar-Rahiem, who was nicknamed "Ezekiel" for his interest in Ezekiel 3:18. In all black, with black hat: Karriem/Black Messiah. To his left, in jacket with hands folded in front of him: Ebeka. Left of Ebeka: Sha Sha. In white jacket and white shirt, hand on hip: Gykee's younger brother Sincere. Behind Sincere in distance, wearing black hat, buttoned black sweater and collared shirt: Universal Shaamgaudd.

Plate 2. Allah with Five Percenters on Seventh Avenue. The youths in matching "crowns" are Barkim, one of the earliest white Five Percenters, and Sha Sha. In front of Barkim are his sister Mecca and younger brother Dihoo. Behind Barkim is Kiheem. Between Sha Sha and Allah, with his back to the camera stands Ra'jab, Allah's "Supreme Investigator."

Plate 3. Front row: Al-Jabbar/Prince, Justice, Uhura, Obey. Back row: Bahar, Yamuse.

Plate 4. Justice, Allah and "Young Akbar" at Mount Morris Park.

Plate 5. Allah in front row at parliament. To his left sit Mecca and Guvasia from the First Born Earths. The child in the center is Harmeen, son of Hasheem. Standing with their backs to the camera are Uhura and Karriem/Black Messiah.

Plate 6. Allah and Barry Gottehrer outside the Glamour Inn.

Plate 7. Allah, Makeba, Barry Gottehrer with Abu Shahid's son "Little Shahid," Omala, unknown.

Plate 8. Allah in NOI: young Muslim with *Muhammad Speaks* newspaper, Harlem, early 1960s. Behind him stands Clarence 13X.

Plate 9. Medina Gods at the street academy: Gykee, Hasheem, Akim and Waleak/Knowledge God, 1967.

Plate 10. Uhura, Allah and Karriem/Black Messiah.

Introduction

The first time I heard of the Five Percenters was during a trip to Pakistan, where I studied Islam at Faisal Mosque in Islamabad. I was joined there by a dear friend, a Jamaican-American convert who had volunteered back home in Rochester, New York as a Muslim chaplain in juvenile detention centers. One evening, while walking through the F-10 Markaz, he told me of his encounters with black teenagers who believed that they were gods.

According to my friend, they based their beliefs on the memorization and application of astronomical data, such as the circumference of the earth and the earth's distance from the sun. These young men even considered themselves to be suns, and referred to their girlfriends as earths. My friend told me that this group—known alternately as the Five Percent Nation, or Nation of Gods and Earths—had originated as a subsect of the Nation of Islam.

I already knew about the Nation; like many American Muslim converts, my introduction to Islam was Malcolm X, who joined the Nation while in prison in the 1940s and later rose to fame as its national minister. But that night in Islamabad, I was not ready to look seriously at the Nation of Islam or any group that sprang from it, less for my whiteness than my Sunni orthodoxy. As a Muslim it was hard for me to look at the Nation as a tradition that stood on its own; at first glance, it appeared to be only a corrupt deviation of my faith.

The Nation of Islam was founded by a man known by over fifty names, most commonly W. D. Fard, who arrived in Detroit on July 4, 1930. He walked through the most impoverished black ghettos of post-depression Detroit, claiming that he had come from Mecca to rescue his "uncle," the black man, from the devil's rule. He did as good a job as any of explaining the presence of evil and injustice in Detroit, or Chicago, or New York or the deep south: the devil was the white man.

Fard taught that there was no creator god in the heavens; the god of Abrahamic tradition was only an unseen "mystery god" used by the devil to oppress and manipulate the masses. Rather than search for something that did not exist, preached Fard, the black man should recognize himself as the only true and living God. After a series of run-ins with the police, in 1934 Fard disappeared. A resulting power struggle within the Nation of Islam was won by his chief minister, Elijah Muhammad, who announced that Fard had revealed himself to be Allah. Within the Nation's theology, the word took on a new meaning. As all black men were gods and there was no phantom "mystery god" in the clouds, Muhammad used the title "Allah" to designate Fard as the best knower among his people. The Nation would believe in a succession of Allahs, all of them mortal men. Fard was the last and greatest Allah, having arrived on the brink of Armageddon to destroy the devil. Though Fard had denounced the worship of mystery gods, in his absence he would become one, while Elijah Muhammad's own status was elevated as the Messenger of Allah.

The Nation maintained its teachings through a series of transcribed dialogues between Fard and Elijah Muhammad, in which Fard, the teacher, asked questions of doctrine and his student provided the answers. These exam-style conversations, known as the Supreme Wisdom Lessons, became the Nation's essential scripture. As access was limited only to registered members of the Nation, mastery of these guarded lessons functioned as a process of initiation within the mosque.

By the summer of 1964, the Supreme Wisdom had escaped Elijah Muhammad's mosques, as exiled or attritioned Nation members began sharing them on the streets. The reasons for members' departures were varied; some could not handle the Nation's strict behavioral guidelines, while others grew weary of the intense social and financial pressures that came with membership. In Chicago, many left the Nation due to allegations of Muhammad's infidelity. In New York, Muslims at Mosque No.7 were torn between their belief in the lessons and their respect for Malcolm X, who left the Nation amid bitter political conflicts and later converted to Sunni Islam.

Many former members of the Nation continued their religious lives outside the mosque, maintaining study of the Supreme Wisdom Lessons and even teaching them to non-Muslims, often teenagers and adolescents. Access to the text was no longer reliant on adherence to the Nation's dress codes, puritanical rules of conduct, *Muhammad Speaks* sales quotas and hierarchical chains of command. The truths of the lessons—that the black man was God, the white man Satan—were now provided a more direct line to frustrated black youth in America's major cities.

In Harlem, this amorphous underground gave rise to two notable movements: the Blood Brothers and the Five Percenters. The Blood Brothers achieved notoriety as outcast Nation Muslims that trained local teenagers as foot soldiers in an anti-white street army. One rumor connected the Blood Brothers to Malcolm X, who was asked about the group while in Africa. There was little proof, however, that the Blood Brothers even existed as an actual organization, and many view them as at least semi-fictitious; others see the Blood Brothers as a precursor to the Five Percenters.

The Five Percenter movement began with Clarence 13X Smith, who left the Nation of Islam in 1963 and began teaching the Supreme Wisdom Lessons to Harlem youth. Outside of the mosque, he declared himself to be Allah, an open subversion against W. D. Fard and Elijah Muhammad. Newspaper reporters and city judges, unfamiliar with the word as Smith understood it, would mistake his claim for a psychotic delusion of grandeur.

Early in his career, Allah was often portrayed as a gang leader threatening racial violence. After an incarceration of nearly two years, during which his name was added to J. Edgar Hoover's Security Index, he reemerged as a legitimate community leader whose work with Mayor John Lindsay won him popular acclaim. In the aftermath of Martin Luther King, Jr.'s assassination, Allah was widely credited with helping to curb riots in New York while other cities burned to the ground. In another radical departure from the Nation of Islam, Allah stated that he was "neither pro-black, nor anti-white" and even allowed whites to become Five Percenters.

Allah tried to make peace but still had enemies among Harlem's Muslims, militants and hustlers. Knowing that bad things were on the way, he tried to prepare the youth that adored him for a time when he would not be there. He told his Five Percenters that if they ever wanted to see him, all they had to do was come together, for they were all Allah. He also said that he did not want anyone crying over his death; if he could, he promised, he would slap them for it. On June 13, 1969 Allah was gunned down while on the way to see his estranged wife Dora. The assassination, which remains unsolved, devastated the Five Percenters. Clarence had been their Allah, but he was also something even greater, a father for fatherless young gods. Without him, some fell hard. Others walked away from the movement.

The ones that held on continued to teach, and remnants of the community could be found in housing projects throughout New York. Before long, a new generation of teens was spreading the "knowledge of self," teaching their friends the true nature of the black man. The lessons also spread in city jails and upstate prisons; a state commission would mention Five Percenters as possible key players during the 1971 inmate uprising at Attica. Five Percenters that left New York State took the message with them, and the movement began to develop branches throughout the country, growing to a level that perhaps Allah himself had never dreamed.

Harlem remained the heart of the culture, the Five Percenters' Mecca. In the 1970s and '80s, Allah's movement became a major influence in another New York phenomenon: hip-hop. The Five Percenters' unique terminology and language, having already entered into street slang, impacted an art form that would in turn be consumed by millions. Artists such as Nas, Busta Rhymes, and the Wu-Tang Clan brought the culture to mainstream America, and Five Percenters have now entered popular consciousness. References can even be found in cartoons: in one episode of the nationally syndicated comic strip *Boondocks*, Caesar salutes Huey with the Five Percenter greeting of "Peace, God!"

Though Five Percenters reject association with the religion of Islam, I came to see them as a critically underdocumented chapter in the story of Islam in America. To me, W. D. Fard represented the essence of that story; as an immigrant who brought Islam to African-Americans, he bridged the country's two primary Islamic experiences. Hoping to better comprehend Fard's life and legacy, I sought the perspective of every group influenced by his teachings. I began corresponding with a Five Percenter named Intelligent Tarref Allah, who suggested that I attend the community's upcoming convention, the "Show and Prove" in Harlem. Given the media's common depiction of Five Percenters as a gang of violent racists, at first I was cautious to approach them; but it did not take long to realize that my fears had been misguided. At the Show and Prove, I was embraced warmly and invited to study further, even receiving the same "kindness and sincere hospitality" that Malcolm X had described during his pilgrimage to Mecca. Through the Five Percenters, I became able to engage Fard on a personal level that was previously unavailable, perhaps even finding a place for myself within lessons that were not meant for me.

Not surprisingly, the proper place for a white Five Percenter was important to my understanding; however, my main interest in continuing to study this culture was its rich history. Most of us are used to engaging only belief systems that are already centuries old; we don't expect to have anything close to direct contact with historically significant figures. However, I first came to the Five Percenters just months prior to their fortieth anniversary, and it was still possible to walk with those that walked with Allah. Comparing this community to my own Islamic background, I can say that I spoke with the Five Percenter equivalents of Abu Bakr, Khadija and the honored *sahaba*. As I absorbed stories from elders, the Five Percenter tradition became real to me, no less real or valid than the Islam that I had practiced, and its own sacred history proved just as compelling.

I write this just ten days from attending my third Show and Prove. As the Five Percenters have spread out geographically, the Show and Prove has taken the role of an annual family reunion, but stays true to its original purpose. Scheduled every June on or near the date of Allah's assassination, the Gods and Earths come together to "show and prove" as the lessons say, that "Allah is God. Always has been, always will be."

For a time in New York, there might have been a man or group of men that could boast that he/they killed Allah, unaware that when Allah rolled the dice on his truth against a gun, his truth would win. Whoever pulled the trigger on Clarence Smith is unknown and possibly dead himself; but Allah is alive and cannot die.

1

Mecca

Harlem! The Mecca of the New Negro! My God!
Carl Van Vechten

There is gold in New York.
Elijah Muhammad

The holy places were quiet as I rolled into Harlem early Sunday morning, the sidewalks empty and pull-down iron gates still covering the storefronts. My Brand Nubian tape offered the soundtrack, a clip of a Louis Farrakhan speech set to a looped groove from Marvin Gaye's "T is for Trouble:"

> the poor have been made into slaves
> by those who teach lies
> they don't teach the law
> of cause and effect
> they make the people believe
> when they see it rain
> that a spook is producing it
> but the rain is real
> how then can the cause be unreal?

Elijah said that the ingredients needed to change the weather could be found at any five-and-dime store. Malcolm used to pester him to reveal the ingredients, but the Messenger always refused.

"The ingredients Malcolm sought in the five-and-dime store," writes Amir Fatir, "were within him."

> the bloodsuckers of the poor make you think
> that God is some "Mystery God"
> well,
> the Honorable Elijah Muhammad said to us
> that there is five percent
> who are the Poor Righteous Teachers
> who don't believe the teaching of lies

1

of the ten percent
but this five percent are all-wise and know
who the true and living God is
and they teach that the true and living God
is the son of man
the supreme being
the black man of Asia

The Honorable Minister Farrakhan went on to explain how the Ten Percent—
the rich, the bloodsuckers of the poor, the slavemakers of the poor—have control
over the masses, the Eighty-Five Percent, and turn them against the Poor
Righteous Teachers. *This is how they've been able to kill the prophets, kill their
communities ...*

I parked and walked up Lenox Avenue, Malcolm X Boulevard. On my jacket
I wore a pin of a man's face with the word "ALLAH" underneath. The man on
the pin did not look deliberately holy in any way, no turban or jewel-encrusted
fez or even a beard, just a regular middle-aged black man that you could find
anywhere with a regular jacket and a shirt with a collar. The pin was my pass-
port, showing that I had traveled among the circles that understood. Sometimes it brought me into conversations that normally wouldn't find me. This
morning I was stopped by a black man who wore a big gold ring bearing a star
and crescent—*excuse me, I just noticed that you had that pin on, do you know
who that is?*

"This is the Father," I told him. "This is Allah."

"I know about him," he said. "I built through all of that. It was just interesting, you know, to see a Caucasian with that on. So you've spent time with the
Gods?"

"I go to parliaments."

"And they're okay with you?"

"They've been good to me."

"Who'd you build with over there?"

"I've built with Abu Shahid, First Born ABG, Gykee, Allah B, Um Allah
and Ja'mella, and I got my Supreme Alphabets and Mathematics from
Azreal—"

"You ever read *Sacred Drift*?"

"By Peter Lamborn Wilson?"

"Yes, but his name wasn't really Peter Lamborn Wilson. That was his pen
name. His real name was Hakim Bey."

"Yeah, I've read it."

"I'm a Moor," he explained, a Muslim in the line of Noble Drew Ali. He
asked about my ethnic heritage. Irish, I told him. Then he asked if I knew the

real story of St. Patrick. "The serpents were really Moors," he said. "I don't celebrate St. Patrick's Day, but I commemorate it."

I exchanged *peace* with the Moor and kept walking. Approaching the corner of 116th Street, I spotted the red-brick mosque with bright yellow trim and a giant green bulb of a dome on top. White curtains in the windows veiled the inside but the strength of this place, its heroes and history seeped through the brick and into the street. Malcolm X was once minister here, succeeded by Louis Farrakhan, and some stories have the Father teaching judo in the basement, back when his name was Clarence 13X.

In those days there was no green dome, which now sits where there was once a fourth floor. After Malcolm's assassination the place was bombed out from the top down, with falling chunks of wall crushing fire engines. The dome came as part of a new beginning. During Farrakhan's time it was covered with gold and topped with a crescent, and then Elijah's son took over and threw Farrakhan out and changed everything. Elijah's son took off the crescent and turned the dome green. Now this old Temple No.7 is a Sunni mosque, Masjid Malcolm Shabazz.

Memorial Day, 1965, the Father stood on this corner with a cluster of Harlem youths and tried to grasp all that had gone wrong. Malcolm was dead and the temple lay in ruins. The Father still had a slug lodged in his own chest. He also had these kids, these "Five Percenters" and a creed that Tamar Jacoby says "combined a bit of Islam with a ganglike esprit de corps."[1] A police officer told them to move on. Forty years later, I followed in Allah's footsteps to Seventh Avenue and made my way up the 120 series of streets, arriving at the lean white tower of the Hotel Theresa.

When Harlem was the black Mecca, this might have been its Kaaba, holding in its years the likes of Dizzy Gillespie, Louis Armstrong, Joe Louis, Nat King Cole, Duke Ellington, Ella Fitzgerald and Ray Charles. This was where Malcolm X, Cassius Clay and Sam Cooke became friends. Malcolm and Cassius tried to make a Muslim out of Sam; when he died out in California, Nation of Islam literature was found in his hotel room. In 1960, the same year that John F. Kennedy addressed a campaign rally in front of the Theresa, Fidel Castro took a room here. When Kruschev came to visit, Elijah's Muslims marched outside with signs reading, "there is no god but Allah" so he could go back to Russia and tell his people how America treated the black man.

It was on this sidewalk that pedestrians heard orations from Malcolm, Charles Kenyatta and James "Pork Chop" Davis-Foreman, who'd preach on his stepladder from the 1940s, when he followed Marcus Garvey, all the way to his death in 1987. And on Memorial Day, 1965, this was where the police showed up again and took the Father away, so I wondered why there wasn't a plaque or anything to commemorate it—Adam Clayton Powell had his own building across the street and even a statue in upward stride with his coat flowing behind him like a cape. The Theresa isn't a hotel anymore, the famous marquee is gone and down in front there's a White Castle. All I could do was stand there for a solemn moment and move along.

I passed the Masonic lodge to the next block and spotted the hand-painted emblem of a star-and-crescent and large 7 within an eight-pointed sun, marking the one-story Allah School in Mecca—headquarters of the Five Percenters, Nation of Gods and Earths. They used to call it Allah's Street Academy, but the place has been through more than name changes: legal wars with the city, repeated arson and Gods with good hearts who couldn't shake the demons. The surrounding sidewalk bears witness to its history, with old wet-cement signatures of Gods who have since gone *warra al-shams*, behind the sun. *Prince*, read one square. In the window sat an old framed photograph of the Father with his best friend, Old Man Justice. As I went in I saw a velvet oil painting of Allah in his collared shirt and jacket, and I remembered an old God telling me that the Father was darker than in those portraits—he was what they called a "knowledge seed" of deep black complexion; when he got a lot of sun his skin would almost turn purple and his features seemed to disappear. After the Memorial Day arrest, he'd go nearly two years without sun. Next to his portrait hung a proclamation from the City of New York, dated June 13, 2004, honoring the Five Percenters for their emphasis on strong families and education, along with contributions to the "tremendously rich history in the Harlem community." On the other wall hung a black and white photo of Malcolm X addressing a street rally with his trademark damning finger-point, and it almost looks like he's pointing at the bar across the street, the Wellworth where the Father would stare down a gunman who hoped to shoot his friend West Indian. I took the back door and sat in a chair outside with my tall can of sweet tea. I could see that where I sat used to be part of the building, destroyed during one of the arsons. It looked like the Five Percenters had started renovations—measuring dimensions, raking debris out of the dirt, getting ready to add on again.

An old God, thin and wiry and wearing a tassled skullcap with the word ALLAH across the front, stepped out and looked at me.

"Is that beer?"

"No, no, it's sweet tea." Relieved that I wasn't disrespecting the School, the God introduced himself as Wise Jamel and told me about his history—he came from the First Resurrection back in 1964, he was with the Blood Brothers and then the Suns of Almighty God Allah, who then became the Five Percenters. He received his knowledge from none other than the famous Black Messiah.

I still had some time before the parliament, so I walked up to the corner of 127th and Malcolm X Boulevard and bought a bean pie from the Muslims.

Walked past the current Masjid Muhammad #7 with its bowtie-wearing Fruit
of Islam out in front. One of them noticed my pin of the Father, so I greeted
him with "peace" and received the same in reply. I crossed over to Seventh and
ate my bean pie on a playground at the St. Nicholas projects.

On the corner of 127th and Eighth I stopped and listened to a gray-bearded
black streetcorner-preacher in suit and tie and cowboy hat, shouting at the top
of his voice in the tradition of Pork Chop:

> "I COULDN'T SAVE MY MOTHER, I COULDN'T SAVE NOBODY! GOD
> PUT ME ON THIS CORNER—"

I headed back down toward the Harriet Tubman School, where the Five
Percenters had been holding parliaments since Mayor John Lindsay gave them
authorization nearly forty years before.

With my blue eyes I stick out like a sore thumb at parliaments, which is usually a good thing because Gods love to share knowledge and speak for their
Nation. Some Gods are naturally suspicious, less for my being white than being
a writer; they have been screwed enough times in arenas of public opinion.

I keep waiting for some justification of what I've heard and read: *security
threat, hate group, racists, dope dealers, cop killers, snipers, militant rappers, radical black terrorists*—but it never comes. Gods introduce themselves and build
with me a little, just to see what I know and make sure I'm coming from a good
place. They're quick to get the important issues out of the way. You know we're
not a gang, right? And you know that we're not Muslims? And we're neither
pro-black, nor anti-white?

One such exchange turned into a minor event, with a circle of Gods surrounding us on the sidewalk in front of the Harriet Tubman. The God with
whom I had been building reached into his bag, pulled out a xeroxed zine and
flipped through the pages to find a photograph of the Father standing next to a
white man. "You see this man?" he asked. "This was Barry Gottehrer, he
worked for the mayor, he was the mayor's man. Look at his face, he doesn't
hate the Father! He's not looking at the Father like the Father is anti-white!" He
was right. Forty years later, Mr. Gottehrer was still firmly supporting the Five
Percenters and had come to their defense on more than one occasion. "We
believe in teaching all human families of the planet earth," said the God.

"That's peace," I told him.

"Did you tell him that we're not anti-white?" asked a middle-aged God in a
Kangol hat.

"That was the first thing I told him." By the end of the dialogue, we were
exchanging phone numbers. The Five Percenters have always been respectful

to me, and the ones that I found most gracious were usually older Gods that actually knew the Father, which should say something.

After going through the security God at the door I walked past the various tables peddling Five Percenter newspapers, bootleg movies, books and shirts and spotted familiar faces among the regulars. I had been to enough parliaments for many Gods to know who I was, and I could receive warm greetings of peace from members of what the FBI had labeled a racist hate-gang in the 1960s. I went into the auditorium, where children rehearsed an African dance routine with their teacher on stage. There were only a few of us in the audience but as soon as the Wisdom hour came, an MTA driver still in his work jacket came up and started the parliament. The kids quieted down and got off the stage. The God addressed the phrase "word is bond" being thrown around too much. "If you're true and just," he announced, "your word is bond whether you say it or not!" He spoke on the devil putting himself deep in the holy land, Iraq, and said that we had a holy land too. "I'm not just talking about Mecca, I'm talking about *your* Mecca: *you.*" He explained that he didn't like Gods using the N-word or trying to change its meaning, "like making S-H-I-T smell good—why try to graft the devil back into the Original Man?" Gods and Earths began to filter in and take their seats. The God described Memorial Day as honoring "those that died for you to not be ruled by someone else." There's nothing wrong with joining the military, he said, though he wouldn't advise his own sons to do so in this day and time. And the Father himself was in the army, decorated with a Combat Infantryman's Badge, Korean Service Medal with one Bronze Service Star, Presidential Unit Citation (Republic of Korea), United Nations Service Medal and National Defense Service Medal.

When the Father stood by himself, said the God, people hated him and said, "if he stands too long, we're going to plot on his death." Same with Malcolm, same with Martin. The God quoted Marcus Garvey—"up you mighty nation, you can accomplish what you will."

After the God relinquished the floor, Ja'mella came and spoke. Ja'mella's time with the Five Percenters goes back to 1967 in Crown Heights, Brooklyn, which had been renamed Kusa Heights after the first God to teach there. Today Ja'mella stands tall as a respected leader in the Five Percent, and when he refers to Allah not as *the* but *my* Father, you get a sense of what the man meant to kids in his time and why they taught their own babies—who had never seen him beyond the Allah School's portrait and maybe wouldn't understand the world and years in which he lived—to love and revere him so.

Wise Jamel from the First Resurrection came to the front and took his turn, telling Gods not to wear their Universal Flags if they used drugs or disrespected women. It didn't take the God long to get his momentum going and then no one in the world could slow him down—he started getting mad and his hands were going fast, jewelry jingling as he punched at the air like he had three speed-bags in front of him, the tassle flying around his skullcap crown as he built all the way back to 1964—"I REMEMBER THE PAIN! DO YOU REMEMBER THE PAIN, GODS AND EARTHS?"

"Peace, God!" shouted a man from the audience.

"Slow down," said another.

After Wise Jamel, a God named Father Divine took the floor to preach about the hazards of eating beef and the healing powers of marijuana. With no priests or imams, parliaments are loosely structured; anyone can come up and offer his interpretations. One God can endorse cannabis and the next can condemn it, with little in the way of party lines to which everyone must conform. The truth behind this egalitarianism is the Five Percenters' understanding that the black man is God—all black men, without any sort of religiously ordered hierarchy, only a loving respect for elders.

I met up with I Majestic Allah from Pittsburgh and we went to the school cafeteria. I enjoyed building with him partly because he had been raised Muslim; he could not only see where I was coming from, but discuss the Father with Islamic terms like *hadith* and *sunna*. And rather than answer questions with memorized catechism, I Majestic stands among the Gods that build like philosophers. Explaining his beliefs to an outsider, he focuses not on which doctrine is objectively true, but what positive effects an idea or value system can have on its adherent and his community. I noticed the same approach with ABG, one of only two survivors of a unique designation in history: Allah's First Born, said to be the first nine Harlem teenagers to call themselves Five Percenters. ABG was also the first to bring the Father's teachings from Harlem to Brooklyn. "We teach that the Original Man was black," he had told me at another parliament, "and the black woman is the mother of civilization." He reminded me that this was pure science. "Today you can hear it all on the Discovery Channel, but back then, forty years ago, people couldn't say that."

I met the other remaining First Born, Al-Jamel, that day; and he was the last living witness of the Father's arrest.

Al-Jamel's life has been hard. His bones are weakening and his posture's bad; he has to lean back as he walks and requires a cane. It's difficult for him to hold his head up and his chin often rests on his collarbone. He's missing four fingers on his right hand. As he built with me, young Five Percenters would come by and lovingly ask their elder if he needed anything.

Al-Jamel told me about that Memorial Day when he arrived at the Hotel Theresa to find Five Percenters fighting off four precincts—the 25th, 26th,

28th and 32nd. "That means four captains," he told me, "four cars pulling up from different directions, and six officers in each car, with riot gear." Al-Jamel spent a full year trying to comprehend the scene of cops making the Father fight for his life while others hung out and watched. Then he learned that on the evening of May 31, 1965, Eighth and Lenox Avenues had been closed off for the whole 120 series of streets. Al-Jamel took my notebook and marker and drew a map showing the directions from which the various precincts would have come. On Seventh Avenue he wrote, "KILL ZONE."

From there he built for me on J. Edgar Hoover and COINTELPRO and the federal government's record of crushing movements like the American Communist Party and the Black Panthers. They tried to destroy the Five Percenters, said Al-Jamel, "but they attacked us from the wrong perspective. They thought we were a political organization—they had a good record of destroying political organizations. But they realized by the late '70s, they failed—" That was when Five Percenter references began appearing in the nascent culture of hip-hop.

Al-Jamel told stories like my grandfather, easily wandering from one topic to another and bringing it all together by the end. He told me how he studied Mao Tse-Tung and read about oppressed peoples all over the world, worked with the Black Panthers, Young Lords, Adam Clayton Powell, various churches and David Dinkins and talked with one of Malcolm's sisters about reopening the OAAU. Then he built on how he used to work downtown for a messenger/courier service, and he was on his way out the door to go to work on September 11th when the announcement came that a plane crashed into the World Trade Center.

"I felt so bad for those people," he said. "They were maintenance people, security, receptionists. That's horrible! They weren't in no war. That's insanity."

He reminded me that the Father wasn't anti-white. "You know your background," he explained. "We don't know ours." Then he said that back in his Muslim years, the Father would go to Chicago for Savior's Day conventions. He told me that Malcolm and the Father were both in Temple No.7 together, and encountered the same problem: "when you have corruption above, you have problems below." The assassinations of Malcolm X and the Father went down only miles apart.

The Five Percenters describe their value system as a culture, not a religion. It makes sense if you spend time at parliaments, which often carry an atmosphere closer to family reunions than a Sunday mass or Friday *jum'aa*. Allah's portrait just gives you a loving Father without any of the cultish power of a Fard or Elijah. It's not there to awe anyone, only to remind those present how they first came together.

"I miss him," said Al-Jamel. "I miss him a lot."

2

Desert Fathers

I walked to the Arab-owned store on the corner of 127th and Eighth, where a middle-aged Five Percenter strolled in with his shirt bearing the 7 over the star and crescent in an eight-pointed sun.

"What's that?" asked the Arab.

"That's the flag of my nation, the Nation of Gods and Earths." The Arab shook his head like a disapproving parent and asked the Five Percenter about the pin on his shirt. "This is Allah, the Father of my knowledge," replied the God, "who came to teach that man is the living manifestation of Allah and it says that in the Qur'an." The Arab started laughing and his brother joined in from behind the other counter. The Five Percenter announced, "this is why I take my business elsewhere" and walked out. They called out for him as I walked back to the Harriet Tubman.

It is often hard for Muslims to see the Five Percent as anything but a vandalism upon their property, and that a God wouldn't automatically drop his beliefs if only he understood "true" Islam. They scoff at the Five Percenters' understandings of *Allah* and *Islam* to be acronyms for "Arm, Leg, Leg, Arm, Head" and "I, Self Lord And Master," since these are not English but Arabic words. Sunni teenagers mock the Five Percenters on Internet message boards, peppering their discussions with emoticons of smiley-faces rolling their eyes or projectile-vomiting. "The 5% use only 5% of their crummy intellect," writes "Abdullah_1417;" "these turkeys believe in some former heroin addict ... this clown got executed in a elevator shaft in 1969, but he stated that he couldn't die? Hmmmmm that is silly in itself!" In the same thread, "AMuslimForLife," claiming to have an in-depth knowledge of the community due to "years" of study, posts that some Five Percenters "pray to a man." He calls the Nation of Islam and Nation of Gods and Earths "the same beast with a different name," and slights them both as *shirk* (polytheism) and *kufr* (disbelief).

In *Why I am a Muslim*, Asma Gull Hasan refers to the Five Percent as a "rogue, unrecognized branch of Islam." The daughter of HMO warlord Malik Hasan and "Muslims For Bush" founder Seeme Hasan, I'm not sure what she knows about Poor Righteous Teachers. More open-minded Muslims try to reconcile the Nation of Gods and Earths enough to get them under their umbrella, sometimes only for the right to claim Five Percenter rap stars like Busta Rhymes and the Wu-Tang Clan as part of an Islamic American legacy. The hard truth for arrogant online phantoms like Abdullah_1417 and powder-puff cheerleaders like Asma Gull Hasan is that Five Percenters make no claim on their religion—not as an "offshoot" of anything, not as a footnote in the Nation of Islam's history, not as the rappers' Islam or convicts' Islam. "You think some Arabs put together a scheme like that?" Father Divine asked the parliament, "to resurrect the black man in America? The black man's no Muslim. Never has been, never will be." I have never heard of a Five Percenter named Muhammad; if the black man is God, why would he follow a prophet?

The Father had declared a formal and emphatic break from Islam years before his death, but he also encouraged Five Percenters to explore all paths and respect the good efforts of others. Some Gods read the Qur'an and speak of Islam as a "science," but others study Eastern philosophy and practice meditation. One is not more "Five Percenter" than the other. As one God told me, Clarence 13X only called himself Allah because he had come up in a mosque. He could have just as easily found his truth in one of the Nubian Hebrew movements and renamed himself Yahweh. One Five Percenter text even refers to Clarence as Christ. From what I could see, he *was* a kind of American Christ, and his cross was the gun.

The meanings of Islamic terms have also changed, and have in fact become English words. Five Percenters could give a rip about how to spell *Allah* in Arabic letters; Allah came to them speaking their own language, and Allah broke down his name as Arm, Leg, Leg, Arm, Head. Though some reach for parallels with medieval Sufism, the Five Percent Nation remains a distinctly American story. Gods and Earths don't bother with schisms between Abu Bakr and Ali bin Abu Talib; the war that moved them was Elijah vs. Malcolm. Five Percenters that undo American white supremacy by adopting names like Majestic and Divine are taking part in an unwritten and largely unacknowledged American tradition. In the time of slavery, Africans and their descendents—having been stripped of their original names and branded with those of their masters—sometimes gave each other titles denoting pride and power. Names such as King, Prince and Queen, writes Allan D. Austin, were awarded for the "proud but politic way" in which slaves carried themselves.[1] The Gods and Earths stand as heirs to their own line of patriarchs and matriarchs who endured the Bitter Passage, toiled through the Worst Part and made the land holy with their struggle.

Islam's place in the story begins with the transportation of captive black Muslims to the New World, where any traces of African culture would be viewed as threats to white control. The slaveowner opposed rituals and ideas that could unite or inspire, suppressed written communication in languages he did not understand and imposed his religion upon his slaves. "I cannot help thinking that the way I was baptized was not right," recalled Nicholas Said, who was born Mohammed Ali ben Said in West Africa around 1833. "I think that I ought to have known perfectly well the nature of the thing beforehand." Some Muslims clung fiercely to their religion. Guinea-born Bilali Muhammad supervised up to 1,000 slaves and led an African Muslim community on Sapelo Island, Georgia. Preparing against a speculated British raid on the island, Bilali told his master, "I will answer for every Negro of the true faith but not for these Christian dogs of yours." Charles Ball's slave narrative quotes a "man who prayed five times a day" as commenting, "I had never seen white people before; and they appeared to me the ugliest creatures in the world."[2] Over time, syncretism and accommodation absorbed slaves' Islam into their masters' Christianity. An 1860 report from South Carolina mentions a woman known as "Old Lizzy Gray," who believed that "Christ built the first church in Mecca and he grave was da."[3]

Remnants of Islam are recognizable in the Ben Ishmaels of eighteenth-century Kentucky, described by Hugo Prosper Leaming as a tri-racial community formed by "chattel slaves or 'free blacks,' remnants of destroyed Native American nations, and European indentured servants or their landless, despised children."[4] They were named for their first patriarch, Ben Ishmael, which could read as the Arabic *bin Ismail*, "son of Ishmael." Abraham's son Ishmael is commonly regarded as the father of all Arabs, and in a certain sense Muslims (Leaming also speculates that the tribe's name may have derived from *Bani Ismail*, "people of Ishmael"[5]). Ben Ishmael and his wife, the "first queen" Jennie most likely passed away sometime between 1802 and 1810. Their son John then led a mass exodus from the developing slavery state of Kentucky, crossing the Ohio River into lands designated by the Native Americans for eastern tribes that had been all but wiped out. Here the Ben Ishmaels were welcomed.

The tribe practiced polygamy and abstained from alcohol. Around the border of Illinois and Indiana they lived as nomads, following annual migratory routes along a triangle that included towns named Mecca, Mahomet and Morocco. In 1870, family names in Mahomet and the surrounding area included some with what Leaming calls an "oriental flavor:" Osman, Gamel, Pusha, Nebeker, Babb, Manser and Fardy.[6] Little is known of the Ben Ishmaels' religion, but they rejected belief in an afterlife and most attempts from missionaries to Christianize them. In the 1830s the tribe engaged in a brief relationship with the Methodist church, attracted to a preacher's declaration that "good things will come to Christians." It took only a matter of weeks to see through the empty promise. When the preacher asked for testimonials after one church meeting, an elderly Ben Ishmael woman stood and announced, "We all joined and we ben waitin' for good things. We ain't got none yit. I h'ain't had a speck of good butter in my house since that day."[7]

Wherever they wandered, the Ben Ishmaels dwelled on society's fringe, living as unskilled laborers, scavengers, beggars and reputed petty criminals. The rising Eugenics movement, branding the Ben Ishmaels as biological aberrations, offered what Hakim Bey terms "salvation by extermination."[8] Reverend Oscar C. M'Culloch, author of "The Tribe of Ishmael: a Study on Social Degradation," proposed to wipe out the community by cutting off public and private aid, removing Ben Ishmael children from their homes and placing adults in asylums or new "correctional" institutions littering the region. Sterilization began at the Indiana State Reformatory, and in 1907 the state of Indiana passed the world's first compulsory sterilization law.[9] The Ben Ishmaels found it best to disperse into nearby cities like Chicago and Detroit, where a nation of thousands might vanish within the larger society. Subsequent decades would yield reports of descendents wandering between Detroit and Philadelphia, living in their cars and still adhering to the tribe's dietary laws.[10]

Allah wasn't the first Father in Harlem, and he wasn't the first black man to come to New York and say that he was God; nor was the Father Divine I heard at Five Percenter parliaments the first to use that name. The original Father Divine was born George Baker, Jr. in "Monkey Run," a black ghetto of Rockville, Maryland in 1879. His mother Nancy died while George was a teenager. At twenty he moved to Baltimore as one of hundreds of black migrants, most of them from rural areas and searching for new opportunities. While absorbing the worst of police brutality and overcrowded slums like "Pigtown," he took refuge in the home of Harriette Snowden, a female evangelist, and attended various black churches and revivals. At one Baptist storefront church, he watched a man get thrown out for proclaiming, "I am the Father Eternal!"[11] George went outside and helped him up. The man introduced himself as Samuel Morris and explained his outburst with a verse from the Bible: "know ye not that ye are the temple of God, and that the spirit of God dwelleth in you?"[12] The two became friends and Morris eventually moved into Harriette's home. Before long, Morris had convinced both George and Harriette that he was God.

Morris changed his name to Father Jehovia, God in the Fathership Degree, while George Baker, Jr. became the Messenger, God in the Sonship Degree. They held services in their home several nights a week and were soon joined by Reverend Bishop Saint John the Vine, who wore a beard, turban and long robes and professed that he had learned Hebrew from his Abyssinian mother. The Bishop's claims drew from traditions of Ethiopianism, an indigenous slave theology in which African-Americans were believed to have descended from the original Jews, and as the true Chosen People would someday be rescued by God and returned to their homeland.[13] After embracing Father Jehovia's divinity, the Bishop was accepted with his own Sonship Degree.[14] The trio got along well until 1912, when the Bishop found a verse stating that "whoever shall confess that Jesus is the Son of God, God dwelleth in him and he is God" and decided that all men were equally divine.[15] Father Jehovia, understandably, was not willing to give up his exclusive position as Godhead. After initially refusing to take part in their debate, the Messenger finally decided to reject them both and claim that he alone was the manifestation of God. The three men went their separate ways.

The Messenger headed south and wandered the countryside, preaching for the empowerment of women and acquiring a large female following. In Valdosta, Georgia a group of black men had him arrested for lunacy. During his booking, when an officer asked for the Messenger's real name, a woman shouted, "he ain't named nothing but God!"[16] While in police custody, his following continued to grow and included white members. On February 27, 1914 he stood trial for lunacy in Valdosta court. The prosecution's star witnesses— Dr. Stafford, a medical doctor and pastor, and Reverend White, a black Methodist minister—used the Messenger's claim to be God to illustrate his level of mental illness. A jury found the Messenger "guilty" of insanity, but not sufficiently so to warrant his commitment to an institution. He was released on condition that he'd leave Valdosta immediately.[17]

Again roaming from town to town as a streetcorner preacher, he tracked down the Bishop, who had established his own church in Harlem. The Messenger attended one of the Bishop's Sunday services, finding him still in his robes and turban. Upon sighting the Messenger, the Bishop blasted his former friend: "He came up to me saying, 'I am as much God as you are, I am as much God as you are.' I said, 'I did not say anything about your not being as much God as I.' I hadn't said a word about it."[18] The Messenger stood and began preaching his own message to the church, managing to win over some of the Bishop's followers. He then resumed his drifting, now with an entourage of disciples, to spread the word in every town. For preaching the equality of the sexes, he continued to win large numbers of female converts.[19] He returned to New York permanently in 1917, during a period of increased African-American migration to northern cities and the early years of the Harlem Renaissance. 1916 had seen the arrival of Marcus Garvey's Universal Negro Improvement Association (UNIA), which held that black Americans could only find peace and prosperity by returning to Africa. "Ethiopia, thou land of our fathers," UNIA members sang at rallies, "thou land where the Gods used to be." Harlem was swelling with a new radical consciousness; between 1919 and 1930, the borough was home to at least eight sects that claimed descent from Ethiopian Jews.

The Messenger, now known as Father Divine, promoted his mission as offering "prosperity, peace and pleasure" in this lifetime.[20] With poverty leaving his followers malnourished, Father Divine encouraged large appetites and even weighed members of his household twice weekly, scolding those who lost weight.[21] Competing not only with casinos and jazz but countless men that he deemed "false prophets," he began making wild promises of the bliss that awaited his followers. One of Father Divine's bolder statements claimed that in the year 2525, he would send ten million people into outer space to live on other planets: "don't you want to go?"[22]

In 1932 Father Divine packed up his believers and moved to Sayville, approximately seventy miles north of the city. As his following in New York grew on its own, he would later return and move into a believer's home in Harlem. Information about his past became sketchy. He reluctantly identified his age as fifty-two, but strictly by legal definition; as God, he had "spiritually and mentally no record."

Believing in the subtle power of words to affect a person's mindstate, Father Divine altered the language of his followers to remove all negative references. The word *hello* was forbidden, since it reminded him of hell; followers were instructed to greet each other with "peace."[23] By this line of thought, sexism and racism could be destroyed by avoiding the words that represented them. Prohibiting his disciples from even using terms like *man* or *woman*, Father Divine spoke of "so-called men" and "those who call themselves women." He also insisted that whites be spoken of as simply "people of light complexion."

Father Divine encouraged black followers to forsake their last names, dismissing a surname like Smith as "your Daddy's master's name;"[24] but despite his struggles for equality, he was often guilty of the same attitudes about black people found in white racism, and at times even blamed African-Americans for the injustices they faced. According to Father Divine, African-Americans "had committed the sin in setting up color in the first place. They set it up in their consciousness and they would find it everywhere they went and they and no one else would be responsible."[25] He went so far as to claim that affiliation with the stigma of blackness doomed African-Americans to continued poverty: "I am not poor because I do not belong to a poor, downtrodden race. If I was attached to a poor downtrodden race like some of you think you are ... then I would be like some of you."[26]

Rather than overcome ingrained notions of black inferiority, Father Divine fed into them. His marriage to a white woman would even be used as proof of

his holy power, as only God himself could win such a victory over racial prejudice. Though probably well-intentioned, he remained seriously out of touch
with growing movements that focused on black pride and cultural empowerment. Another Father, George Hurley, who formed his Universal Hagar's
Spiritual Church in Georgia in 1923, insisted that black Americans call themselves Ethiopians. Black people, he taught, were the original race, original
Hebrews and creators of civilization while whites were descended from Cain
and "cursed with a pale color because of leprosy."

Worshiped as the "black God of this Age," Father Hurley taught that God
existed within all of humankind and gave his followers the status of "minor
gods and goddesses." He stressed an improvement of conditions in this lifetime, rather than dreaming of otherworldly solutions, as clearly stated in two
of his "10 Commandments:"

> 2. Thou shall ignore a sky heaven for happiness and a downward hell for
> punishment.
> 3. Thou shall believe in heaven and hell here on earth.[27]

The era's most notable leader to disagree with Father Divine's denial of race
was Marcus Garvey, who advocated a "real patriotism" centered around blackness. "There must be a real recognition of the Negro Abyssinian," he told his Universal Negro Improvement Association. "He must not be ashamed to be a
member of the Negro race. If he does, he will be left alone by all the Negroes of the
world, who feel proud of themselves."[28] Garvey arrived in Harlem on March 23,
1916 and began preaching his racial patriotism on the sidewalks of Lenox Avenue:

> When Europe was inhabited by a race of cannibals, a race of savages, naked
> men, heathens and pagans, Africa was peopled with a race of cultured black
> men, who were masters in art, science and literature; men who were cultured
> and refined; men who, it was said, were like the gods.[29]

"The Negro is crying for a Mohammed," Garvey declared, "a Prophet to come
forth and to give him the Koran of economic and intellectual welfare."[30]

> The official sources describe Noble Drew Ali as founder of the first black
> Islamic sect in America. In truth he was less than this, for there were black
> Moslems here before him; but he was more than this—he was an American
> prophet. He could have stepped from the pages of Melville or Ishmael Reed, "a
> thought of allah clothed in flesh," a fact, a poetic fact.
>
> Peter Lamborn Wilson

Ali was born Timothy Drew in 1886, in North Carolina, a child of ex-slaves and
allegedly raised among the Cherokee. As the stories go, at sixteen he began

traveling as a circus magician, later arriving in Egypt, where he was initiated into the Egyptian Shriners and the High Priesthood of the pyramid of Cheops. He would cross the Atlantic with a new scripture, the *Circle 7 Koran*, and a mission to uplift humanity's fallen towards its "Father Allah" and proper religion of "Islamism."

Ali distinguished between Islamism and "Arab-Islam," since the latter came from a "slave master's orientation" and "no Arabian seed sought to propagate the faith among members of our race."[31] True Islamism included not only Semitic prophets but figures such as Buddha and Confucius, and could not be contained within ritual or laws. Man and Allah were one, and all men were priests unto themselves.

He moved to Newark, New Jersey, renamed the city "New-ark" and in 1913 founded a Canaanite Temple, named for his belief that African-Americans were descended from the biblical Moabites and Canaanites. In 1919 his leadership was allegedly subverted by one Abdul Wali Farrad Mohammed Ali, a "Russo-Syrian peddler of silks and raincoats"[32] who swayed enough followers to stage a temple coup. Noble Drew Ali fled New-ark for New York, where he believed that his John the Baptist had appeared in one Marcus Garvey. Ali admired Garvey's aggressive racial pride, pageantry, enterprise, articles in *Negro World* on Moorish and Egyptian history and his call for a new religion with a god who reflected "the physical beauty and characteristics of the Negro himself."

"Marcus accused the Deity of being a Negro," joked humorist George S. Schuyler; "no wonder luck went against him!"[33] Kelly Miller wrote that Garvey's plea to "paint God black" was "revolting even to the Negro,"[34] but for many it was the most necessary truth offered by Garvey's movement. "God made black skin and kinky hair," read a letter from a UNIA women's auxiliary, "because He desired to express Himself in that type." Garvey's UNIA Chaplain General and principal theologian, Bishop George Alexander McGuire, reported that an elderly African-American woman gave him five dollars after he preached of a black Christ. "No white man would ever die on the cross for me," she told him.[35] During Garvey's 1924 convention, UNIA members paraded through Harlem under a giant portrait of a black Mary and baby Jesus. "Let us start our Negro painters getting busy," announced Bishop McGuire, "and supply a black Madonna and a black Christ for the training of our children." He would demand not only a reimagining of God, but also a new Satan. The American Negro was the only black man in the world, he cried, who would allow white men to tell him that the devil was black. The bishop predicted that the future church of a black god would have its own white devil.[36]

For Noble Drew Ali, an important element in the coming black religion was a redefining of terms. The black man was neither Colored nor Negro; "colored" meant "anything that had been painted, stained, varnished or dyed," and "Negro" meant a "four-legged animal." Ali believed that African-Americans were actually Moors, with a heritage that entitled them to a certain legal and social privilege. As far back as 1682, citizens of Morocco were distinguished from ordinary "Negroes" and could not be enslaved, and in 1786 Morocco became the first country to recognize the United States as a sovereign nation. Booker T. Washington had written in *Up From Slavery* of a black man who, after being refused service at a hotel, showed himself to be a citizen of Morocco and received not only service but profuse apologies from the staff.[37] For Noble Drew Ali, what separated this man and the African-American was a knowledge of self, a proper consciousness of identity. What America's Moors needed to do was reclaim their nationality.

It was in 1924 that Ali, given a proper herald in Garvey, felt ready to be revealed as the prophet for his people. Sensing that the midwest was "closer to Islam,"[38] in August 1925 he arrived at Chicago, which he dubbed a "new Mecca." But here he would start from scratch: preaching on street corners to strangers, receiving derision for his fez and enduring stones thrown by children. For Chicagoans, he was only one of countless black migrants who gave their street hustles an exotic flair by posing as Arabs or Indians. The city hosted numerous self-described "Moslems" who sold lucky numbers for the lottery,[39] and the *Chicago Defender* told of "Abd El Mustaph Bey Mohammed Allah Kismet," a coffee vendor whose accent would slip between Turkish and southern, and whose real name was revealed to be George.[40]

Noble Drew Ali preached to the migrants, finding early support among those that spoke of themselves as "Ishmaelites" and members of a "tribe of Ishmael" that had come from downstate.[41] His very first disciple is considered to have been a morbidly obese woman named Lily Sloane, who had one foot in the doorway of the "number house," planning to place two cents on the night's drawing, when she spotted Ali jumping up and down on a wooden crate, waving his arms. The tassel on his fez flew around his head as he moved. Lily stepped away from the number house and walked toward him, nearly tripping over a dirty white dog asleep on the sidewalk. "Goddamn dog," she cursed, "get out of the way." She then heard the strange fez-headed man softly calling her name.

"Lily Sloane: I, your Prophet, command you to come to me and learn the truth and be free in your Father-God-Allah Holy Name!" Then the vision disappeared, leaving only the crate behind. Lily stood alone, believing that she had gone crazy in the heat. She regained her composure and went into the number house with a good feeling about 5–7–4.

"Forty cents on the first six," she told "Jackpot," the tobacco-chewing numbers man, "ten cents straight." Lily crossed the street and sat on the crate where just moments ago stood her tassled hallucination. "Damn hoodoo stuff," she told herself—only to again see the man in the red fez, his arms outstretched. For the next four hours she sat on the crate, mesmerized as he called out to her.

The next time she saw the prophet was on State Street, surrounded by pedestrians that apparently shared her hallucination. Before she was close enough to make out his words, she heard the laughter of the crowd.

"Laugh!" Drew yelled back at them, "but the day will come when you will weep! When the wrath of my Father God Allah is poured out upon the earth, you will regret that you did not heed His prophet! That is why you are so easy to trick; that is why the Europeans—who you call the white man—can keep you in bondage. Oh, and you will listen to him! Anything he tells you is all right. He took you out of Asia and gave you slave names; he calls you black folks, colored folks, Ethiopians and you believe him! I tell you, brothers and sisters, there ain't but one race on the earth, and that's the human race. That race has got two branches: the Europeans, the man you call the white man, and the Asiatic—us. But you don't know that 'cause the European don't want you to know it. He wants to call you by your slave name and keep you working for him. It's your own fault, brothers!

"Come all ye Asiatics of America, and learn the truth about your nationality and birthright—because you are not colored, you are not black folks, you are not Ethiopians. You must claim a free name; a Moorish name. Learn of your Forefather's ancient divine creed that you will learn to love instead of hate."

He stopped and let them process what he had said. Some gave encouragement. Some still laughed. After a few moments they all walked away, leaving only Lily Sloane. She watched the tired prophet take off his fez to wipe the sweat from his forehead. "Sister," he called out to her, "your friends are gone. Why do you remain behind? Why don't you go with the rest of the unbelievers?" Lily stammered out that he must not have remembered her because she was "crazy in the head." Ali looked her, smiled and replied, "Why of course, sister, of course I remember you. Have you a lodging for me tonight, sister?"

Lily Sloane took in the prophet and became the first disciple of his new sect, standing at his side when he preached in vacant lots. Her intuitive feeling about the lottery numbers 5–7–4 had manifested the truth, via the time-honored numerology of "digit summing:" $5 + 7 + 4 = 16$; $1 + 6$ resulted in the divine number 7. She shared the prophet's teachings with her upstairs neighbors, Mr. and Mrs. Mealy, who then became Mr. and Mrs. Mealy *El*. For Moors, the suffixing of El or Bey to one's "slave name" reclaimed his or her lost nationality. As Noble Drew Ali's following grew, Els and Beys became distinguished from one another by the color of their fezzes: Els green, Beys red. They greeted each other with "Islam," right hands on their hearts; they bid farewell with "peace."[42]

Ali obtained a charter for the first "Temple of Islam" of his new movement, the Moorish Science Temple of America, drafted a Divine Constitution and began issuing "passports." His Moors also embraced their natural religion, "Islamism," which a member expressed by wearing a button of the star and crescent on his coat. Ali taught his catechism through a simple question-and-answer format, similar to those used in Masonic lodges:

57. Who were Adam and Eve? They are the ones who brought about a discord in the Holy City of MECCA and were driven out.
58. Where did they go? They went into Europe.
59. What is the modern name given to their children? Roman.
60. What is the shade of their skin? Pale.
61. Who is guarding the Holy City of MECCA to keep the unbelievers away? Angels.
62. What is the modern name of these angels? Arabian.
63. What is the shade of their skin? Olive.
64. Are the Moorish Americans any relation to those Angels? Yes, we all have the same Father and Mother.
65. Give five names that are given to the descendents of Adam and Eve. Lucifer, Satan, Devil, Dragon and Beast.
66. What is the Devil sometimes called? The lower self.
67. How many selves are there? Two.
68. Name them. Higher and lower self.
69. What people represent the Higher self? The angels who protect the Holy City of MECCA.
70. What people represent the Lower self? Those who were cast out of the Holy City, and those who accept their teachings.
71. What is the Higher self? The Higher self is the mother of virtues and the harmonies of life, and breeds Justice, Mercy, Love and Right.
72. Can the Higher self pass away? No.
73. Why? Because it is ALLAH in man.[43]

Like his herald Marcus Garvey, Ali's rhetoric of black empowerment accompanied a growing business enterprise. The prophet sold "Moorish Healing Oil" and his Moors operated their own grocery stores, newspapers and even schools. Ali's rising power—and the habit among some Moors of flashing their passports at whites—may have frightened authorities. One official in Detroit remarked, "What a terrible gang! Thieves and cutthroats! Wouldn't answer anything. Wouldn't sit down when you told them. Wouldn't stand up when you told them."[44] Hoping to get the authorities off his back, Ali later forbade his Moors from engaging in aggressive public behavior or flashing their passports at whites. The Moors began working their way from the fringe. They promoted their temple as a fraternal order, leading colorful marches in regalia not far removed from the faux-Arab aesthetics of Shriner parades.[45] Sheik Claude Greene became butler to revered philanthropist Julius Rosenwald, who purchased the MST a building at 3640 Indiana Avenue. The new headquarters, named Unity Hall by Ali, hosted the first Moorish national convention from October 15 to 20, 1928. Like UNIA conventions, the event opened with a parade. On the second day, Ali kissed a boy wrapped in the Moorish national flag and declared his Moors a sovereign people.

Moorish Science was becoming politically entrenched, as local candidates played up Ali to win his followers' votes. Moors helped south side alderman Oscar S. DePriest into the House of Representatives, and Ali attended the January 14 inauguration of Illinois Governor Louis L. Emerson. At the apparent height of his power, Ali told the Moors that he wasn't long for the world; according to Moorish sources, this was also when "every evil spirited pone was moving now against him."[46] Lomax Bey announced before 1,500 Moors that Noble Drew Ali should be deposed as leader, and even attempted a courtroom coup to wrest control of the movement. Then Ali learned that his wife Pearl was sleeping with Claude Greene.[47] On March 11, Greene emptied the prophet's Unity Hall office and tossed his furniture into the street. Greene was later shot and stabbed to death, causing the Chicago police to apprehend Ali. On May 20 he was indicted as an accessory to homicide.

On July 27, less than a month after his release on bail, Noble Drew Ali returned to Allah. The *Chicago Whip* attributed his death to tuberculosis; the Moors believed that police abuse—such as forcing the prophet to sit on giant blocks of ice—had aggravated his health problems and brought on martyrdom. Moorish history records the exact time of death as 10:10 p.m., and Noble Drew's final words as "Carry on." His body would lie in state for five days. The funeral service at the Pythian Temple included songs by the MST choir and a eulogy delivered by C. Kirkman Bey in English, Arabic and Spanish.

The Moorish Science Temple began to fall apart before its prophet was even in the ground. Ali's attorney Aaron Payne tried to hold the movement together, but had none of the "spiritual charisma" required to capture Moors' imagination. Majority opinion held that Noble Drew Ali had chosen to reincarnate himself into his chauffeur, John Givens El. Mealy El, Grand Sheik of the Chicago Temple, claimed to be Ali's personally appointed successor, only to be voted out by the general membership. Complicating the issue was Ira Johnson Bey, also known as the "Nazarene," an enforcer who had been sent from Pittsburgh to Chicago to squash the Claude Greene revolt. Bey stormed into Mealy El's office and demanded recognition as Grand Sheik. His men kidnapped Mealy El's opponent C. Kirkman Bey, believing that Kirkman possessed Noble Drew Ali's last will and testament. Kirkman's wife Peasie called the police; a resulting gun battle left two officers and one Moor dead, and sixty-three Moors arrested. Ira Johnson Bey managed to escape back to Pittsburgh, where "the spirit of Jesus reincarnated into his form." Receiving permission from his Father to come in His Name, he then declared himself "Allah El, son of the most High God-Allah." Despite being a vessel for Jesus, Allah El insisted that he was but a mortal man with a simple role to play: "I am no Christ and I have no wings, I am an old man, I am Spirit. I am going to my father when I return." Allah El returned to Chicago, surrendered to police and was institutionalized at Illinois Security Hospital for the Criminally Insane in the town of Menard.[48]

A stranger then appeared in Detroit's Paradise Valley, selling silks from door to door in post-Depression ghettoes and regaling customers with tales of Muslim lands. His stories were so enthralling that he would often be invited to stay for dinner. After the meal, he would exhort his hosts to give up pork and adopt the diets of their brothers and sisters in the east. Soon the stranger was preaching to crowded basement audiences on the superiority of Islam and the coming destruction of the white world.[49]

Various far-flung theories name him as David Ford El, Grand Sheik from Chicago, or Abdul Wali Farrad Mohammed Ali, the Russo-Syrian peddler of raincoats who had taken over the Canaanite Temple in New Jersey, or even Arnold Josiah Ford, the Barbados-born black rabbi and former UNIA choirmaster. He has been identified as a Syrian Druze, Indian Ahmadiyya, Turkish Nazi, cockeyed Greek and New Zealand drug dealer, and he could have been one of the last Ben Ishmaels. He might appear in old photos with Noble Drew Ali and Moors standing outside the Unity Hall, everyone in turbans and headdresses and robes with sashes; in the upper left corner there's a fair-skinned man wearing a bowtie. The Moors swear that it's *him*, but who knows—?

His official biography would depict him as the son of a black man named Alphonso and Baby Gee, white woman of the Caucus Mountains, who gave birth to him in Mecca. After making himself known in Detroit on July 4, 1930 he went by over fifty aliases, including Mohammed Ali, Wali Mohammed, Wali Farrad, Farrad Mohammed, Wallace Mohammed, W.F. Muhammad, Wallace Farrad, Wallace Don Ford and W. D. Fard. As the Moorish Science Temple's Chicago nucleus was split by rival factions, he collected wayward followers in Detroit with tweaked Moorish doctrine.

Noble Drew Ali had taught that Allah and the Devil existed within man as "higher" and "lower" selves, with the lower (devil) self represented by Adam's descendents, the Europeans. W. D. Fard took Ali's religion and made it science. Within the black man existed two germs: a dominant black germ and recessive brown germ. For trillions of years there were only pure black men, who lived in peace and enlightenment. As the brown germ lay dormant, black men fathered civilization. This natural order was challenged approximately 6,000 years ago, when a "big-headed" youth named Yacub told his uncle, "I'm going to make a man that will rule you." His uncle's reply mimics the Qur'an, when angels question Allah on His decision to create Adam: "What will you make other than something that will cause bloodshed and mischief in the land?"

"That's all right," answered the youth. "I know what you do not know." In his college years Yacub discovered the weak brown germ and endeavored to create a man from it. The new man would of course be weaker than the black man from which he was grafted, but with Yacub's instruction would come to rule the world.

At eighteen years old, Yacub had graduated from every college and university and took to preaching his ideas on the streets of Mecca, slowly gathering converts until he became a legitimate threat to the government. The King called for Yacub's arrest, which only made him more popular among his followers. Eventually, the jails were overcrowded with Yacub's party and he still had disciples teaching on the street. The King asked to be taken to Yacub's cell.

The two of them worked out an agreement: Yacub and his followers would go into exile, and the King would financially support them for twenty years. They sailed to the island of Pelan (Patmos) in the Aegean Sea, where Yacub set up a social hierarchy topped by doctors, ministers, nurses and a cremator. After two hundred years of strictly enforced breeding laws, including regulated marriages and even infanticide of black babies, Yacub's government had completely weeded out the black germ to create a brown race. As many of the brown people migrated to other areas of the world, Yacub kept his remaining population under the eugenics laws and in another two hundred years had created the yellow race. After the third and final stage, he had made his devil: the white man.

Yacub was Arabic for Jacob. The biblical story of Jacob stealing Esau's birthright had been read by the Moors as an allegory for the white man robbing them of their nationality. The devils of Fard's interpretation would come to the Holy City of Mecca; but like the pale people of Moorish Science narrative, they would be chased out, driven across the desert and exiled to the caves of Europe. After "half-original" prophet Musa (Moses) came to civilize the devils and teach them the forgotten science of "tricknology," they would rise up to over-power the original people. Six hundred years it had taken to make the devil fit into a mathematical theme. Yacub was only six years old when he discovered magnetism; his fol-lowers numbered 59,999, himself making 60,000; his created devil had only six ounces of brain, compared to the original man's seven. The devil, who used six million square miles of land, would rule the earth for six thousand years. Jeho-vah's Witnesses understand the number six, "being short of the biblically com-plete, or perfect" seven to signify imperfection, emphasized in the Beast's mark of 666.[50] Fard encouraged his Muslims to listen to Jehovah's Witness radio programs, which contained hidden truths that could only be unlocked with his help. Charles Taze Russell, founder of the Jehovah's Witnesses, believed that Christ had secretly arrived in the year 1874. Using the book of Daniel to calcu-late a period of 2,520 years, Russell deducted that Christ would emerge to lead a "Battle of Armageddon" in 1914. After the year came and went, 1914 was then interpreted as the "beginning of the end." Fard, who was likely born after 1890 but would be portrayed with a birthdate of February 26, 1877, professed that the reign of Yacub's devil had expired in 1914. At that time, however, the original people in the wilderness of North America were not prepared to reclaim their position. They still worshiped the hocus-pocus god that the devil had taught them to fear, and ate the devil's poison foods that made them sick. The devil was thus allowed a "grace period" during which Fard arrived to res-cue his people. If original people lived true to the laws of Islam, Fard promised, they would be rid of the devil by 1934.[51]

Both Noble Drew Ali and W. D. Fard aspired to create an identity for African-Americans greater than that offered under the United States flag. Ali claimed that black people could reclaim their true names, culture and religion by embracing Moorish heritage; Fard taught his followers that they were registered in the "Nation of Islam"—which had no birth record, beginning or ending, and was older than the sun, moon and stars.[52] Rather than suffix his followers' "slave names" with Bey or El, Fard sold original "righteous names." Joseph Shepard based his new name on his old, becoming Jam Sharrieff. Some took the surname Allah, such as Lindsey Garret (Hazziez Allah) and William Blunt (Sharrieff Allah).[53] New names marked the beginnings of new lives, a resurrection from mental death; sociologist Erdmann Doane Beynon, who studied the Nation of Islam in 1936 and 1937, observed that Fard's Muslims "became so ashamed of their old slave names that they considered that they could suffer no greater insult than to be addressed by the old name."[54] "I wouldn't give up my righteous name," remarked Rosa McCoy, renamed Rosa Karriem; "that name is my life."[55] The names were only part of Fard's intricate use of words, numbers and symbols to stimulate his followers and restructure their world. Europe was broken down into *Eu*, meaning hillside, and *rope*, meaning to bind in, to illustrate how Caucasians had been "roped in." The white man's continent was no longer the beacon of civilization, but his prison. Fard's unique terminologies and memorized phrases were the work of, in the words of Warith Deen Mohammed, a "genius of powerful reform psychology, he created the kind of strange language environment that would just shock dead brains, dead sentiments into living form."[56]

There might have been no telling where a shocked brain would lead its owner. Henry James Moaning, known within Fard's group as Ahmed Ullah, was arrested for writing threatening letters to the mayor of Detroit and judged insane by Probate Court.[57] In November 1932 police arrested unskilled laborer Robert Harris for performing a bloody human sacrifice. Harris had convinced his friend, a former Moor named James J. Smith, that in death he could become "savior of the world." Smith voluntarily placed himself on a makeshift altar in Harris' apartment and allowed Harris to stab him in the chest. Harris then took the rod from an automobile axle and brained Smith before stabbing him four more times. In police custody Harris, who had been renamed Robert Karriem by Fard, called himself the "King of Islam" and freely admitted that he had to kill four people to "gain his reward" from the "gods of Islam." Robert's brother Edward Harris, also a follower of Fard, remarked that financial worries had caused Robert to "lose his mind."[58]

The gods of Islam were Fard and his lieutenant, Ugan Ali. After arresting Ali at the Allah Temple of Islam on Hastings Street, Detroit detectives read from the open book at Ali's lectern: "Every son of Islam must gain a victory from a devil. Four victories and the son will attain his reward." Fard was later seized outside his room at the Fraymore Hotel.

"They apparently misunderstood my teachings," he told police. Fard and Ali were subjected to a lengthy psychiatric examination and then joined Karriem on the Detroit Receiving Hospital's psychopathic ward, restrained in straitjackets and padded rooms. Ali's "mental processes," read the exam reports, "are radically deviated. His sanity is extremely doubtful," while Fard was seen to be "suffering from delusions that he is a divinity. He has a pattern of religious precepts and patterns which, taken literally, are dangerous to those influenced by them." Ali bargained his way out of jail time by promising to help "disband the Allah Temple of Islam" and Robert Karriem was shipped off to Ionia State Hospital for the Criminally Insane. Fard was released after agreeing to a permanent exile from Detroit.

Ugan Ali was nowhere to be found; his role in Fard's organization now filled by Elijah Poole, a factory worker who had migrated to the Motor City from Sandersville, Georgia and was renamed numerous times by Fard before finally becoming Elijah Muhammad. Fard continued to teach in Chicago. He soon resurfaced in Detroit, was apprehended and given another order to leave the city. It was during Fard's second Chicago exile that the Detroit Muslims began withdrawing their children from public schools for enrollment at various "Universities of Islam" throughout the city. In addition to normal curriculums, these storefront campuses offered such courses as "General Knowledge of the Spook Being Displayed for 6,000 Years," "Prophecy" and "General Knowledge of Spook Civilization." Teachers and administrators were eventually arrested in a mass raid and charged with contributing to the delinquency of minors. Elijah was arrested while leading five hundred Muslims on a march to the police station.

"What are you taught at the University of Islam about white people?" prosecutor George Schudlich asked fifteen-year-old witness Sally Ali. She answered that if she cut off the heads of four devils, she would "win a trip to Mecca and a button with Allah's picture on it." Elijah was found guilty but received a sentence of only six months' probation on the condition that he close the schools.[59]

Fard disappeared for good that June. One day he had Elijah drive him to the airport, provided his student a list of books to read, and then he was gone— back to Mecca, maybe, or New Zealand or Japan or Pakistan, having done all that he could for his uncle in the wilderness. In August Elijah began publishing his own newspaper, *Final Call to Islam*, which at first praised Fard as "the great prophet." Before long, however, Elijah had elevated himself to the role of messenger and raised Fard's status to Allah. The innovation caused many Muslims to reject Elijah as Fard's successor. Fearing plots on his life, Elijah took flight and in exile built temples in Milwaukee and Washington, D.C. The message later spread to Baltimore and Cincinnati, inevitably making its way to New York, where Fard had predicted the rise of some "very wise men."

During his travels, Elijah made attempts to teach among the Beys and Els. He was barred entry from a Moorish temple in Baltimore and twice rejected in Newark. "They were so afraid and jealous of that which Noble Drew Ali gave them," he would later claim, "that they thought that my strong teachings of God and Islam may put some of them out of office." One Newark Moor reportedly told him, "I just wish I were the Sheik, I would let you teach all night because you were telling us things we never heard."

For registered Muslims, teachings were shared in *Secret Ritual of the Nation of Islam*, a series of transcribed dialogues between Master Fard and Elijah Muhammad, better known as the "Supreme Wisdom lessons." In a format taken from Noble Drew Ali's Questionary, the lessons outlined basic beliefs through a series of question-and-answer exchanges. The text's "English Lesson No. C-1" gives a precis of Fard's mission:

1. My name is W. F. Muhammad.
2. I came to North America by myself.
3. My uncle was brought over here by the Trader three hundred seventy-nine years ago.
4. My uncle cannot talk his own language.
5. He does not know that he is my uncle.
6. He likes the Devil because the devil gives him nothing.
7. Why does he like the devil?
8. Because the devil planted fear in him when he was a little boy.
9. Why does he fear the devil now that he is a big man?
10. Because the devil taught him to eat the wrong food.
11. Does that have anything to do with the above question, No.10?
12. Yes, sir! That makes him other than his own self.
13. What is his own self?
14. His own self is a righteous Muslim.
15. Are there any Muslims other than righteous?
16. I beg your pardon? I have never heard of one.
17. How many Muslim sons are there in North America?
18. Approximately three million.
19. How many original Muslims are there in North America?
20. A little over seventeen million.
21. Did I hear you say that some of the seventeen million do not know that they are Muslim?
22. Yes, sir!
23. I hardly believe that unless they are blind, deaf and dumb.
24. Well, they were made blind, deaf and dumb by the devil when they were babies.
25. Can the devil fool a Muslim?
26. Not nowadays.
27. Do you mean to say that the devil fooled them three hundred seventy-nine years ago?
28. Yes, the trader made an interpretation that they receive gold for their labor—more than they were earning in their own country.
29. Then did they receive gold?
30. No. The Trader disappeared and there was no one that could speak their language.
31. Then what happened?
32. Well, they wanted to go to their own country, but they could not swim nine thousand miles.
33. Why didn't their own people come and get them?
34. Because their own people did not know that they were here.
35. When did their own people find out that they were here?
36. Approximately sixty years ago.[60]

"Actual Facts" consists of geographic distances and measurements, including the square mileage of oceans, islands, deserts and mountains. The Earth's circumference is given as 24,896 miles, which becomes the basis for original men dividing the history of the universe into 25,000-year cycles known as "Korans:"

> The Nation of Islam is all-wise and does everything right and exact. The planet earth, which is the home of Islam, is approximately twenty-five thousand miles in circumference. So the wise man of the East (Black man) makes history or Koran equal his home circumference—a year to every mile. And, thus, every time his history lasts twenty-five thousand years, he renews it for another twenty-five thousand years.[61]

The number also has its roots in the work of Charles Taze Russell, who based his Armageddon year of 1914 on a 2,520-year period.

Fard had avoided offering mere spiritual redemption, instead focusing on the real world in front of him. Rather than "talking to us about holiness, righteousness, divinity, God and the saints,"[62] writes Warith Deen Mohammed, Fard instructed Elijah Muhammad to "hold out to them the bait that represents to them the things that they need and want right now ... good homes, money, and friendship in all walks of life."[63] Fard, teaching that black people had been deprived of such joys in part by otherworldly dogmas, advocated a sort of pragmatic atheism. Prayers offered to an unseen, unknown entity were useless in uplifting the downtrodden; rather, this imagined "mystery" has been used as a tool of oppression:

> 10. Who is that mystery God?
>
> ANS. There is not a mystery God. The son of man has searched for that mystery God for trillions of years and was unable to find a mystery God. So they have agreed that the only God is the son of man. So they lose no time searching for that that does not exist.
>
> 11. Will you sit at home and wait for that mystery God to bring you food?
>
> ANS. Emphatically No!
>
> 12. Tell us why the Devil does not teach that?
>
> ANS. Because he desires to make slaves out of all he can so that he can rob them and live in luxury.[64]

In the absence of creator gods, the NOI developed a cosmology going back trillions of years in which the universe and all that it contained stemmed from the divine Black Intellect. The son of man had created himself.[65]

The "son of man" was specifically the black man, but both W. D. Fard and Noble Drew Ali had broadened their scopes to unite all nonwhite peoples under the "Asiatic" umbrella. This perspective was connected to growing pro-Japanese sentiments in the black community. As with Islam, the Empire of Japan offered nonwhiteness a prestige not available within the American experience. Following its victory over Russia, Japan had become the center of near-messianic hopes as a liberator from white oppression; in 1918, Marcus Garvey had promised that black Americans would win a race war with Japan on their side.[66] The federal government initially targeted the NOI and MST as seditious pro-Japanese groups. Elijah Muhammad boasted of the "Mothership," a giant spacecraft loaded with bombs, that had been designed in Mecca but built in Japan and would play a key role in the final battle of Armageddon. At the height of World War II, some MST members claimed that when Japan eventually invaded the United States, only those with Moorish identity cards would be spared.[67] Both movements had connections to Satokata Takahashi, a Japanese national who had settled in Detroit. Takahashi had taken over a political organization, The Development of Our Own (of which Fard once claimed to be the founder[68]), and reportedly used it to "urge Negroes to join with all other colored people—yellow, brown, and black—against all white people."[69] Takahashi went on to form two new organizations with similar aims, the Onward Movement of America and the Pacific Movement of the Eastern World, which in turn begat offshoots such as the Ethiopian Pacific Movement. Elijah Muhammad is quoted as having said in 1933 that "the Japanese had sent a teacher to the black people."[70] Ten years later, an article in the *Detroit News* attributed rising black pride to "Moslem and Shinto cults."[71] In Harlem, Ethiopian Pacific Movement leader Robert Jordan was arrested for spreading pro-Japanese propaganda, and New York's black weekly *The People's Voice* reported of a Japanese "B.B. Plan" to convert African-Americans to Buddhism.[72] Mentioned in the article was one Sufi Abdul Hamid (Eugene Brown) who had dabbled in quick-cure schemes and activism in Chicago before arriving in Harlem. Abdul Hamid preached from stepladders on 125th Street, wearing a purple turban, gold-lined cape and large Van Dyke moustache, claiming birth from the Sudan and promoting a theology that mixed Buddhism with the Qur'an. He founded the Buddhist Universal Holy Temple of Tranquility on Harlem's Morningside Avenue and titled himself "His Holiness Bishop Amiru al-Muminin." *The People's Voice* alleged that the temple had been funded by Japan; the story in part moved J. Edgar Hoover to authorize microphone surveillance of Brooklyn's Moorish Science Temple.[73]

Takahashi was eventually deported and the dream of a non-white superpower faded. Elijah Muhammad's triumph in the NOI civil war would again unite the movement under one leader, but the Moors continued to fight among themselves and create new splinter groups. In the second half of the 1940s, the Kirkman Bey faction exiled Charles Mosely Bey from its Cleveland temple for promoting astrology, after which he formed his own group. A self-proclaimed "Free Moorish-American and Master Mason, 3rd, 33rd and 360-degrees, Ph.D and LL.D," he drafted a "Zodiac Constitution" and wrote volumes on the Clock of Destiny, a wheel featuring the twelve astrological signs with a sun—the "only Sun of God"—in the center. Despite the mystical overtones, C. M. Bey spoke of Islam as a science, not a religion, and insisted that his Clock of Destiny Moors composed not a faith-based sect but a *Cultural-National Club.* "I am not interested in religion," he declared, "and the 'GOD' no one has ever seen. I am interested only in the solving of my economic problems and helping others to solve their problems in the most reasonable and intelligent manner."[74] Beyond an occasional reference to the "science of Islam" and criticisms of orthodox Islam's "mystery" teachings, Islamic material remained largely absent from Bey's movement. When three Clock of Destiny Moors were tried for draft evasion during the Korean War, however, Bey was barred from the courtroom for refusing to take off his fez.

Though apparently influenced by Fard, C. M. Bey differed in his assertion that the true Creator was not the "son of man" but the black Asiatic woman, whom he described as "definitely not a secret nor mystery. She is a reality,—the living God of humanity."[75] The Asiatic woman was the actual author of the Qur'an, and "declared some thirteen hundred and sixty-seven years ago: 'Inni Anallahum La Illaha Illa Ana'—Truly I am God-Allah, Besides Me There is no Other."[76] Moorish Men found their own divinity as *sons* of God. "Do you know of any being," asked Bey, "that is superior to you and your mother?"[77] Believing that Muslim and Christian scholars held a "monopoly on mystic religious superstition, but not on mathematics," Bey taught that women could harness their true power through an understanding of numbers:

> If women on national scales possessed the applied knowledge of the secrets of the number 9, they would be supremely qualified to educate their children to the practical side of life during its 9 months maturity from conception to birth. Then, there would be no need for the institutions of religious mystery worship, Idol or image God. Jail houses, prisons and insane institutions would not be needed for there would be no racial hatred or crime.[78]

In Bey's 0–9 code, 0 represented the 360 degrees of a perfect circle and 9 symbolized the months a developing fetus spent in the womb. The number 333 took a special significance with each 3 representing a trimester of pregnancy, and "3 into 9 goes 3 times, which equals the 3rd and 33rd degrees" of Masonry. Bey also taught a "Moorish Color Code in electronics" in which each number from nought to nine corresponded with a specific color. 0, the "sun of life," was black; 1 was brown. 9 was white.

"Our Moorish forefathers' code of alphabet and mathematics," wrote Bey in *Clock of Destiny*, "have proven that the 'white people' have no culture of their own."[79] His numerology included interpretations of letters. Examining the biblical transformation of Abram into Abraham, Bey found that *Abram* contained five letters while *Abraham* contained seven. Adding them resulted in twelve, representing the twelve signs of the Zodiac.

Like Noble Drew Ali, C. M. Bey was influenced by the Rosicrucians, who believed that the manipulation of numbers would reveal new meanings; adding all of the numbers from 1 to 6 would equal 21, which digit summing then turns into 3, representing the Trinity. In the Rosicrucian system, 5 symbolized Man; the union of Adam and Eve (5+5) thus produced 10, the number representing Completion. Bey worked with the central numbers of his "Moorish Mathematics"—three, nine and twelve—to reveal God: "The number twelve reduces to three as: (1) and (2) equals (3). Three into nine equals three times. And three into twelve equals four times ... The preceding division of nine and 12 by the figure three represent the (Circle Seven) of the science of ISLAM. (3) and (4) equals (7)."[80]

The placement of *I* as the ninth letter in the alphabet proved "the great I,"[81] affirming the divine nature of man. Bey broke down the word *Islam* as "I Am," which "expressed the highest phrase of creation, namely: Ourselves which symbolizes the letter one (1) or (I)."[82] He gleaned the phrase from the "I AM" movement founded by Guy Ballard in 1932. Ballard believed that God was present in the "higher being" of man, and if one tapped into this power of "the Mighty I AM" he or she would make serious changes in the world. "We are the Great I AM," announced Bey, "cloaked in flesh and having the supreme power to dominate everything in creation." Including, as Master Fard said, rain, hail, snow and earthquakes.

Bey traveled to promote his Clock of Destiny club from 1947 until 1957, when a stroke left him with speech impairments. He continued to teach from his home and spread the message through published works. Despite the apparent perfection of his mastery over numbers and the Zodiac, Bey understood that truth would be lost on the masses: "If you should attempt to establish an argument against this absolute code of mathematical and alphabetical facts, then you might be considered as the living dead, that is mentally dead, or insane. Well, due to religious mystery 95% of the population of the U.S.A. will attempt to establish an argument against the preceding absolute facts."[83]

C. M. Bey's "Sons and Daughters" did manage to score considerable influence in Cleveland and Detroit and are believed to have reached New York in the 1960s.[84] Meanwhile, Ira "Allah El" Johnson Bey upheld his own sect from prison; over the years, hundreds of "fez wearing men and long skirted outfitted women" traveled from all over the country to see him at Menard, believing, according to a 1948 reporter, that "he is god."[85] His son founded a temple in New York in the 1940s, blending with other factions into an ideological soup for the "very wise men" that Fard had prophesied. The Five Percenters would emerge from Harlem's chapter of the Nation of Islam, but may also reveal Moorish Science influence in the 7 on their flag and the precedent of Allah El. Allah's own science of numbers, as well as the urban legend that Malcolm X had asked Allah to teach him astrology, point to a Clock of Destiny connection. The claim has been made that before or after his NOI stint, Allah did in fact join a branch of the Moorish Science Temple;[86] however, official membership would not have been required for Allah to syncretize the lessons of various movements in New York.

Five Percenters today, while respecting the Nation of Islam and Moorish Science, commonly view themselves as fulfilling these generations of resistance theology, and Allah saw himself as arriving at the perfect time in history to end America's illusion of white supremacy. Elijah Muhammad, maintaining suspense for the Battle of Armageddon, alternately promised the end of bondage in 1955, the fall of America in 1965 or 1966 and the expiration of the devil's respite in 1974. The Five Percenters would teach that the devil had received fifty years of respite, expiring in 1964.[87] It was time to take him off the planet.

3

Clarence and Malcolm

Muslims in the Nation of Islam were forbidden from participating in the American military. Elijah Muhammad in the Nation of Islam even went to prison for draft evasion during World War II. Prior to becoming Clarence 13X, Clarence Edward Smith was a light-weapons infantryman who had nearly given his life defending freedom on foreign soil while it was denied him in his own land.

The first-class private was born a second-class citizen in Danville, Virginia on February 22, 1928. When he was two years old, Virginia state codes were introduced requiring segregation in every school, theater and other public venue that accommodated both whites and blacks. "Race classification" codes and a "Miscegenation" bill, designed to "preserve the integrity of the white race," identified a Negro as anyone possessing Negro blood. "Whiteness," meanwhile, was defined as having "no trace whatever" of non-white blood.[1] Given the choice between the "colored" movie theater or the balcony of the white theater, young Clarence and his six siblings (five brothers, one sister) would sometimes take the balcony and look down at the whites, laughing at how "silly and trivial" they seemed. Clarence once watched his father defend his mother's honor by beating a white man who had cursed at her, and Clarence helped fight off the man's son and daughter.[2]

New York had only a handful of Muslims when eighteen-year-old Clarence came to Harlem in 1946 to live with his mother. Eight years later, there still weren't enough Muslims in Harlem to fill a bus,[3] but 1954—the year that Clarence returned from a two-year stint in Korea—also saw the arrival of Minister Malcolm X, who had led successful temples in Detroit and Boston. "The white man has taught us to shout and sing," Malcolm X would preach outside black churches, "and pray until we *die*, to wait until *death*, for some dreamy heaven-in-the-hereafter, when we're dead, while this white man has his milk and honey ... right here on *this* earth!"[4] Under Malcolm's leadership, Temple No.7 grew into the Nation's flagship mosque.

As with NOI mosques across the country, male members of Temple No.7 engaged in "Fruit of Islam" training, which included self-defense and military drills. The head of Harlem's Fruit of Islam (FOI), Captain Joseph X, was the son of Joseph Gravitt El, one of Elijah's old friends from the Moorish Science Temple. Before encountering the Nation of Islam, the younger Joseph was an alcoholic who couldn't hold a job; in Detroit he was arrested for "involuntary molestation of women" after exposing himself to urinate on a street corner. Fearing that Joseph would wind up dead in a gutter, his father (at the time leading Detroit's Moorish Science Temple) sought help from Elijah. The Messenger told Joseph that he'd be spending seven weeks with Malcolm X. After the seven weeks, Elijah promised, Joseph would be free to stay with the Muslims or go on his way. Joseph did join the Nation of Islam, and Elijah kept him close to Malcolm by naming him the minister's bodyguard. Joseph later followed Malcolm to Harlem, where Malcolm became minister of Temple No.7 and Joseph was named captain of the Fruit.

In 1956, Captain Joseph went to Elijah Muhammad with the unfounded rumor that Malcolm had impregnated one of the Apostle's teen secretaries. Malcolm demanded that Joseph be punished for spreading lies, but the captain had a direct link to the Muslims' roots in Moorish Science and could have caused a scandal if pushed too hard. Elijah named Joseph head of the Fruit of Islam for the entire East Coast, putting him under only Supreme Captain Raymond Sharrieff and Elijah Muhammad Jr.

Despite internal tension between Joseph and Malcolm, the New York Muslims scored a major victory in 1957, after a Temple No.7 brother named Johnson Hinton had his skull split open by members of the NYPD. The bloody, half-dead heap was then carted off in a squad car to the precinct. Police brutality was nothing new in Harlem, and Temple No.7's Fruit of Islam had been trained for this situation. Malcolm put the Fruit in formation and sent them marching single-file to the 28th precinct. While scared white policemen looked out from their windows, a growing mob of up to five thousand non-Muslims swelled behind the FOI. Malcolm X went inside and demanded to see Hinton. At first the officers denied that he was there; then they admitted that he was, but refused to let Malcolm see him. The minister informed them that until he was assured that Hinton had received medical care, his FOI would stay in front of the precinct. Malcolm was finally taken to see the blood-soaked, semi-conscious Hinton and demanded that an ambulance take him to Harlem Hospital. An ambulance was called and the Fruit of Islam, along with throngs of supporters, followed it up Lenox. When Malcolm learned that Hinton was received at the hospital and properly treated, he gave the sign for his FOI to disperse. The crowd of spectators broke up on its own. Hinton had a steel plate inserted in his head, and with the NOI's help sued the NYPD for $70,000. At the time, it was the largest amount that New York City had ever paid for police brutality.

Accepted Five Percenter tradition holds that Clarence had returned from overseas duty in 1960 to discover that his wife Dora had joined the Nation of Islam. She now wore long dresses and covered her hair with a headwrap, forbade their children from eating pork and refused to drink alcohol, dance or listen to music. Her husband, bewildered but intrigued, allowed her to take him down to Mosque No.7 (on the corner of 116th and Lenox) for a meeting with Malcolm X.

With most legendary history, details don't always hold together. Clarence actually served in Korea from 1952 to 1954. He would have been in Harlem during the years that Malcolm built up Temple No.7, appeared on national television specials and made the FBI nervous by meeting Fidel Castro at the Hotel Theresa. It is not unthinkable that Clarence was one of the twenty thousand at a rally in Harlem's garment district to protest the Emmett Till verdict, at which Adam Clayton Powell, Jr. announced that "no crisis facing America is more serious than the crisis of racism." Clarence remained in the Army Reserve until September 30, 1960. It is possible that he was away from New York on a Reserve commitment during the time that Dora converted. The FBI dates his earliest appearance with the Nation of Islam as September 1, 1961.[5] In the rapidly growing Muslim community, however, the first time that Clarence was noticed by an informant would not necessarily have been his first time in the temple.

Upon registering as a Muslim with Temple No.7 (renamed Mosque No.7 in 1961), Clarence dropped his "slave name" Smith in favor of 13X, signifying that he was the thirteenth member named Clarence. The life of a Muslim turned out to be harder than he imagined. In December 1960, Malcolm returned from a lengthy stint on the road to learn that in Captain Joseph's hands, the temple was falling apart: a number of recent converts were selling and smoking marijuana, dealing in cocaine and heroin and engaging in illicit sex. On December 23, Malcolm conducted a mass trial in which various Muslims stood for their crimes. Malcolm told the suspected drug dealer that he was fortunate to have been caught by Muslims instead of police, as the police would use it against the Honorable Elijah Muhammad. The guilty Muslims were suspended for periods ranging from ninety days to five years. The new Clarence 13X, a self-proclaimed "master gambler" who enjoyed marijuana and women, had some adjustments to make.

As a neophyte, Clarence embarked on the Nation's process of induction: committing the entire Fard-Muhammad dialogue, the Supreme Wisdom Lessons, to memory. Amir Fatir recalls that converts were issued the text in sections, mastering each lesson to receive the next:

the student did not receive Lost-Found Lesson No.2's first question and answer until each question and answer of Lesson No.1 was recited exactly as written. Then the student could receive just the first question and answer of the 40 which comprise Lost-Found Lesson No.2. When that first one was recited perfectly, then he or she would be given the second question and answer to learn and memorize.[6]

"Like all initiation systems," Fatir adds, "the process Master Fard used on Elijah Muhammad is intended to bring about an inner change that lights a spark and, suddenly, renders understanding. The Messenger taught his students to memorize the lessons. Through memorization and repeated recitation, the true power within the lessons begins to unveil itself."[7]

Clarence's military background helped him attain the level of AFOI (Advanced Fruit of Islam), a sort of unofficial lieutenant. Highly disputed tales have Captain Joseph assigning Clarence the role of judo instructor, Malcolm naming him an assistant minister and the Honorable Elijah Muhammad congratulating him on his progress with the honorific title of Abdullah ("servant of Allah").[8] The FBI began monitoring his appearances in Mosque No.7 and at NOI events. On February 16, 1963, informants observed him at a Muslim rally on 125th and Seventh, where Malcolm X preached that the so-called Negro had helped the white man fight his wars, giving his life for the white man in Korea, Japan and Germany, and the time had come for so-called Negroes to die for their own freedom.[9]

Despite his apparent rise through the Muslim ranks, Clarence's deep explorations of the Supreme Wisdom led him to an intellectual crisis. Initially he accepted Elijah's teachings that Allah had appeared in the person of Master W. D. Fard, the child of black Alphonso Shabazz and white Baby Gee. In the Supreme Wisdom Lessons, however, he learned that the True and Living "God of the Universe" was the Black Man; so why were Muslims worshiping a half-black man?

After a long day of selling Elijah's newspapers in Queens, the Muslims waited for their train home on the L platform, where John 37X Brooks overheard Clarence arguing with one of their comrades about W. D. Fard's divinity.

"I'm Master Fard's uncle," Clarence told him; "that means I'm his father, Alphonso Shabazz's brother and Alphonso was Allah before Fard." Clarence could support his argument with Fard's own lessons. "Who is the Original Man?" he asked his challenger, quoting the first question from the Supreme Wisdom's "Student Enrollment."

"The Original Man is the Asiatic Blackman," replied the Muslim, reciting his lessons by heart, "the Maker, the Owner, Cream of the Planet Earth, Father of Civilization, God of the Universe."

"I am an Original Man," Clarence shot back, "and the Original Man is God and that makes me Allah."[10]

John 37X, who had joined the mosque in 1958, approached Clarence after the debate and the two would talk for the entire ride to Harlem. They became inseparable friends and were nicknamed the "High Scientists" for the way that they constantly poured over the Supreme Wisdom Lessons.

Clarence would later say that the Fruit of Islam "played with him."[11] Five Percenter tradition narrates that Captain Joseph X and the FOI once pulled him from the elevator and mockingly demanded, "brother Clarence, come up here and minister."[12] They pushed Clarence to the podium. From the back of the mosque, Malcolm X heard the commotion, raced to the front and rang a small bell—a signal for silence. The Fruit immediately came to attention. Clarence stood before the crowded room and announced that what Fard had given to Elijah, Elijah had given to him. The shocked FOI began to approach the podium. Clarence then added, "and I am Allah."[13] The episode should be read with an understanding of Nation of Islam nuance, in which the Arabic *Allah* and English *God* did not always carry the same meaning. The distinction is illustrated in a 1959 exchange between Louis Lomax and Elijah Muhammad in the Mike Wallace documentary, *The Hate that Hate Produced*: " 'Now, if I'm to understand you correctly,' said Lomax, 'you teach that all members of the Nation of Islam are God, and that one of you is supreme and that one is Allah. Now, have I understood you correctly?' 'That's right,' answered the Messenger."[14] The statement of Clarence 13X in the mosque was indeed bold, heretical and an open challenge to the Nation's power structure; but it was also dependent on Elijah Muhammad's theology. The NOI believed in a succession of Allahs; Clarence may have been insinuating that Fard's term had expired and he would now carry the mantle.

In addition to his thought-crimes, Clarence's everyday behavior had fallen out of line. On one occasion he was barred entry from the mosque for wearing shorts, a violation of the NOI dress code.[15] At increasing odds with the organization, he drifted to the fringe of the fringe. He found a place for himself within the Supreme Wisdom Lessons, which broke down humanity into a system of percentages:

14. Who is the 85%?

ANS. The uncivilized people; poison animal eaters; slaves from mental death and power, people who do not know the Living God or their origin in this world, and they worship that they know not what—who are easily led in the wrong direction, but hard to lead into the right direction.

15. Who is the 10%?

ANS. The rich; the slave-makers of the poor; who teach the poor lies—to believe that the Almighty, True and Living God is a spook and cannot be seen by the physical eye. Other wise known as: The Blood-Suckers Of The Poor.

16. Who is the 5% in the Poor Part of the Earth?

ANS. They are the poor, righteous Teachers, who do not believe in the teachings of the 10%, and are all-wise; and know who the Living God is; and Teach that the Living God is the Son of man, the supreme being, the (black man) of Asia; and Teach Freedom, Justice and Equality to all the human family of the planet Earth.[16]

In its standard interpretation, the five percent would have been the Nation of Islam, while the eighty-five percent was made up of black Christians that had been exploited by the ten percent, the religious establishments. The ten percent, of course, kept the eighty-five percent pacified by teaching them to believe in a "mystery god" that could not be seen. But within the Nation of Islam, Clarence could perhaps see eighty-five percent of the population laboring while an elite ten percent (Elijah, his family and the inner circle) lived in mansions and rode in luxury cars. And how did they do it? By selling W. D. Fard, a man who disappeared thirty years before and hadn't been seen or heard since, a man who had become, in every sense of the word, a *mystery*, as Allah. It may have dawned on Clarence that he wasn't only in the Five Percent, but a special five percent *within* the Five Percent, the truest and poorest of Poor Righteous Teachers.

Clarence traveled to Philadelphia for the September 29 "Muhammad Speaks" rally at which Elijah Muhammad embraced Malcolm X and told the audience, "this is my most faithful, hard-working minister. He will follow me until he dies." But by the end of 1963, both Malcolm and Clarence would be effectively out of the Nation of Islam.

It is widely believed that Malcolm expelled Clarence for any of a variety of reasons such as gambling and smoking. Clarence's friend Les Matthews of the *New York Amsterdam News* reported years later that Clarence was called a "rebel" by Malcolm, who had supposedly said, "he refuses to abide by the rules and we gave him many chances. I think he would fare better out of the mosque."[17]

Clarence may not have sat well with the Nation's strict adherence to monogamy. In 1949, the year that Willieen Jowers gave birth to their son Clarence Jowers, he was treated for syphilis. In 1950 he wed his sweetheart Dora; one year into their marriage, he fathered another son (Otis Jowers) by Willieen. In 1953, serving in the army thousands of miles from both women, he received treatment for chancroid and is alleged to have impregnated a Korean woman.[18]

Around the same time that Clarence left the Nation, rumors of Elijah's adultery provoked mass defections in Chicago. Beginning in 1960, the Apostle had not only fathered children with seven of his young secretaries, but punished at least three of them with the standard NOI penalty for unwed mothers: complete isolation from the Muslim community. Malcolm began investigating the matter, even defying Nation protocol by visiting the three secretaries who had been placed in isolation. He heard the allegations confirmed by Elijah's own son Wallace, who had come to doubt his father's theology while studying the Qur'an in prison. It became clear that the rules for a lowly laborer in Harlem were not the same as those for the Messenger of Allah. If infidelity had caused Clarence to fall out of grace with the mosque, the hypocrisy could not have been lost on Malcolm.

Minister Akbar Muhammad, the NOI's international representative, has stated that Clarence was exiled not for adultery but domestic violence. Muhammad alleges that Clarence first received a thirty-day suspension, then returned and beat his wife again, after which he was suspended for ninety days.[19] The last time Clarence set foot in Mosque No.7, he was said to have been escorted out by the Fruit. It made for a "tense situation," claims a member of the Nation of Islam who spoke on condition of anonymity. Vincent Chambers, who at the time attended Mosque No.7 with his father, refutes the story. According to Chambers, Clarence simply stopped attending meetings, and any charges (possibly for stealing funds from the mosque[20]) were only brought upon him later as rationale for his absence.[21] For whatever reason, when Clarence permanently parted ways with the mosque, Dora chose to stay, and Clarence moved into his mother's apartment uptown.[22]

While investigating the death of a Muslim, the Bureau of Special Services had determined that Clarence 13X was employed by the Earth Painters Improvement Company in Brooklyn, run by Muslims George X and Ben X. John 37X, also employed by Earth Painters, told me that meager wages were the true impetus behind Clarence and his leaving the mosque: "we weren't making enough money to take care of our families, so we went for ourselves ... doing things to get paid that weren't a credit for the Nation, making money from the street."[23] Without providing too many details, he had given the same explanation in 2001, in a videotaped interview conducted by Five Percenters: "We decided to separate ourselves from the mosque so we could get paid ... we recognized that we was going to have to do some unscrupulous stuff to get money and that was not conducive to the image that the Nation presents, you know, the Nation of Islam."[24] John 37X agrees that Clarence had been under no disciplinary action. However, one week after Clarence left the mosque, John was suspended for continuing to associate with his friend. Rather than wait out his suspension, John abandoned the Nation of Islam and hit the streets with Clarence. "First he went," said John, "and I came behind him."[25]

Following the November 22, 1963 assassination of President John F. Kennedy, Elijah Muhammad, worried that false accusations would be thrown at his Nation, placed a moratorium against his ministers issuing any statements on the matter. He cancelled his December 1 appearance in New York, perhaps to avoid the issue himself, and assigned Malcolm to speak in his place.

The rally took place at the Manhattan Center and was open to the public; the audience of seven hundred included members of the press, Muslims, non-Muslims, and Clarence 13X. Malcolm gave his speech, entitled "God's Judgment on White America," and then allowed a question-and-answer session. When a reporter inevitably asked about the forbidden topic of President Kennedy, Malcolm gave his most famous soundbite (with the exception of "by any means necessary" and possibly "the ballot or the bullet"): "It was a case of the chickens coming home to roost."

Elijah suspended Malcolm for ninety days and transferred temporary leadership of Mosque No.7 to Captain Joseph X and later James 3X, minister of the Newark mosque. Malcolm is said to have paid a visit to Clarence 13X, who respected the ousted minister too much to buy the brandings of "hypocrite". While Elijah ruled from Chicago like a distant monarch, Malcolm had been the general on Harlem's front line. Malcolm was the man on the street corners, preaching to Harlemites in their own language and knowing their stories. In a previous life he ran those very streets as a pimp and hustler; when he admonished Clarence for shooting dice, it came with the authority of having been there. During Malcolm's visit, Clarence explained the unique roles that they were meant to play: Malcolm's job was to teach the old, while Clarence would teach the young.[30]

Malcolm went to Miami and vacationed at the training camp of Cassius Clay, who was preparing to challenge Sonny Liston for the heavyweight championship of the world. Fielding questions from the sports press, Malcolm claimed that his suspension would end after the ninety-day period. "If you think Clay was loud," he told one reporter, "wait until I start talking on the first of March!"

Malcolm described Liston-Clay as the "Cross and the Crescent in a prize ring" but Clay went in with such long odds (8–1) that *Muhammad Speaks* made no mention of the fight or Clay's interest in the NOI, lest the Crescent lose. Malcolm, however, was certain that Allah had provided three signs of a Clay victory, starting with the date of the fight, February 25. Malcolm added two and five together to get seven, which Elijah had taught was a lucky number (along with twelve and its reverse, twenty-one, which equaled seven + seven + seven) for the black man. At the Convention Hall, Malcolm was happy to find that his ticket placed him in the seat numbered seven. Allah's third sign was the fight taking place just a day before 1964's Savior Day—the thirty-fourth anniversary of W. D. Fard's arrival in the wilderness of North America. Again, Malcolm added the digits together and got the lucky number: three plus four equals seven. "Seven has always been my favorite number," he would reveal in his autobiography. "It has followed me throughout my life."[31] Clay pulled off the upset when Liston, claiming shoulder injury, failed to come out of his corner for the seventh round. The next morning Clay announced that he was in fact a Muslim in the Nation of Islam.

Malcolm's usual role at the Savior's Day Convention was filled by Louis X (Farrakhan), his pupil who had succeeded him at the Boston mosque. On March 8, two days after Clay was renamed Muhammad Ali by the Messenger, Malcolm X announced his complete break with the Nation of Islam. He had not desired to leave, he told the press, but had been forced out by internal politics. Malcolm stressed that he still considered himself Elijah's follower, and that Elijah still had the best solution to America's racial problems. Rather than blast the Messenger, Malcolm exhorted Muslims to "stay in the Nation of Islam under the spiritual guidance of the Honorable Elijah Muhammad" and insisted that he'd best spread Elijah's message by staying out of the Nation and focusing his work on non-Muslims. Four days later he announced the start of his own organization, "Muslim Mosque, Inc.," which would provide a "religious base" but focus on social and economic black nationalism. The Mosque would encourage participation by all, regardless of their religious or non-religious leanings.

On March 11, Malcolm sent a telegram to Elijah insisting that his decision to leave had come under pressure from a conspiracy between the national officials in Chicago and Captain Joseph X in New York. His intention was only to preserve Muslims' faith in the Messenger and the Nation of Islam. "I will always be a Muslim," he wrote, "teaching what you have taught me, and giving you full credit for what I know and what I am." The telegram ended, "I am still your brother and servant." The FBI suspected that Malcolm was leaving a door open for Elijah to take him back.

Malcolm announced at an April 12 rally that he would be leaving on a three-week tour of Africa and the Middle East. The next day he departed for Cairo as Malik Shabazz, which is commonly misunderstood to be Malcolm's "post-NOI" name. Malcolm had been using the name for more than ten years, and there is at least one instance of Elijah publicly referring to him as

"Minister M. Shabazz" during his time in the Nation. As roughly forty Muslims were said to leave Mosque No.7 with Malcolm, including a lieutenant in the FOI (James 67X), it meant a great deal that he still used Shabazz, the name of Elijah's Lost-Found Tribe. Fellow Muslim outcasts like Clarence 13X, who continued even in exile to revere Elijah and the Supreme Wisdom Lessons, saw no reason that they couldn't follow Malcolm upon his arrival home. For those tired of "talking tough, but never doing anything,"[32] Malcolm would manifest Elijah's message with direct action. Harlem had a new militancy, born in the Nation but free from its leader's control.

The life of Malik Shabazz, however, had been a series of sharp 180 degree turns and was about to take another.

4

The Blood Brothers

I tremble for my country when I reflect that God is just; that His justice cannot sleep forever.

Thomas Jefferson

1964 threatens to be an explosive year.

Malcolm X

At first the Harlem Six were seven, and they were teenagers when they heard Malcolm speak at a Nation of Islam meeting in 1963. Older non-Muslims had already given them the truth about Satan, which had trickled from the mosque into the streets; but hearing it delivered in Malcolm's voice changed their lives. "The knowledge and wisdom that the white man is a devil was so thick in the atmosphere," remembers Amin, "we left the meeting feeling completely different about ourselves."

Rather than register as official Muslims, the teenagers took holy names on their own and taught Islam to the younger brothers at their schools and on 129th Street between Seventh and Lenox, while learning karate from the older brothers. "We took up the art," states Amin, "because the police had started messing with us." With their new skills they could mess back. When patrolmen offered a challenge with nightsticks and guns, the teenagers took a fighting stance and dared them with "Allah is God! C'mon suckers!" The group also acted as Harlem's Robin Hoods, stealing entire bags of groceries from white-owned stores and leaving them on the doorsteps of needy black families.

On April 17, 1964, just two days before Malcolm X arrived in Mecca, the seven were part of a crowd of roughly eighty—most of them students at Cooper Junior High School—that Amin describes as "hot headed, and wanting to destroy whitefolks." Ranging in age from seventeen to nineteen, Amin and his friends stood as elder statesmen in the adolescent mob. On 125th and Lenox a black youth jumped a white man who was getting a shoe-shine just as a mostly white school on 124th was letting out its students. While Lenox Avenue fell to a miniature race-war, Jahad, Walik, Amin, Rahim, Malik, Akbar, and Latif walked up to 129th, where they discovered a fruit stand and helped themselves to what they wanted. As the NYPD rushed to the scene, Walik tried to prevent three officers from beating a youth with a stick and received a beating of his own. Latik was apprehended after standing between young children and a gun-waving cop. Walik and Latik were handcuffed together and thrown into a squad car. "When they got us to the precinct station," said Walik, "they beat us practically all that day." According to Latik, there were as many as six to twelve officers beating them at a time, and "all the time they were beating us they never took the handcuffs off." When the cops grew tired of beating, they began to spit on the boys.[1] The events of that day came to be known as the "Fruit Stand Riot."

On April 29, the seven reunited teenagers were hanging out with Amin's cousin Al-Jabbar (Leslie Stanley) in the night center of P.S. 144, where they held a karate class, played music and danced. Akbar (Robert Barnes) left, and later his six comrades—Amin (William Criag, 19), Walik (Wallace Baker, 19), Malik (Robert Rice, 17), Al-Rahim (Ronald Felder, 18), Jahad (Walter Thomas, 18), and Latik (Daniel Hamm, 18)—were picked up by NYPD for the murder of Margit Sugar, a Hungarian refugee. The six youths had allegedly walked into Sugar's Eve and Pete Clothing Store at 3 West 125th Street and asked to try on second-hand suits. "We don't have your size," replied Sugar, allegedly prompting one of the youths to stab her. Margit's forty-seven-year-old husband Frank tried to get the knife and received some jabs himself. Famed civil rights lawyer William Kunstler agreed to represent Latik, who along Walik had also been accused concerning the stabbing death of Eileen Johnston. Latik eventually confessed and named Malik as the other killer.

The Harlem Six all came from around the high 120 streets and Seventh Avenue. While in custody, Amin remembers, the group was visited by Clarence 13X, who provided "a whole new look at life, white folk and ourselves."

According to a series of *New York Times* articles by African-American reporter Junius Griffin, these six teenagers at the Brooklyn House of Detention were only the first glimpse at white America's new nightmare: throngs of young, angry black bodies coming together, getting trained and organized, building a force to counter police and take the heads off devils.

The "Blood Brothers" ranged in age from twelve to their mid-twenties. "Making traditional street warfare in Harlem obsolete," they had been recruited away from small-time gangs into something bigger, an army fighting not for turf but race. The leaders of the Blood Brotherhood were supposedly attritioned Muslims who had left Mosque No.7 with Malcolm X but would in turn abandon Malcolm when he wrote his famous post-*hajj* letter from Jedda, Saudi Arabia, dated April 20, 1964:

Never have I witnessed such sincere hospitality and the overwhelming spirit of true brotherhood as is practiced by people of all colors and races here in this ancient holy land, the home of Abraham, Muhammad and all the other prophets of the Holy Scriptures. For the past week I have been utterly speechless and spellbound by the graciousness I see displayed all around me by people of all colors ... There were tens of thousands of pilgrims from all over the world. They were of all colors, from blue-eyed blonds to black-skinned Africans, but were all participating in the same ritual, displaying a spirit of unity and brotherhood that my experiences in America had led me to believe could never exist between the white and non-white ... America needs to understand Islam, because this is the one religion that erases the race problem from its society ... The whites as well as the non-whites who accept true Islam become a changed people. I have eaten from the same plate with people whose eyes were the bluest of blue, whose hair was the blondest of blond, and whose skin was the whitest of white—all the way from Cairo to Jedda and even in the Holy City of Mecca itself—and I felt the same sincerity in the words and deeds of these "white" Muslims that I felt among the African Muslims of Nigeria, Sudan and Ghana. True Islam removes racism, because people of all colors and races who accept its religious principles and bow down to the one God, Allah, also automatically accept each other as brothers and sisters, regardless of differences in complexion.[2]

"Malcolm taught a lie," John 37X would snap at me in February 2005; "Malcolm told us that the devil could not enter the holy city. Then he came back and said, 'I *slept* with the devil! I *ate* with the devil! I *prayed* with the devil!' "[3]

A new Black Islam was forming on the streets, inspired by both Malcolm and Elijah but owned by neither. Blood Brothers shared their martial arts training with youths on rooftops around the area of 135th and Lenox, but operated mainly around 129th. Staple weapons of the group included makeshift wooden knives and three-inch razor blade holders in which the blade protruded half an inch. The Blood Brothers taught their disciples to greet each other with *as-salamu alaikum* and never attack another black man. They were said to be divided into two camps, one advocating indiscriminate violence against whites while the other taught its members to fight only if attacked. Requiring each member to share his training with ten other youths, the Blood Brothers had the potential to grow exponentially through the city. The group had already spawned an offshoot, the "Black Mollyzuls," distinguished by their wearing of red, black and green.[4]

The story snowballed. In his first piece, dated May 3, Griffin speculated that about sixty Blood Brothers roamed Harlem streets in search of white victims. On May 5, Griffin reported an unnamed researcher from HARYOU (Harlem Youth Opportunities Unlimited) announcing that the Blood Brothers numbered four hundred. On May 7, Griffin wrote of forty African-American detectives moving into Harlem to scope areas in which the group was believed to hang out after school hours. Morris Levy, lawyer for Al-Rahim, stated that he had heard "reports and rumors" of an anti-white gang but Al-Rahim assured him that he was not a member. Blood Brothers were even said to be secretly working their way into the fabric of local leadership, through positions on committees at public schools and community centers. Eric M. Javits, candidate for the Republican nomination for State Senator, demanded a grand jury investigation while the NAACP's New York chapter demanded proof that the Blood Brothers existed. James Farmer, national director of the Congress of Racial Equality (CORE), viewed the Blood Brothers—real or imagined—as emblematic of greater issues: "I think the Blood Brothers are merely another indication of the sickness of our society. They reflect the growing anger, frustration and sense of hopelessness in the Negro ghetto, especially among our youth, most of whom are unemployed."5

Minister James 3X denied any connection between Blood Brothers and Mosque No. 7. Malcolm X was still overseas as rumors blossomed of his involvement. Police informants reported that Blood Brothers had attended Malcolm's nationalist meetings and members earned the right to replace their surnames with "X" after killing a white person. One alleged Blood Brother was quoted as declaring that "chickens are coming home to roost." Another member who had been taken into police custody asked his mother to send word to James 67X, Malcolm's secretary at the Hotel Theresa. 67X denied that Malcolm had anything to do with the group, and addressed the issue at a meeting of the Militant Labor Forum. "I don't know if there is such a neighborhood Mau Mau," he said; "I wouldn't be surprised if there were one."6

The Blood Brothers did display some political sophistication, referring to the recently passed "no knock law" (allowing policemen to enter homes without knocking) as the "passbook law," an allusion to apartheid. In South Africa, the passbook law required nonwhites to carry passes as a means of restricting their movement.

The Militant Labor Forum arranged a panel on the "Harlem Hate Gang Scare," featuring Malcolm X, who had been asked about Blood Brothers while in Nigeria, Quentin Hand from the Harlem Action Group, William Reed from the Harlem chapter of CORE, Socialist Party presidential candidate Clifton DeBerry, and Junius Griffin. On May 29, the date of the panel, Griffin cancelled his appearance by telegram: "Regret that cannot participate in your symposium. Professional ethics restrain me from such participation."

When asked whether the Blood Brothers existed, Malcolm replied that it was possible and that it wouldn't surprise him at all. Such a group had every right to exist, he said, given the treatment that African-Americans received from police. As long as police continued to function as "occupation forces" in Harlem, said Malcolm, "you will find that there is a growing tendency among us, among our people, to do whatever is necessary to bring this to a halt ... I'm not here to apologize for the existence of any Blood Brothers."[7]

The same day of the panel, Griffin's "Harlem: the Tension Underneath" appeared on the front page of the *Times*, complete with fuzzy photos of black youths practicing karate kicks, tosses and blows to the Adam's apple. Today the Blood Brothers are commonly viewed as Griffin's invention, another cold black phantom to scare whites into buying newspapers. Though you can find Five Percenters today who identify as former Blood Brothers, it's questionable that Harlem's scattered pockets of renegade Muslims viewed themselves as an organized movement before Griffin gave them a name. In the Five Percenter community, the title marks an elder as present during the group's prehistory, that transitional period between Elijah's lessons escaping the mosque and their birthing a whole new culture.

The Harlem Six would ultimately receive guilty verdicts, thanks in part to the prosecution's star witness, Robert "Akbar" Barnes. After shouting anti-white slogans in the courtroom, Walik and Amin were sent to Bellevue for psychiatric examination. The remaining four each refused to comment when asked if they would like to say a word before their sentencing, standing expressionless with arms folded across their chests. The years to come would bring verdict reversals, appeals and retrials. Akbar recanted his testimony, saying that the police had coerced him to implicate the Harlem Six; he later recanted his recantation, claiming that Malik had threatened him. The trial judge, State Supreme Court Justice Gerald P. Culkin, caused further controversy by remarking that "these boys wouldn't know a good attorney from a good watermelon."[8] The youths became folk heroes, inspiring Truman Nelson's book *The Torture of Mothers*, supported with benefit rallies by the Charter Group for a Pledge of Conscience and a petition written by James Baldwin, which carried the signatures of Ossie Davis, Bertrand Russell, Günter Grass and Allen Ginsberg. Baldwin explained why support of the youths was a crucial and natural response from the black experience: "No one in Harlem will ever believe that The Harlem Six are guilty—God knows their guilt has certainly not been proved. Harlem knows, though, that they have been abused and possibly destroyed, and Harlem knows why—we have lived with it since our eyes opened on the world."[9]

Clarence 13X spent the summer of 1964 wandering across battle lines in Harlem's Muslim civil war, unsure of where he belonged. A June 16 confrontation with thirty-five Fruits led to the arrest of six armed men from

Malcolm's camp, forcing Malcolm into temporary hiding. Clarence was frequently seen in front of the Hotel Theresa; in the first week of June, the NYPD had determined him to be a member of Muslim Mosque, Inc. But on June 28, while Malcolm held the founding meeting of his secular nationalist group, the Organization of Afro-American Unity (OAAU), Clarence went to the 369th Regimental Armory on 142nd Street and Fifth Avenue to hear Elijah Muhammad address a rally.

Outside the Armory, a squad of Fruit swooped down on a suspected Malcolm supporter and beat him for a few minutes while policemen made hapless attempts to intervene. The Muslims, sporting armbands reading, "WE ARE WITH MUHAMMAD," then carried him across the street and left him for the cops. The New York Times described the beating as the only fight that day, but the New York Amsterdam News reported that two other alleged members of Malcolm's camp had been beaten for trying to attend. One of them might have been Clarence, whose sister Bernice claimed that he was barred entry following a scuffle.[10]

Inside, a mass of FOI appeared onstage and separated to reveal the Messenger in a velvet fez. He took his seat in a rose armchair until it came time for the "short, meek-looking" man of sixty-seven to address the crowd. The podium was covered with microphones and surrounded by Fruit. Elijah greeted the crowd of nearly seven thousand, roughly half of whom were Muslims, with as-salamu alaikum. Though neglecting to mention Malcolm by name, Elijah alluded to "some person who wants to be what I am, but that person is not able to be what I am." After an hour and fifteen minutes, he announced the end of his speech. As members of the audience got up to leave, Louis X took the podium and scolded those who would walk out on the only man who had ever told them the truth. Next to speak was Muhammad Ali, recently returned from Africa, who presented the Messenger with a miniature gold mosque on behalf of the Supreme Council of Islamic Affairs in Cairo. At another time Clarence 13X would have been on that stage, standing in a phalanx between the masses and the Messenger with a cold Fruit stare burning through and beyond the crowd. At another time it would have been Malcolm X, not Louis, who welcomed Elijah to the podium. Instead Clarence watched the Honorable Elijah Muhammad, Minister Louis X and the Heavyweight Champion of the World from the Armory stands, while some twenty streets away Malcolm struggled to get his new group off the ground.

The rumors that Clarence had joined Muslim Mosque, Inc. were later refuted; though he admired Malcolm, and the two occasionally met at a Chock Full of Nuts on 125th and Seventh,[11] Clarence couldn't identify with the new message. There was no place in Malcolm's *al-Islam* for Supreme Wisdom Lessons or the Yacub story, all essentials to Islam as Clarence understood it—but there was no room in that Islam, Elijah's *Nation* of Islam, for Clarence. As the Holy Apostle squeezed tighter and Malcolm moved toward his own immolation, odd men out were stumbling on the margins.

5

Allah

Clarence 13X and John 37X smoked herb and studied their NOI lessons at "the Hole," a hangout for hustlers, number-runners and riff-raff in the basement of Clarence's tenement building at 200 West 127th Street. "It wasn't uncommon in Harlem," says Vincent Chambers, "for the gambling spots to be in basements, and if you weren't from around there, you'd walk by and have no idea."[1] Reciting the Lost-Found Lesson No.1, John would ask a question such as, "why isn't the devil settled on the best part of the planet earth?" and Clarence provided the memorized answer:

> Because the Earth belongs to the original Black man. And knowing that the Devil was wicked and there would not be any peace among them, he put him out in the worst part of the Earth and kept the Best Part preserved for himself since he made it. The Best Part is in Arabia, at the Holy City (Mecca). The Colored man or Caucasian is the Devil. Arabia is in the Far East and is bordered by the Indian Ocean on the south.[2]

Out of the Nation, they dropped their X's and took new names. As the "best knower," Clarence 13X renamed himself Allah; bearing witness to Allah, John 37X took the Arabic name Shahid (Witness), which turned into *Abu* Shahid after the birth of his son, "Little Shahid."

During his stint as an AFOI, Abu Shahid had discovered a copy of *Teaching for the Lost Found Nation of Islam in a Mathematical Way* (also known as the "Problem Book") while shaking down Muslim officers' quarters in the Bronx. "I had offered it to the Father," says Shahid, "but he said that he didn't have any problems."[3] The former John 37X became "caught up in its science"[4] and was determined to solve the book's thirty-four riddles. He had been fasting for three days when he reached the thirteenth problem:

> After learning Mathematics, which is Islam, and Islam is Mathematics, it stands true. You can always prove it at no limit of time. Then you must learn to use it and secure some benefit while you are living, that is—luxury, money, good homes, friendship in all walks of life.
>
> Sit yourself in Heaven at once! This is the greatest Desire of your Brother and Teachers. Now you must speak the language so you can use your Mathematical

49

Theology in the proper Term – otherwise you will not be successful unless you do speak well, for she knows all about you.

The Secretary of Islam offers a reward to the best and neatest worker of this Problem.

There are twenty-six letters in the Language and if a student learns one letter per day, then how long will it take him to learn the twenty-six letters?

There are ten numbers in the Mathematical Language. Then how long will it take a Student to learn the whole ten numbers (at the above rate)?

The average man speaks four hundred words – considered well.[5]

Abu Shahid sought to find the "alphabetical computation of the mathematical evaluation."[6] Because there were twenty-six letters in the "Language of the Alphabets," he began by attempting to break down the number twenty-six. Because ten numbers constituted the Language of Mathematics, and two plus six equals eight, Abu Shahid believed there to be something missing from the Alphabets that was not absent from the Math.[7]

Shahid would find his truths in opposing sets of three. "Deaf, Dumb and Blind" were negative attributes countered by "Knowledge, Wisdom and Understanding." Shahid understood Knowledge to be the foundation of all things, and thus assigned it a mathematical value of 1.[8] Wisdom (2) was the application of Knowledge, and Wisdom added to Knowledge produced Understanding (3). The concepts occurred several times throughout the Bible, but not always in the same order:

For this cause we also, since the day we heard it, do not cease to pray for you, and to desire that you might be filled with the *knowledge* of his will in all *wisdom* and spiritual *understanding*.

Colossians 1:9

By *wisdom* the Lord laid the earth's foundations, by *understanding* he set the heavens in place; by his *knowledge* the deeps were divided, and the clouds let drop the dew.

Proverbs 3:19–20

For the Lord gives *wisdom*, and from his mouth come *knowledge* and *understanding*.

Proverbs 2:6

Abu Shahid denies the legend that he and Allah argued for three days over the proper placement of Knowledge and Wisdom, with Allah advocating Knowledge-Wisdom and Abu Shahid favoring Wisdom-Knowledge. "How can you have Wisdom," Shahid asked me, "if you don't *know* a goddamned thing?"

Describing this period, Shahid writes, "you must remember that I was fresh out of the Mosque, and that information was foremost in my mind."[9] Searching for the next set, he remembered the chalkboard at the mosque. On one side of the board was the United States flag, under which was written "Suffering, Slavery and Death." On the other side was the flag of the Nation of Islam, said to represent "Freedom, Justice and Equality." Shahid now had his four, five, and six. To the Rosicrucians, 7 symbolized divine influence in the physical realm, which became Noble Drew Ali's "Circle Seven." "Seven is God," writes Shahid, "because 6 days shall you labor, but the 7th day is the Lord's day or so it is written." In the Rosicrucian view, 8 was seen to represent "Evolution." Shahid determined 8 to be a "Transitory Period," symbolized by the opposing forces of "Build or Destroy." He also related the numbers to a baby's development in the womb: a child born in the seventh month was "lucky" to have matured early, but now faced the urgent struggle to "Live or Die." Then "following the analogy of the 'Child Birth Process,' " 9 was defined as "Born" or "Birth."[10]

> All male babies are sons of nine—9 months from conception to birth.
>
> C. M. Bey[11]

Shahid saw 10 as "Islam," but believed that 6 could not represent "Equality" in a system of only ten numbers; he needed two more. 11 became "Supreme Wisdom," since one plus one equals two and the Supreme Wisdom Lessons taught that there were eleven Original men for every devil. To unlock the meaning of twelve, Shahid looked once more to Elijah Muhammad, who wrote that Messengers were selected by a panel of twelve divine scientists:

> When Messenger is chosen, these 12 confer to see if whether or not he can do the job that he is now chosen for. The 12 Gods decide on all of this. We call them the 12 Great Scientists. This is why your ruler was made with 12 inches; it's after the number of the 12 Major Scientists, and without this, you cannot live. We call it a ruler when you have 12 square inches in it.[12]

With Elijah's foundation and an artful twisting of logic, Abu Shahid found 12 to be "Supreme Ruler:"

> if you want to be God then you have to be a Righteous Ruler, because the God of Righteousness is a Righteous Ruler. You must stand on your own "two feet," there are twelve (12) inches in a foot, two feet is twenty-four (24) inches. Six is half of twelve (12), 24 = 2 + 4 = 6, six is half of twelve and half of that is Equality. Now that is the way that I worked it out over a weekend of fasting.[13]

He now had a completed 1–12 system, which he called the "Living Mathematics:"

1 Knowledge
2 Wisdom
3 Understanding
4 Freedom
5 Justice
6 Equality
7 God
8 Build or Destroy
9 Born (or Birth)
10 Islam
11 Supreme Wisdom
12 Supreme Ruler

The search for Mathematical Language had spanned the entire tumultuous journey of John 37X into Abu Shahid. "I started it in the mosque," he told me, "and finished it in the street."[14]

While "sciencing out" the Living Mathematics and fasting, Shahid was also dealing and using drugs[15] and running a numbers business in the Bronx. He cites his big mistake as turning numbers money into heroin, which led him to get "strung out like a research monkey." He eventually got caught and did six months for gun possession. By the time Shahid got out, his fellow "High Scientist" had become the center of a small cult of personality. Allah was teaching the Supreme Wisdom to upwards of forty kids at a time,[16] mostly fatherless boys who had graduated from adolescence in the Hole's league of hustlers and gamblers. Several of them, including Al-Jabbar, had already learned "basic Islam" ("white man is the devil, don't eat no pig and be strong"[17]) and techniques to "smack police off horses"[18] from members of the Harlem Six on the eighth floor of 275 Atlantic Avenue.[19]

Allah also had a new running partner: James "Brother Jimmy" Howard, who "knew all of the street hustles and cons"[20] and went by a variety of names including Akbar, Arbar, Four Cipher Akbar, Free Cipher Akbar and Jimmy Jam. The two had met while shooting dice at Mount Morris Park. Howard's brother, "Karate Bob," had been a bodyguard for Malcolm X, and his wife, an NOI Muslim, left him because he wouldn't quit gambling and serve the Nation. Abu Shahid recalls that Brother Jimmy had attended enough meetings to become James 109X, but never stuck with it. To the former John 37X, Jimmy appeared to be little more than Allah's gopher: "He copped for the Father. Whatever the Father wanted, he went and got it."

"Like what?" I asked him.

"C'mon, man. I know you're not that naive."

Shahid soon learned that during his short prison stint, Allah and Brother Jimmy made changes in the Living Mathematics.[21] 4 was changed from Freedom to "Culture" (later taught as "Culture or Freedom"). 5, formerly Justice, had become "Power" (later to become "Power or Refinement"). Allah and Brother Jimmy's arrangement followed 9 with 0 ("Cipher"), which symbolized, as in C. M. Bey's Moorish Mathematics, the "circle of 360 degrees."[22] Faithful to the Problem Book, they had reduced the "mathematical language" back to ten numbers. There were no unique attributes for numbers after nine, instead combining values (12, for example, would be Knowledge Wisdom). Allah and Brother Jimmy had in fact turned Shahid's Living Mathematics into a whole new "Supreme Mathematics:"

1 Knowledge
2 Wisdom
3 Understanding
4 Culture or Freedom
5 Power or Refinement
6 Equality
7 God
8 Build or Destroy
9 Born
0 Cipher

While Allah and Brother Jimmy spread their version, Shahid was written out of the text's intellectual history. According to Al-Jabbar, Allah claimed that he had based his Supreme Mathematics on a 1–7 system formulated by Elijah Muhammad and taught within the confines of the mosque.[23] Enthralling uninitiated teenagers with his NOI arcanum, Allah taught that 7 in Elijah's mathematics represented "Islam" and took credit for changing it to "God."[24]

After completing the Math, Allah and Brother Jimmy set to work on uncovering the "twenty-six letters in the Language." Their efforts birthed a second system, the Supreme Alphabets, in which each letter carried its own meaning.

A   Allah
B   Be or Born
C   Cee
D   Divine or Destroy

E	Equality
F	Father
G	God
H	He or Her
I	Eye or Islam
J	Justice
K	King
L	Love, Hell or Right
M	Master
N	Now, Nation or End
O	Cipher
P	Power
Q	Queen
R	Rule or Ruler
S	Self or Savior
T	Truth or Square
U	You or Universe
V	Victory
W	Wisdom
X	Unknown
Y	Why
Z	Zig Zag Zig

The Alphabets gave rise to a stylized slang and could even serve as code. To refer to a police officer, Allah might have said "Cee Cipher Power," representing the letters C, O and P. While numbers had fixed meanings, letters were flexible and a word could be creatively broken down without each letter coming from the Supreme Alphabets. The word *job* could be broken down as "Justice Cipher Born" or "Just Over Broke." Allah broke down his own name as "ALLAH Leave Hell—Allah He."

With a legion of street kids to back him up, Allah held growing power in the hustlers' underground. Abu Shahid maintained his Living Mathematics and beefed with Brother Jimmy, who had interloped on Shahid's role as "brown seed" to Allah's "black seed." Jimmy had also seduced Sister Carmen, the mother of Shahid's son. "She deserved whatever she got from him," Shahid told me, "and she got her ass whipped by him." Shahid once laughed in Jimmy's face and made a trigger-pulling hand gesture; Jimmy tried to send the kids after him. "He was a punk motherfucker," says Shahid,[25] who remembers that Allah stayed out of their feud; in other versions of the story, Allah took the view that "if he fucked your girl, she wasn't your girl."[26]

Allah had attracted other apostate or exiled Muslims from Mosque No.7, such as Eugene 32X White, who adopted the African name Ebeka. As elders and initiated Muslims, they were respected by the teenagers who kept coming to the Hole and bringing friends to receive the lessons. The youths' daily lives gave proof enough to believe in savage, swine-eating devils who had crawled from the caves of Europe to rape the world. Many of them were no older than James Powell, only fifteen when shot and killed by the NYPD's Lt. Thomas Gilligan. Two nights after the shooting, a confrontation between demonstrators and police led to a storm of rocks and bottles hurled from rooftops, rioters smashing windows, sirens wailing, cops discharging firearms and black smoke choking the sky. The riot spread from Harlem to Brooklyn's Bed-Stuy section, and with the help of media exposure reached cities like Philadelphia and Rochester.

It was in this Harlem that young men left the sidewalks for basements and listened while outlaw Muslims preached that those white cops were genetically engineered beasts with smaller brains. For Allah, however, the most vital truth was not the wicked nature of the white man, but the inherent holiness of being black—as Al-Jamel remembers those early lectures in the Hole: "We were ... ingesting the knowledge that we are of a noble ancestry, god-kings upon this Earth. We were there learning that we were of the original people—a link between Divinity and humanity—a noble legacy, with godly identity, honored memory, sacred destiny."[27]

Al-Jamel had first been brought to the Hole by a kid named Akbar. A Christian at the time, Al-Jamel was originally not impressed. "God is dead," he told Akbar; "God died on the cross."

"You have a lot to learn," Akbar replied.

"If you can disprove what it is I say to you," Allah challenged Al-Jamel, "then disprove it, but I tell you: you are all of the Original inhabitants of the planet—you are a godly people; a people of the God of the Universe. You are of the first, with no known birth records short of millions of years."[28]

One tradition marks October 7, Elijah Muhammad's birthday, as the official start of the Five Percenter movement. According to Leslie Stanley, who had become Al-Jabbar during the summer of the Blood Brothers, Clarence 13X first made "knowledge born" that he was Allah on October 10. Allah used the date as a means of calling attention to the tenth degree of the Lost-Found Muslim Lesson No.2:

10. Who is that mystery God?

ANS. There is not a mystery God. The Son of man has searched for that mystery God for trillions of years and was unable to find a mystery God. So they have agreed that the only God is the Son of man. So they lose no time searching for that that does not exist.

Allah demonstrated his ideas by transforming words. He broke down *Allah* to mean "Arm, Leg, Leg, Arm, Head," thus representing man, and *Islam* as "I, Self (or Savior), Lord and Master." He also taught with an airtight argument of numerology: in the Supreme Alphabets, *G* stood for God; in the Supreme Mathematics, 7 stood for God; and *G* was the seventh letter in the alphabet. Hip-hop mogul Russell Simmons writes that "slick, smooth-talking, crafty niggas" embraced Allah's message and in turn proselytized "with as much flair as possible. A true Five Percenter could sit on a stoop or stand out on a street corner and explain the tenets of the sect for hours on end—and be totally entertaining!"[29]

Matthew "Black Mack" Johnson, who was only fifteen years old when he witnessed Clarence 13X being turned away at Mosque No.7, accepted him as Allah and was renamed Karriem, one of W. D. Fard's early names for Elijah Muhammad. Allah explained to Karriem that he was the "Cream" that would inevitably rise to the top. He was said to have favored Karriem because the youth was dark-complexioned (a "black seed") and would thus have the respect of his peers. According to Five Percenter literature, the youth's arrival held heavy symbolism, as "the Old Testament closes with God (ALLAH) visiting the Temple of Elijah in the book of Malachi and the New Testament begins with the Gospel according to St. Matthew."[30]

All sources name Karriem as present during an early Five Percenter cataclysm, Allah's first trial by fire. Details have been lost and added on as the story abandoned fact to become legend. As Karriem's pamphlet biography has it, the events of December 9, 1964 begin with him in a second-floor apartment on 126th Street between Sixth and Seventh Avenue, preparing to go outside. As he dressed for the cold, Karriem caught a sense of what evil the day could bring. On the street he grew cautious as Seventh Avenue was a "very busy avenue in those days."[31] Bumping into someone as he turned the corner onto Seventh, he instinctively assumed a martial-arts stance before realizing that it was Allah and Abu Shahid. They exchanged greetings of *as-salamu alaikum*. Allah told Karriem that they were going to the Hole, and that he should go home. What Karriem didn't know was that Allah had been summoned to the Hole by gun-wielding men that had trapped Brother Jimmy.

Karriem followed Allah and Abu Shahid as far as the basement entrance, at which point Allah told him again to go home. Karriem watched them descend the steps, counted to ten and went after them just in time to witness a confrontation between Allah and two men armed with a shotgun and high-powered rifle. Fearing that he'd have to defend Allah, Karriem tried breaking off a pipe from the furnace.

One of the gunmen asked Allah whether he knew the meaning of the Last Supper and Allah replied, "come on with it, lollipop." So they gave it to him. The crowd of hustlers, pimps, pool-sharks and Muslims scrambled for cover. After six shots Karriem rose to his feet but Ebeka pulled him back down and warned, "Karriem, they got more guns than you think, stay down."[32]

Forty years later in Harlem, I asked a Five Percenter named Ja'mella why they shot Allah.

"Because he was Allah," he answered. In the climate of 1964, that could have pinned a motive on anyone—NYPD, FBI, NOI, Sunnis. This early attempt on Allah's life then weaves itself into the greater sacred history; the failed assassination forebodes a later success, and Allah's character is reinforced as a Christ whose truth was so dangerous that it marked him for death.

Not all tellings raise the event to a biblical matter. In the late 1960s, it was believed that the attack had taken place during a crap game; Allah, a notoriously sore loser, was known for having his followers intimidate winners to get his money back. In another story, Abu Shahid and Allah were doing a deal with a hustler named Carlos, when Shahid spotted Carlos reaching into his jacket. Allah rushed Carlos, and Carlos pulled the trigger.[33]

The most detailed account of the shooting appears in an August 16, 1991 letter from Al-Jabbar to Knowledge Born Azee. Al-Jabbar attributes the beef to a Glamour Inn barmaid who had loaned Allah twenty dollars. Angered that Allah would keep coming into the bar and ordering drinks without offering to pay her back, on December 9, 1964 she refused to serve him. Allah walked out and went to the Wellworth. Later a man known as "Lil' Walter" ran in and told Allah that three men in the Hole were holding guns on Shahid and Brother Jimmy. Allah rushed to the Hole and pushed his way through the crowd, shouting "Who got the fuckin' guns?" Shahid and Brother Jimmy were there, along with Ebeka and Karriem, but there were no gunmen. Allah then arrived at Carlos, a "known stick-up kid" with a sawed-off shotgun under the right side of his coat and a rifle under the left. Carlos drew his shotgun and blasted Allah in the chest, knocking him to the floor. As Allah began to get up, Carlos went for the rifle and shot him in the left collarbone. Carlos then turned and shot two Hole denizens known as Pop and Billy; Al-Jabbar would later theorize that Carlos had intended to use Allah's debt as an excuse to rob everyone in the place. On his way out, Carlos aimed right at Jimmy's face and pulled the trigger, but the gun jammed and the shell ejected.

Allah was taken out of the Hole and back to Harlem's surface with at least two bullets in his chest and powder burns on his back. Karriem ran upstairs to

Allah's apartment where Al-Jabbar, Al-Salaam and Niheem were studying their lessons. All four sprinted to Harlem Hospital and met with Shahid and Brother Jimmy at the emergency room. Roughly twenty minutes later, a doctor informed the group that "the man who called himself Allah died on the operating table." Jimmy turned to Shahid and said, "it's almost two o'clock, it's time for us to pray." After performing Muslim *salat,* they learned from the doctor that a mistake had been made and Allah was not the one who had passed away.

Al-Jabbar writes that the next day, Allah confirmed to Shahid that he had in fact died for a time. Shahid ran down the hall to tell Pop, who, unable to speak, only pointed to himself and seemed to mumble, "me too!" Allah later related his near-death experience to the youths: the doctors cutting through his flesh in search of the bullet had caused him so much pain that he briefly left his body, during which he watched as they pronounced him dead. One legend claims that Allah actually spent three hours in the hospital's morgue and scared a janitor with his tears. Allah insisted that he was returned to his body by the prayer of Shahid and Brother Jimmy, after which he in turn brought Pop back to life.

Carlos was unable to shoot Brother Jimmy, Allah claimed, because Jimmy had a special role as his brown seed. Allah believed that Carlos had been sent by the Glamour Inn barmaid to collect the twenty dollars, and Lil' Walter's luring him to the Hole was part of the setup. His young followers were ready to get them back but Allah refused all offers of revenge, breaking down "gun" as "God U Not." According to Ja'mella, Allah said that he wouldn't even pick up a gun if Malcolm did, and taught youths to never carry weapons, "not even matches."[34] Refusing both fight and flight, Allah's only response was to stand firm on his square: "I don't run from no Muslim and nobody else. 'Cus I know, if I'm telling you the truth and *that* don't stop you, then nothing else will."[35]

Al-Jabbar took his friend Benjamin Gathers to Harlem Hospital to meet Allah, introducing Benjamin as Bilal.

"How do you spell that?" asked Allah from his bed.

"B-I-L-A-L," Benjamin answered. He had been named for an Ethiopian companion of the Prophet Muhammad who rose to elevated status within the early Muslim community. Allah would later break it down as *Build-Al.*

"I am Allah," he told Benjamin. The name kept ringing over and over in Bilal's head, causing him to miss most of the conversation between Allah and Al-Jabbar. Drawn back in after hearing Al-Jabbar say, "he has a better handwriting," Bilal was then chosen as scribe while Allah gave them the 34th question and answer from the Supreme Wisdom's Lost-Found Muslim Lesson No.2.[36] Bilal wrote the words as he heard them from Allah: "Can you reform devil? Answer: No! All the prophets have tried to reform him (devil), but were unable. So they have agreed that it cannot be done unless we graft him back to the original man which takes six hundred years. So instead of losing time grafting him back, they have decided to take him off the planet—who numbers only one to every eleven original people."

Allah's faction became known as the "Suns of Almighty God Allah." Five Percenters today recognize nine early followers of Allah, at the time ranging in age from thirteen to twenty-one, as his "First Born:" Karriem, Al-Salaam, Al-Jabbar, Niheem, Uhura, Akbar, Bilal, Al-Jamel and Kiheem. One story has Allah teaching the first four, then asking them to select five more. Standard history today places Karriem as the first youth to officially accept Allah; the claim is also made that Al-Salaam preceded him. Al-Salaam, however, went crazy, breaking a seven-day fast with pork and then telling Allah, "I did something that you can't do," so Allah exiled him and forbade fasts longer than three days.[37]

Bilal has speculated that each of the teenagers chosen as First Born reflected one of Allah's attributes.[38] Uhura has been described as a thug, while Niheem was considered "quiet but steady" and Kiheem was an especially skilled teacher.[39] Allah broke down Al-Jabbar's name as "I'll Jab Her" because Al-Jabbar would always "jab his way out of things." To Bilal, the First Born resembled characters from the 1963 science-fiction film *Children of the Damned*, as "when one of the children learned something, or was taught something, or internalized knowledge, and wisdom the others automatically knew."[40]

Uhura's chosen name, often spelled *Uhuru*, was the Swahili word for "freedom" and had been popularized by the famous Mau Mau revolt against British rule in Kenya. That Five Percenters commonly adopted non-Islamic African names such as Uhura and Ebeka may reflect not only the growing Afrocentrism of the time but also the presence of other alternative religions in Harlem's black nationalist discourse. At 28 West 116th Street stood the Yoruba Temple founded by Oba Ofuntola Oseijeman Adelabu Adefumni I in 1960. Adefunmi had been born Walter Eugene King in 1928 in Detroit, his father a member of the Moorish Science Temple. Cuthrell Curry writes that "a number of Black Americans received their African names from Adefumni and some of those began to wear African dress whether they converted to the Yoruba Religion or not."[41] In 1961 Adefunmi started the African Nationalist Independence Partition Party (with the aim to acheive an "African State in America by 1972") and the Harlem People's Parliament. Adefunmi's Minister of Arts and Culture was Jomo Kenyatta, who in 1961 named his newborn son Uhuru and in 1964 became the first president of liberated Kenya.[42]

Allah instructed his Suns to commit the entire Supreme Wisdom to memory and then destroy their printed copies. Abu Shahid often found Uhura and Karriem in his Bronx apartment, studying and smoking. Brother Jimmy did not know the lessons well enough to quote degrees, but could listen to others' recitations and correct them if they were wrong.[43] Captain Joseph X sought out Allah and Abu Shahid and pleaded with them to stop sharing NOI canon with youths that had not been registered Muslims, as they were "making the Nation look bad."[44] The Supreme Wisdom was a prized secret; as with a fraternity's pledge-book, to have knowledge of the document placed one within an exclusive brotherhood. Moreover, Allah had required each of his First Born to go forth and teach ten others ("First Fruit") that were younger than themselves, who in turn were each required to find ten younger seeds of their own. The NOI's lessons were fast becoming public knowledge at playgrounds. Kiheem, then a student at Junior High School 120, would dare peers to try staring at the sun. When they failed he'd smirk, "that's because of the pig in your system"[45] and proceed to enlighten them. Karriem taught youths who had adopted righteous names such as Rajeem, Sahammad, Alhambra and Omar. His First Fruit also included Vincent Chambers, the twelve-year-old Muslim who had known Allah as Clarence 13X in Mosque No.7. Vincent later ended up in a juvenile center in Otisville, where Al-Jabbar became his teacher and named him I-Jabar. Allah, careful to avoid doctrinal confusion, was said to have allowed each new Sun only one teacher lest he receive contradictory interpretations. Suns were known for "bombing" each other with the lessons, on threat of verbal or even physical embarrassment. "It wasn't based on someone not knowing his or her lessons," clarified a Five Percenter in a 2005 interview for *FEDS* magazine. "It was based on deliberately lying and deceiving somebody. If you know your lessons, then you will manifest them. If you don't know them, then you won't be able to. If you tell lies, then you will receive a Universal beatdown."[46]

"Universal beatdowns" were nearly administered to Clarence and Otis Jowers. Allah often visited his sons in Brooklyn, and Willieen sometimes brought them to Harlem, where she'd see her ex-boyfriend on a street corner telling kids to "hate white folk and don't eat no pork."[47] "My father's not Allah," jeered young Clarence, almost leading to a fight between Allah's sons and his Suns. After they relented, Allah renamed Clarence "A-Allah" and Otis "B-Allah."[48]

Suns were often thrown out of their mothers' homes for following Allah and refusing to eat pork. A number of destitute youths around fourteen and fifteen years old made their home at Akbar's place on 125th and Amsterdam, which became a sort of Five Percenter commune. "They'd go out and do their hustle or whatever," explained Jamar, "and then buy groceries."[49] Five Percenters sold weed and formed "boosting crews" to steal from department stores

ALLAH   61

downtown. Infinite Al'Jaa'Maar-U-Allah writes that the Brooklyn House of
Detention, "the only holding pen in the City for adolescents," played a major
role in the First Born's proselytizing:

> Allah's chosen would do minor, yet intentional violations of the law, so that
> they may be detained. These slight violations consist of: disorderly conduct,
> harassment, loitering, unlawful assembly, etc., and the quoting of lessons in
> front of the Masonic temple, or in front of the police station ... they would be
> taken to the Brooklyn house of detention ... these, the Nine Born, would
> instruct, teach and show the future members of the Five Percent Nation.[50]

In jails and reform schools, the Supreme Wisdom Lessons were regarded as
contraband. Youthful offenders taught each other verbally with coded references to lessons as "degrees" and the complete text as "the 120 (one-twenty)"
due to the document's combined number of degrees. Released Five Percenters
later turned the prison code into street slang, with "degrees" and "120" finding
general use.

Allah had not yet fully set himself apart in Harlem's underground culture of
Muslims and Muslim apostates; some of his Suns even attended NOI rallies.
After a visit to the mosque, Suns approached Allah and questioned him on the
10th degree in the Lost-Found Lesson No.1:

> 10. Why did Muhammad and any Muslim murder the Devil? What is the Duty
> of each Muslim in regards to four devils? What Reward does a Muslim receive
> by presenting four devils at one time?
>
> Answer: Because he is One Hundred Percent wicked and will not keep and obey
> the Laws of Islam. His ways and actions are like a snake of the grafted type. So
> Muhammad learned that he could not reform the devils, so they had to be mur-
> dered. All Muslims will murder the devil they know he is a snake and, also, if he
> be allowed to live, he would sting someone else. Each Muslim is required to
> bring four devils. And by bringing and presenting four at one time, his Reward
> is a button to wear on the lapel of his coat. Also, a free transportation to the
> Holy City Mecca to see Brother Muhammad.

According to the Suns, the minister had given a literal reading to the degree
and alluded to the coming Battle of Armageddon. Without further comment,
Allah told his Suns not to go to the mosque anymore.[51]

While recovering from his wounds, Allah made a slight reform to distance
himself from both Sunni and NOI Muslims. Al-Jamel recalls greeting Allah
with Islam's traditional *as-salamu alaikum* and receiving only "peace" in reply.
The exchange was repeated two more times, after which Allah asked, "what do
you mean by that?"

"Peace," replied Al-Jamel.

"Then why don't you say it in a language you understand?"[52]

Allah told Bilal that they walked the earth in humility, and should approach the ignorant with "peace."[53] As I heard one Five Percenter explain it, "we're not Arabs, and we're not in Arabia." Like the seventh-century Muhammad when he changed his *qiblah* from Jerusalem to Mecca—or Elijah Muhammad, who, when angered by Arab Muslims, told his NOI to pray facing Chicago[54]—Allah was breaking away from the parent religion; the Suns were being "debriefed from Islam."[55]

His body torn and scarred, Allah sensed that he wouldn't last the decade. In one of several cryptic statements about the future of the group, he said that the First Born would eventually go their separate ways. Drawing from the Supreme Wisdom, he told his Suns that each had to "swim his own nine thousand miles." They would find numerous obstacles in life, but also people to guide them. When Bilal asked how they'd be able to identify these guides, Allah replied simply: "you will know."[56]

Allah also told Bilal, "in order to keep what you have, you have to give it away."[57] Bilal understood; on the 19th, he took a train to Brooklyn to give away his knowledge. His friends Gypsy and Geno, at the time members of the Fort Green Chaplains gang, noted that he looked and spoke differently and tried to mock him. Bilal stifled them both, and neither would eat pork again. Gypsy became known as Gykee. Though today Five Percenters pronounce it *ja-kee*, Gykee writes that originally the *G* was silent and the first *Y* pronounced, but he did not know why;[58] *ya-kee* might have derived from *y'akhi*, the Arabic greeting "O brother." Geno took the name Shaamgaudd, which appears to be an Arabic-English mash of *shams* (sun) and God. Bilal spent six days and nights teaching the lessons, resulting in what would come to be known as Brooklyn's own First Born (which actually consisted of fourteen youths, not nine): Gykee, Shaamgaudd, Gamal, Bali, Ahmad, Lakee, Akim, Siheem, Ali, Raleak, Waleak, Sha Sha, Byheem and Hasheem. Bilal returned to Harlem on Christmas Day and the Brooklyn First Born began a three-day fast, subsisting on coffee and water. Their devotion may have been powered by apocalyptic fervor: according to Shaamgaudd, many Suns believed that because the devil's time ran out in 1964, "they could go out and do wrong, rob and steal and go to jail, and on New Year everything would be all right because the devil would be off the planet."[59]

Sha Sha and Akbar began teaching on the basketball court at the Good Shepherd Center on Sutler Avenue and Hopkinson, telling kids that if they didn't want to learn, they'd have to leave after their games. The civilization class opened with "Peace, Allah is God!" followed by each Five Percenter stating his name and how far he was in the Supreme Wisdom. Akbar taught on the history of Yacub and the day's math, after which Sha Sha would ask each student to explain what Akbar had said. As a class ended, Akbar and Sha Sha announced the date, time and place of the next lesson and reminded their students to bring notebooks and pencils.[60] Born Justice recalls that good study habits were not only encouraged, but enforced: "When we had our lessons, if you didn't know your lessons, you got chastised. I never got physically jumped on and beat down but I have seen brothers do that, because they were serious about the Mathematics but other people were not serious about the Mathematics. And if you're not serious about something that is of a serious nature, expect to get your behind Mathematically checked."[61]

According to the Supreme Wisdom Lessons, Jerusalem had been founded by Original men, who called it Jebus Salem or Oreil. "We took the city from the devil 750 years ago," says Lost-Found Muslim Lesson No.1. The text inspired a motif among Five Percenters; when the teachings are brought to a previously untouched city, the area is "reclaimed from the devil" and given a new name. The practice also follows a historical root back to Noble Drew Ali, who dubbed Newark New-ark. As birthplace and emotional center of the new movement, Allah understandably designated Harlem his Mecca (Harlem had also been called an African-American "Mecca" since the Harlem Renaissance of the 1920s). Across the bridge, Brooklyn became known as Medina, parallel to the second holy city of Islam. New York's largest borough, Queens was renamed the Desert after the 2,200 miles of hot sand that Yacub's devils were driven across in exile from the Holy City. Application of the Supreme Alphabets led to Staten Island becoming Savior's Island. Allah referred to the Bronx as Pelan, which in the lessons was another name for Patmos, where Yacub made the devil. Two rationales for the name both revolve around Abu Shahid, who lived in the Bronx as a Muslim and during the early history of the Five Percenters. Shahid ascribes the name to a comparison with the New Testament: Patmos was where St. John received the Book of Revelation, and it was in the Bronx that Shahid (John 37X) first uncovered the Problem Book which led to his Living Mathematics.[62] A more controversial story claims that Allah had deemed Abu Shahid a devil—perhaps during Shahid's feud with Brother Jimmy—and "banished" him to the Bronx, much as Yacub and his followers were exiled to the Greek island.[63]

Allah quickly grew popular as an alternative to both the Nation of Islam and Muslim Mosque, Inc., scooping up unaffiliated teenagers and Muslims who could take neither side in the schism. "Malcolm and Elijah were fighting," Abu Shahid told a Harlem audience in 2004; "we loved Malcolm, we loved Elijah, and we weren't down with that."[64] The division of Harlem's Muslims was not only between the parties of two heroes, but a split of rival philosophies. Malcolm was far more politically militant than Elijah, but his religion went soft on the devil; Elijah put the white man in his place but avoided taking real action. Like the semi-mythical Blood Brothers, Allah in his early years most likely saw value in both camps. As his basement sect grew in notoriety, it remained unclear to some where Allah's loyalties stood—even among his young Suns, some of whom believed that Malcolm X was the group's leader.[65]

Allah also provided the NOI's validating message without Elijah's uniforms and rules. Malcolm X acknowledged that harshly enforced moral puritanism had turned away potential members from the Nation of Islam;[66] however, Malcolm and Black Muslims who followed him to *al-Islam* shared Elijah's emphasis on self-discipline and rigid organizational roles. A saint only of the street, Allah lived like anyone else—he called wine "wisdom" and taught that reefer "referred" the mind, while cocaine made one "see"[67]—and appealed mainly to adolescent boys who may have respected Elijah's anti-white rhetoric but held no interest in wearing bowties or quitting music and girls. While Malcolm would have scolded youths for gambling, Allah assured them that shooting dice revealed the mathematical properties of the universe. Rather than impose rules and regulations, he gave the powerless a means by which they would command the unknown.

6

The Burning Mosque

I feel sorry for Malcolm. The sheer weariness of the man during his year of trial was overwhelming. On some level I think the poor man wanted to die, to gain a modicum of peace or, at least, a cessation of pressure and pain ... Malcolm, spiritually, was going through the kind of suffering, death and rebirth you read about in scripture.

Amir Fatir

As Allah spent December 1964 healing from his wounds, Minister Louis Farrakhan declared Malcolm X "worthy of death" in *Muhammad Speaks*. Allah later took one of his First Borns, sixteen-year-old Al-Jamel, to the Hotel Theresa for a meeting with Malcolm at his office. Al-Jamel recalls that the two leaders shared a brief but friendly interaction before Malcolm excused himself to accept a phone call.[1]

Malcolm held meetings every Sunday at the Audubon Ballroom on Harlem's Broadway and 166th, which in January also hosted a Nation affair, "A Night with the FOI" which was attended by top-tier Chicago officials such as Elijah Muhammad, Jr., John Ali and Raymond Sharrieff, the FOI's national Supreme Captain.

The night of February 14, Malcolm's house was bombed with Molotov cocktails while Malcolm, his wife Betty, and their four young daughters slept inside. The family escaped unharmed. Captain Joseph later visited the scene, claiming that the attack was on "Elijah Muhammad's property" and most likely committed by Malcolm himself. Two days later Malcolm confided in friend James Shabazz that he had been marked for death within the next five days, and knew the names of the five NOI Muslims assigned to kill him. He planned to reveal the names at his upcoming OAAU meeting on February 21.

As Malcolm began a speech at the Audubon Ballroom, two men began fighting in the audience. "Nigger," yelled one of them, "get your hand out of my pocket!" One reached into the other's coat, pulled out a German Luger and shot Malcolm in the chest. A third member of the team threw a smoke bomb. Malcolm was still upright as a fourth man came up from the third row and blasted him, again in the chest, with a sawed-off shotgun. A fifth man then shot him in the left leg and hand before shooting his way out of the room.

Growing throngs of people gathered outside the Hotel Theresa to hear updates on Malcolm's condition. When word came that he died, the crowd quietly dissipated. "A good brother is gone," Allah told his Suns. Malcolm's attorney, Percy Sutton, accompanied Betty Shabazz to Columbia Presbyterian Hospital to identify the body.

Four of the five assassins had escaped. At the scene police arrested Talmadge Hayer (also known as Thomas Hagan), who had been trapped by the crowd. Norman 3X Butler and Thomas 15X Johnson were picked up later. It was immediately assumed that the shooting had been ordered by the NOI's upper echelon. Rumors abounded of pro-Malcolm squads heading to Chicago to take Elijah's head, and shots would be fired at Elijah's house in Phoenix, Arizona. At 2:15 a.m. on February 23, Mosque No.7 was destroyed by an explosion on the building's roof, resulting in a five-alarm blaze that took over seven hours to subdue. A collapsing wall of the building injured five firemen and a pedestrian and ruined two fire engines. Firemen later found an empty gasoline can and rags on an adjacent roof.

During preparations for the February 26 celebration of Savior's Day, Elijah surrounded himself with Fruit of Islam and Chicago police. The festivities would have little to do with W. D. Fard; for Elijah, the three-day convention came at a perfect time to restore order in the flock. First he paraded out Malcolm's brother, Wilfred X Little, whose succinct address served to praise Elijah for saving Malcolm in prison, blame Malcolm for his own assassination and plea for the Muslims to remain united behind the Messenger:

> It was through the guidance of the Honorable Elijah Muhammad that he became known all over the world ... but he chose to go off on a reckless path. And the recklessness of his choice is what has, no doubt, brought about his early death. Let you and I not fall victim to becoming confused, now, and running in different directions. Let us stay in unity. Let not anything divide us and confuse us from our main purpose.[2]

Next in Elijah's pageant of conciliation was his own Prodigal Son, Wallace D. Muhammad, who had sided with Malcolm and embraced orthodox Islam:

> In the name of Allah, the Beneficent, the Merciful, may His peace and blessings be upon His Messenger, my father, the Honorable Elijah Muhammad. Brothers and sisters, I am thankful to be present here today to, in truth, make a confession of guilt for having made public a dispute that I should have taken privately with my father and perhaps I wouldn't have assumed a position that was not mine to assume, and that was to judge my father, a man who has a title

and a history that makes it permissible for God Almighty to judge him and not me. I regret my mistake and I pray, Allah, that my father accept me and I pray, if it's necessary, that you also accept me and permit me back in your midst as a brother. And I wish to say, at this moment, that I did use a hammer to knock, but in my ignorance I wasn't knocking to destroy. In my ignorance, I was knocking to repair, but I made a great mistake and I'm sorry for it. As-salamu alaikum.[3]

Wallace was welcomed back by his father and received warm applause from the crowd. "Brothers and sisters," remarked the National Secretary, "how can you express the joy?"[4] In just two moves, Elijah had washed his hands of Malcolm's blood and won a surrender from his own challenging seed. Louis Farrakhan then took the stage and lashed out at Benjamin Holman, a Chicago journalist who had gone undercover as a Muslim—and sat in the audience that day. "Put the light on him!" commanded Farrakhan. Muslims circled the reporter, shouting "Uncle Tom!" and "Kill him!" until Elijah Muhammad, Jr. ordered, "Go back, brothers!"[5]

Finally, Farrakhan introduced the Messenger himself, who stood to address his faithful:

For a long time, Malcolm stood here, where I'm standing. He was my intro-ducer. Every time a Mass Meeting was brought forth, he was the man to intro-duce me. In those days, Malcolm was great. In those days, Malcolm was loved. In those days, God Himself protected Malcolm. In those days he was a light. He was a star among his people, as long as he was with me. Now, here lay a man, his body now, on the way into the winds of the earth, that could have been here helping us to give praise to his own God and salvation, but turning against that God, he criticized the God who brought to him salvation and liberation. He criticized it, he called His teachings a tuxedo religion.

He criticized that God for even speaking of separating us from our own enemy, whom He has declared them to be. He went and gave the lie to what He had said. He came back preaching that we should now not take the enemy for an enemy, as God have made them manifest—that they had as much right to the kingdom of heaven as we ...

I have worked hard. These followers of mine, some of them has been following me for the whole of the thirty-four years. They saw, lived and heard everything, and I am thankful to Almighty Allah for opening up my son's heart and under-standing to return again to his father who has never did an atom's worth of harm against him, nor anyone else. And I am thankful to see him bold enough to come before you and to ask your forgiveness for the foolish mistakes that he made. I could not accept him because of what he had done with talking. You know it. You heard it. And therefore, I told him I could not accept him until you accept him because in the faith of Islam I have no choice among the believers ...

I ran from hypocrites and enemies of mine for seven long years on these terms. They ran me out of this state in 1935. I did not go and buy a pocket-knife, nor did I go and buy a gun. I could have armed myself but Allah bids me not to arm myself, nor are my followers to arm themselves. Therefore, I had to fly for my life. I stayed on the east coast from 1935 to 1942, slipping in to see my family under the cover of darkness ... on the eve to that flying from my hypocrites and enemies, I was arrested by the FBI and sent to the federal penitentiary for five years. This gave me twelve long years away from my family in all. This I was suffering before Malcolm ever knew that I was on the scene.

I suffered this, that I may be alive to help Malcolm when he returned from prison. I corresponded with him in prison. His two brothers knew all about it. They stand here like men, like Muslims. They know me. They know their brother. They know I didn't harm their brother. They know I loved their brother. He had been given the highest place. And when he made accusations among the public, he foolishly acted like Lucifer. He turned, then, to make war against me. I looked at him and laughed. I said to Malcolm, I said, "Go up on the mountain top, anywhere you want. Yell out anything you want to against me ... but Malcolm, I have the key."

Not that I mean that I had a key to kill Malcolm, I mean this: that Malcolm and not one of the twenty-two million people of mine, here, can get out of here without a key from me ... I am the door of this people and they have this to learn the hard way ...

Now, here you are agitating. You're always wanting to know why [don't] we admit white people in our Nation. The orthodox Muslims in Asia seem to be dissatisfied. And it's not that white people cannot believe. It is true, we have lots of white people in this country that is Muslim in just belief. We have people in Europe that believe. We have a whole country over there called Turkey, Muslim country. Now, here is what I'm teaching: Allah said to me, "by nature they are not Muslims ..."

Islam is as old as Allah Himself. It is not an organized religion. It is the very nature of God ... but this excludes the white race. The white race are not the people that was created in the nature of Islam ...

I want you to listen to this, you that is grieving and worshiping Malcolm. What was he teaching that you think, that you would benefit from? He was teaching a bloodbath ... arming yourself to attack a well-armed people of whom you would have just committed suicide ... he was a man upset, had lost his mind and [was] running all over the country saying, "let's kill him" when no one was around but himself. We didn't want to kill Malcolm, and didn't try to kill him. We knew that ignorant, foolish teaching would bring him to his own end ...

If God had wanted to save Malcolm, He would have saved him ... we did not try to interfere with Malcolm, especially when he came right in my door. I didn't tell my followers to go out there and kill Malcolm. I wanted him to be brought to a naught by that which he preached. I let God take care of him. I know you don't have a chance against me if God is with me ... but I warn you in my conclusion, leave us alone if you don't like us. Leave us alone, lest you find yourself playing with fire. Leave us alone. We will leave you alone. On an instant that we find that you don't like us, we let you go. Be just, do the same by us. Let us go. If you don't like us, leave us alone.[6]

Malcolm's funeral was the next day. Al-Jabbar planned to see the casket after getting high. Not sure how Allah felt about attending the service, Al-Jabbar only told him, "I'm going to go smoke a joint." Allah could tell that something was up.

"Why did Musa have a hard time civilizing the devil?" Allah asked. Al-Jabbar gave the proper answer from Lost-Found Muslim Lesson No.1, that Musa was savage and half-original. Then it hit him that Allah knew he was being "half-original," telling only half the truth. Al-Jabbar confessed that after smoking he would attend Malcolm's funeral. Allah asked Al-Jabbar why he would want to see a dead body.[7]

One month after the assassination, the Nation of Islam held a rally in New York. It is likely that speakers addressed the subject of Malcolm, perhaps reiterating the themes of the Savior's Day convention for those that weren't there. FBI informants noted the attendance of one Clarence 13X.[8]

As the Harlem Muslims sank in disarray, Captain Joseph X relieved stress with trips to Mount Morris Park—where he could chase Allah's Suns around, yell nasty things at them, hit one if he got the chance, and drive them away. It did not take long for Allah to catch word and make an appearance at the park. "These are my Suns," he told the captain; "never, ever bother my Suns again." Joseph went back to the mosque.[9]

On May 28, leadership of Mosque No.7 was handed to Louis Farrakhan, catapulting him to national prominence as it had for Malcolm before him. Given the minister's comments regarding his former mentor, the move could have done little to build bridges in Harlem's devastated Muslim community; if anything, it might have been a final stamp on Elijah's condemnation of Malik Shabazz. Three days later, Allah walked with Brother Jimmy and a handful of Suns to the corner of 116th Street and Lenox Avenue, site of the ravaged Mosque No.7. They stood before the ruins of what had been a psychological nexus for various currents of black nationalism, from the liberation theology of Elijah to the political urgency of Malcolm. On that day in 1965, the bombed-out building served as a monument, a tombstone, the terrible conclusion. As he stood on the corner, what ran through Allah's mind? In the last five years, his story with that temple had changed him from Smith to 13X to God. Allah had been there through all of it: the glory days and the growing tension, Malcolm's suspension and exodus and finally his own. Despite everything, Allah loved both the mosque and Malcolm, even if the mosque had shut him out, even if Malcolm had prayed with the devil, even if the two had now destroyed each other.

According to FBI files, Allah and his group caused a "disturbance" and were told by a policeman to move on. They cursed at the officer but complied, turning onto Seventh Avenue and heading north for the 120 series of streets. Roughly ninety minutes later, they were breaking windows in stores and bars. When an African-American named Wilbert Lee tried to pull his revolver, Allah dropped him with a stick. Black patrolman H. T. Webb would claim to have rescued Lee from the group.

They stopped at the Hotel Theresa, whose front sidewalk was cluttered with the usual stepladder preachers and impromptu rallies. From the NOI's ruins on 116th and Lenox to the headquarters of the all-but-dead Muslim Mosque, Inc., Allah had led his Suns on a furious tour of the Elijah-Malcolm tragedy. At 9:15 p.m., police were called with reports that the Suns were blocking traffic and harassing pedestrians in front of the Hotel. When three white patrolmen arrived, the Suns allegedly turned on them and shouted for bystanders to join in. Allah shouted for Karriem to get away. Karriem refused and Allah repeated his command until the youth finally relented, sprinting around a corner to flee down 124th Street. "Allah knew that I wasn't going to leave him," Karriem later explained, "so he gave me an order to get away. Them Cee Cipher Powers were no match for my arts."[10] Al-Jamel and other Suns arrived to find Allah with his back against the wall, throwing wild punches. Enough backup arrived that some officers just stood around and watched as Allah was subdued.

"Don't murder my Suns," he finally pleaded. "I'll go with you."[11]

Allah, Brother Jimmy (at the time known as Akbar), Gumal, and three sixteen-year-old Suns—Leon (Uhura) McCray, Hasan Jamel and Ronald (Al-Raheem) Perry—were taken into police custody. Gumal and Hasan Jamel refused to give their legal names. Brother Jimmy Howard gave his last name as Howell. Allah gave his residence as Harlem Hospital, his birthplace as Mecca and refused to further identify himself. He confessed to assaulting Wilbert Lee but asserted that Lee had first threatened him with a gun. The six were charged with felonious assault, conspiracy to commit felonious assault, resisting arrest, assault with a deadly weapon and disorderly conduct. Allah was additionally charged with malicious mischief and possession of marijuana.

Barely twenty-four hours later, the FBI's New York office sent a teletype marked "urgent" to the Bureau's national director, J. Edgar Hoover, relating that all six men had identified themselves as members of a new organization, the "Five Percenters," which they claimed were the "five percent of Muslims who smoke and drink." They denied membership in the Nation of Islam or Muslim Mosque, Inc. and claimed no headquarters beyond various Harlem street corners.

The next day roughly sixty black teenagers, some wearing "fezzes," appeared at Allah's arraignment. "Police fill court for Muslim case," read a *New York Times* headline, which described the arraignment as taking place "under the tightest security measures seen in the Criminal Courts Building for at least 10 years," including fifty uniformed patrolmen and thirty detectives.[12]

When the defendants arrived in the courtroom, Allah wearing a black fur hat, gray windbreaker and tan pants, the sixty youths rose to their feet and shouted "Peace" with their palms upraised. Judge O'Brien cleared the courtroom of spectators.

The charges were read. "Lie, lie, lie," mumbled Allah. "You're wrong for accusing righteous people," he told Judge Francis X. O'Brien. "The city will blow up. We're going to cause much trouble, you watch. We're not charged with anything. You can't charge Allah."

"He's not a patrolman," Allah remarked on Webb, "he's a bum! You have no right to come to Harlem and ask us to move. We don't come to your city. We could have killed many officers." Concerning Wilbert Lee, Allah stated, "if he tells the lie we hit him he'll never see the street no more."

Judge O'Brien asked Allah if he had a lawyer. "*I'm* the lawyer," Allah snapped. "We don't want your people to do nothing for us. They called me to stop fighting. They attacked me."[13]

The case was adjourned at the prosecution's request. The teenaged Suns were held in lieu of $2,000 bail. Bail for Gumal was set at $3,000; Brother Jimmy, $9,000; Allah, $9,500. The arraignment was covered in both the *New York Times* and *Daily News*, which referred to the men as "Black Muslims." Photographs of the six defendants were shown to police informants in the NOI, OAAU and Muslim Mosque, Inc. while a list of forty-eight known Five Percenters, all between the ages of twelve and nineteen, was circulated to various government agencies.

At 10:00 a.m. on Friday, June 18, upwards of fifty Five Percenters arrived at Manhattan Criminal Court, matched by a comparable police detail. Assistant District Attorney Alan Broomer suggested to Judge Walter H. Gladwin that

Allah's case be held off until 12:15, hoping the crowd of teenagers would get bored and leave. Instead it doubled, prompting the police detail to call in thirty more officers. The Suns "milled around the courtroom and courthouse" without incident.[14] Felony charges against the underage defendants were dismissed, while the adults (Allah, Brother Jimmy and Gumal) were transferred to New York Supreme Court. Because they did not have attorneys, their hearing was postponed until June 24.

Eight Five Percenters—five from Harlem (Karriem, Omar, Dubar, Lubar and Allah's son Clarence "A-Allah" Jowers), three from Brooklyn (Gykee, Akim and Gamal)—left the courthouse and later followed Ebeka in Muslim prayer in the schoolyard of P.S. 168, between Seventh and Lenox Avenues on 127th and 128th Streets.[15] They then parted ways with Ebeka and climbed onto the roof of 131 West 128th to fly their pigeons.[16] At 7:10 p.m., police showed up, allegedly found the Suns with a gallon can of gas, a funnel, cloth, piece of hose and four empty bottles and arrested them for unlawful possession of combustibles. The NYPD claimed that three molotov cocktails had been thrown in the same area of Harlem. The New York Times was fed reports of a "witness" observing one black youth point to the police station as he announced to his friend, "Tonight we'll take care of them. Inside. We'll give it to them with molotov cocktails."[17] A-Allah and Lubar, both sixteen years old, were released, while the others were held on $500 bail. Because Gykee would not stop smiling, they raised his bail to $1,000. Gykee, Akim, Gamal, Omar, and Dubar remained in police custody from June 18 to July 5. Karriem was held for an extra week. The FBI noted that while one suspect (most likely Clarence Jowers) was a known Five Percenter, the youths all gave "Muslim type names."[18]

A memo to J. Edgar Hoover observed that "Due to Smith's actions, rantings and ravings, particularly in front of the judge at his hearing, he appears to have a 'psychological problem', but the court has taken no action in this regard."[19] The FBI might have nudged the court; on July 9, Allah was committed to Bellevue Hospital for psychiatric examination. At Bellevue Allah found new disciples, including a "scientifically miraculous" latin man named Jesus and Armando X, a Muslim from Mosque No.7.

On July 29, seventeen Five Percenters between the ages of fourteen and eighteen were arrested for throwing bricks, rocks, garbage cans and bottles at a police officer. An article the next day in The New York World Telegram didn't seem to take Allah or his Five Percenters seriously, quoting casual dismissals by Harlem residents. "That cat ain't got nothing but the blues," said one. "That ain't God," said a barmaid, "that's Puddin. That's what we always called him—Puddin." A man described as Smith's friend of twenty years called him a "nice friendly guy, who used to work pushing trucks down in the garment district."[20]

Allah was still at Bellevue when eighty-six-year old Father Divine passed away in September. Father Divine had started a gradual withdrawal from the public in the late 1950s, and stopped making appearances altogether in 1963. His *angels* declared that since Father Divine was God, he couldn't die, and had merely decided to "lay his body down." Over the years, numerous angels had been locked behind the same walls that now caged Allah. In April 1932, two women were taken to Bellevue after police broke up a Peace Mission event in Harlem. One of them had been dancing and singing while dressed only in a sheet, while the other told officers, "we're older than Methuselah."[21]

Louis Farrakhan appears to have viewed Allah's incarceration as a chance to bring the Five Percenters under his control. Supported by a Fruit of Islam "Doom Squad," Captain Joseph X announced that anyone who knew the Supreme Wisdom Lessons should immediately register as Muslims with Mosque No.7. Upon hearing the news, Karriem walked to Bellevue and called to Allah from the sidewalk. Allah came to the second-floor window and Karriem shouted up the story. Allah told him to go to Mosque No.7, ask for Captain Joseph by his "real" name—Captain Yusef—and tell him that he said, "I know who I am and he knows who I am. My Five Percenters are not Muslims and they never will be Muslims, and he better leave my Five Percenters alone." Karriem went back to the mosque restaurant and exchanged greetings of *as-salamu alaikum* with the Doom Squad. He asked to see Captain Yusef but the Muslims weren't sure who that was. One of them found Captain Joseph, who asked for Karriem to be sent to him. Karriem told the captain what Allah had said. Joseph replied, "tell Clarence—"

"You mean Allah?" interrupted Karriem.

"Yes," Joseph relented. "Allah. Tell Allah that I will pull back my people."[22]

At least for the moment, the Muslims and Five Percenters had agreed to a peaceful coexistence; but Allah had enemies much bigger than the Doom Squad.

7

Matteawan

There does exist a group that refuses to accept grievous social injustices—and they are prepared to rebel.

Livingston Wingate

I know absolutely nothing about the Five Percenters. Maybe Mr. Wingate does.

Adam Clayton Powell, Jr.

Wingate was the director of HARYOU-ACT, a unification of the Harlem Youth Opportunities Unlimited and Associated Community Teams programs. At a National Urban League conference in Harlem, he told the leaders of approximately fifty poverty programs that unless conditions changed, an uprising would occur to "make Watts look like a tea party," referring to that summer's riots in South Central Los Angeles that left thirty-four dead, a thousand injured and four thousand arrested. Wingate warned that the next outbreak of bloodshed would start in Harlem, move to the Bedford-Stuyvesant section of Brooklyn and then spread upstate to Rochester and Syracuse. Meanwhile, Wingate himself was under investigation by local and federal authorities for charges of fiscal mismanagement. He defended his spending as essential to preventing a race war, but refused to identify a particular "armed group" for fear that it would come after him. "These kids don't give a damn," he said. "They are willing to die."

At least one already had. Fifteen-year-old Cedric Avery was bragging about the Five Percenters on the St. Nicholas projects' playground when Earl Green, a twenty-one-year-old veteran, laughed him down. Avery attacked Green and Green stabbed Avery to death. Avery's body was then decorated with "Muslim medals" while his friends shouted, "Get up. You're not dead. We can't die." He did live on through his Five Percenter name, Kaseim,[1] which was given to a new member.[2]

A group of hecklers that caused Adam Clayton Powell, Jr. to end his walking tour of Harlem with Democratic mayoral candidate Abraham D. Beame were identified as members of the Black Arts Repertory Theater, home to director and playwright LeRoi Jones. Reporters immediately asked Jones if he had anything to do with the Five Percenters. "I've never met one," he replied. "It sounds like it might be an idea for another TV show."[3] Jones then remarked that if the Five Percenter mission was anything like he had heard, then he supported them as he would "any idea to end white domination of the world." A month later, FBI informants observed Jones "affiliating and hanging around" with Five Percenters at his theater.[4]

Assemblyman Percy Sutton explained to journalists that he had first heard the term "Five Percenter" from Malcolm X, in prophecy of a "Negro elite" that would act as freedom fighters.[5] City papers reported the chaos that Five Percenters wreaked at public schools: at Harlem's Junior High School 120 there had been at least two assaults and a telephone threat, while teens and preteens received five-day suspensions for insisting on using their "Muslim names" and terrorizing fellow students and teachers alike. Anticipating assaults from Five Percenters, "several pork-eaters brought weapons from their homes on the way to school," wrote James W. Sullivan in the *Herald-Tribune*. "They checked their weapons with the principal when they arrived." One man was quoted as claiming that he could identify Five Percenters by the way they looked at a store window: "they're not looking in it, like other people do; they're looking in it, like they want to break it."[6] Five members were arrested by the Transit Authority police after cursing at passengers. When warned by a patrolman, the group allegedly turned to attack him. Taken to the 24th precinct, they gave only their righteous names—Omar, Krean, Dumal, Semik and Shariff—and named their birthplace as "earth."[7] A front-page story in the *New Pittsburgh Courier* called Five Percenters a "mysterious gang of thugs" led by "subversive older men," but writer John E. Moore at least gave them credit for being well-read: "they avidly devour anything written by the radical Negro and can quote much of it verbatim."[8] "They're a pure growth of the slums," a city youth worker told the *New York Times*.[9]

The *New York Amsterdam News* claimed that Allah had threatened to kill white babies and black policemen, and start riots unless his Five Percenters received some "poverty money" to build their own mosque.[10] "There's no evidence that they are advocating violence," insisted Rev. Eugene Callender, HARYOU-ACT's chairman. "I hope we will be able to involve them in meaningful programs that would channel their energies into more constructive pursuits."[11] Dr. Kenneth B. Clark, founder and former director of HARYOU, accused Wingate of "black McCarthyism" and referred to his warnings of Five Percenter revolt as "fantastic, dangerous and irresponsible." "These kids don't go around armed," said a youth worker, "and anyone who says that doesn't know what he's talking about. The cops have been picking these kids up left and right and not once have they been charged with a violation of the Sullivan

Law."[12] Though certain that the youths were robbing and extorting their own mothers, Moore placed the blame on their unseen leaders: "these mentally pliable children have no way of knowing that the older 'Svengalis' who are indoctrinating them, are merely using them as the means to support their own selfish greed and unwillingness to work honestly for a living."[13]

Speculation continued to run wildly out of hand. Five Percenter membership was placed as high as a thousand, "organized into cells in every New York City project with a substantial number of Negro residents," while the number of Five Percenters said to have shown up for Allah's arraignment had ballooned to 150. A twenty-one-man police detail that had been created specifically to deal with the group was assigned to St. Patrick's Cathedral during a visit of Pope Paul VI, due to fears of a Five Percenter assassination attempt.

The day after the Urban League conference, while provocative headlines ran in the *New York Times* ("Wingate Warns of Negro Revolt"), *New York Amsterdam News* ("Harlem Hit by Five Percenters") and *New York Herald-Tribune* ("Harlem's '5 Percenters'—Terror Group Revealed"), agents from the FBI's New York Office (NYO) met with the NYPD. The Special Agent in Charge (SAC) was informed that a "Special Unit" of the Youth Division had compiled information on the Five Percenters by "daily interrogation of gang members and nightly surveillance of them."[14] These investigations were said to result in numerous arrests of Five Percenters on charges of "assaults, mugging and marijuana smoking."[15] In contrast to the media panic, the Special Unit reported a more subdued estimate of two hundred members with ages ranging from twelve to twenty-one. Over half of the Five Percenters roamed Harlem's 120 streets, bordered by Seventh and Lenox Avenues, but there were also reported concentrations in Brooklyn's Fort Green area and the region around St. Mary's Park in the Bronx. One month prior to the meeting, NYPD's Bureau of Special Services (BSS) reported that Clarence 13X Smith had sometimes gone by the name Clarence Smith Jowars, and was unsure whether Smith or Jowars was Allah's real name.

City police requested that the information they provided be kept strictly within the Bureau, due to the ongoing "extensive" investigation and "recent publicity given to the matter." The NYPD had refused comment to "numerous incidents of newspaper speculation" and feared any public suggestion that they were actively pursuing the Five Percenters. In a communication to the SAC on October 23, 1965, however, J. Edgar Hoover ordered that all material on the group be disseminated to officials in the military, Justice Department, and Secret Service. He told the SAC to remind the police of their responsibility to share pertinent information, with assurances that the NYPD would be concealed as the source. Besides, Hoover noted, much of the info had already appeared in newspapers—including suspicions that Five Percenters were linked to Chinese or Cuban Communists and a group that had plotted to dynamite the Statue of Liberty. While agreeing that Five Percenters posed a "local police problem" and dismissing Allah as a "Harlem rowdy," Hoover advised a continuing FBI effort to find possible links to foreign elements. The NYO began an investigation of Ebeka, "the third leader of the gang," to determine whether he was involved with "any organization inimical to the internal security." Ebeka, who had assumed a leadership role during the incarceration of Allah and Brother Jimmy, was himself arrested in August for selling a marijuana cigarette. On October 19, Bronx County Supreme Court sentenced him to two years in prison.[16]

According to the SAC, the District Attorney's office and the court consistently pushed Allah's hearing to later dates. The results of his psychiatric exam were also delayed: after "examining" Allah for four months, Bellevue requested an additional ten days to complete its evaluation. The judge stated that in all likelihood Allah would be placed in a mental institution, and an SAC memo to Hoover, dated November 16, 1965—the exact date of Allah's final hearing—predicted that Allah would be found insane. When Bellevue finally submitted its report, the judge indeed found Allah "unable to understand the charges against him" and remanded him to the custody of the New York State Department of Mental Hygiene for an "indefinite confinement." It was another victory for a man who had given his whole life to squashing voices of dissent.

J. Edgar Hoover began his career in 1917 as a clerk at the Justice Department. With most of his potential competitors overseas fighting World War I, he enjoyed a meteoric rise through the ranks. Landing a major promotion as head of the Enemy Alien Registration Section, Hoover observed and studied Department battles with labor movements such as the IWW. When Attorney General A. Mitchell Palmer's home was bombed by an anarchist, he assigned Hoover the task of collecting and organizing information on all radical organizations and their leaders. Palmer even gave him a new agency: the General Intelligence Division (GID). From his new authority, Hoover saw a particular threat in the rising Communist movement and declared open season. In what became known as the "Palmer Raids," over ten thousand suspected Communists were detained; most enjoyed quick releases due to a lack of substantial evidence. Hoover continued obsessively collecting names. In 1921 he moved up to Assistant Chief of the Bureau of Investigation; three years later he rose to the top of the Bureau and would retain his position through six presidents. Over time, Hoover *became* the Bureau, with such a paternal and domineering presence that his own prejudices dictated agency culture. In 1956 the FBI established COINTELPRO (Counter-Intelligence Programs) with Hoover's stated intention to "expose, disrupt, misdirect, discredit and otherwise neutralize" radical organizations. Just as his WWII-era fears of Japan-sponsored black revolt led him to pursue the Moorish Science Temple and Nation of Islam, his 1950s fear of Soviet-inspired black revolt inspired him to pursue the civil rights movement. Hoover enlisted roughly eight thousand "ghetto informants" to provide him with names and information on groups like the Southern Christian Leadership Conference. He investigated Martin Luther King, Jr., who had first been brought to his attention for having socialized with a Communist. Both Elijah Muhammad and Malcolm X were well aware that the FBI had infiltrated their organizations. An agent of the Bureau of Special Services actually landed a job as Malcolm's bodyguard and even attempted mouth-to-mouth resuscitation while Malcolm lay dying in the Audubon Ballroom.

By 1965 Hoover had spent nearly half a century compiling his lists of suspected troublemakers, grouped into over one hundred indexes. Some were simply photo albums of petty criminals, with almost-cute titles like Known Gambler Index and Con Man Index; others constituted a serious and secretive effort to keep track of political dissidents. The Communist Index included nearly twenty thousand known Party members, while the Reserve Index held roughly half a million names of authors, journalists and others (such as Martin Luther King, Jr.) who could possibly wield a Communist influence on public opinion. As Hoover's passion turned from reds to blacks, he created a new Rabble Rouser Index (later known as the Agitator Index) that included Jesse Jackson. Taking precedence over all was the Security Index, which could nearly create martial law during times of crisis. In the event of a national emergency, persons on the Security Index could be apprehended and detained without warrant.

Word reached the FBI of a major subversive act planned for January 15, 1966, possibly involving Five Percenters and/or gangs such as the 129th Street Deacons and the Dragons, which hung around 140th. The rumor went unfulfilled, but two days later the NYO suggested that Clarence 13X Smith be added to the Security Index.

The FBI forwarded a thirty-page report and photograph of Allah to the Secret Service. On a form to indicate which classifications of security threats he fell under, Hoover put checks in the third box ("Because of background is potentially dangerous; or has been identified as member or participant in communist movement; or has been under active investigation or member of other group or organization inimical to U.S"), and the fifth ("Subversives, ultrarightists, racists and facists"), which included its own sublist of criteria. Of the three subcategories, Hoover checked: "a) Evidence of emotional instability (including unstable residence and employment record) or irrational or suicidal behavior" and "c) Prior acts (including arrests or convictions) or conduct or statements indicating a propensity for violence and antipathy toward good order and government." With Allah a decorated veteran of the Korean War, Hoover left "b)" unchecked: "Expressions of strong or violent anti-U.S. sentiment."[17]

The indexed Allah was effectively a political prisoner. Had the United States suffered a major catastrophe or foreign attack, he would have been merely shipped from a mental institution to a concentration camp. However, for a time the FBI had no idea where he was being held. There was also confusion among the Five Percenters. Brother Jimmy had heard that Allah was in Pilgrim State Hospital; however, in February the SAC issued a memo advising that the Index list his residence as "Matteawan State Hospital for the Criminally Insane."

> In addition to people who were truly insane, people who were not in favor with society were also stored in Matteawan State Hospital.
>
> Ron Casanova, *Each One Teach One*

> And Matteawan is a place, when you go there, they say you are criminally in what? Sane. That means that you cannot control your emotions. And I had just been ... I had been out there too long. The people have taken advantage of me ever since I said I'm Allah. And I knew when I said I was Allah, the Mus—the whole world was what? Against me. I don't care.
>
> Allah[18]

In 1892, the Asylum for Insane Convicts was moved from Auburn, New York to the town of Beacon and renamed Matteawan State Hospital. A second institution, Dannemora, was added to the grounds in 1899. The 1940s saw the introduction of treatments such as group therapy, hypnosis, shock treatments and lobotomies. By the mid-1960s, both facilities emphasized "moral treatment" and "low-stress routines." A "Rec Room" consisted of chairs, books, magazines and a television. More than one straitjacketed inmate committed suicide by smashing his head through the Rec Room's window and impaling his throat on shards of broken glass.[19]

Matteawan offered the worst conditions in both America's criminal justice system and its treatment of the mentally ill. "Confinement in Matteawan is universally regarded as a disgrace," wrote David N. Fields, general counsel for the Association for Improvement of Mental Health, in a 1965 letter to the ACLU; "medical care at Matteawan is below the standard of civil hospitals." Ron Casanova, who was fifteen years old when he arrived at Matteawan in

1961, writes that "just walking in the door meant you got beat up." After Casanova's introductory beating, staff worked over his fresh bruises with a scalding hot shower.[20] Years later he'd be offended by a photo in the *Daily News* showing a Matteawan cell complete with bed, lamp and chairs; while he was there, he had only a torn mattress on the floor and a pot for his toilet.

"Moral treatment" and "low-stress routines" included the rape and murder of patients. Casanova writes that sexual assaults occurred several times a night, and once watched as attendants wrapped towels around a patient's neck and dragged him down the halls until he died. In October 1961, African-American inmate John Stevens died after a struggle with three attendants. After staff placed him in a straitjacket, Stevens had both of his kidneys kicked in, his testicles kicked completely off and ribs broken on both sides. Bleeding from the mouth, bruised from head to toe, screaming and shaking, he was then strapped into a bed. In a letter to the ACLU on the incident, anonymous hospital employees refer to fellow staff as "sadistic" and Matteawan as "the snakepit."[21] Beginning in 1965, the hospital was used to train guards for prisons throughout the state.

Jails disguised as hospitals, Matteawan and Dannemora played by their own rules, treating criminals like they were mentally ill and the mentally ill like they were criminals. Patients (and "certain visitors") were fingerprinted. Patients' hospital records included their FBI/DOC files. Visitors' belongings were searched. Patients were forbidden use of telephones and restricted in their letter writing. There were no home visits, passes or convalescent status. All visiting was done indoors. "The conclusion is inescapable," wrote Fields, "that Matteawan is basically a prison." By placing the mentally ill in jail, New York State was "imposing punishment without authority of law," constituting a legal definition of cruelty.

Victor J. Whitree was beaten by attendants, stripped and placed in the "Blue Room" for eight days without a toilet, running water or mattress, receiving only bread and water and a full meal every three days. During a six-year period, he was examined by doctors only seven times. After serving fourteen years for an assault charge (of which he was never found guilty) with a maximum sentence of three years, in 1968 the New York Court of Claims would award him $300,000 in damages. The judge in the case spoke of Matteawan as "no more than a pen into which we are to sweep that which is offensive to 'normal society.' "[22] Daniel N. Fields charged in October 1964 that fifty-seven patients had been committed to Matteawan in error.[23]

Matteawan held mentally ill individuals who had not been convicted of any crime, while Dannemora was established for convicts who had been found insane while in prison. State law granted the Commissioner of Mental Hygiene the power to transfer patients from civil to criminal hospitals for demonstrating "criminal tendencies" or even having previous records. Matteawan and Dannemora could both hold inmates for as long as the inmates were deemed ill; in 1964, it was estimated that roughly half of the 1,800 "patients" had been imprisoned longer than the maximum sentences for their alleged crimes. Paul Shappet served fifteen years for a charge of vagrancy, while Joseph H. Negro was committed for twenty years after his indictment for a five-dollar robbery. For the court to find Allah unable to understand his charges came as great news for the FBI. Allah could theoretically spend the rest of his life in prison without a fixed sentence or even a guilty verdict, and the Five Percenters were expected to wither away in his absence.

Allah was admitted to Matteawan on November 26 and placed in Ward 8. The facility's clothing register records that on November 29, a "Clarence Allah" was issued one jacket (dark), one pair of pants (tan), one shirt (black and white), one t-shirt and one pair of shoes.[24]

He wasn't the first Five Percenter in Ward 8; May had seen the admission of an "Al Jabbar."[25] Dannemora had earlier received members of the Harlem Six who were deemed insane at Elmira Reformatory for saying that they were Gods. Allah's own claim of divinity stuck him with a diagnosis of schizophrenic reaction, paranoid type, with delusions of religious grandeur and persecution. He reportedly described himself to examiners as a "master gambler" who had "never worked productively." One thickly accented Eastern European doctor considered Allah quite funny, but also believed him to be mentally ill.[26] One officer hit Allah for no reason, and Allah knew enough to let the incident slide: "I was under the doctors ... if I wanted to protest, I couldn't protest, 'cus they'd send me to the court in Beacon and boy, whatever the doctors say, that judge will not go against it."[27] Separated from his loving Suns and against all odds, Allah was determined to stand his ground: "I didn't ask for one thing in Matteawan ... I wanted to show them exactly who I said I was and I was going to prove it. All I wanted them to do was to ask the question. And I knew I was the only one who could give it to them."[28]

With Allah, Brother Jimmy, Ebeka Shahid, and members of the First Born locked up at various times, the Five Percenters maintained a sense of structure through the appointment of ministers (First Borns Karriem, Uhura and Niheem were specially designated as *divine* ministers[29]) and holding of "house parliaments." During a house parliament, Five Percenters would assemble in a circle (*cipher*) and take turns "building" on the date using Supreme Mathematics or the date's corresponding degree in the 120.

A day to God is 1,000 years.

The RZA

Since man renewed his history at twenty-five thousand-year cycles, a house parliament would take place on the twenty-fifth day of the month (the "parliament period" extended to the end of the month). On the twenty-fifth, Five Percenters greeted each other with the Math: "through your Wisdom (2) I see your Power (5), and through your Power I see your Wisdom."[30]

Though Matteawan's logs have no record of a single visitor for Allah,[31] Five Percenter traditions and literature contain numerous accounts of youths traveling upstate to see him. Waleak is said to have visited Allah twenty-four times during his twenty-two-month incarceration. Allah's earliest visitors would meet him in the hospital cafeteria, among the patient population; later visitors were relegated to a separate room. Allah attributed the change to his Five Percenters acting "savage."[32] Hakeim would later claim that the separate room was considered "Allah's office" and furnished as a gesture of respect by Matteawan officials. The room contained a number of antique wooden chairs arranged in a circle, while Allah sat in a throne-like antique chair behind a desk on which he kept his own personal phone.[33] "Allah's office" and its details can be taken as religious hyperbole; the odds are slim that Allah enjoyed regal treatment from the authorities behind an environment such as Matteawan.

Gykee made a trip to Matteawan with Waleak and Sha Sha, during which Sha Sha asked Allah, "which was right, what or why?" Allah told them that these things were not as important as understanding the nature of God. The group then asked Allah why it had rained for their entire journey upstate. It was the nineteenth day of the month, equaling Knowledge Born. Allah explained that when a baby is born, the water breaks. At the train station later, Waleak and Sha Sha were so fired up by the visit that they ventured to the nearby town of Newburgh to teach, while Gykee sat in the train station, "alone with the thoughts that had just been given to us by the Father."[34]

As the movement continued to grow on the streets of New York, Allah— sometimes in regular clothes, sometimes in a striped hospital gown—began receiving visits from Five Percenters who had never met him before. Shameik was a new convert in the summer of 1966 when Al-Jabbar, Dubar, Hakeim and Akbar Islam walked him to the Metro-North train line for his first trip upstate. Shameik and Akbar Islam got on while the others waved them off. They were joined by four Five Percenters that Shameik didn't know. During the train ride Akbar Islam started to build on the lessons, getting so worked up that Shameik would claim to see smoke rising from his head. Akbar Islam began testing the Five Percenters on their degrees. Because Shameik was sixteen years old, Akbar asked him the sixteenth degree from the Lost-Found Muslim Lesson No.2: "Who is the 5% in the Poor Part of the Earth?"

"They are the poor, righteous Teachers," Shameik answered, "who do not believe in the teachings of the 10%, and are all-wise, and know who the Living God is; and teach that the Living God is the Son of Man, the supreme being, the black man of Asia; and teach Freedom, Justice and Equality to all the human families of the planet Earth, otherwise known as civilized people, Muslim and Muslim Sons."

At Matteawan, the *devils* allowed the Five Percenters to enter the visiting room—except for Akbar Islam, because his pants were torn. Akbar shouted at the hospital staff and then sat down directly across from one of the white guards. Shameik and the others left their friend in a staredown with the devil.

After Shameik's group waited fifteen minutes in the visitors' room, a door opened, and in came a guard with a "Blackman around 5'9," about 150 lbs and dark in complexion, smiling ear to ear."[35] He had an overwhelming presence that betrayed his modest physical stature, and an aura that filled the atmosphere around him.

"Peace, Suns," said Allah as he took a seat.

"Peace, Allah!" they replied.

They sat with Allah for hours, during which he lectured about numerous topics, including the mastery of time. "Suns," he said, "the people's minds are on the clock; they wake up at a certain time, they go to sleep at a certain time, they work at a certain time." He told them that without a clock, they could know what time it was just by watching people.

"Now I want to hear you speak," he told his Suns. Shameik tried to make a good impression with his knowledge.

Uhura joined them as Allah was beginning to lecture on the "magnetic." He told the Suns that they were the "piece with the magnetic," and must share this knowledge with their brothers, then come back to get more. When a guard announced that the visiting time was over, Allah told his Suns not to take a cab, but walk to the train station and teach the whole way. They again exchanged peace and Allah returned to his cell.

In the front lobby, Akbar Islam had won the staring contest—the devil had fallen asleep—but Akbar still kept his eyes locked on him. As they walked back and the Five Percenters spoke about their visit, Akbar's eyes filled with tears. Then Uhura shouted "peace!" at a group of children playing, and they yelled it back, having already received the knowledge. Shameik was amazed that there could be Five Percenters so far from the city.[36]

Ronald Robinson was sixteen years old in 1964 when he passed some young men on 128th street and heard a greeting of "as-salamu alaikum." He was unaware of the proper reply, but they asked if he wanted to be a Blood Brother. From then on he was learning martial arts and the Supreme Wisdom Lessons.

He later hung out at the Afro Hut on 133rd and Eighth, which was frequented by Karriem and various First Borns. Ronald had still not met Allah when he agreed to join Five Percenters on a visit to Matteawan on August 25, 1966. Ronald was far from awe-struck: "who's this little guy saying peace, peace?" By the end of their session, however, he was enlightened. "Allah had a way to make you feel what he was saying," he told me. That day Allah taught the Five Percenters how to treat each other, as well as women, discussing the issue of a woman in the Bronx who had been mistreated for having a hard time with her lessons. It was also during this visit that Allah corrected someone who referred to his group as *Suns of Almighty God Allah*: "no," he told the young man; "you're the Five Percent."[37]

The cover of *Life*'s June 10, 1966 issue proclaimed that "red-hot young Negroes plan a ghetto war." Inside, readers learned about the Five Percenters, a "super-gang" of adolescents with "evidence of adult leadership." Writer Russell Sackett described them as extremists "without all the intellectualizing" of other black militants: "they have their own arsenal and their own creed, based on a pseudo-religious mystique that they borrowed in part from the Black Muslims, which leans on astrology, numerology and voodoo."[38] The piece claimed that each Five Percenter paid a monthly due of $30, but Sackett could not discern where the money went. "Wild as it sounds," said a youth counselor, "we're pretty well convinced most of the money goes for the parties— well, you could call them orgies—after their weekly meetings. Pot-smoking is a big part of the group ritual."[39] One official described a child's refusal to eat pork as an indicator that he had joined the Five Percent, and warned of what could come next:

> A kid who's never taken any more interest in dietetics than wanting to know what's for dinner suddenly wants to know whether his mother cooks with oil or with lard. If Mama's hair isn't gray already, that's when it starts turning. Most ghetto adults know that, under the Five Percenters' code, parents are expend- able—especially if they're working for "The Beast." These kids are so hot that they don't just threaten to leave home or to hit the old man. They threaten to kill him—and some of 'em could do it.[40]

"It's the Superman thing all over again," a school official told Sackett. "Some- how being Five Percenters pumps these kids full of their own strength and power ... they'll tear a school apart for no stronger reason than that it doesn't provide an adequate course in African history."[41] One junior-high teacher offered a more humanizing view:

> It sounds strange to say it after some of the things they've pulled off, but most of these are not bad kids. This ghetto life is stacked awfully high against them, and

the wonder is that any of them make it at all. How do you reconcile the life of a boy who's a pretty fair student in school and a Five Percenter on the outside? I've asked kids this question, and I've seen them cry, really cry, trying to explain it. Sure, some of the Five Percenters are psychotics and have no business in school, but if they were all as bad as they'd like to have us think, I'm sure we'd all be dead. Something's going to have to be done to help these kids or the place is just going to blow up. It's a failure our society can't afford. I wish *I* had the answer.[42]

It's hard to fathom the panic afflicting Allah at this time, desperate to "save the babies" but powerless behind Matteawan's walls. The previous summer's chaos of molotov cocktails, Fruit Stand Riots, Blood Brothers, Harlem Six, police assaults and the stabbing of Cedric Avery stayed fresh in his mind, but nothing would have devastated Allah more than the sights in front of him: scared black youths marched to their new cells, their own torn mattresses and piss-pots, already broken by their first beatings and scaldings and hunched over like invisible crosses weighed down on their backs. As Allah endured the hell of Matteawan, writes friend and journalist Les Matthews, "he changed the thinking of his group. He taught them not to hate, impressed upon them to go to school, learn a trade or profession. He sent them lessons from the hospital and sent me word that he had a new look at life."[43]

Allah would state that during his incarceration, someone told him that "the Negroes and the Puerto Ricans are the hardest people to educate," to which he agreed, because "a child don't have no one to look after him or take care of him."[44] Years before, Allah had told Malcolm that he would teach the young. When Gykee made an upstate pilgrimage with Sihiem, Waleak, and Lubar, Allah counseled them to get jobs, pursue their education, and stay out of trouble. During another visit, Allah told Gykee and Hasheem to give up alcohol and drugs. They returned to the city and tried spreading the word to their brothers with limited success; Allah later withdrew the prohibition. Some Five Percenters began sniffing heroin with the justification that they had to be "Lords of all the Worlds." Allah condemned the practice, commenting that "the only way to master it is to leave it alone."[45]

Allah also collected students from among the Matteawan inmates. One adherent, a Texas-accented teenager named Robert Walker, had already built with the Five Percent in Brooklyn's Fort Green section, which by then was known as the "Head of Medina." Some Five Percenters believe that Walker was actually Armando X from Bellevue. Like Armando, Walker impressed Allah as a "very sharp understudy."[46] Allah honored his apprentice with the title *Ibn Allah* (Son of God) and later named him Allah the Sun.

Perhaps the best-kept secret about Allah is the fact that while at Matteawan, he even taught his lessons to a grafted seed. The kid's name was John Michael

Kennedy and he came in as a seventeen-year-old transfer from Elmira on December 31, 1965. In his first twenty-four hours at Matteawan, John witnessed the staff's murder of a six-foot-seven Black Muslim and learned firsthand how things worked:

> Their main therapy there, the corrections officers, is knuckle-therapy. They don't tell you the rules, they give knuckle-therapy to anybody that tells you the rules, and you learn as you go along. You gotta sit in your chair all day; you got to go to the bathroom, you can't verbally ask to go to the bathroom, you get knuckle-therapy. You can't get up and go to the bathroom, and if you piss in your chair, knuckle-therapy. You have to raise your hand, and wait till they call on you and ask you what you want. And if you speak to them, say "I gotta go," knuckle-therapy.[47]

According to John, the guards were all in the KKK or American Nazi party and didn't like his name. He tried to fight them off, in the process kicking through a honeycomb-glass window. After working the kid over, the guards gave other inmates a chance on him, two at a time. Then they put him in a Thorazine coma. When John first opened his eyes, he found Clarence Smith standing over him. Allah said simply, "you are a righteous man." He then asked John if he knew who he was.

"You must be God," the teen exclaimed.[48]

From that point on, John stayed at Allah's side. Allah named him Azreal after the angel of death, and said that he was in charge of the "inhabitants of the hellfire." After memorizing the lessons, John destroyed his written copies to keep them from falling into the guards' hands. When Allah the Sun crafted his own plus-lessons with Allah's help, they chose Azreal for the role of scribe.

Both Allah and Allah the Sun instructed Azreal in the martial arts. While Allah the Sun demonstrated various attacks, Allah (the Father) only taught self-defense. Allah the Sun once approached Azreal in a bathroom and asked him, "who are you to be Azreal? How do *you* get to be Azreal?" to which Azreal replied, "why would you want to be Azreal when you're a born God?" As Allah the Sun continued writing plus-lessons with titles such as "General Monk Monk," "Islam in 90 Degrees," "Magnetic Analysis," "The Magnetic Field," and "Magnetic Flux," Allah (the Father) suggested that his Sun separate and form his own nation.

Allah and Azreal were later transferred from their individual cells to one large ward in which fifty beds were jammed head-to-head. Allah, who broke down *Matteawan* as "for the Maddest Ones," was confronted on every side with the shocked and tranquilized and straitjacketed, the screaming, moaning, crying, and babbling, the sounds of guards cursing and hitting patients or strapping them in bed with restraint sheets, the choking smells of urine and feces and industrial-strength cleaners. He took to sleeping with the sheets pulled over his face. Azreal would sing to make him feel better.

In 1966, the Supreme Court ruled that persons committed to institutions for alleged crimes possessed the same rights as anyone considered mentally ill, including proper treatment and a fair trial. In compliance, New York State began quietly transferring patients from criminal hospitals to civil institutions, after which many would be completely discharged. Dannemora lost nearly half its prisoners. Matteawan identified roughly 250 inmates for release and began reviewing the cases of 200 more. Allah's hospital records were reviewed by the New York SAC, who placed a stop on his file ordering that the FBI be alerted of any change in his confinement.

Back on the streets of New York, police hailed the decline of old-time gangs like the Cobras, Enchanters, Corsair Lords and Social Crowns. The Youth Investigation Unit, once assigned to monitor over two hundred fighting gangs, now spoke of only one: the Five Percenters, suspected of beating random white youths that came around their base of the St. Nicholas projects. The group was also accused of intimidating "blood-sucking preachers and their churches." At a November 1966 meeting of the National Committee of Negro Churchmen, New York pastors claimed that the Five Percenters were so named for demanding at least five percent of ministers' monthly salaries.[49] The NYO alerted Hoover that a park near Bed-Stuy's Tompkins and Lafayette Avenues hosted gatherings of over eighty black teenagers at a time. During these meetings, said the memo, "no individual is considered the floor chairman ... anyone who desires to discuss anything simply stands and can be heard," including one afro-wearing nineteen-year-old who called himself "Allah." An informant reported this Allah as saying that "the devils ('meaning the white man,' the NYO clarified) will not allow young Negroes to have anything and that you are supposed to beat them up when they come around." He also told his audience that they were all brothers and sisters, "since Allah was their father."[50] The Allah in Matteawan disapproved, as the Five Percenters "were not yet strong enough to carry his name," and he reportedly told Gykee "what was to come at anyone who did."[51]

On New Year's Eve, Gykee, Sincere and Shamdu were involved in a drunken brawl at a youth center on Myrtle Avenue. "We wrecked and caused havoc and destruction," remembers Gykee, "and that was before the other brothers even got there."[52] The next day an urgent NYO teletype warned that several Five Percenters had promised "actions, disorders, riots" in the Jamaica section of Queens, east Brooklyn and Harlem if Allah was not released. The Five Percenters were said to be awaiting Allah's arrival at 116th and Lenox—in front of Mosque No.7. The FBI contacted officials at Matteawan, who advised that Allah be released no sooner than March.

Azreal describes Allah's March 6, 1967 departure as coming with no prior advance: "one day he was just told to pack up and then he was gone."[53] A group of state legislators would later visit the hospital and declare it worse than Sing Sing Prison. Learning that some patients were seen by doctors only once every six months, Assemblyman Bertrand Podell remarked, "these people weren't sent here for therapy at all; they were sent here to vegetate." Matteawan's entire 1967 population of six hundred patients was in the care of fourteen foreign doctors, many unlicensed and speaking limited English. Matteawan superintendent, Dr. William C. Johnston, told the legislators, "this has been our problem down through the years—to get enough money to run this as a hospital, not as a jail."

From Matteawan Allah returned to the Manhattan House of Detention (famously known as "the Tombs") and then the street. He viewed his release as an endorsement of his teachings: "if they didn't believe I was Allah, why did they let me out? Would they let out a crazy person?"[54] On one occasion he claimed that Matteawan had given him proof that he was God; he then revealed the waistband of his underwear, on which had been inked *Allah*, his name in the hospital.[55]

Allah's name was removed from the Security Index, but J. Edgar Hoover still wanted tabs kept on him: "In view of the subject's background and his current mental condition, the Bureau feels that upon release from his incarceration at the Matteawan State Hospital for the Criminally Insane, Beacon, New York, you should determine his whereabouts and ascertain whether he resumes his participation in Black Nationalist activities."[56]

Agents observed that Allah had no job or permanent residence but "could almost always be found at 127th Street and Seventh Avenue." He was watched at the Hotel Theresa Coffee Shop and made his first public appearance at a bar called the Glamour Inn, described by Barry Gottehrer in *The Mayor's Man* as a "long, thin room with an air conditioner that didn't work."[57] On April 5, Allah finally stood trial for events that were nearly two years old. Pleading guilty to unlawful assembly, possession of marijuana and disorderly conduct, he received a three-month suspended sentence.

His official welcome home came at Harlem's Mount Morris Park, which interrupted Fifth Avenue from 120th Street to 124th, and according to Gottehrer hosted a mess of winos with their broken brown-bag bottles and discarded drug paraphernalia. Greeted by hundreds of Five Percenters, Allah delivered his equivalent of the Sermon on the Mount: "You are all pace setters of the world," he told the young men and women, "you are guardian angels. Keep teaching and you will take over the world." He abolished the First Born's practice of holding house parliaments; the gathering that day was the first of a new practice, a "Universal Parliament" on the last Sunday of every month. He also declared an end to the ordaining of ministers and warned to avoid leaders whose teachings were not "right and exact." Specific reference was made to Robert "Allah the Sun" Walker, whose plus-lessons had found their way to the city. Allah spoke of Walker's false degrees as "pins and needles," instructing his Five Percenters to burn all copies and refrain from teaching or quoting them to others.

Prevailing Five Percenter history reports that a group of Muslims from Mosque No.7 arrived on the scene, heckling the former Clarence 13X for his claim to be Allah. What is given as Allah's response illustrates the ostensible paradox of Five Percenter thought: that a rebellion against Elijah Muhammad's authority could be endorsed by Elijah himself as more true to his theology than his own words:

> The Muslims of the Nation of Islam have never seen W. D. Fard, and they worship him as Allah. But they say that they don't worship a mystery-god. So you are worshipping on blind faith. Elijah said we had to stand up on our own two feet. You can bring Elijah and any of his ministers to Rockland Place and he will tell you that I am Allah. You or any Muslims can't judge me or my Suns and your lessons say that anything made weak and wicked from the Original Man is devil, and you are running around worshipping a Half-Original Man and not the Blackman.[58]

While the Muslims departed, Five Percenters celebrated with "thunderous cries" of "all praise is due to Allah."[59] The Sermon on the Mount was followed by three other Five Percenters, each speaking on behalf of his borough: Karriem for Harlem, Waleak for Brooklyn, and Hakeim for the Bronx.

The Muslims were not done. Farrakhan's powerful New York territory came second only to Elijah's base in Chicago; the destroyed Mosque No.7 in Harlem was actually "7A" of twenty NOI mosques in the city, including 7B on Northern Boulevard in Queens, the particularly strong 7C on Brooklyn's Madison Street, 7D on Prospect Avenue in the Bronx, and on up to 7T. During a meeting at one of the branch mosques, Farrakhan's men complained to "Brother Clarence" that because Five Percenters in police custody gave "Muslim names" like Omar and Karriem and claimed to hail from the Tribe of Shabazz, the NYPD and the press considered them members of the NOI:

> Police are concerned by the fanaticism of the youngsters who the source said, believe that if Allah tells them to kill they must obey, and that the policeman's

bullets either will not hit them, or will not penetrate their bodies. The Black Muslims disclaim any connection with the Five Percenters, the source said, but police do not believe them ... Policemen believe that a man who calls himself "Allah" could not continue his organization in the Negro community without the tacit approval of the Black Muslims.[60]

To keep peace between his Suns and the Doom Squad, Allah told Five Percenters to invent new names for themselves. "The Father told us that we could not have Muslim names," writes Shaamgaudd, "so that they would not have to take the weight for the unrighteous actions of our fruit ... it's hard enough being righteous or a Muslim in Hell without a bunch of knuckleheads running around on the warpath causing confusion."[61] The compromise had a parallel in the life of Elijah Muhammad, who in 1935 banned his Muslims from wearing fezzes to avoid association with the Moorish Science Temple.

Al-Jabbar became Prince. Allah rewarded Karriem for his struggles by personally naming him Black Messiah. Ronald Robinson considered the breakdown of *Islam* as "I Self Lord and Master" and took the name Understanding Islam. Allah discouraged Ronald, arguing that Islam was "not a name, it's a religion" and renamed him Understanding Master.[62] Some Five Percenters who were previously named Islam became Tislam. Five Percenters named Omar became Amar. Lil' Armin wrote to Abdul, who was incarcerated at New Hampton Training School for Boys, and told him to change his name. Abdul found his new name, Kalim, by choosing attributes from the Supreme Alphabets, then adding vowels and putting them in order.[63] Benjamin (Bilal) Gathers caused an uproar when he called himself Allah Born God (later ABG), but Allah now endorsed the taking of his name; all black men had to be the Allahs of their own lives. Five Percenter literature quotes him as telling Hakeim (who adopted the name Born Allah), "Sun, know you are Allah, never deny yourself of being Allah, even if the whole world denies you, never deny yourself, because it's your own doubt that can stop you from being Allah."[64]

Increasing numbers of Five Percenters, qualified by demonstrating mastery of at least 100 of the 120 degrees, called themselves Allah or God, usually for a surname.[65] Gykee became Gykee Mathematics Allah. Shameik became U-Allah. G-Islam changed his name to Infinite Al'Jaa'Maar-U-Allah. Kalim became God Kalim, but is said to have refused the name Allah because he considered himself unworthy of comparison to the Father. Gamal became God Def. Waleak took the name Knowledge God. There was still occasional Islamic overlap. Niheem became Bisme; though not a typical "Muslim name," his new full name, Bisme Allah, formed the Arabic *bismillah* ("in the Name of God") from the opening line of the Qur'an.

Five Percenters had also been using a star and crescent for their emblem, bearing too close a resemblance to the NOI's National—the "Holy Flag of Islam" and the "greatest and only flag known."[66] They later adopted their own flag, the "Universal:" a circle containing a black 7 over a yellow crescent and black star, enclosed within an eight-pointed compass rose similar to those used on maps to indicate direction. For Five Percenters, their black and gold compass rose would represent the rays of the sun.[67]

The Universal was created during Allah's imprisonment by Shaamgaudd Allah, who had recalled a conversation with Allah on 126th Street in which Allah spoke about suns, stars, planets and black holes. A talented artist who made portraits of W. D. Fard, Elijah Muhammad and Allah and had painted the solar system on his ceiling, Shaamgaudd decided to make a birthday gift for Allah "to show him what I had seen and learned from the experience, as well as its relationship to us as a Nation." According to Gykee, "many of the Medina born had seen the flag in the making, not knowing what Shaamgaudd had in mind."[68] Shaamgaudd recalls that "when some of my brothers saw me adding the 7 and points, they thought I was flaking out."[69] The star-and-crescent and 7 design appears to be an amalgamation of the NOI's National with the Circle 7 of Moorish Science. Gykee considers that it might have been inspired by the insignia of the Cross Park Chaplains gang, but assures that "our beloved brother knew better than that."[70] Shaamgaudd showed an early version to Jesus/Brother Jimmy, who remarked that it wasn't an appropriate flag but still "enough to take the head off of the Messenger." The young Sun went back to the drawing board.

In May 1966, Shaamgaudd, Gykee and God Def (then Gamal) reportedly brought a finished painting on a trip to Matteawan, but hospital staff would not allow them to bring it inside. When Allah finally saw Shaamgaudd's design after his release he remarked, "that's our Universal Flag!"[71] Shaamgaudd then proudly added Universal to his name, becoming Universal Shaamgaudd Allah.

With new names and a new flag, the Five Percent Nation came into its own. Having taken the ideas of Moorish Science and the Nation of Islam as far as they would go, Allah reached that road's logical end. Marcus Garvey had called for a new religion with a black God, and both Noble Drew Ali and Elijah Muhammad tried to produce it; Allah made black men their own Gods and did away with religion altogether. "Religious people fight against one another," he said. "You can't tell me they don't, 'cus they do."[72] Disapproving of the "Our Father," Allah taught only one prayer, in which each worshiper affirmed himself as the only object of worship: "Allah is the God, and He cannot die."[73]

8

Allah and the Mayor

"**D**uring the late sixties," wrote David Dawley, "the energy that street gangs once used in preparation for gang warfare increasingly was directed toward creating viable community organizations."[1] Dawley was a member of Chicago's Vice Lord Nation, which claimed at least twenty-six branches—including the Unknown Vice Lords, Spanish Vice Lords, Invisible Vice Lords and Insane Vice Lords—and eight to ten thousand members.[2] The Vice Lord supergang was itself part of an even bigger confederation, the People, which battled another umbrella group called the Folks.

Founded in 1959 in an Illinois reform school, by the late 1960s the Vice Lords had reinvented themselves as a non-profit community development group. Funded by Alderman Collins and Sears Roebuck, they obtained a gutted storefront and turned it into "Teen Town," an ice cream parlor. With a grant from the Field Foundation of Illinois they founded the African Lion, a "soul shop" for literature, clothing and accessories celebrating black history and culture. They also started a venture with Sammy Davis, Jr. to distribute cosmetics designed especially for black skin. Using the slogan, "Where there was glass, there will be grass," the Vice Lords obtained one hundred Neighborhood Youth Corps positions from the Catholic School Board and spent a summer "sweeping streets, picking up trash, and planting grass."[3] They protested with Jesse Jackson against welfare cuts, set up a tenants' rights action group, and through an arrangement with Malcolm X Community College opened a Vice Lords Street Academy for high-school dropouts.

Counted among Vice Lord-friendly "People" gangs were the Blackstone Rangers, who claimed a similar metamorphosis and attached themselves to Rev. John Fry, a radical Presbyterian minister. Fry's First Presbyterian Church became the Rangers' headquarters, hosting at least one hundred gang members at any given time of day or night. On August 1, 1966, the Rangers picketed a War on Poverty office, and two weeks later secured a package deal from the youth welfare establishment. Fearing violence at the Bud Billiken's Day parade, a group of youth agencies bused 900 Blackstone Rangers for a day trip to South Bend, Indiana, where they were treated to a picnic on the football field of Notre Dame University. The Blackstone Rangers and other South Side gangs later scored a piece of the federal antipoverty pie, sharing a $927,341 education and job-training grant from the Office of Economic Opportunity (OEO). Through the grant, gang members were getting paid up to $58 a week for attending classes. The program would come under investigation when the Blackstone Rangers used their grant money to stockpile guns, grenades and drugs in the basement of First Presbyterian.

Despite Mayor Richard Daley's claim at an NAACP convention that "Chicago has no ghettoes,"[4] others understood that the Windy City's slums—like those in New York and Los Angeles—were, to paraphrase Malcolm X, powder kegs with numerous sparks around them. The growing political consciousness and revolutionary potential of street gangs was recognized by both sides of the struggle. FBI agents would sometimes call the Vice Lords' ice cream parlor, wanting to know the mood on the streets in times of potential riot.[5] Years later it was revealed that the FBI had also deliberately sparked hostility between the Blackstone Rangers and Black Panthers in the hope that the Rangers would then block the Panthers' development in Chicago. In 1966 the Rangers were contacted by Martin Luther King, Jr.'s Southern Christian Leadership Conference (SCLC); in 1967 they met with members of the Revolutionary Action Movement (RAM), which had been joined by Malcolm X in 1963 and Bobby Seale in 1964 (Seale had gone on with RAM-influenced Huey Newton to form the Black Panther Party). Considering the cultural impact of the Watts riots, RAM developed a strategy to manipulate riots as political uprisings. Reverend Fry had warned of the possibilities in a sermon:

> There are on Chicago's South and West Sides four major constellations of gangs: the Vicelords, Cobras, Devil's Disciples, and Blackstone Rangers. They have shifting alliances and historic animosities. But recently the big leaders of these four gang constellations have been meeting privately in order to talk things over. And what do you think they talk about? A basketball league? No. You are wrong. What is the matter with the Bears? Wrong again. They are talking about how they can create a series of incidents in such a way that the Mayor would be forced to call in the National Guard, and then they would openly invite the colored boys in the Guard to join them![6]

When protests against police in Newark, New Jersey sent a wave of riots across the nation, Daley gave a press conference to warn that as long as he was mayor in Chicago, "law and order will prevail." Reminded by a reporter of Martin Luther King, Jr.'s warning that Chicago suffered from the same problems that caused riots in other cities, Daley replied, "We don't need him to tell us what to do. He has been asked to join our constructive programs and he has refused. He only comes here for one purpose—or to any other city he has visited—and that is to cause trouble."[7] Daley notified Chicago that the National Guard would soon be on the streets with live ammunition.

The old machine boss Daley stood in contrast to New York's JFK-evoking mayor with Hollywood good looks and matching idealism, John Vliet Lindsay. To keep New York calm through the summer of 1967, Lindsay established programs such as the Citizens Summer Committee and Summer Task Force. The Citizens Summer Committee was charged with creating various programs for city youth such as Operation Beat the Heat, which bused children to public parks, and Operation Plane Ride, which provided them their first rides on airplanes. Meanwhile, the Summer Task Force aimed to "establish a continuing dialogue between the city administration and neighborhood leaders." It would later become the year-round Urban Action Task Force, headed by a former *Herald Tribune* reporter named Barry Gottehrer.

With the aim of building credibility in the African-American communities of Harlem and Brooklyn, Lindsay took to semi-spontaneous walking tours through impoverished neighborhoods. The walks were coordinated by political general Sid Davidoff, who remembers Lindsay often calling to ask, "where are we going today?" and Gottehrer, who developed relationships on Lindsay's behalf with neighborhood leaders. Rather than elected politicians, Lindsay wanted support from the *real* leaders, local heroes who often commanded more respect than those with official positions. They included men like legendary number-runner Bumpy Johnson, who would send his sister and other proxies to accompany Lindsay on his Harlem strolls, and Charles 37X Kenyatta, a former bodyguard to Malcolm X who carried a machete and wore a pith helmet. Lindsay viewed men like Kenyatta as necessary to maintain a city's balance; he told Davidoff that "to maintain center, you have to have extreme rights and extreme lefts" because when extremes move toward the center, the center itself moves.[8] As Lindsay's liaison to those extremes, Barry Gottehrer would come to be "alternately praised or condemned for buying off militants."[9]

The mayor's office requested that the NYPD provide them with lists of the "thousand worst kids in the city" and the "handful of adults who could cause real problems,"[10] with hopes of dissuading radical leaders from sparking riots and other public disturbance. Topping the list as New York's most feared subversive was Allah.[11]

City Hall sent feelers to Allah through street informants but heard no reply. Davidoff suggests that Allah was playing hard-to-get, and believes that for a man found unable to understand a charge of felonious assault, Allah was quite shrewd: "he knew what he was doing."[12] Then one Saturday morning, as Davidoff played basketball at a schoolyard in Queens, he was interrupted by an

NYPD patrol car with its lights on, tearing across the yard and up to the basketball court. The car stopped in front of him and an officer stepped out to deliver the message: "someone named Allah is looking for you."[13] Allah was willing to talk. Davidoff facilitated a meeting between Allah and Gottehrer for May 11 at the Hotel Roosevelt. After Allah no-showed, they rescheduled for 3:00 p.m. the next day at the Glamour Inn. The bar was "drab enough," writes Gottehrer, "and empty enough, to discourage the few customers who might show up there."[14] Gottehrer ordered a rum and Coke and noticed two men seated several barstools from him, one of them matching Allah's description. Gottehrer came over with his drink and introduced himself. Allah's companion that night was Brother Jimmy, who introduced himself to Gottehrer by his new name, Jesus. The mayor's man had arrived at the setup for a joke: *Allah and Jesus are sitting in a bar ...*

Jimmy/Jesus offered to show Gottehrer a good time: "any kind of women you want, all the women you want," for one hundred dollars. Gottehrer declined and ordered another drink. Allah broke down the percentages for him so that he knew what it meant to be a Five Percenter, and then they talked business. Allah wanted the city to provide buses to take his Five Percenters on picnics. When Gottehrer said it sounded feasible, Allah moved to a second request: his own school.[15] The Urban League ran numerous storefront "street academies" with various functions; one was designed specifically for young drug addicts, others focused on vocational training and roughly ten street academies were devoted to formal education.[16] "Each academy has its own atmosphere," writes Joseph Featherstone, who visited street academies as a journalist for the *New Republic,* "but what is taught is roughly the same: a mixture of basic, often remedial reading and math, and subjects like African and black history, sometimes Arabic or Swahili, and sociology which usually means discussing life in Harlem."[17] Staple reading included Langston Hughes, Richard Wright and Malcolm X,[18] whose portrait adorned more than one street academy's wall.[19] Featherstone described a conversation he had with an academy "streetworker" and student, in which

> both insisted there was a growing mood of racial pride and anger, and it was important that courses be given that interpreted this mood to the kids. The streetworker said that a few intensely serious students needed—he didn't want to say a religion or an ideology—but something that gave them an idea of how to interpret the world, some coherent body of ideals: "They can work out their own lives, you know, but they need a start, especially the ones going on to white colleges, because that's a hard scene." I wondered whether African history or even the personal example of a militant streetworker would lead to a coherent body of black ideals. He wasn't sure; nor did he know if a school could offer what he was talking about as well as, say, a Muslim organization.[20]

What Allah was offering might have filled the gap. He had already approached the Urban League, which was unwilling to hand over a school to the most feared gang in New York. Gottehrer said he'd look into it, still shocked at what he was hearing from a man who had supposedly threatened an armed revolt: "All the time we talked, my mind kept drifting back to the police report on Allah. It didn't go together. I began to wonder if I was talking to the right man."[21]

The meeting ended with Allah inviting Gottehrer to attend his upcoming parliament and speak to the youth. Allah gave the numbers of the Glamour Inn's pay phones as a means to reach him; Gottehrer wrote them on a matchbook and promised to call him within the week. As they parted ways, Allah greeted the mayor's aide with a simple "peace."

Sunday, May 28, Gottehrer attended the second Universal Parliament at Mount Morris Park. Flanked by two black police officers, one in uniform and one in street clothes, the City Hall deputy watched as Allah—with Jesus and a Glamour Inn regular, Al Murphy, at his side—lectured roughly two hundred Five Percenters, some as young as eight or nine, on the virtues of clean living and taking care of their own community. After Allah's speech, the youths formed a circle and took turns addressing each other. Allah then introduced Gottehrer and let him explain the city's interest in working with the Five Percenters, offering free trips to state parks and beaches. The mayor's aide even announced that Allah could be getting an Urban League street academy. The Five Percenters were silent. Gottehrer could tell that not a single one of them, including Allah, believed him.

Plans were announced for a trip to Long Island State Park. The following Sunday, a scowling, skeptical Allah stood on the corner of 127th Street and Seventh Avenue, smiling only when Gottehrer showed up with six buses. "It wasn't really the buses," Allah told him later, "even though I wanted them. But you kept your word."[22] Three hundred young Five Percenters piled onto the buses and Gottehrer filled his own car with sandwiches provided by a restaurant chain through the Citizens' Summer Committee. On the way to the park, Gottehrer remembered Allah telling him that Five Percenters did not eat pork. He pulled over and examined a sandwich, discovering ham and cheese. One by one, Gottehrer spent two hours removing the ham and rewrapping the six hundred sandwiches (two to a child).

Three days after the successful bus trip, Allah attended a meeting between Mayor Lindsay and black community leaders at Gracie Mansion. Among those present were CORE's Floyd McKissick and Manhattan borough president Percy Sutton. The purpose was not to negotiate, says Davidoff, but lay the foundations for dialogue between the mayor and the community. Originally

scheduled for 5:00–6:00 p.m., the meeting ran nearly five hours as each politi-
cian delivered a long prepared speech. "Everyone was hustling for a slice of the
anti-poverty pie," recalls Gottehrer.[23] At one point Lindsay tried to dip out of
the room, only to be pulled back in by leaders threatening riots if they were
denied the chance to speak. The only men that refrained from addressing the
mayor were Allah and Charles Kenyatta.

On August 5, Lindsay accompanied eighty-six Harlem youths on a walking
tour of Harlem before joining them on their first plane ride: an hour-long
flight on a four-engined Eastern Airlines Constellation that flew over the
Hudson River, parts of Brooklyn, Staten Island, and New Jersey.

"Lindsay goes aloft with slum group," announced the *New York Times*. The
article mentioned the participation of Five Percenters, who the Urban
League's Herbert Miller described as "a militant group of teen-agers, mostly
school dropouts, who have chips on their shoulders which we are trying to
remove." *Times* writer John P. Callahan lacked a sufficient background in
Supreme Wisdom to know what "Five Percenter" meant, but he at least
skipped the accusation of ties to Communists:

> The Five Percenters take their name from their contention that only 5 per cent
> of all Negroes are militant enough to redress their grievance against what they
> felt was ill treatment by whites. However, according to Barry Gottehrer, assis-
> tant to the Mayor and head of the Summer Task Force, about a year ago they
> abandoned their militance.
>
> Mr. Gottehrer said, "They now believe that everyone—whites and Negroes—
> should learn to live together in harmony and understanding, and that is pre-
> cisely why we are working with them in every way to help themselves."[24]

For Sid Davidoff, working with Five Percenters was strictly business. Allah
"knew we weren't there because we liked the guy, but because we needed him;"
likewise, "Allah saw us as a way of stopping police oppression and meeting his
own needs."[25] Barry Gottehrer, however, felt a growing personal attachment to
the group through his long nights at the Glamour Inn and corner dice games,
and developed such a close friendship with Allah that Deputy Mayor Richard
Aurelio asked him whether his priorities were in order.[26] Davidoff also grew
concerned. He once accompanied Gottehrer to the Glamour Inn for a night
with Allah, "who was in rare form," remembers Gottehrer, "high less on
cocaine than on his wit." Davidoff was later shaking his head. "Anyone who
likes to spend time with a guy like that has got to be either stupid or crazy," he
told Gottehrer. "And I know you're not stupid."[27]

Gottehrer called Rev. Eugene Callender, who had become head of the Urban
League in 1966, and Allah did get his school: a small building with a storefront

that the city had won in a tax case, adjacent to the Wellworth and just five doors from the Glamour Inn. It had most recently been home to a barbershop. Through the Urban League, Gottehrer arranged for the Five Percenters to acquire the building at a cost of a dollar a year. The new headquarters was situated in harmony with Allah's Supreme Mathematics, located on Seventh (God) Avenue. Even the address, 2122, held up in the "science of everything in life," as $2 + 1 + 2 + 2 = 7$. A large 7 was painted on the front door. For Five Percenters, the school meant everything from the promise of a better future to the mayor embracing their beliefs.

Allah, however, would grow wary of the arrangement as his dream of an autonomous Five Percenter school met its disappointing reality, governed by more than one hostile agenda. The Urban League's educational director, Harv Oostdyk, was a white Christian who ran classes for drop-outs at the Church of the Master on Morningside Avenue. Oostdyk had initially staffed his street academies with members of the "Young Life" outreach ministry, and the future author of *Step One: the Gospel and the Ghetto* prayed to bring drop-outs not only diplomas but eternal salvation. "Used to be every other word was Jesus," remarked a streetworker to Featherstone, "but Jesus hasn't all that much of a following in Harlem, and now he's stopped that kind of talk."[28]

Featherstone describes Oostdyk as envisioning "great corporate involvement in the renewal of the ghetto, arguing that business is the one segment of white society black people do not regard with disillusion."[29] Street academies were mostly funded through a $700,000 grant from the Ford Foundation, with lesser funds coming from the city, and Oostdyk procured sponsorship from companies including IBM, American Airlines, American Express, Citibank, and Chase Manhattan. "The price of involvement with public schools and corporations may, in the end, be too high," Featherstone muses.[30] "There are so many billions of dollars coming out in the people's hands," Allah commented, "but the children are not getting any benefit from it."[31] Featherstone considered that the street academy experiment might have been doomed by opposing interests that could not be reconciled: "The program needs to be as various as the streets, and yet it is hard to envision militant streetworkers toeing a line chalked by the city schools, just as it is hard to believe that many corporate officials would be pleased by the tone of some of the discussions I heard."[32]

The city hoped to keep academy rhetoric in line. One storefront school was closed because its director was considered "too extreme,"[33] and Allah's street academy received impromptu check-ins from NYPD Deputy Chief Inspector Eldridge Waith.[34]

The Five Percenter school followed a standard Urban League program, serving a range of ten to thirty students with three certified teachers and three streetworkers.[35] Upon graduation a student would move on to an "Academy of Transition" before being recommended for the third and final level, a college preparatory school. Allah offered suggestions for how his school should run, but they mattered little to Harv Oostdyk, his corporate sponsors, or the Urban League that had not wanted to work with Five Percenters in the first place. According to Featherstone, "Allah complained of neglect. In his view, 'the children' need more training for jobs and literacy; only a few could take advantage of college preparatory courses, and without basic skills they were going to fall prey to 'savages and wolves in the streets.' "[36]

Gottehrer also witnessed Allah's Suns challenging the relevance of their classes, for different reasons: "The academic curriculum took a beating right from the start, as the Five Percenters had their own ideas. They believed that the most important thing is to have knowledge of self and, as everybody is godly inside, so everybody is Allah. As a consequence, they felt free to reject as much as they accepted from the teachers the Urban League hired."[37]

"I just want the government to give the children more qualified teachers than those people they are giving this money too," Allah pleaded.[38] Discussing a teachers' strike with Eldridge Waith, he remarked, "we're going to do the job right for our children, even if they don't."[39] It was eventually agreed that youths would seek their state-mandated curriculums at other street academies, and Five Percenters would take over instruction at Allah's school. According to Prince, Allah hoped to maintain classes in five subjects: mathematics, history, English, Arabic and self-defense. Amar Education taught math. Divine God taught English. No youths could be found to teach history or Arabic. Zumar, who began studying martial arts in 1961 under Shariff X and received his first black belt in 1967, was assigned to train Five Percenters in self-defense. A native of Jamaica, Queens who was sometimes called "Green Eye" Zumar, he had a reputation as a "walking weapon" and considered himself Allah's personal bodyguard.[40] Like many street academies, classes were gender-segregated; Knowledge Allah taught the sisters.

The math, English and defense classes "didn't last very long as I remember," wrote Prince.[41] "The Five Percenter academy is being allowed to languish," observed Featherstone; "the street academies will have to begin thinking of other challenges besides college to offer the mass of angry black youth in the cities."[42]

Allah continued to search for ways to help his young Gods. Through a Five Percenter named Dumar he met with Ed Carpenter, headmaster of Harlem Prep, which had been founded by Rev. Eugene Callender.[43] At the top of the Urban League's three-level program, most of Harlem Prep's seventy students had come from street academies. The school's logo read "Umojo Undugo,"

Swahili for "Unity and Brotherhood," and its history teacher was none other than famed scholar Yosef ben-Jochannan, who wore a Marcus Garvey UNIA pin on his lapel.[44]

Ed Carpenter and Allah became instant friends. Carpenter came to be known as "God Carp," hung a Universal Flag in his office and agreed to accept any Five Percenter that Allah sent him.[45] Al-Shakeim and Born Allah were elected president and vice-president of Harlem Prep's first student government.

Regardless of the success or failure of his street academy, Allah's growing "Five Percent Nation" would evolve on its own terms. As an NOI lesson stated that by bringing the heads of four devils, a man would be rewarded with a button to wear on the lapel of his coat, Allah asked Barry Gottehrer to print the Universal Flag on pins for his Five Percenters to wear. City Hall opposed the idea, fearing that "a medallion would give them legitimacy" and spark increased recruitment or even violence. Gottehrer went ahead and made the pins, along with full-sized flags that Five Percenters signed with both their "honorable" and "righteous" names; i.e., their born names and adopted Five Percenter names. Ronald Robinson's righteous name, Understanding Master Allah, was too long to fit so he shortened it to Um Allah. Vincent Chambers, the Mosque No.7 youth who became I-Jabar in Otisville, came to the school with his newborn niece Yakeema to pick up his pin. Allah put the pin on Yakeema, remarked, "that's hers" and told I-Jabar that he'd get his own pin when he changed his name. I-Jabar later became Allah Supreme God.[46]

And the Five Percenters, Gottehrer notes, "did not start a war."[47]

In the mid-1940s, one of Elijah's Muslims wrote a "national anthem" with the refrain, "So let us rise ye Moslems, Fight for Your Own," which entered into NOI ritual and was sung by Muslim men like Clarence 13X before prayer at Mosque No.7. The Five Percenters would adopt their own anthem, composed in its earliest version at Rikers when Knowledge Allah (then Dihoo) was planting flowers around the administration buildings. To pass the time, he played with Supreme Mathematics in his head and came up with the foundation for a new song. After his release, he continued to work on his lyrics with help from Amar Education and other youths at the street academy. One day Allah walked in, heard them and asked what they were doing.

"It's a song we made," replied Knowledge.

"Let me hear," Allah told the boys,[48] so they clapped the rhythm and sang:

Chorus:
Peace Allah, Allah-U-Justice
Peace Allah, Allah -U-Justice
each and every day

each and every way
I'm going to Show and Prove
and teach the righteous way
(Chorus)
the Knowledge [1] is the Foundation
the Wisdom [2] is the way
the Understanding [3] shows you, that you are on your way
(Chorus)
the Culture [4] is I-God the Power
[5] is the Truth Equality
[6] only shows you that you have planted your roots
(Chorus)
God [7] came to teach us of the righteous way how we must Build [8] with that
which he taught us build to be Born [9] on this glorious day
(Chorus)
the Knowledge [1] of the Cipher [0]
is to enlighten you
just to let you know that GOD is right amongst you
(Chorus)
PEACE!

"Yeah okay," Allah exclaimed, "that's our national anthem!" He had the young
men present their song, titled "The Enlightener," at the next rally. The chorus'
"Peace Allah, Allah-U-Justice" is often sung as "Allah *and* Justice" in respect
for Brother Jimmy, who had changed his righteous name from Jesus to Justice—a move inspired by Colossians 4:11 ("And Jesus, which is called Justus,
who are of the circumcision"[49]) and/or the question-answer catechisms of
Noble Drew Ali:

36. What does the name Jesus mean? Jesus means Justice.[50]

The meaning would also be recast in a Five Percenter light, to bring down
the mystery god and present man's divinity in a Christian context as "Arm,
Leg, Leg, Arm, Head" had done within an Islamic one: "Jesus is Just Us."[51]
Moorish Science retained an influence on the group, as found in one of the
more suspect narratives from Allah's hagiography. Universal Shaamgaudd
was walking down Brooklyn's South Oxford Street, wearing his Five Percenter
"crown" (tassled skullcap) when he was stopped by a fez-wearing Shriner. "I
felt like a fire breathing dragon," writes Shaamgaudd; "I was going to roast this
old 10%er alive." The Shriner was impressed with Shaamgaudd's knowledge
and invited him back to his den for tea and cookies. Shaamgaudd joined
him but declined the tea and cookies. The Shriner tried to get the best of

Shaamgaudd with his books and pictures, but Shaamgaudd provided break-downs of their true meanings. For every question the Shriner asked, Shaam-gaudd would "serve it to him fried." The Shriner ate it up, exclaiming "yes, Lord!" He said that if Shaamgaudd agreed to teach his and his brothers' children twice a week, he would donate five or six brownstone houses on South Oxford to the Five Percenters. Shaamgaudd answered that he first had to ask Allah.

Upon arriving in Harlem, Shaamgaudd excitedly told Allah the story. "That was no ordinary man, son," said Allah, "that was Satan. He was trying you as he did Jesus before you." Allah warned Shaamgaudd that the Shriner would try three times to tempt him, and wouldn't be alone.

At the next encounter, Shamgaudd met two more Shriners. The first one asked Shaamgaudd a question, to which he answered, "It is written, man shall not live by bread alone, but by every word that proceedeth out of the mouth of Almighty God Allah!" The Shriners smiled and offered another question. Shaamgaudd replied, "Have you not heard that thou shalt not tempt the Lord thy God?" At this point the Shriners were kissing their aprons and rubbing their fezzes. They asked their third question and heard Shaamgaudd answer, "Get behind me, Satan! Have you not heard that thou shalt worship the Lord thy God and Him alone shall you serve?" The overjoyed old Shriners fell to their knees and kissed Shaamgaudd's boots, crying, "We bear witness, you are truly the son of Allah!"

"Allah is the God," replied Shaamgaudd. "Always has been, always will be." He greeted them with "peace" and continued down the street, tears streaming down his face.[52] Shaamgaudd's account is reminiscent of C. Kirkman Bey's *The Mysteries of the Silent Brotherhood of the East*, which, like Noble Drew Ali's *Circle 7 Koran*, was lifted from Levi Dowling's *Aquarian Gospel*. Bey retells the story of Jesus passing various tests to enter new Adept chambers. After his master names him "Logos of the Holy One, the Circle of human race, the Seven of the time," Jesus visited by a "tempter" dressed in the "somber garb" of a priest. Jesus sees through the tempter's deception, then encounters two more men in the same disguise and thwarts them in turn. For passing this second test, Jesus is rewarded by his master with a scroll bearing the word, "JUSTICE."[53]

Brooklyn's Flatbush section offered a young rival to Allah in Dwight York. After his release from prison, York embraced Sunni Islam at the Islamic Mission of America, Inc. Mosque on State Street and took the name Isa Abdul-lah. He was only one of a growing number of African-American converts at the mosque, which had been founded by a West Indian named Daoud Faisal, Pakistan-born Maqbul Ilahi, and a handful of Yemeni seamen. Faisal proved unwilling or unable to address the needs of converts, and in 1967 demanded that the mosque's black members carry "Sunni identification cards" to prove that they were not in the Nation of Islam. Many broke away to form the Dar ul-Islam, a politically charged Sunni movement. York formed Ansar Pure Sufi, which blended Five Percenter teachings with those of Elijah Muhammad, Sufism, Judaism and the Sudanese Mahdi movement. Members wore a crescent, ankh and the Star of David on green and black shirt and pants. Through the late 1960s and early 1970s, York's movement went through a series of name and uniform changes, from Nubians in African robes and caps to Nubian Islamic Hebrews in dashikis and black fezzes and finally the Ansar community in white robes and turbans, with its own mosque on Bushwick Avenue. York himself became Isa al-Mahdi, built ties with the Sudanese government and created his own personal army, modeled after the FOI: the Swords of Islam (SOI). Ansars and Five Percenters occupied opposite ends of Bushwick Avenue and engaged in minor confrontations. Allah Supreme God recalls walking down Pitkins Avenue when an Ansar saw his Universal pin and mocked him: "You're not Allah, you're not Allah." A crowd quickly gathered around the ensuing verbal battle. Allah Supreme God had them laughing at the Ansar, who insisted that God was unseen and omnipresent.

"Is He standing by that fire truck?" asked Allah Supreme God.

"What fire truck?"

"Well, if He's everywhere—"

Other Five Percenters showed up and gave their own intellectual bombings to the Ansar while Allah Supreme God continued on his way.

Oral apocrypha within both the Five Percenter and Ansar communities speak of a prison encounter between the Mahdi and Allah. Five Percenter legend says that York met Allah in Matteawan and became his student for a time. The Ansar version maintains that York spotted Allah while they were both at Elmira Reception Center in Beacon, where new male commitments were held before going to their assigned prisons. York had received a three year maximum sentence following his October 1964 arrest for assault, possession of a dangerous weapon and resisting a police officer. At Elmira York supposedly approached Clarence, scoffed, "so you're supposed to be Allah?" and then punched him in the face.[54]

Neither story is true. York was never at Matteawan, and Elmira Reception Center only took men aged sixteen to twenty-one. When nineteen-year-old York entered Elmira on January 6, 1965, Allah would have been approaching his thirty-seventh birthday.[55]

The Five Percenters' fable of York in Matteawan seems a misplacement of Robert Walker. "Allah the Sun" later wound up at Great Meadows, where he told inmates that he was "Great God Allah in the Wisdom Body." Despite his claims to be the true Allah, Walker's new name was based on his mentor's numerology. "Wisdom" expressed the number two; Allah in the *Knowledge* Body would have been the first (Clarence). After release Walker founded his own Brownsville, Brooklyn faction, the "First Born Muslims," with a core of thirteen "Archangels:" Lord Eternal Allah, Lord God Allah, Mallah God Allah, Infinite God Allah, Eminent God Allah, Lord Allah, Lord Blesseth Allah, Gallah, Boundest God Allah, Organic Allah, Glorious God Allah, Exziel Allah, and Victorious God Allah. "My wings are 4 feet wide and 7 feet long," Archangels bragged. The First Born Muslim logo, a thirteen-pointed star, came in two versions: one with a 7 in the center for men, the other with a star and crescent for women. "Walker's teachings were beautiful," remembers Infinite Al'Jaa'-Maar-U-Allah, "but his actions weren't."[56] Walker won converts by rendering Five Percenters susceptible with free drugs[57] and requiring female followers to sleep with any jailed First Born Muslim upon his release.[58] First Born Muslims engaged the Five Percenters in verbal confrontations, challenging them not only with the 120 but Walker's own "3rd Prophecy Lessons/1–30" and an added weaponry of questions such as, "Tell us how did God Allah create the sun in the above?" and "How fast does a fly's heartbeat go beep beep?"[59]

Among the Five Percenters mesmerized by Walker were Brownsville natives General Wise-Allah, who trained the First Born Muslims in martial arts, and Katanga Ali, regarded as a rising scientist of the 120. After a disagreement with Walker in the summer of 1968, Katanga Ali broke away and organized a small cache of followers who all took Ali for their surnames. Walker's sect—the offshoot of an offshoot of an offshoot—had now spawned its own heresy, the "Ali Family." Accidental meetings between Walker and Ali in public parks or on sidewalks resulted in impromptu "teaching battles" in which each attempted to show up the other.

Katanga Ali later renamed himself Notorious Victorious Great God Allah and opened his own "street academy" on Blake Avenue between Amboy Street and Hopkinson Avenue. Shortening his new name to God Allah and hanging one of Robert Walker's flags in his school, he managed to offend both the Five Percenters and First Born Muslims. Walker took over the school and kept the flag while Five Percenters tried in vain to convince him to take it down, pleading that the thirteen-pointed sun was not "right and exact." Eventually a group of Five Percenters entered the school and destroyed the flag, exiling both Robert Walker and Katanga Ali from the premises.[60]

Members of the First Born Muslims and Ali Family did recognize Clarence Smith as Allah and use his Supreme Mathematics, and eventually the offshoots were absorbed back into the Five Percent. Walker would change his name from Great God Allah in the Wisdom Body to Al-Champaine, abandon the lessons for full-on pimping and ultimately disappear from the scene.[61] Ali would drown in 1969.[62] Infinite Al'Jaa'Maar-U-Allah, an active Five Percenter who considers Ali one of his early educators, continues to "wear the Ali Family."[63]

As the Five Percenters took turns speaking at a Harlem parliament, an unknown man used his turn to denounce Allah's teaching and put himself over as a new leader. The Five Percenters stood up and walked toward the man, ready to take him out ("GODS didn't PLAY back then," writes Kalim on the incident). The rising tension could have reminded Allah of his own rebellion at Mosque No.7 years before, when the FOI started moving in on him as he spoke at the podium. Perhaps recognizing the moment's parallel in his life, Allah stood up and told his Five Percenters to stop.

"He can have all those that want to follow him," said Allah, who then walked away from the parliament with most of his young Gods in tow.[64]

While fending off aspiring prophets and their scriptures, Allah was also challenged by the secular Black Power movement. To the new wave of militants, Allah's sin was not his claim to be God, but his statement of being "neither pro-black, nor anti-white" and cooperation with City Hall. Allah taught Five Percenters to respect the government, and hoped that rather than separate, they would become part of mainstream America and change it from within. Through Lindsay's programs, Five Percenters were going to free movies and shows, even catching the Jackson 5 at the Apollo (some thought that Jermaine Jackson was a Five Percenter, because he had a "Five Percenter-sounding name"[65]). Reporters from the local media, hovering around the Street Academy with hopes of catching revolutionary rhetoric, found interviews with Allah to instead be "free commercials for the Lindsay administration."[66] Meanwhile, extremists warned Allah's followers, "you can't deal with Whitey. Don't go to his schools, don't work for him. Stay on the street."[67] Allah assured Gottehrer that he'd bat away all "tempters" like flies.

In June 1967, sixteen RAM members were arrested for plotting the assassination of moderate black leaders. A police raid found "over thirty weapons, a machine gun, three carbines, a dozen rifles, a machete, 1,000 rounds of ammunition, police riot helmets, walkie-talkies, and 275 pounds of heroin."[68] On September 18, an NYPD officer confided to the Special Agent in Charge that police were planning a similar "secret raid" on Five Percenters in the Bronx. Some time between 12:00 and 2:00 a.m. on an undetermined date, officers would storm several apartments in a five-story brick tenement building on Clay Avenue between 166th and 167th Streets, expecting to find "numerous weapons." The next day it was revealed that there had been no raid planned and the whole thing was a hoax.

After the closing of his Black Arts Repertory Theater, LeRoi Jones/Amiri Baraka returned to his hometown of Newark, New Jersey and established a black community theater called the Spirit House. In addition to performances of Baraka's plays, the Spirit House played host to a developing scene of black nationalism. At a winter 1967 rally, Baraka's opening speaker made an electrifying appearance, pulling up in front of the Spirit House in a chauffeured Cadillac with the personalized license plate, "ALLAH."[69] The rear passenger-side door was opened to reveal the man himself, sporting a shiny gold suit and matching fez. Despite his headwear, Allah's personal vibe was said to resemble that of a Christian minister[70] as he drew his speaking style from black Baptist street-corner preachers who competed with each other to give dazzling raps and capture the attention of passersby.

For an audience of black Marxists, Allah might have been expected to speak on white devils or the class war between bourgeois Ten Percenters ("bloodsuckers of the poor") and proletariat Five Percenters ("Poor Righteous Teachers"); but in his fifteen-minute address, he spoke only of the need to respect women ("Queens") and then launched into his favorite topic: numbers. Teaching from the Supreme Wisdom, Allah skipped its ideologically loaded sections in favor of "Actual Facts," which dealt with geographical measurements ("Mount Everest is 29,141 feet high"[71]). He then built on the statistics with his own numerology.[72] It might have been an odd choice of material for this crowd of leftist intellectuals, but Allah was often finding himself out of place.

The 1967 "Cops and Robbers" Christmas party in Barry Gottehrer's Urban Action Task Force office was intended as a surreal sort of social experiment. Inspired by the film *Ten Little Indians*, he hoped to bring together characters from all walks of New York life—"movie stars, revolutionaries, businessmen, politicians, clergymen, police, union leaders"—and see how they'd interact for an evening. For the role of revolutionary, Gottehrer invited Allah.

For Gottehrer, the highlight of the night was a discussion between Allah and Bronx district attorney Burt Roberts in which a smiling Roberts told him, "I have no problem with you being Allah, you can be Allah all you want—in Manhattan, in Queens, in Kings County. But you come up to Bronx County and tell people you're Allah and I'll have your black ass in jail." The surrounding crowd, which included a Wall Street broker, Hollywood director and high-ranking members of the police and fire departments roared with laughter.[73] Perhaps unknown to Roberts, Allah had already established a presence in the Bronx. The borough had a Five Percenter stronghold at the Hewitt Place home of Al-Jamal (not to be confused with First Born Al-Jamel), who had been taught by First Born Bisme. "Gods from all over Pelan would come up to the crib," says U-Allah (the former Shameik), part of the cipher's "hardcore" along with Born Allah, Shara, El-Bar-Sun, Little Bish-me, Obey, Kindu and Warkim. "We would see if they were strong or weak. If you were weak you wouldn't come back, because we wasn't playing, you might get seriously hurt, and a lot did."[74] In 1967 Born Allah, who along with Shara organized the first parliament in the Bronx, taught the Supreme Wisdom in a school on Prospect Avenue. At the end of the year, perhaps in reaction to the Burt Roberts comment, Allah designated Born Allah and U-Allah as Captain and Lieutenant of Five Percenters in the Bronx.[75] The pair soon obtained work with a community-based organization called Bronco S.I.A. and impressed the director so much that she let them use her storefront for weekly rallies. They later started a high school diploma class.

The apparent saltation of Allah was a boon for Lindsay's cause in Washington. Accompanied by Gottehrer, the mayor appeared before Senate Appropriations Committee hearings in February to justify his summer programs' $37 million budget and secure increased funding for the fiscal year. His report to the committee asserted that through programs such as the Urban Action Task Force, the city had established positive ties with organizations once deemed unreachable: "the Five Percenters, a group of some 500 to 700 Negro youth who were supposed to be violently anti-white but proved to be quite different, is an excellent case in point."[76] Such groups were often considered "ready to riot" but turned out to be "far more constructive and cooperative in face-to-face confrontations and relationships."[77]

It would never prove more true than on April 4, 1968. Lindsay and his wife were at the opening of a Broadway play when his media consultant called the theater with news that Martin Luther King, Jr. had been assassinated. An NYPD detective found the mayor and informed him during the start of the play's second act. Lindsay immediately left the theater, called Barry Gottehrer and Police Commissioner Leary and learned of growing mobs in Harlem and Bedford-Stuyvesant. The mayor, convinced that "somebody white just has to face that emotion and say that we're sorry," decided against all advice to walk through the streets of Harlem.

Gottehrer was the first of Lindsay's men to head uptown. Loudspeakers from Harlem record stores, usually blaring soul or Spanish music, now played King speeches. As he moved out of one store's range into another, the speeches mangled together as though a Martin Luther King stood on every corner, preaching from a stepladder. "King's presence was so palpable," Gottehrer remembers, "you half expected to see him moving through the crowd that spilled into the streets." Gottehrer headed for the Glamour Inn, found Allah and told him that the mayor was coming. Allah left to round up his Five Percenters and give them instructions: prevent fights, protect the stores and spread word that Martin Luther King stood for peace and wouldn't want anyone honoring his memory through violence and destruction.

The mayor was driven to Frank's Restaurant on 125th and met with Joe Overton, head of the Harlem retail clerks' union, who offered his men as bodyguards. Also present was at least one representative sent by Bumpy Johnson.[78] Someone entered the Glamour Inn to tell Gottehrer that Lindsay was walking down 125th. Gottehrer ran outside and entered the sidewalk-to-sidewalk mob, hoping to wade his way through the people to Lindsay. The six-foot-four mayor was easy to spot, towering over most men in the crowd. "Jesus," feared the mayor's man, "this is just the night for someone to take a shot at him, too." Lindsay put his hand on the shoulders of men he passed, offering silent, solemn nods in recognition. Occasionally the mayor heard sounds of breaking glass.

Lindsay's group converged with Allah's assembled Five Percenters, who angered Joe Overton's thugs by acting as an informal security team. Overton, as Barry Gottehrer remembers, "was more interested in exploiting the mayor than in helping us."[79] Lindsay and Allah turned onto Seventh Avenue together and walked toward the Glamour Inn. One of the union bodyguards began pushing Five Percenters out of his way, causing some Five Percenters to push back. When Allah himself was pushed, the scene erupted. A confused Lindsay was almost knocked down in the mêlée before getting whisked away in Percy Sutton's limousine. Lindsay remarked that he felt as though one group was trying to kill him while the other was trying to save him, but he didn't know which was which.[80]

Lindsay's later published account would refrain from naming names, brush over the turmoil, and deny any discord within his entourage:

> Finally, I looked up and saw several very large black men on either side of me, all of whom I knew and had worked with. We edged to a clearing in the crowd, when another group of men moved close—also men I knew. The two groups began arguing about which was the better route for me to take. (It was later reported that I had been wedged in between hostile groups and had been driven off the street. In fact, the opposite was true. I was in the best of hands.)[81]

The march through Harlem was a defining moment in the careers of both the Mayor and the Father. While riots destroyed urban centers across the country, New York suffered minimal damage. Lindsay was praised in the *Village Voice* as "the only white Mayor in America ... to have the grudging trust of the black underclass." *Life* ran a cover story on "the Lindsay Style," with photographs of the mayor cleaning up a city street and "rapping" with Charles Kenyatta.

Chicago lay in ruins. At least eleven people were dead, three hundred arrested for looting and thousands left homeless. Fires ravaged West Madison Street for twenty-eight blocks and power and phone lines were dead across the city.[82] A ragged and emotionally drained Mayor Daley surveyed the damage from a helicopter. The next day he delivered an incoherent tirade about violence in public schools, "beatings of girls, the slashing of teachers and the general turmoil and the payoffs and the extortions. We have to face up to this situation with discipline. Principals tell us what's happening and they are told to forget it."[83] Daley later blamed the police for their restraint in dealing with rioters and delivered orders that he had assumed were already policy: "shoot to maim or cripple arsonists and looters—arsonists to kill and looters to maim and detain."[84] In the aftermath of the riots, members of the Vice Lords set up emergency relief services and distributed three thousand fliers asking the community to "be cool and to honor our dead brother with the non-violence that he preached." A *Washington Post* editorial pinned Chicago's destruction on Mayor Daley's failure to embrace groups like the Blackstone Rangers, who had kept the South Side's Woodlawn section safe while the West Side burned: "the Daley system is inappropriate to the ghetto. Unlike Mayor John V. Lindsay of New York, Daley has refused to deal with militant neighborhood Negro leaders as autonomous peers ... Chicago has neither independent political leaders (as in Los Angeles) nor communication links between the Mayor and the militants (as in New York)."[85]

In New York, Allah received public commendation for his efforts and his followers were praised as peacekeepers, despite one television report that identified looters as Five Percenters.[86] "The Five Percenters," says Sid Davidoff, were "as important as anyone" involved with preventing riots that night.[87] A photo of Allah and Lindsay hung in the street academy's window, signed by the mayor: "to Allah, thanks a lot." Allah signed a duplicate print that would later hang in Gottehrer's City Hall office: "to the greatest mayor that ever been in New York City." At a memorial ceremony for King in Central Park, Mayor Lindsay, Percy Sutton, and Charles Kenyatta were among those looking on as Allah was embraced by Governor Nelson Rockefeller.[88]

Not everyone was impressed. Militants passed around mimeographs claiming that Allah had not only sold out to white interests, but was also guilty of "cutting black women."[89] A group called the "Kufere Muslims" took strong offense at the photo of Allah and Lindsay. One Kufere Muslim named Azream stormed into the school, tore down the picture and ripped it to shreds while his friends assaulted the young Five Percenters present. Uhura led a mission to "return the favor in spades."[90] At the other end, Lindsay's outreach to the black ghetto and leaders like Allah distanced him from white ethnic groups and the

NYPD. Lindsay made the cover of *Time* in November, but the article inside mentioned two thousand policemen picketing in front of City Hall with signs declaring, "Dump Lindsay" and "We want Daley."[91]

The partnership reached an odd apex when Allah handed over the Supreme Wisdom Lessons to City Hall, as part of his "Book of Life" to be printed at the city's expense. The Book of Life also contained a manual to assist interpretation, as well as the first and last *suras* of the Qur'an.[92] For Allah the book was a practical move, with only the lessons' integrity in mind; Five Percenters teaching strictly by word of mouth had spawned differing versions of the text. To Muslims, however, and perhaps a few Five Percenters, he had done the unthinkable: Master Fard's key to destroying the devil was now in the hands of the mightiest devil in New York.

But what was a devil? Allah's understanding of the term had changed since 1964. When one of his challengers asked him the 38th degree in the Lost-Found Muslim Lesson No.2, "Then why did God make devil?" the question might have been a mockery of his claim to be Allah—or a test of his command over the 120, in the same manner that Allah and Abu Shahid practiced their lessons in the Hole. Allah was expected to recite the 38th degree's entire answer, perfectly word for word:

> To show forth His power – that He is All-Wise and Righteous. That He could make a devil, which is weak and wicked, and give the devil power to rule the earth for six thousand years and, then, destroy the devil in one day without falling victim to the devil's civilization. Otherwise to show and prove that Allah is the God – always has been and always will be.

Instead of rattling off the memorized response, however, Allah replied simply: "I didn't make no devil, son." The man asked two more times and received the same answer.

One cloudy morning on 125th and Seventh, Allah was drinking his coffee and took Universal Shaamgaudd through the 8th, 13th, 35th, and 37th degrees in the Lost-Found Muslim Lesson No.2. The 8th and 13th degrees asked what brought rain, hail, snow and earthquakes. The 35th degree addressed the end of the devil's civilization, while the 37th asked what the devil taught the Eighty-Five Percent about God. As they walked, Shaamgaudd noticed that it was raining on one side of the street and snowing on the other.

"All right, son," said Allah, well aware that the Sun had something on his mind. "Tell me about it."

"You teach me all these things," answered Shaamgaudd, "you show me all of these miracles, yet when I go back and tell people these things they tell me I'm lying or that I'm going crazy, I tell them that I'm your son and that the Son is just like the Father, and they be sayin' that if you God then do this or do that, show me your powers if you are like your father! And those things make me wonder, when are you going to give me the power to have and do as I want to?" "If I give you that power right now," replied Allah, "what would be the first thing you would do?" Shaamgaudd paused to consider his answer. "I would take the devils off the planet Earth."

"Son," said Allah, "you would have just killed a lot of people that you love and that I love as well, not only your friends and relatives but a lot of your brothers. You see, anyone who does devilishment is a devil. Anyone who lies, steals or cheats and tries to master other people is a devil. Those who break the Ten Commandments are devils. You see, son, I'm Allah and I'm the God of all the people. Do you think that I do not hear the prayers of people who are not black? If a person has lived a good life and tried to help other people and has kept the faith of their religion as it was handed down to them from my messenger, prophet or apostles and does not do devilishment, then that person is not a devil; even if they do not know that my proper name is Allah."

It may be hard to take Shaamgaudd's inflated apologues seriously, and the idea of Allah "hearing prayers" betrays the heart of his doctrine, but the parable illustrates Allah's very real evolution. Like Malcolm X in Mecca, Allah (in his own Mecca, Harlem) had outgrown the Nation of Islam's racial antagonism. Willieen Jowers, who remembers Allah preaching hatred of whites early in the movement, says that he had "seen where he was wrong."[93] Allah would say that he felt as though Muslims and the "whole world" opposed him because he was neither "anti-white, nor pro-black. They really against me 'cus everybody is against the whites. Why let me tell you something. Who is man if he ain't man? Tell me."[94]

Both Gottehrer and Davidoff insist that Allah was friendly towards whites. Davidoff sees parallels between his own Jewish heritage and Allah's belief that African-Americans were "Chosen People." He refuses to condemn Allah as teaching black supremacy: the message was only "to instill spirit and self-confidence in his followers, to take some pretty bad kids and give them self-respect."[95] Like Davidoff's Judaism, Allah celebrated the unique history and struggle of a specific people.

Even Allah's concept of what a Five Percenter was, or who could be one, had changed over the years. During one of his lectures at the street academy, Allah told the youths that he trusted Gottehrer and Davidoff and considered them both to be Five Percenters. "Since I didn't eat pork anyway," jokes Davidoff, "it didn't make much difference." But in reality, the City Hall general saw deeper meaning in the gesture: "it was a way of saying 'we're partners,' and ensuring that partnership."[96]

John "Azreal" Kennedy, Allah's white student at Matteawan, was released in September 1968 and went home to Guttenberg, New Jersey. He made his first trip to Harlem that following February, during one of the worst snowstorms in New York history: the infamous "Blizzard of 1969" that caused the entire city to shut down. Also known as the "Lindsay Storm," City Hall's ineffective response to the storm would almost cost the mayor his reelection. Azreal was practically skating up the frozen Seventh Avenue when he found the street academy. Spotting him from the window, Allah ran outside, picked up Azreal and swung him around. "If any of you have a problem with Azreal," he told the Five Percenters, "you have a problem with me." A *probably* joking Allah then blamed Azreal for the blizzard.

"Anybody can be a Five Percenter," said Allah, "white, I don't care who they are, could be a Five Percenter, 'cus a Five Percenter is one that is civilized."[97] Gottherr was sitting with Allah in a bar one night when Allah suggested that he quit his job at the mayor's office and work for him. Gottehrer said that he didn't know what kind of work he could offer; Allah told him that if he moved to Harlem, he could be Moses. Besides, according to Gloria Steinem, Allah believed that he had a better chance than Lindsay of becoming president.[98]

"It's all very well for you to be Allah," Gottehrer replied, "but I know I'm not Moses."

"But Barry, if you're not Moses—who is?"

If the mayor's aide had been more learned in Nation of Islam canon, he would have seen what Allah was getting at: Moses (Musa) was the "half-original" prophet that God had sent to Europe, to civilize the savage white men and bring them out of their caves.

Allah's movement remained focused on pride and empowerment. On the streets with Harlem's youth every day, he could directly engage the culture of black nationalism. Allah embraced Afrocentrism and sometimes wore dashikis; his Suns, often with African names such as Yamuse and Uhoso, adopted a trademark Five Percenter "crown," a knit kufi with one tassel. The brightly colored headwraps worn by many Five Percenter "Queens" owe less to Islamic dictates of *hijab* than to the late-1960s boom of interest in African history and culture. It came as a stark contrast to Elijah Muhammad, who in June 1968 threatened women that wore "traditional African tribal styles and garments with gay colors" with expulsion from their mosques. From his isolated mansion Elijah declared that he would not "adopt any of those jungle styles of our people," dismissed African culture as "uncivilized" and "degrading" and condemned the afro as "bushy hair the style of savages."[99] Elijah's lessons from 1934 taught that Africans had "strayed away from civilization and are living a jungle life." Muslims were even taught to distance themselves from the shameful word "Africa," which had been used by the devil to divide Original people. Elijah in his jewel-encrusted fez and bowtie was the product of another time, old enough to be grandfather to the average 1960s black nationalist. Like a grandfather, some of what he said was outdated, even embarrassing to younger men who nonetheless owed him their existence.

Allah had his own contradictions. As Gottehrer had realized at their first meeting, what the man said did not always match what was said about him. Earlier in the year, state law had been passed that prohibited police officers from using guns unless their lives or the lives of others were threatened.[100] During an interview with religious ministers at Otisville Training School for Boys, Allah bemoaned the law, as well as New York's rejection of capital punishment, as signs of the United States "going backwards; you're gonna see."[101] The Allah from this interview does not match the Allah of Gloria Steinem and Lloyd Weaver's New York article, speaking openly of self-defense against officers:

> Bakar Kasim and two sisters got busted over in Brooklyn where they were teaching. Some cops come messing with them, and one of the sisters bit him on the hand. He shouldn't have had his hand on her, and the man should have took his head! Now, you know we believe in peace, but I didn't say if we are attacked don't fight! You say you are God, and a sister is in jail for biting a policeman on the hand. Malcolm said he'd rather have the women than the niggers.[102]

In both the Otisville interview and New York article, Allah stressed respect for the American flag and government. The Otisville interview's most shocking moments occurred when Allah continually harped on the topic of foreign policy:

> I am not against the United States ... I say go to war, if the country calls them ... if the country treats them what? Right! I say go! Now, because I don't think I rather for them to go up under anyone else command, such as other countries. Now, you know for a fact that other countries are strong ... this country is falling because we see it even through the hippies ... the what? The children now are leaving what? Home! They don't want to fight no more, do they? Do they? If they don't fight, how you going to win? How? Tell me, if everybody keep protesting against war, how you gonna win? The earth gotta be builded on and it's your duty to teach the uncivilized people. I don't care if they are black or white. That's your duty. That's the law of nature. Now, Russia is building up against this country, right? They got people coming here protesting no war, right? Who you think going to win after a while, if the children are not kept strong. Unite for one common cause, huh? You show me! The children are not fighting children no more. They don't care no what? More.[103]

"I'm not against the United States of America in Vietnam," Allah said later in the recording. "They should go there and kill all them people that don't want to build and become civilized."[104] He also criticized Muhammad Ali, who had refused to fight in Vietnam on religious and moral grounds, for "not fighting for his own country he came from." "Where did his teaching come from?" asked Allah. "Did it come from me?" Allah then asserted that Ali's views came from the white community.

"The wealth of any country is the children," said Allah. "If you don't keep the young people strong, how you gonna win? Bombs won't do it. The bombs haven't made Vietnam submit ... you've got to have the manpower! Feed them the right food. Don't teach religion." In the most bizarre application ever made of the Supreme Wisdom, Allah gave the 120 an ultra-right reading: belief in the *mystery god* keeps American soldiers soft and thus inefficient killing machines. "If you continue to teach that child about religion," he exclaimed, "the first thing that boy gonna be hard on is Jesus comin'. He ain't gonna fight!" Allah's observation actually echoed statements of Elijah Muhammad: "the white man hates to go to war, even to fight for his own country. They don't want to fight another week."[105] Allah knew the mentality of a soldier:

> You got to kill all religion or else you're gonna lose all fighting men. And they will not have the heart to kill. And you've got to have the heart to kill. You've got to! Everyone has to have the heart to what? To kill ... Now I don't tell the children, "don't go to war." 'Cus I'd go back with 'em. I enjoyed it [unintelligible] when I was over there. I enjoyed it. 'Cus it's somethin' to kill and don't worry about it ... Now when I was in the army, I knew I was fighting for the country and also myself. And I was the one to come home when many didn't.[106]

"You can't say that Russia's not strong," said Allah, " 'cus Russia's strong. Because the children here have used drugs, they're going back to sleep." He then warned the white ministers, "and now they're getting to *your* people ... and sooner or later you're going to see the downfall." Allah was candid about the "trials and tribulations" of his own drug use: "I have messed with cocaine, I've messed with everything but LSD. I'm not gonna take none of them trips. Now, did I gain from using cocaine? Yes. I know what it do for me."

Discussion went everywhere from Allah's experience in Matteawan to his views on relationships. He said that he had no problem with youths attending church if they were not forced: "Go. Go! You'll benefit from it." Mentioning Barry Gottehrer's upcoming Christmas party, he added, "Muslims don't believe in Christmas. I would like to have a Christmas party for the Five Percenters."

Asked whether he was nonviolent, Allah stated that fighting when it was necessary for survival could not be called violence. "I'm civilized," he said.

"You want the boys," asked one of his interviewers, "to follow these ..."
"I want them to obey your orders," Allah replied.
"Personal, cooperative approach?"
"You try to force them under religion, you can't win." As the interview wrapped up and Allah was thanked for his time, he took the final seconds to drive home his main point: "All right, gentlemen. I'm not against nobody." He repeated that he was only trying to make young people strong and keep the country safe: " 'Cus this is a new country, you know that this is a new what? Country!"[107]

It was one thing for Allah to "sell out" to City Hall; but his hidebound views now overstepped the liberal Lindsay, who had earned resentment from both war supporters and the police. Allah's conservatism may be understood with a sense of what he had to work against. He was the leader of a movement that rumor linked to Black Muslims, Blood Brothers, street gangs and Chinese Communists, accused of plots that ranged from muggings to blowing up the Statue of Liberty. Five Percenters went in and out of reform schools and juvenile centers; Allah himself had arrived fresh out of a State Hospital for the Criminally Insane. And here he was at a youth prison, advocating for his Suns, attempting to get them out of mandatory church attendance or at least spare them from beatings for getting caught with the lessons. With teenaged Five Percenters locked up at Otisville, Allah might have said what he could to get guards off their backs.

Allah was also permitted to visit Five Percenters at New York's Juvenile Center, addressing a group of boys on a ballfield and receiving invitations from the Center to return. Director Wallace Nottage allowed Five Percenters to hold parliaments on Sundays while other youths attended church, and respected their dietary requirements: "if the boys in this group do not want to eat pork, we don't force it on them or make them get along on bread and milk for a meal." A fourteen-year-old Five Percenter known as Salik remarked that the Juvenile Center was "all right now that they give us some kind of consideration so we can keep our rules." Salik also said that he was serving his sentence "without complaint."[108] Allah taught Five Percenters in trouble to turn themselves in and accept the consequences for their actions. Universal Shaamgaudd claims that Five Percenters would waltz into court with their towels and toothbrushes, announcing that they had come to surrender because they wanted to be righteous; "I wish you could have seen the look on some of the judges' faces."[109] To foster a better rapport with the NYPD, Allah sent U-Allah, Shareik, Zumar and El-Bar-Sun to Fire Island to befriend a graduating class from the police academy.[110]

On May 22, 1968 Allah attended a meeting of a youth parole agency after a parolee invited staff members to a parliament. Accompanied by Dumar and his girlfriend, a parolee named Omika, Allah gave the board a brief introduction of himself and his teachings. He stated that Five Percenters were being attacked by Elijah's Muslims and black nationalists, who called them "Toms" for their work with the mayor's office. While admitting that the majority of Five Percenters had been in prisons or other institutions, Allah told the board that *true* Five Percenters gave up crime and drugs. He then offered his help to the agency in working with "parolees who are declaring their allegiance to the 5%ers and yet are violating the basic teachings of the group." A memo on the meeting describes Allah as "a very bitter, angry man, who became impatient with questions that members of the staff directed to him. He later expressed his amazement ... at the 'narrow mindedness' and 'inability of so-called professional social workers to accept or even try to understand' the reality of a philosophy that is foreign to middle-class idealists."[111]

According to the memo, Allah had also stated that he would soon be leaving the movement. Without saying when or where he'd be going, he mentioned that each Five Percenter would have to continue the teaching in his absence.

9

Swarms of Devils

If even a tenth of the threats against Allah were actually voiced, there were plenty of people around with a motive.

Barry Gottehrer

When he said he wasn't anti-white, all the black revolutionaries turned against him. When he said he was Allah, all the Muslims turned against him. When he told us not to use dope, all the hustlers turned against him. So now here he was on Seventh Avenue, at the time where there was nothing but hustlers, revolutionaries and Black Muslims, he was standing alone.

Gykee Mathematics Allah

The new brown and yellow Mosque No.7 was completed in January 1969, built at 116th and Lenox on the ruins of the old. "We'll top it with a dome, a crescent and a star in a few weeks," said Minister Louis Farrakhan. Captain Joseph X boasted of plans for a new Salaam restaurant on Lenox with carpeted floors, chandeliers and Pakistani delicacies. Amidst all the optimism, the mosque's Lenox side neighbored a tenement still gutted from the fire of five years ago.

The factional warfare that nearly annihilated Harlem's Black Muslims, Sunni Muslims, and Five Percenters had seemed a faded memory until Gloria Steinem featured Allah in a 1968 article for her *New York* magazine. In "Special Report: The City on the Eve of Destruction," Steinem and Lloyd Weaver blamed the NOI for the 1964 attempt on Allah's life and claimed that he was "on the list after Malcolm X." Steinem was far from an expert on the Nation or its divisions, attributing the strife to Allah's supposed claim that Elijah Muhammad should serve as his messenger. Regardless, the story weighed heavily with Allah.

Like Malcolm before him, Allah's experience with the Muslims prepared him for their techniques. On one occasion, a Muslim peddling *Muhammad Speaks* approached Allah and suddenly dropped his newspapers. As he bent over to pick them up, Allah went down too, their eyes locked until both men were again standing upright. The Muslim walked away with his papers and Allah explained that it was an old FOI trick to bend over, ostensibly to pick up a dropped item, and then take down your mark by the cuffs of his pants. The foiled Muslim later became a Five Percenter and took the name Bohar.[1] Though he had thwarted one attempt, Allah knew that his days were numbered; Harlem remained covered in battlelines and not all of the combatants were known. With the same stoicism with which he treated Malcolm's death, Allah told his Five Percenters that if he died, "I don't want you standing over me crying; because if I could, I'd reach up and slap you." In increasingly frequent allusions to his own death, he told youths that they'd have to carry on without him and "never let anyone stop this." Likewise, Five Percenters were aware of the danger and remained fiercely protective of their Father. When Born Allah noticed a man who was arguing with Allah reach into his back pocket, he "set it on this cat."[2] Youths such as God Kalim were willing to give their lives for Allah. Kalim had joined the Five Percent in May 1966, while Allah was in Matteawan; the two did not have a face-to-face encounter until December 20, 1967, the day of Kalim's release from New Hampton. "I was finally meeting Allah," remembers Kalim, "who I had been told of and believed in for 18 months. I was ready to submit to him and make him my God." The first thing Allah said to him, however, was "Sun, all I can tell you is that you are God." A stunned Kalim found that the weight he had put on Allah was placed back on his own shoulders.[3]

Later thrown out of his mother's house and forced to live at the street academy, Kalim told Allah that he'd "take care" of anyone that planned harm for him. Allah only smiled. One night Allah and his friend Old Man Streets came into the school after a night at the Hole, where Allah had been shot five years earlier. While they spoke, Allah pointed at a half-asleep Kalim and asked, "how can I die if he keeps on teaching?"[4] To make Kalim feel better, Allah would cut back on explicit mentions of death, instead saying that he'd soon "go home" and replacing talk of "when I die," with, "after this year."

It has been said that Allah was ready to go; being the father figure for hundreds of teenagers had taken its toll. "He couldn't get no rest," says Azreal, who remembers young Five Percenters climbing a fire escape just to watch Allah sleep.

Allah continued teaching nonviolence, stating that a gun was the new cross since "they tried to crucify me with a gun." He had two crosses at the street academy, a Winchester 30.30 and 30.06. The 30.06 was kept in a locked cabinet, the 30.30 in an open one. One night he put Kalim in charge of the 30.30 and left for the neighboring Wellworth Bar, where Allah's friendship with manager "Tuttie" had secured weekend jobs for Five Percenters.

When word hit the school that someone had trapped Allah in the Wellworth, Kalim loaded the 30.30 and ran over to find Allah staring down a gunman who hoped to shoot his friend, "West Indian." Allah was standing between the two men, blocking the gunman's shot. As Five Percenters formed a circle around the scene, Kalim prepared to take aim. Allah saw the kids and ordered, "get out of the line of fire." The Five Percenters retreated back to the school. Allah later emerged unharmed but furious at his Five Percenters for the way that they panicked. He threw everyone out and confiscated their keys to the building, but returned them before the night was over.

In May, the 30.30 rifle was stolen from Allah's cabinet. Rumors accused various Five Percenters. When a witness tried telling Allah who he had seen leaving the school with the rifle, Allah put his hands over his ears and shouted that he did not want to know.

On June 7, Charles Kenyatta was shot in his car in the Bronx. "The Black Muslims are out to get me," he told paramedics on the scene. He was rushed to Fordham Hospital and later transferred to Bellevue, where nurses constantly moved him from one room to another to prevent further attempts on his life.

State Assemblyman Charles Rangel accused New York's narcotics syndicate of the attack, due to Kenyatta's tireless anti-drug efforts. Kenyatta survived and would later blame the Nation of Islam and/or corrupt officers in the NYPD who themselves benefited from the drug trade.

Allah spent the night of June 11, 1969 at his mother's apartment. The next morning he said he'd enjoyed the best rest of his life. Allah's mother asked if there was any way he could "get out of it," to which he replied: "when they are ready, they will kill you."

Later he went out with Al Murphy and Barry Gottehrer, who was still shaken from the attack on Kenyatta. Though much of their conversation remained light, Gottehrer expressed serious concern for Allah. Allah in turn worried about the mayor's aide, but didn't seem to fear for himself. "Who can kill God?" he asked. Gottehrer couldn't answer, as the basement shooting had all but proven Allah invincible.

They eventually parted ways. Murphy went club-hopping, Gottehrer went home and Allah went to play craps on a corner. Across from the street academy, protesters were squatting to prevent the construction of the State Office Building, hoping that the city would instead give them a Malcolm X/Martin Luther King School.

At some point Allah headed over to the street academy and spoke at length to God Kalim, Um Allah, Radu, and Al-Raheem about women and relationships. He called two of them "faggots" for letting their women tell them what to do. He told one that he wasn't a faggot, but said to the last, whose girlfriend had cheated on him, "I can't call you a faggot, but if you go back to that woman, you are a faggot too!" He punched one of the "faggots" in the chest.[5] Other Five

Percenters came in and out of the school, including the First Born's Al-Jamel, who had taken part in the protest. Sometime around 2:00 or 3:00 a.m., June 13, Allah left his final message on the chalkboard: "Teach On!" and went outside to hail a Yellow Cab. As Allah climbed in, according to Kalim, Prince ran to the taxi and handed something to him.[6] The Five Percenters that lived in the school at that time—Kalim, Islam Ubeka, Ladu, and Raheem—went inside and called it a night.

Sometime near 4:00 a.m., Allah headed over to Dora's apartment (his habit after winning at craps) at 21 West 112th Street, in Martin Luther King Towers. A short time later, Murphy called Gottehrer, sounding intoxicated.

"Are you all right?" he asked.

"Sure," replied Gottehrer. Murphy asked if he had taken Allah home; Barry answered that he had last seen Allah in the street, gambling. Murphy then told the mayor's man that Allah was dead, that "somebody shot the shit out of him."[7] Allah had been ambushed from behind by three black men, shooting him in the head, back, chest and legs. The assailants fled in a white Chevrolet.

Gottehrer arrived at Martin Luther King Towers to find that the body had already been taken. He examined the splattered blood in the elevator and Allah's chalk outline in the lobby, and even spotted a shard of bone on the floor. After Murphy arrived the two went to the fifth floor to see Dora and the children. Gottehrer later called two of his secretaries, both black women, to tend to the family. Allah's sons by Willieen Jowers, A-Allah and B-Allah, were both incarcerated at the time. His son "Little Allah" (by Guvasia) might have been less than a year old.

Word spread among the Gods. Uhura called Abu Shahid at his hotel room on 136th and Lenox. Born Allah called U-Allah in the Bronx, who rushed with Shareik to Mecca. Al-Raheem went to the street academy and woke up the kids that lived there. They ran to the corner of 127th Street, where a friend of Allah's offered to drive them to the scene. The Five Percenters jumped out of the car at 116th and Lenox to run the rest of the way.

Though Allah had just won at craps, police found no cash on him; his wallet contained only receipts indicating that he had been on the city's payroll ("Tension Reduction Fund"). At 9:45 p.m. the NYO sent a teletype marked "urgent" to J. Edgar Hoover, informing him that "the leader of the Five Percenters, a Negro youth group" and "recent aide to Mayor John Lindsay" had been gunned down. Reporters exaggerated the mutual respect between Kenyatta and Allah into a close alliance of NOI apostates, directing fingers to be pointed at Mosque No.7. "Kenyatta's Pal Killed," cried a *Daily News* headline, "Cops See Muslim War." The article quoted an unnamed police spokesman as stating that the Black Muslims were sick of "splinter groups" and the Kenyatta/Smith

attacks were opening shots in an "all-out war." Gottehrer believes that the
rumors were started by an individual "fairly high up" in the NYPD.[8] During an
emergency meeting at Gracie Mansion, a furious Lindsay erupted at Chief of
Detectives Frederick M. Lussen: "I don't give a damn what kind of leads you
have, that kind of story does not get into the papers. You stop those rumors."[9]

Louis Farrakhan expressed outrage at "white insinuations," claiming to
have a healthy relationship "with the Five Percenters and many other black
groups who disagree with our views." Meanwhile, some Five Percenters suspected Bohar, the former *Muhammad Speaks* salesman who joined Allah after
trying to attack him. Bohar changed his name to Gohar and moved to New Jersey, where he later reverted to Islam. According to Gottehrer, both Muslims
and Five Percenters began arming themselves in preparation for a war that
could go down "simply because enough people expected it."[10]

On Monday the mayor and Gottehrer went to the street academy and
expressed their condolences to the forty or so Five Percenters present. "Brothers," said Lindsay, "I hope you know the sadness in my heart at Allah's death."
In all likelihood, says Sid Davidoff, Lindsay would not have been able to
explain the Five Percenter philosophy if asked, but he did grasp Allah's "discipline and intention ... Lindsay understood that better than any of us."[11] The
mayor told the group that Allah had made an important contribution in the
last few years, especially in education, and pointed out that six of the youths
present would be attending college in the fall. The Five Percenters gave Lindsay their word that they would stay in school and refrain from any violent retaliation for Allah's murder. One youth stated that the only way to show their love
for Allah was to "build—to get our own carpenters, doctors, lawyers, painters,
electricians." The city continued offering bus trips, free admission to theaters
and "all sorts of things to appease and console us," remembers Gykee, "not
knowing how we were going to react, [but] nothing seemed to matter to many
of us at that point."[12] One week after the assassination, four Five Percenters—
Wabu, U-Allah, Warkim and Shara—would be arrested for assault and sent to
Rikers.[13] "This was a horrible time for us," recalls U-Allah. "We was at our
most dangerous mood. A couple of people got hurt just by looking at us."[14]

While the *Washington Post Times-Herald* misunderstood the group's name
as meaning that "95 percent of the blacks did not care about improving the
community, but 5 percent did," the media's treatment was mostly positive.
The *New York Times* even reported that the street academy had one white
enrolee, twenty-year-old John Kennedy. Allah "gave me knowledge of self,"
Azreal told the reporter. "Allah loved everybody."

The truth of Allah's incredible journey was best expressed accidentally in an
understated *Washington Post Times-Herald* headline: "Harlem Moderate is

Murdered." Just four years earlier, the Harlem Moderate's "youth group" received comparisons to the Hitler Youth. He had gone from a Korean War hero to the Fruit of Islam to a feared "gang leader" to a "moderate" that kept Harlem safe by marching with its mayor. Once accused of conspiring to kill the Pope, he later earned public commendation and hobnobbed at City Hall Christmas parties. Gloria Steinem's magazine and the *New York Times* put him on coffee tables throughout the city, he was featured on Canadian television, and a sociologist came from Sweden to interview him. It was even rumored that this former shoe shiner, shipping clerk, house painter, and master gambler had scheduled a formal meeting with Chinese delegates for later in the month.

Allah's funeral was held on the Monday afternoon at Unity Funeral Chapel on Eighth Avenue and 126th Street, just a block from the Glamour Inn. Up to four hundred people attended the service, including dozens of on-duty police officers. "Allah cannot die," cried Five Percenters as they approached the walnut casket and beheld the Father in his double-breasted suit, a gold crown on his head: "Allah is God, and God lives forever!" The funeral procession, which included seven buses packed with young black men, rode through Harlem to Ferncliff Cemetery. A minister delivered the eulogy and a prayer. A young girl performed a song she had written, titled simply "Allah." A latin God known as "Puerto Rican Kendu" was appointed to be Allah's cremator, pulling the lever to destroy his physical remains. A reception was held at the home of Allah's brother, attended by Gottehrer and marked by heavy drinking. Meanwhile, a large circle of youths gathered on a softball field, sang the Five Percenter anthem and vowed to teach until they died.[15]

> Some Gods never got over it, that night as I laid in my bed, I thought about the "Father" and the influence he had on my life. I thought of how one time Allah punched me in my chest, because I wouldn't take money that he was offering to me ... I thought of the first time that I met him. I laid in my bed thinking about the Man, who we called "Father" and cried.
>
> U-Allah[16]

With Malcolm, Martin and Allah wiped out in a five-year span, the Bureau looked to what targets it had left. June 15, just two days after Allah's assassination, J. Edgar Hoover issued the following statement: "The Black Panther Party, without question, represents the greatest threat to internal security of the country." Investigation of the Allah case was left to local authorities. A June 24 article in the *Daily News* reported Chief of Detectives Lussen as stating that the Kenyatta and Allah shootings could have been linked to a ten-man extortion ring. The extortionists usually acted in groups of three and pretended to

be seeking "contributions to advance the civil rights cause." While claiming to
have already identified the suspects, Lussen refused to give names. He did
reveal that his investigation would look into the $43,000 bank account of
Edwin Ellis, former editor of black nationalist magazine *The Liberator*. On
June 22, Ellis was arrested for the shooting of thirty-four-year-old Bronx resi-
dent James Howard, which Lussen suggested was a case of mistaken identity;[17]
was the intended target Allah's right-hand man, Jimmy "Justice" Howard? The
NYPD speculated that the extortionists were active members of the Fair Play
for Cuba Committee and had hired Anthony Reed, Jr. to kill both Allah and
Kenyatta, either for their work with Mayor Lindsay or the possibility that they
were "cutting into territory" by extorting local businesses themselves. Reed in
turn was killed only six days after Allah; perhaps, as police guessed, "because he
knew too much."

Gottehrer calls Lussen's extortion-ring story a "blatant example of managing the news," meant only to cool off the tension that Lussen had caused
between Five Percenters and the NOI.[18] It did not seem that the NYPD ever
treated Allah's murder seriously; the Fair Play for Cuba Committee had dis-
banded in 1963. The police weren't even sure of Allah's real identity: his sister
Bernice had to publicly refute NYPD insistence that their family name was
Jowars.[19]

The final pages of Allah's FBI file mention a police inquiry at the Apollo
Theater. The largely censored summary offers little more than a cryptic passage: "three negro males who told him he had not done enough for the black
community and if he did not cooperate with them he might not leave the
building alive." It appeared that a limited amount of NYPD questioning followed, in which someone with a censored name was identified as having once
belonged to the Revolutionary Action Movement and Black Panthers.
Another censored party requested that the above information be kept inside
the Bureau, as "investigation into this matter is still pending and much of the
information is to date unsubstantiated." The FBI file on Clarence 13X Smith,
opened while he was at Bellevue Hospital, was closed on June 25, 1969. In
August the NYPD arrested twenty-nine-year-old Aubrey Cline, an unemployed African-American with a "long police record" of arrests for assaults and
narcotics, and charged him with shooting Allah. Cline awaited trial in the
Tombs, where he was confronted by Five Percenters and denied any involvement in the murder. "Police are expected to arrest other suspects momentar-
ily," reported the *Amsterdam News*.[20] But they never did, and on March 27,
1973, charges against Cline were finally dismissed.

Allah had stopped identifying as a Muslim years before his death, and what
he once practiced as "Islam" had very little to do with the Muhammad of

seventh-century Arabia; but parallels do run between the Prophet and the Father, highlighted first by the Five Percenters' renaming of Harlem as Mecca and Brooklyn as Medina.

Both Muhammad and Allah were well-known as men of character before embarking on their prophetic careers. In the beginning, they intended only to purify existing traditions: Muhammad stressed that he was simply a continuation in the line of Abraham, Moses and Jesus, while Allah remained a faithful believer in Elijah Muhammad. However, when differences became irreconcilable, both men broke away and forged ahead on new paths.

Muhammad and Allah both started as renegades, persecuted by the establishment, but ended their careers as political leaders.

Considering the companions of Muhammad, one can see their counterparts in the early Five Percenters. Muhammad's first male follower was his nephew Ali, who through years of righteous struggle evolved from a feeble youth into the Lion of Islam, the Prophet's right-hand lieutenant. Revered likewise for his steadfast devotion and bravery on the battlefield, the Ali of 1960s Harlem was Karriem, the Black Messiah. The *Sahabas*' Umar bin Khattab might have been the First Born's Uhura. Both Muhammad and Allah had soldiers and willing martyrs, but placed a greater value on education. Muhammad taught that the ink of scholars outweighed the blood of martyrs and that a Muslim should seek knowledge from the cradle to the grave. Allah, while topping a list of New York's most feared subversives, asked the mayor to give him a school.

As with Muslims following the death of the Prophet Muhammad, Allah's murder left his Five Percenters faced with the difficult issue of succession. In Islam, the crisis of who could lead in Muhammad's absence resulted in the Sunni-Shi'a schism that continues to bring division, persecution and occasional violence throughout the Muslim world. Barry Gottehrer writes that in the summer of 1969, "all kinds of people were trying to take over the Five Percenters."[21] He asked Abu Shahid who would now lead the community. "Whoever thinks he can handle it," Shahid replied.[22] Some Five Percenters believed that Allah had groomed Knowledge Allah to succeed him.[23] Others looked to A-Allah and B-Allah, Allah's sons by Willieen Jowers, but she warned her boys that they would inevitably be killed too.[24] Both refused leadership roles.

Black Messiah was in prison upstate and read in the newspaper that Allah was murdered. His fellow inmates kept telling him, "when you go home, you have to take over the nation." After his release he heard more of the same in Harlem, with the lost and confused begging him to lead the Five Percent. "They were wrong for putting that weight on him," said Allah Supreme God, "the Father told us to share that weight." Black Messiah sank into a deep depression and used drugs to escape the pressure. According to Allah Supreme God, he "never really bounced back."[25]

For many the logical choice to lead was Justice, but he "made only a dutiful gesture toward carrying on for his friend"[26] and fell into increased drug use.[27] Gottehrer observed that Justice lacked not only Allah's charisma, but also his heart and nerve. This became apparent one night as a coked-out Justice was riding around town with Gottehrer and Murphy. Justice, suddenly convinced that the two had killed Allah and were going to take him next, tried jumping out of the car as it turned the corner. Gottehrer and Murphy then jokingly threatened to toss Justice in the river, causing him to tremble uncontrollably.

Justice lived at the street academy and then briefly with a woman before drifting away from the Five Percenters for some time. During his stint at the school he managed to solve the question of leadership by declaring that the Five Percenters should have no leader, so that "no one could kill a leader again."

"That's bullshit," Abu Shahid told me. "The Father was the black seed, I'm the brown seed, it's mine by nature. No one can take that away from me until I'm gone, then it's the next one."[28]

Abu Shahid was addicted to heroin and eventually caught an arrest in Brooklyn for armed robbery and attempted homicide. Despite acquiring a lawyer through Livingston Wingate, he was sentenced to four years at Auburn Prison.[29] Ebeka, once considered by the FBI to be third-in-command behind Allah and Justice, had returned to the Nation of Islam—allegedly by Allah's order—and later went to prison.[30]

Barry Gottehrer estimated that in 1969 there might have been four hundred Five Percenters in Harlem and one hundred and fifty in Brooklyn, but they quickly dissipated. Allah's street academy was all but empty as members moved on or found themselves in jail. Uhoso had started trouble at a Steak House on Dekalb Avenue and got himself stabbed; he lived but was sent upstate for three years. Jamar Allah, who learned of the assassination while watching the six o'clock news in Rikers, states that over half of Allah's followers there abandoned the Five Percent. Prince received a sentence of 5 to 20 for shooting and killing Dahu, the older brother of Black Messiah and student of the Harlem Six's Walik, after Dahu had robbed his apartment. Azreal returned home to Guttenberg, New Jersey and went roughly two years without leaving his mother's house. Bisme, an especially close friend of Black Messiah and once regarded as skilled with the lessons, took hard to the bottle. Some Five Percenters that came up through the street academy or Harlem Prep left New York for college. Dumar went to the University of Massachusetts; Um Allah, whose journey to Allah began with the Blood Brothers in

1964, flew to California to attend the Polytechnical Institute. A handful of youths continued to use the street academy as a clubhouse, trading stories about Allah until going their separate ways.[31] When asked how many Five Percenters there might be in the future, Justice considered that it might come down to nine or seven, maybe five, perhaps three or only one.[32]

Meanwhile, criticisms that John Lindsay had spent city funds "buying off militants" put him at odds with his party. Opposing the mayor's reelection bid in the 1969 Republican primary were Long Island state senator John Marchi and Brooklyn assemblyman Vito Battista, who named the election's key issues as "anarchy in the schools, terror in the streets, and runaway welfare." Accused of abandoning the city's white ethnic groups to reach out to blacks and hispanics, Lindsay hustled for votes in Irish, Italian and Jewish neighborhoods.

The primary was scheduled for June 17, following a week in which the *New York Times* reported Allah's assassination, rumors of a Black Muslim war and Lindsay's visit to the Five Percenters' Street Academy. Marchi took the nomination with 113,000 votes to the mayor's 107,000. President Nixon gave Marchi his endorsement: "The American people in our cities, in our small towns and in this country are fed up to here with violence and lawlessness, and they want candidates who will take a strong stand against it." Lindsay would have to run against the party that put him in office.

The Democratic nominee, Controller Mario Procaccino, was described by journalist Nicholas Pileggi as "ethnic in the extreme," "unabashedly patriotic," and "unsophisticated." Jimmy Breslin wrote of Procaccino as "short, waddling, crying, sweating Mario, his mustache from Arthur Avenue, his suit from the garment center, his language from all the years of all the neighborhoods of New York."

"The forces of reaction and fear have captured both major parties," said Lindsay after the primaries. "These parties have been captured by the very forces of hatred, fear and negativism." He formed his own party, the Independent Party of New York City, designed to last only through the November election. The incumbent mayor was now a third-party dark-horse, with few giving him even a remote chance at reelection. "If John Lindsay wins against Mario Procaccino," wrote a *New York Times* reporter, "it will be like Montclair State Teachers College beating Notre Dame."

The work that characterized Lindsay's relationship with Allah was exploited by both his campaign and its opponents. Lindsay ads showed off his record of keeping New York calm while other cities burned in race-riots—a legacy that he largely owed to Allah.

During a debate at the studios of WABC-TV, Procaccino charged that the mayor used city programs to employ "hardened criminals and troublemakers,"

claiming evidence that would indict a prominent Lindsay aide: Barry
Gottehrer. "Is it proper for John Lindsay to buy off hardened criminals?" asked
Procaccino. "As Mayor, I'll stop this practice. I will deal only with the respon-
sible persons in the troubled neighborhoods." Lindsay compared the attack to
McCarthy's Communist witch-hunts of the 1950s. "You know," Procaccino
told the mayor, "you boast of your relationship with the black community.
Well, I know the black people better than you ever will ... I understand their
hopes, their dreams, their aspirations, because I know what they are."

"I don't boast of anything," countered Lindsay, "because I know how much
has to be done in this great city ... that night that Martin Luther King was killed,
which you referred to, Mr. Procaccino, I could have used you at two o'clock in
the morning on 125th Street in Harlem." After the debate aired on television,
Lindsay issued a statement demanding a "full list of names and facts" by
6:00 p.m. Lindsay's deadline came and went, after which his spokesman cited
Procaccino's refusal as proof of "the irresponsibility of the charges."

Procaccino's evidence turned out to be the Malcolm X Afro-American Cultural Center in Queens, described as an outgrowth of the Urban Action Task
Force and one of fourteen "satellite" storefronts founded in the summer of
1967.[33] The Malcolm X center, with walls covered by murals of African tribes-
men and Black Panther posters, was responsible for free lunch programs,
clothing programs, classes on black history, drug education, recreation programs and a new public library named for Langston Hughes. An internal
NYPD memo described the center as working to turn "hard core youths of the
area" into "useful citizens" and claimed that funding for salaries and rent was
overseen by Gottehrer and Davidoff.

One of the youths employed by the center, Fred Fernandez, was a former
RAM member who had been arrested in the 1967 raid and charged with plotting the assassinations of moderate black leaders Roy Wilkins and Whitney
Young. The center's director spoke of Fernandez as one of over one hundred
leaders "we finally were able to reach" in 1967.

Gottehrer appeared before a grand jury in Queens and denied that Lindsay
was throwing around city money to keep the streets calm: "if you buy off kids
for peace, someone might buy them off at a higher price for war." The case
against him fell apart. Assistant District Attorney James Robertson, who
thought he could prove that Gottehrer had paid young hoodlums with his own
money, did not know the difference between the Youth Board and Urban
League or how programs were funded. Gottehrer did not even know why he
was asked to testify. After the hearing, Robertson praised him to reporters.

Between the mayor and the Jewish vote stood Rabbi Meir Kahane, who
wrote anti-Lindsay op-eds for the *Jewish Press* and heckled him at public

appearances. Deputy Mayor Richard Aurelio described Kahane as "showing every sign of being unstable and unbalanced and hostile beyond reason." The rabbi founded a Zionist answer to the Black Panthers, the Jewish Defense League, which used as its logo a Black Power-esque fist inside a Star of David and chanted slogans such as "Every Jew a .22." Lindsay's team invited Shalom Klass, publisher of the *Jewish Press*, to Gracie Mansion. Klass expressed his reservations about endorsing Lindsay, as many of his readers feared that the mayor was anti-Semitic. Lindsay stormed out of the room. Before the meeting's conclusion, however, Klass had agreed to fire Kahane—in exchange for an old Brooklyn train station to use as his newspaper's headquarters, leased from the city for a dollar a year.

One month before the election, Lindsay was getting doused with champagne by New York Mets pitcher Tom Seaver, catcher Jerry Grote and outfielder Rod Gaspar in the team's Shea Stadium clubhouse. After seven seasons finishing last or second to last, the "Miracle Mets" had won the World Series in five games. Photos of Lindsay celebrating with the team helped humanize the opera-attending, tux-wearing WASP that Procaccino had derided as a "limousine liberal." The mayor hoped for the team's underdog charm to rub off on his third-party campaign. At a dinner he introduced himself as John "Met" Lindsay and declared, "now New York needs just one more miracle."

And the miracle came through, with Lindsay receiving 1,012,633 votes in November to Procaccino's 831,772 and Marchi's 532,411. The mayor took 85 percent of the total black vote and 65 percent of the Hispanic, a strong 45 percent of the Jewish vote and even 25 percent of Catholic voters while running against two Catholic opponents.

Personal attacks, empty political friendships and the death of Allah had left Barry Gottehrer jaded. He recalled:

> A new term meant a new kind of administration and new kinds of problems. I tried to imagine what Allah would have thought. It didn't seem too incredible to me that maybe some of the people I worked with every day were members of that wicked 10 percent he used to talk about, and the growing list of friends of mine who were dead, shot up or in jail, just might, from time to time, have been in touch with the True Wisdom of the 5 percent.[34]

It was all bad news. In March 1970, the *New York Times* reported on a small black cult charged with the murder and mutilation of a white teenager in Detroit. The sect's founder, known as "Enoch," had attracted followers through karate and culture lessons at an Urban League street academy.[35] Though unconnected to Allah's street academy or Barry Gottehrer, it did not help the credibility of either in New York. Meanwhile, the Five

Percenters were showing all the signs of an early extinction. Gatherings at Mount Morris Park and the Harriet Tubman School, once overflowing, had thinned out. Gykee recalls a parliament attended by only nine people.[36] When Gottehrer left New York in 1971, he was sure that he had heard the last of the Five Percenters.

10
The Lives of Nations

Pulp novel *Black Angels* depicted the Nation of Islam as governed by a shadowy group of elders, the "Guardian Angels," who manipulated events among Muslims from behind the scenes. In the early 1970s, author Sterling Hobbs was Sterling X, a student minister at Mosque No.7. During his stint in federal prison (Lewisburg, 1979–1982) for murder, the FBI allegedly offered him freedom if he'd kill a prisoner who had been transferred from Atlanta. When Hobbs refused, the agents told him that he should be their hit man, since they believed that he had already been one for the NOI; they apparently had him confused with the Sterling X Hobbs at Philadelphia's Mosque No.12, regarded as a "gangster" in Muslim circles.[1] After the Philadelphia Hobbs attacked a group of Wallace Muhammad's supporters, an FBI memo named him as "the individual usually called upon by mosque officials when the need for physical force is anticipated." On December 29, 1964, when Malcolm X and his bodyguards arrived at a Philadelphia radio station, they were ambushed by Sterling's doom squad. Malcolm later called Betty and told her to put his shotgun near the door.

The Guardian Angels of the Harlem Hobbs' fiction carried out much of their operations through a network of secret agents, known as "Five Percenters," who smuggled themselves into minor administrative roles at temples throughout the country.

Later, one of the Five Percenters named Clarence 13X defected and started his own cult which he also named the Five Percenters.

When Clarence declared himself "Supreme Allah" and began attracting hundreds of followers from prisons and reformatories in the New York area, the Guardian Angels decided to give him some assistance. One of his "followers" arranged a meeting to prove beyond all doubt that Clarence, the Father, was in fact the Supreme Allah.

He gathered a group of believers around Clarence and screamed: "I know you are Allah. You are He who lives and dies not!" Then he emptied a revolver into Clarence's body. Clarence died on the spot.[2]

The fiction illustrated a serious crisis for the real Five Percenters. The

Father's primary representatives were high-school and junior-high boys with a tendency toward hyperbole, who used his survival of the 1964 shooting as proof that he was Allah. His initial victory over bullets won him some awe-stricken youths, but he lost many with the rematch.

Allah had allegedly predicted that after his death, his nation would itself lie dead for a year. He also taught his Five Percenters that if they ever wanted to see him, they needed only to come together and say his name. The rebirth of the poor and righteous began with a December 4, 1970 dance in Queens. The event was organized by Born Allah and featured entertainment from Sabu & the Survivors, with Five Percenters Emmanuel "Rahiem" LeBlanc doing lead vocals and Keith "Sabu" Crier on bass. The group, which also arranged music for the "Enlightener," would later form GQ and score a top 100 hit with "Disco Nights" (during their appearance on *American Bandstand*, Dick Clark would ask Sabu and Rahiem, "what happened to the regular names, like James and Charles?"[3]). A New Year's party at the street academy had Five Percenters again sharing stories, while a party in Hollis, Queens reunited Five Percenters from Harlem Prep.[4] Agreements were made that each Five Percenter would bring one new person to the next parliament; when the time came, some were described as bringing entire "tribes." Born Allah, Kassiem Allah and God Kalim were known as prolific teachers in Pelan (the Bronx), and Chauncey "God B" Milliner, Allah Mathematics, and Rasheem reclaimed the Desert (Queens). Medina (Brooklyn) had Allah-U-Akbar, Father Ubeka, and the new Five-Percent "Father Divine." Classes were held in the community room of the Marcy projects with the likes of Big God Lord Supreme, Justice Foundation, Kendu Foundation and Melson. Knowledge of self reached a new crop of Five Percenters who had never walked with the Father, but could nonetheless hold fast to the rope of his word.

To these youths, the Father seemed distant. He was unknowable, a "legend, a myth," says Beloved Allah, who joined in 1972 at the age of fifteen.[5] Some of those touched by Five Percenter discourse were too young to really comprehend the philosophy. During work with the Thunderbirds, a preadolescent gang in a Harlem housing project, researcher Clarence Robins interviewed two eight-year-old members who might have misheard some Five Percenter dialogues:

GREG: And sometimes I'll curse with "B.B."

CR: What's that?

GREG: Oh, that's a "M.B.B." Black Boy. 'Merican Black Boy.

CR: Oh.

GREG: Anyway, 'Mericans is same like white people, right?

LEON: And they talk about Allah.

CR: Oh yeah?

GREG: Yeah.

CR: What they say about Allah?

LEON: Allah–Allah is God.

GREG: Allah–

CR: And what else?

LEON: I don' know the res'.

GREG: Allah i–Allah is God, Allah is the only God, Allah–

LEON: Allah is the son of God.

GREG: But can he make magic?

LEON: Nope.

GREG: I know who can make magic?

CR: Who can?

LEON: The God, the real one.

CR: Who can make magic?

GREG: The son of po'—

CR: Hm?

GREG: I'm sayin' the po'k chop God! He only a po'k chop God![6]

Shabu was ten years old when his cousin Supreme Shabazz Adew Ali brought knowledge from the Albany projects to the Cypress Hill Houses. Supreme told Shabu that he'd have to fast for seven days, living on only water and ice cream. Shabu gave up on the Five Percenters because he couldn't maintain the fast, but in fifth grade he regained interest after questioning that blond-haired Mystery God who put black people in chains. For post-1969 "newborns," the Five Percent worldview would be less about Allah's charisma or paternal love than an intellectual and political stand.

At the April and May 1971 parliaments, plans were announced for an "Educational Show and Prove" that would be held at Harlem Prep, showcasing talent and scientific exhibitions by Five Percenters. Intended to demonstrate that Allah lived on through his Five Percenters, the Show and Prove would be scheduled for June 13—the second anniversary of his assassination. Harlem

Prep headmaster Ed "God Carp" Carpenter offered his full endorsement to the event, not only waiving the school's usual $500 rental fee but donating $500 for supplies.

Admission was $1.00 in advance, $1.50 at the door and free for children, who each received a free dictionary. Five Percenters started coming in after 2:00 p.m. Around 4:00, Kundalini Isa Allah showed up with a van full of children from the Bronx.

Serving as the night's emcee, Dumar introduced performers. A female Five Percenter named Latisha sang a song entitled "Allah's Blessings," which had been written by Eye God (William Craig/Amin of the Harlem Six). Five young drummers from Queens, having previously practiced on empty boxes, cans and cars, performed on congas donated by African drummer La Roc Bey. Ranging in age from nine to thirteen, each youth performed a solo and received his own standing ovation.

During intermission it was announced that Amar, a visual arts student at Harlem Prep, was showing his film—the first documentary on the Gods produced *by* a God, with Prince providing commentary—in the screening room downstairs.

Children's science exhibits served to "show and prove" Allah's teaching. The Allah Science Award was bestowed on a boy for his exhibit, "What Makes Rain, Hail and Snow." Using an AC/DC battery, 100-watt bulb and pan of water, he proceeded to make vapor and turn it back into water. Another youth earned a Headmaster Award for his exhibit, "Spook in the Bag."

At 7:00 p.m., Gods watched karate demonstrations by Born Allah's brother Jabar Abdul Jabbar and the Father's former bodyguard Green Eye Zumar, who took on six opponents at a time. After the karate came a fashion show and then African dancing courtesy of the Ndgu Dancers, who in 1973 would be featured on CBS' *The People's Show*. Luasia, the troupe's choreographer, performed a "Supreme Alphabetic finale" with female Five Percenters (referred to as "Queens" or "Earths") Mecca, Makeba, El-Latisha, Tykina, Shalaysa, Asia, Shalema, Guvasia (mother of Allah's son "Little Allah") and two "young princesses," each girl spelling out her name in rap style. Sabu and Rahiem then led a sixteen-piece band including Knowledge Allah, Kaseem Allah and Kiheim, playing original and popular music while Gods and Earths danced until two in the morning. The Show and Prove had been such a success that it would become an annual event.

Like the Father said, all they needed to do was come together. The Harlem street academy (renamed Allah School in Mecca) was again packed with Gods, while in Brooklyn Five Percenters pooled their resources to establish similar programs in Brownsville, Fort Green, and Bed-Stuy and acquired a building on Sterling Place and Washington Avenue for a free-lunch program. For a time in the mid-1970s, most of the students at Westinghouse High School were Five Percenters; students were even given a special African Studies class in which to build, drawing Gods from throughout the city for one period in the school day. U-Allah, who had been incarcerated at Rikers and Elmira from June 1969 to February 1971, looks back on a resurrected cipher in the Bronx:

> In the year of 1971, we was teaching all over Pelan. Around my way (158th Street off of 3rd ave) was Harmeen and his brother Bish-me, Jabber, Al-Raheem from Mecca who came and lived with me and family for a little while. We were real strong in my area. We had Jamar, Knowledge-Born, Dihu, Uhuru, Dakiem, the young gods of Bathgate Ave., were older now, and still strong. Pelan at this time was united from one end to the other. A lot of new Gods were on the scene now, I didn't care, as long as they were strong and had Islam in their hearts.[7]

Allah's nation stretched even beyond the five boroughs. Ernest Allen, Jr. calls it an "extraordinary growth" that "remains, for the most part, an undocumented process."[8] The Gods have maintained limited oral and written history on their expansion, which rarely amounts to more than the names of early Gods who blazed trails in a given area. Wise Allah and Dakim maintained ciphers in Beacon and Newburgh, regarded as legacies of early visits to Matteawan. Knowledge God and Trusan carried the teachings to Asbury Park, New Jersey. Kashiem Allah traveled from Queens to New Haven, Connecticut, where he gave lessons to students at Jackie Robinson Middle School, spawning the city's seven First Born—Be Wisdom Allah, Just-I-C Equality Allah, Supreme Allah, Rahiem Allah, El-Sun Allah, Universal Allah, and Sincere Allah.

In 1971 Amar Self, who had been taught in Harlem by the Father, moved to north Philadelphia. To avoid the escalating gang conflicts he relocated with Queen Asia to Powelton Village, where he met three youths named Jimmy, Larry and Kevin. One summer afternoon on the corner of 36th and Baring, he told them that they were gods. Jimmy became Jamel, Kevin became Ramel and Larry took the name Kahim. The group made a pilgrimage to Harlem and returned home determined to teach. Ramel would build at the dice and card games along the south side's Webster Street, attracting students who became Satu, Knowledge Divine, Tauhid, and Born Divine. During this time, a graduate of Allah's street academy named Messiah had come to Philadelphia to attend Gettysburg College, where he recruited Salim, Rahiem, and Sharrief. Philadelphia now had two ciphers developing simultaneously, one in the streets and one on the campus. The city's sections were renamed as parallels to New York: south Philly, where the knowledge originated, became Mecca; west

Philly was renamed Medina; the east side became the Desert; and north Philly, because of its gangs and strife, was renamed Pelan. The city as a whole would come to be known as Power Hill.

Ramel's student Satu went to jail, where he encountered hostility from NOI Muslims. Though "heavily outnumbered and threatened daily" he continued to teach until his death in 1973. One of Satu's students in the prison, Rshine Justice, would teach in Power Hill after his release.[9] Philadelphia's Five Percenter history seems representative of what took place in cities across the country: the culture first came by way of Gods from New York and spread among a variety of circles (as rapper Lord Jamar puts it, "from the jails to the college dorms"), despite threats from Muslim squads, common gangs and law enforcement.

Sha Sha (from Brooklyn) and Raheem God (from Queens) taught in North Carolina; Freedom (from the Bronx) taught in South Carolina. Hasheem became the first God to teach in Atlanta, which he named Allah's Garden. Bisme brought the message to Washington, D.C. Back in Harlem and Brooklyn, meetings were packed; according to Kalim, "you had to get to Parliament early just to get a seat."[10] Despite everything, the Five Percenters had managed not only to carry on but penetrate the greater consciousness of black America, even influencing those who may have never heard the term "Five Percenter." Omar Abdul-Malik, Research Fellow in Islamic Studies at Harvard Divinity School, cites the Five Percenters as at least partly responsible for the popularity of "Muslim names" such as Karriem in the African-American community at large.[11] La Shu Bee, a member of the early hip-hop group Crash Crew, was often mistaken for a Five Percenter because of his name. In the film *Wattstax*, comedian Richard Pryor seems to be spoofing Five Percenters—or at least Five Percenter-styled characters:

> In my neighborhood, used to be some beautiful black man would come in the neighborhood dressed in African shit, really nice shit, you know, and he'd be "peace, love. Black is beautiful. Remember the essence of life, we are people of the universe, and life is beautiful." And my parents would go, "that nigga's crazy." I used to go to the meetings, though. I got ultra-black for a while and brothers be rappin', I never knew what they were saying, though. But the brother be havin' emotion: "you see, the first thing you gotta know is by eatin' pork, now you eat a piece of pork, you don't realize the suffocations of this individuality's prospects! What the Man is tryin' to lay on you through *porkitis*, you will not understand because the *trickinosis* of your mind will not relinquish the thought of individuality!"[12]

As Five Percenters came together, the Muslims tore themselves apart. During Sterling Hobbs' time in Harlem he saw the NOI, permanently disfigured after the slaughter of Malcolm, spiral further into collective madness. Imagining someone behind the scenes with a beautiful master plan might have been the only way to make sense of it.

The Messenger turned seventy-three in 1970. He had seen his Nation through the post-Fard power struggles, accusations of pro-Japanese subversion and criticisms from Sunnis, Moors, and civil rights leaders. In the early days he lived as a fugitive from his own congregation, fled across the country, sat in prison for a time and still heard Fard's voice coming to him like thunder out of a clear blue sky. He lost and won back a son. He survived Malcolm, Martin, Allah and even the Black Power movement that called him outdated; COINTELPRO had effectively squashed the Black Panther Party in five years or less but couldn't bring down the Nation of Islam in four decades. Through three wars and six presidents it was J. Edgar Hoover vs. Elijah Muhammad, move for move. Hoover gave a newspaper reporter the material to pump out an article accusing W. D. Fard of being a white con-man; Elijah offered $100,000 to anyone that could come forward with proof. Hoover sent word of Elijah's extramarital affairs to his wife and daughters, and in 1969 it became known that the FBI had tapped the Messenger's phone for at least six years. Elijah lashed out against the "ever-evil snoopers" who followed him around. In 1972, after nearly four decades of back-and-forth, Hoover passed away and Elijah was still in power.

But he was so old and frail now that the Feds no longer called him a security threat, instead watching his fading health with high interest. With the Messenger's days clearly numbered, both the Muslims and FBI anticipated a war of succession and recognized two clear contenders. Dialogues in *Black Angels* between the shadowy rulers of the NOI seem at least inspired by real arguments that Hobbs overheard among Muslims in Harlem:

"Louis is only forty years old," pleads an Angel named Isaac. "He has served the cause faithfully and tirelessly."

"The Saviour himself chose Wallace," counters Jacob (Ya'qub). "He taught Clara the proper way to raise him, what to teach him and what to feed him. His most formative years were spent in accord with the Saviour's instructions. The boy is a genius. And you say that Wallace is spiritually inclined. I dare say not a man alive is as spiritually inclined or as theologically enlightened as Wallace."

"I don't trust him, Ya'qub. He's always in and out, never settled. If he can't settle his own life, how can he stabilize the Nation? And all of that Arab motif. He's too much in love with the Arab style, Arab culture. He has no loyalty to his father."

The Angels finally decide that in a time of crisis, the Muslims would look to the "royal family" for guidance. But to secure the throne for Wallace Muhammad, his father must pass soon; a few years down the road and Farrakhan could pose a serious threat. The Angels then agree to assassinate the Messenger.[13]

In real life, Elijah was losing his grip on the empire; mosques throughout the Nation fell into discord, with the conflicts sometimes getting physical. Some Muslims waited impatiently for Elijah to loosen his ban on political action while others resented the Nation's existing power structure of men like Raymond Sharrieff, Supreme Captain of the Fruit of Islam, and Elijah's family. New movements popped up with names like "Young Muslims" and "Saudi Arabia," some pledging their spiritual allegiance to the Messenger yet existing beyond his control.

In October 1971, four men who had plotted on the life of Sharrieff were found dead. One of Sharrieff's assistants was later shot in a restaurant, and his secretary was almost hit by gunfire at the headquarters of *Muhammad Speaks*.

On April 14, 1972, two patrolmen from the 28th Precinct responded to a false call of 10–13 (officer down) on the second floor of 102 East 116th Street, on the corner of Lenox. Philip Cardillo and Vito Navarra entered Mosque No.7 and were met on the stairs by up to twenty Muslims. Police reenforcements arrived and stormed the mosque. As "Muslims and cops swung fists and billy clubs at each other, the high-ceilinged hallway resounding with screaming and cursing," a beaten Navarra managed to make it out. The battle spilled through the main entrance to the sidewalk, and the Muslims locked their doors with three officers trapped inside: Cardillo, Ivan Negron and Negron's partner, Victor Padilla, whose gun was lost in the attack. Cardillo had been shot and a Muslim later identified as Lewis 17X stood over him with a gun. Police broke down the mosque door, fired at the Muslims and forced them into the basement. Louis Farrakhan and Congressman Charles Rangel arrived, warning the police to leave immediately: "If you stay, there is nothing we can do to protect you. You'll be overrun. There'll be rioting. People may be killed." Chief of Detectives Albert Seedman was ordered by his superiors to release the seventeen Muslim men from the basement.

Members of a growing mob outside screamed at police, "I hope you die, you pigs. I hope you drop dead." A police car was overturned and set ablaze, bottles and bricks were thrown at officers from neighboring rooftops, a detective was smashed in the head with a brick and a white female reporter was knocked down and trampled. Mayor Lindsay, who just a week before had pulled the plug on his disastrous bid for the White House, refused to classify the incident a riot. "What's a thousand people, twelve hundred people?" he scoffed at the NYPD deputy commissioner for public affairs, Robert Daly, who had estimated the mob at reaching upwards of twelve hundred people. "You can't have a riot with a thousand people or twelve hundred people."[14]

On January 18, 1973, at 4:00 p.m., two men arrived at the Washington, D.C. headquarters of Hamaas Abdul Khaalis, who had left Harlem's Mosque No.7 to start his own group following the Hanafi school of Sunni Islam. Khaalis had recently circulated letters condemning Elijah's Muslims as "eaters of their dead brothers' flesh" with "polluted minds." The men knocked on the front door and were answered by a young man named Daud. After exchanges of *salam*, one of them introduced himself as Tommy and said that he had called earlier with interest in purchasing Hanafi literature. Tommy gave Daud money for the books; as Daud left to get him change, the men stormed into the house, joined by five or six other men, yelling "this is a stickup." They shot Daud, shot Abdul Nur in his bedroom, found Khaalis' wife Bibi and made her watch them drown her one-year old girl and newborn boy in a bathtub. Then they dragged her to the basement, let her witness the drowning of her nine-day old granddaughter in a sink and then shot her. They killed her toddler Abdullah in a powder room, and Khaalis' ten-year-old son Rahman on Daud's bed, and put Daud's mother Amina in a closet and shot her in the head.

As the assailants left, one shouted, "Don't mess with Elijah!"

"They were so threatened," mourned Khaalis' student, pro basketball star Kareem Abdul-Jabbar, "that they had to take the lives of children." The next issue of *Muhammad Speaks* called Khaalis a "modern-day Uncle Tom." According to Farrakhan, the killers were agents of the United States government who hoped to divide the Muslims. Four members of Philadelphia Mosque No.12 would later be convicted and each receive seven consecutive life sentences.

Two days after the Khaalis massacre, a Muslim was murdered execution-style with two shots to the head. Then four gunmen shot and killed Hakim Jamal, relative of Malcolm X and leader of the Malcolm X foundation.

In September, two members of the "New World Nation of Islam" sent a bullet into the eye and through the brain of Newark's Minister James Shabazz in retaliation for the deaths of NWNOI members in prison. Two weeks later, twin brothers Roger and Ralph Bankston were found dead; police suspected two Muslims, who were in turn found beheaded in a vacant lot. The New World Nation of Islam had been founded in 1960 by Muhammad Ali Hasan, who claimed to be under the direction of Elijah Muhammad. In 1965, Hassan was arrested in Newark, NJ after the city mayor witnessed him fleeing a bank robbery. Hassan crashed into a telephone pole, leapt out of his car and shot at the mayor's windshield. He continued to lead his sect from Trenton State Prison.

The 10th degree from Lost-Found Lesson No.1 ("Why did Muhammad and any Muslim murder the devil?") found its way to national headlines in early 1974. As with Robert Karriem forty years earlier in Detroit, Fard's requirement that a Muslim kill "four devils" received a literal reading and was carried out by believers in the San Francisco area looking to earn their trips to Mecca. A series of black-on-white attacks (nicknamed the "Zebra" killings, ostensibly after the "Z" radio band assigned to the crimes) yielded the discovery of the Death Angels, an underground circle of Muslims said to earn "points" by killing Caucasians, earning extra credit for decapitations, mutilations and female or child victims. The Death Angels successfully took fourteen devils off the planet (all but one by shooting) and seriously wounded seven others. One victim was kidnapped and raped. San Francisco Mayor Joseph Alioto blamed the group for over eighty unsolved murders throughout the state. One police informant claimed that the Death Angels were not limited to the San Francisco mosque but actually belonged to a nationwide network with roughly two thousand members.

On February 25, 1975, the Honorable Elijah Muhammad died of chronic heart failure. The timing of his death—as with Malcolm's ten years and four days earlier—gave incredible weight to the next day's start of the Savior's Day convention. Again, the celebration of W. D. Fard's birth became an opportunity to put on heavily symbolic displays, reassure the faithful and carry the Nation of Islam through a turbulent time.

Elijah had never officially named a successor, saying that the matter was completely "up to Allah." The family closed its ranks behind Wallace, who had been prophesied by W. D. Fard to become a great spiritual leader. The Savior's Day speech of Wallace's primary threat, Louis Farrakhan, erased any rumor of an NOI civil war: "I, like all the rest, submit and yield to see that the work of Elijah Muhammad is carried on by his son Wallace D. Muhammad." Wearing a Fruit of Islam uniform, Wallace was hoisted upon the shoulders of FOI and congratulated before a giant portrait of his father.

"No one can really say how he will act now," an unnamed source told the *New York Times*. "He might not turn out as they expect."

In his own address, Wallace made reference to white devilry only as a mental state.[15] The distinction may seem negligible to outsiders, but Elijah's son had made the first cautious step in pulling his Nation to *al-Islam*. At heart Wallace had been a Sunni for years, repeatedly leaving the Nation over its worship of W. D. Fard as God. Reconciliations with his father in 1965 (after the death of Malcolm X) and 1969 or 1970 (after the death of Allah) might have been purely for his survival.

He later abolished the Fruit of Islam and dismissed old hard-liners like Raymond Sharrieff. With NOI mosques formerly modeled after churches,

Wallace took out the seats to allow for traditional Muslim prayer. He spoke of African-American Muslims as "Bilalians," in reference to Bilal, an Ethiopian companion of the Prophet Muhammad, and renamed the NOI newspaper *Bilalian News*. He appointed a Pakistani imam, Muhammad Abdullah, to head his Oakland mosque. After Abdullah's death, Wallace would claim that the imam had been none other than a repentant W. D. Fard, having returned in disguise to undo his work.

At a June 16 rally in Chicago's McCormick Place, Wallace dropped his biggest bombshell in front of twenty thousand believers: the Nation of Islam would allow white members.

"There is not even a ripple of discord in the Nation," insisted Louis Farrakhan, who had renamed himself Abdul Haleem Farrakhan. "We are all happy over the emergence of the Honorable Wallace Muhammad ... no one among us is high enough to tie the shoelaces of Wallace." Eventually giving the Nation of Islam a complete rebirth as the World Community of Islam in the West (WCIW), in barely a year Wallace removed all traces of Elijah's legacy. He'd cap it off by changing his own name; to wash his hands of Wallace D. Fard and assume a more "Muslim" aesthetic, he became Warith Deen. To gain distance from his father, he changed his spelling of Muhammad to *Mohammed*. In a move to heal the wounds of the past, and perhaps demonstrate who had really won the war, Wallace renamed Mosque No.7 in honor of its former minister: Masjid Malcolm Shabazz. He then removed Minister Farrakhan from his post, appointing him an "international representative."

As Wallace methodically dismantled forty years' worth of labor, thousands abandoned the WCIW, most to go their own ways. Silas Muhammad scooped up a handful of supporters and formed his own hardline group. By 1977, Farrakhan was again teaching Elijah's doctrines. On March 7, 1978, tired of being a "prostitute" for a "cheap hypocrite," he officially left Warith Deen's WCIW to resurrect the Nation of Islam. "Family don't make you right," he announced, "family don't give you no power." Still, to counter Warith Deen's gravitas as Elijah's son, Farrakhan recruited the Messenger's six former secretaries and thirteen illegitimate children. With the 116th and Lenox mosque under Warith Deen's control, Farrakhan established a new "Muhammad Mosque #7" in Brooklyn.

Farrakhan may have looked to the Gods as a possible constituency; during Warith Deen's reforms, many dissatisfied Muslims joined the Five Percenters. The resurrected Nation of Islam would move its flagship mosque to 127th Street and Lenox Avenue in Harlem, barely a block from the Allah School. A story also spread among the Five Percenters that Allah had told his First Born, "if anything happens to me, go back to Elijah." The NOI would even develop mathematical exegesis influenced by Allah's Supreme Mathematics.[16]

At Arizona State University, Farrakhan delivered a lecture entitled "Is the House Divided?" and fielded questions from the audience. One youth stood and asked,

What do you think about the Five Percent Nation of Islam? Because there are a lot of Muslims who say that the Five Percent Nation of Islam is a bunch of gangsters and street—uh, street, you know, garbage. And that we don't give, that the Five Percent Nation of Islam do not tell the true righteousness and that the true righteousness is in the *Bilalian* and *Muhammad Speaks*—also that a lot of the brothers that are Muslims started off as in the Five Percent Nation of Islam and they forget all about it.[17]

"Thank you," said Farrakhan. "You heard him, didn't you? There was a brother who was in Temple Number 7 in New York City under the name of Clarence 13X—" Immediately a member of the audience shouted his disapproval, to which Farrakhan answered, "no, don't do that. The Holy Qur'an says evil is a bad name after faith." The minister then praised Five Percenters for keeping to Elijah Muhammad's lessons when many did not, and even offered posthumous approval from the Messenger:

I'm telling you that the Honorable Elijah Muhammad respected those young brothers and sisters who called themselves the Five Percenters. Now, I talked to the Honorable Elijah Muhammad about that group that was developing in New York and now spreading. He said, "That's good. That is good. They are studying that which Allah questioned me on and they are studying my answers to those questions."[18]

At his final Savior's Day celebration in 1974, Elijah's address had revealed the very fine line between Nation of Islam and *Five Percent* Nation of Islam teachings—a line that, for many, continued to blur:

Every time you look at a black man, you're looking at God. Maybe some of us will say, "Oh no! I'm no God and you're no God." Okay, get your God out and show him to me. You can't do that. You say that God is a spirit. Show him to me. You can not show me your spirit God. Then you say, he's not to be seen. Well then, I don't want to see him if he don't want to see me ... for 43 years, I have been teaching that God is man![19]

11

Warrior Stripes

When the gangs I hung out with in the '70s gave way to '80s hip-hop culture, it was the street language, style and consciousness of the Five Percent Nation that served as a bridge.

Russell Simmons

There may be no easier way to offend Five Percenters than to call them a gang—neglecting the members that have parlayed their beliefs into a rehabilitating influence, Gods and Earths that have never been involved with criminal activity, and not least of all the "seeds:" children of loving Five Percenter parents, who often excel in school and stay out of trouble. The Five Percenters were labeled a gang from their inception, viewed originally as an outgrowth of the Blood Brothers and old-fashioned fighting gangs and later confused with the Zebra Killers. Allah's journey from "Harlem rowdy" to legitimate community leader, as well as his oft-repeated vow to be "neither pro-black, nor anti-white" are forgotten today by columnists like the *Washington Post*'s Daniel Pipes, who calls the Five Percenters a "more aggressive NOI offshoot" full of "violent ex-cons, hoods, unsocialized individuals."

In the years immediately following Allah's assassination, his post-Matteawan transformation of the Five Percenters into a "youth group" encouraging civic pride and education, embraced by the mayor and hailed for preventing riots, was viewed as a model by New York gangs. During the first half of the 1970s, Bronx and East Harlem gangs clashed not over turf or respect but access to city programs, including summer jobs and recreational activities. A five-gang coalition called the Brotherhood arranged meetings with the Bronx borough president, hoping to acquire its own clubhouse for the purpose of hosting high-school equivalency classes. No less than sixty-eight Bronx gangs later came together as the Family in an attempt to wrangle antipoverty funds from the city, but by then Lindsay was out of office and the funds had dried up.

While Mecca Gods went unchallenged on Seventh Avenue along the 120 series of streets, Medina Gods navigated through a well-defined map of gang mandates. "If you traveled five or ten blocks in any direction," writes First

Born ABG, "you were off your turf, most likely in hostile territory." Gykee describes Brooklyn as "the land of the warriors." In 1973, police estimated that Brownsville and Bed-Stuy were each home to roughly twenty-five fighting gangs. The Jolly Stompers ruled Crown Heights with a membership of 165. The Tomahawks, believed to be responsible for at least eleven homicides that year, achieved notoriety after the alleged nine-man rape of a thirteen-year-old girl led police to raid its headquarters. Classic blaxploitation film *The Education of Sonny Carson* employed actual Tomahawks, Jollystompers and Black Spades for a major fight scene at Prospect Park.

In 1974, police estimated that roughly 2,500 Brooklyn youths were participating in a sophisticated extortion ring. Some local businesses worked openly with the gangs; Tony's Theater on Sutter Avenue printed cards that entitled any Tomahawk to free admission. In the summer of 1972, members of the Black Hebrew movement B'nai Zaken (Sons of the Ancient Israelites) formed a Brooklyn version of the Family, uniting fifteen gangs and five thousand youths under their control with aims to teach the Torah and self-defense. According to police, B'nai Zaken supplied guns to Tomahawks and Outlaws for a cut of the money they made extorting local stores. Gang members who could not obtain real guns had homemade "zip-guns" that were crafted from ballpoint pens and could shoot .22 caliber bullets.

Beyond neighborhood beat-down squads, Brooklyn Gods faced ideological rivals and their respective paramilitary wings. They still had to contend with Farrakhan's FOI, and the Ansar in Flatbush had their SOI (Swords of Islam). The Dar ul-Islam, at the time the largest indigenous Sunni group in the U.S., had its *Ra'd* (from the Arabic word for thunder). According to the Dar ul-Islam's Sheik Sulaiman al-Hadi, "it became a dynamic of life and death over our religious beliefs to secure our turf."[1] Brooklyn was also home for Rabbi Meir Kahane's Jewish Defense League, which would be linked throughout the 1970s to attacks on Arabs, harassment of Russians, vandalism, firebombings, kidnapping threats and even the attempted hijacking of a plane bound for the United Arab Emirates. The summer of Allah's assassination, Kahane held his first paramilitary training camp in the Catskills, where students between the ages of fifteen and twenty woke up at 5:00 a.m. for daily routines that included four hours of karate, two hours of weapons training, one hour of close-order drill and four hours of Jewish history. Graduates then taught riflery and self-defense to rabbinical students and patrolled the margins between Jewish and African-American neighborhoods, wielding baseball bats and looking for *situations*. When black militant James Forman was rumored to plan an appearance at Temple Emanu-El, Kahane dispatched a mob of forty men, some armed with bats and chains. In 1970, Kahane organized a protest against black and hispanic harassment of Jews and was placed in police custody for throwing bottles at officers. He then sued the Board of Education to prevent a meeting between Black Panthers and Young Lords at Thomas Jefferson High School, denouncing both groups as violent and radical. Less than a year later, Kahane would plead guilty to conspiracy charges involving manufacture of explosives.

As the Father had reportedly forbidden his Suns from carrying weapons, Gods in the Brooklyn battlefields kept a close watch on each other and made a point of traveling in pairs. ABG writes that Brooklyn's Five Percenters developed a "warrior spirit," but defines the phrase in the "language of the Gods:" warriors are those who know their brothers better than their brothers know themselves, and understand that the civilized are responsible for the uncivilized.[2] The Medina Gods viewed themselves as *righteous* warriors. In 1971, the NYPD believed an alliance of Five Percenters, Muslims, and Rastafarians to be responsible for the vigilante-style killings of ten suspected drug dealers. Black youths in the Brower Park area, some wearing "star-and-crescent emblems," told reporters that drug sales had decreased in the area after "the brothers did a thing," refusing to identify both the *brothers* and the *thing*.

The first Five Percenters in Brooklyn, Gykee Mathematics Allah and Universal Shaamgaudd Allah, were originally members of the Fort Green Chaplains. Gykee recalls that before their mental rebirths, they had already "broken the land with our war-like tactics and actions." Waleak from the Medina First Born was previously known as "El Cid," leader of the Homicide Lords. Some left the gang to follow him into the Five Percenters.[3] In later years, Brooklyn Gods recruited whole gangs at a time: all forty members of the Together Brothers, the fifty-member Ministers and all one hundred Fugitives. When Tomahawk president Derrick "Champ" Ford, who played "Wolf" in *The Education of Sonny Carson*, went Five Percent and changed his name to Akbar (he later renamed himself Allah-U-Akbar after the war cry of Gods at Rikers Island), the gang's entire three hundred-man roster followed. In 1976 these crews accounted for 141 arrests, 18 percent of all gang-related arrests in Brooklyn, causing the NYPD to identify the "Five Percent Nation" as a loose alliance of gangs. In 1978 they were responsible for 418 arrests, 28 percent of Brooklyn's gang arrests. One year later, the various gangs had apparently dissolved into the Five Percenters, which were then considered a single gang; 113 known Five Percenters were arrested in Brooklyn, nearly half for robbery or criminal possession of a dangerous weapon.[4]

Eighteen-year-old Father Bushawn was building constantly in Tompkins Projects, which had been renamed Truth City. "The way we conducted ourselves," he remembers, "whenever you saw one team of Gods, the other team wasn't far away and they would soon be coming together."⁵ Students of Victorious Shabazz and Lord Graceful Malik would often test each other, "like steel sharpening steel."⁶ Malik brought Bushawn to Mecca to meet the legendary Justice, who Barry Gottherer believes might have found a job with the city.

By then they spoke of Justice as *Old Man* Justice; the young Brother Jimmy who swung sticks at cops' heads in front of the Hotel Theresa was only sacred history. He walked with a cane now, broken down by years of drink and drugs and struggle. Long-term cocaine use often brings a chronic depletion of dopamine, impairing functioning of the extrapyramidal motor system and resulting in Parkinsonian movements. Old Man Justice began getting seizures; one episode caused him to fall into a tub of hot water and suffer scaldings on his entire body. Following his hospitalization, he returned to the streets and the young Gods that looked to him as an "example of the power."⁷ In the years of his declining health, the *New York Times* described the Five Percenters as "fragmented" and "nearly defunct," and the *New York Amsterdam News* reported that Gods were caught up in their own "raging" power struggle.⁸ It was during this time that the Harlem Planning Commission tore down Allah's old block, starting with the Wellworth Bar where he had saved West Indian. Bulldozers were then aimed at the Allah School. At first the Commission claimed that the building was unoccupied; after Five Percenters protested, the Harlem Commonwealth Council's president wrote a letter to Percy Sutton, claiming to speak on behalf of the Five Percenters and the Allah School, asking that Sutton do something to remove the Gods from the land. On October 12, 1977, the Five Percenters appeared en masse at a meeting of the Planning Commission. Ja'mella God, Kundalini Isa Allah and Born God Born made pleas to the board. A number of Five Percenters signed up to speak and then handed their turns to God Kalim, who gave the board a summarized history of Allah, Lindsay, the Urban League, the dollar-a-year lease for ninety-nine years and the dirty tricks pulled by the HCC. For confirmation the Gods tracked down Barry Gottherer in Connecticut, who was stunned to hear that the Five Percenters had even existed so long, let alone maintained the school.

In June 1978, Old Man Justice told Azreal that he could sell "Popeye," his sister's myna bird for her. Azreal brought Justice the bird, then walked down to the Nation of Islam's Shabazz Restaurant on 125th. "I was still hostile towards them," Azreal remembers, "not knowing who did what" and having no way to strike back. So he looked at the giant portrait of W. D. Fard and shouted, "which half did Elijah listen to, the Original half or the Caucasian? Was it God or the devil?" The FOI security guard jumped up and tried putting himself over as a police officer, threatening to arrest Azreal. Azreal told him that if he was a real cop, he'd like to see his gun. The Fruit took out a stiletto knife and gave him a quick stab in each thigh. Azreal knocked him down and escaped the restaurant, running down the sidewalk with blood spurting from both legs. The Fruit chased Azreal until they reached the police precinct, where officers spotted Azreal's bleeding legs and the Fruit's dripping knife.

The next time Azreal stopped at the Allah School, he learned that Old Man Justice had died in a seizure. Five Percenters collected money for a funeral and cremation. The eulogy mentioned a long list of Gods that had been taught by Justice over the years, including Raheem Asiatic Shabazz, whose name was Melvin when he met Justice in 1965 at Karate Bob's dojo. Justice had given him his holy attribute, explained that it meant "most merciful" and said that he'd have to "display aspects of being merciful and be a warrior at the same time; defend righteousness and uphold righteousness." Raheem described Justice to me as "quiet, laid-back, but serious in what he knew and what he taught."

Father Bushawn joined the army and was stationed in Augusta, Georgia. One night his friends came back from a club and bragged about getting the best of a Five Percenter in front of the building. Two days later Bushawn saw the God wearing a Panama with "69 Pro Keds" on it and shouted, "Peace, where you from?"

"Physically I'm from New York," replied Victorious Shabazz, "mentally I'm from the universe." Together they opened an Allah School at Fort Gordon and ran it until Bushawn's 1980 discharge. July saw Father Bushawn and Victorious Shabazz make their return to Medina's Truth City (Tompkins Projects) and join forces with Bed-Stuy Gods under the leadership of Minister Allah and Rahiem. "At that time of our development," states Father Bushawn, "we understood that we had to stick together in everything that we did. So if you messed with one then you had to deal with all."[9]

Shabu had been building with Gods in Cypress Hill Houses and reading Eldridge Cleaver, and his best friend's brother got him a "Book of Life" containing lessons by Robert Walker. When his friend Divine was shot and killed by a Cee Cipher Power in the back of the projects, Shabu stepped up his study. Then he ran into Allah's old bodyguard Zumar, who told him that Walker's lessons were not *right and exact* and provided a copy of the Supreme Wisdom. Mastering every degree would earn Shabu a pin of the Universal flag from "half-original" Monik, who "used to come out to the park jams with some Universal Flags pinned inside of his coat with our names already on them, all we had to do is get 120 lessons in our heads."[10] While Zumar encouraged Shabu to go to college and helped him attain a degree in Business and Administration, Minister Allah served as Shabu's "educator in the streets:" "Minister took all of the fear out of the young Gods and told us that we was the cream that would rise to the top, that's where I get my Medina warrior stripes from and yes back then we had to do 'whatever was necessary to protect our way of life.' "[11]

Five Percenters claimed the park behind P.S. 92, renamed it Born Wisdom Park and kept gangs out of the area. "No one would come in and start any trouble with Gods," remembers Infinite Al'Jaa'Maar-U-Allah; "the people in the community knew that their children were safe."[12] Minister Kassiem (also known as D-Islam) was regarded as head of the Five Percenters in Bushwick. When two 85ers known as Harry and Tweety tried to rape his sister Mecca and girlfriend Medina, they were stabbed up by a joint effort of Minister Kassiem, A-Islam (Lord Serious) and B-Islam. The Five Percenters exiled A-Islam after he turned state's evidence; Minister Kassiem and B-Islam went upstate for seven years.[13] Protecting the Gods' way of life also included actions against fellow Five Percenters who exploited the movement for personal gain. In 1976 Prince A Cuba opened a Brooklyn shop that sold Universal Flags and crowns. "He was 10% profiting economically, using our Nation," writes Born King Allah.[14] In 1982, Five Percenters destroyed the store.[15] Cuba himself would go to prison for second-degree attempted murder. Questions of sincerity and devotion to the Five Percenters resulted in murder near the Allah School, when Jamar Allah and two companions confronted Larry "Messiah" Scott and his friend Edward Greene over Scott's lack of attendance at parliaments.[16] Scott insisted that he was God; one of Jamar's friends told him that he was neither God nor Messiah[17] and Scott challenged them to fight. Jamar's companion pulled out a gun. Greene tried to interfere, prompting Jamar to draw his own gun and shoot him in the back. Jamar's friend shot and killed Scott while Jamar shot Greene again, then pistol-whipped and robbed him.[18]

It was not only men that found the knowledge through gang life. While researching gang activity among females, Anne Campbell followed a young woman named Sun-Africa who first encountered Five Percenter boys while running with an all-girl gang known as the "Puma Crew." In April 1981, Sun-Africa's Five Percenter boyfriend Shamar was killed during an attempted burglary. His close friend Shasha died soon after, during an argument at a numbers spot. Campbell identified the Five Percent Nation as a gang for the purposes of her study.[19]

In 1983, an assistant minister from Louis Farrakhan's Brooklyn mosque ventured to nearby Truth City to watch the Gods build. Impressed with their grasp of the lessons, he invited them to the mosque to meet Minister Kareem Muhammad. At the mosque, Father Bushawn was shocked upon entering the lunch room to find FOI building in the manner of Five Percenters, using the date's corresponding degree in the 120. The Gods joined the *cipher* and gave peace to the Fruit. Kareem Muhammad was unable to meet with the Gods that day but forwarded them an invitation for dinner the following week.

Over dinner, Muhammad told Bushawn and the Truth City Gods that he had spoken with the Honorable Minister Farrakhan, who expressed high hopes for the Nation of Islam and Five Percenters to work together. Courtesy of Farrakhan, Muhammad offered the Five Percenters use of the mosque. He suggested to the Gods that Victorious Shabazz run their lessons, with Father Bushawn serving as Captain of Security. Though concerned that they'd appear to have been bought by the Muslims, the Five Percenters accepted.

For four months they held their Civilization Class in Mosque #7 without incident, and it appeared that a new unity was forming. When a Sunni wanted to fight Kareem Muhammad, the Fruit and Gods banded together, piling into cars and heading for Muhammad's hometown of Plainfield, New Jersey. Though Captain of Security, Father Bushawn was not allowed to come along because he had just beaten an attempted murder rap. The combined teams successfully defended Minister Muhammad, but ran into trouble when Farrakhan learned of the mission.

Farrakhan immediately called a meeting with the Fruit of Islam and Five Percenters. He started by explaining the meaning of his name, incorporating Supreme Mathematics, Supreme Wisdom Lessons and the Bible. Then he got to business, promptly dismissing Kareem Muhammad and replacing him as minister with Abdullah Muhammad. Next he fired the Captain of New York's FOI, who happened to be his son-in-law. Farrakhan then asked everyone who had gone to New Jersey to stand. One by one, he relieved the Fruit. Though the Honorable Minister was unable to formally discipline the Five Percenters, they would no longer be allowed to hold classes in the mosque.

Father Bushawn continued associating with the Muslims, even wearing both NOI and Five Percenter flags until Abdullah Muhammad told him that he couldn't serve two masters. Bushawn then had to show and prove "one nation as well as one god" and was accepted into the mosque. As with the Father twenty years before him, Bushawn's military background made him valuable; appointed as an FOI security officer, he assisted Farrakhan in Harlem and was the only male allowed in Mosque 7 during Muslim Girls' Training classes.

In 1985, when Farrakhan addressed an audience of twenty-five thousand at Madison Square Garden, Father Bushawn was part of the Minister's personal security detail. During the speech, Farrakhan specifically addressed his "beautiful brothers and sisters of the Five Percent Nation" to an ovation from several hundred Gods and Earths in the crowd.

Father Bushawn's relationship with the NOI ended after another fight. Protesting when an Arab tried to disrespect his Earth, Bushawn was jumped by the man's three sons. Bushawn later received visits to his home from Five Per-centers, Fruit of Islam and the NYPD. The police offered to take care of the matter. Bushawn declined assistance, agreed to end his work with the Fruit and ultimately moved from Medina to the Desert, "where we are still counting the miles of history as we make it."[20]

> I am at war with the Five Percenters. It fills me with sadness and chagrin that this band of hoodlums and thugs could capture the minds of hundreds of teenagers. I will not allow it.
>
> Joseph Clark, principal, Eastside High School (1984–1991)

Principal Joe Clark, who would be immortalized by Morgan Freeman in *Lean on Me*, complained to the *New York Times*' Sandra Gardner of his male stu-dents calling themselves by names such as King, Justice, Knowledge and Star, as well as female students wearing "bandanas." In the December 1984 article, Gardner explained to readers that the Five Percenters were a movement classi-fied at times as "a cult, a gang, a fad and a jailhouse religion" that was "linked with gang fights and a killing, but also has been praised for turning delinquents into serious, law-abiding students."

> When a 5% goes among the 85% one of two things happen. Either the 85% start acting like the 5% or the 5% start acting like the 85%.
>
> God Kalim[21]

To some extent, Gods and gangs may have conquered each other. Like the Black Panthers, Young Lords and Zulu Nation, Five Percenters countered the senseless violence of gang life with a message of unity and respect. At the same time, old gang beefs sometimes resurfaced in new settings, causing trouble between Five Percenters and the Zulu Nation through the late 1970s and early 1980s. Beloved Allah remembers two types of Five Percenter: some Gods, empowered by the black man's divinity, used the knowledge to uplift themselves and their community, while others abused the notion of Godhood to justify criminal behavior. While Zumar and Minister Allah personified these opposites in Brooklyn, Queens had Prince Allah (not to be confused with First Born Prince), a "family man on his way to becoming a doctor," and Chauncey Milliner, a stick-up artist who used the righteous name God B but still lived for the streets.[22] In the 1970s, while the Five Percent became infested with gang entanglements, Freedom Allah (who considered himself "the Nation's cook") and other Gods acquired a building at Sterling Place and Washington Avenue to establish a free-lunch program.[23] Universal Shaamgaudd Allah taught that the Father broke down *gun* as

"God-U-Not," but complained of other Gods calling guns their "God-U-Now" or "God-U-Nation."[24]

Five Percenters at one Bedford-Stuyvesant high school were described as a "difficult, volatile group, almost pathological in its actions, who purportedly justify their antisocial actions by quoting the Koran."[25] New gangs formed specifically to oppose the Gods, such as the HBOs (Home Boys Only), who took shape in 1985 in Asbury Park and Neptune, New Jersey, and the Cazzeeks, who enjoyed a reputation as the only group in its area that would rob Five Percenters. Like the Five Percent Nation, both gangs moved toward positive roles in their communities; the Cazzeeks maintained a "stay in school" message and participated in neighborhood clean-up programs, and in 1988 the Home Boys Only became the Healthy Black Organization.[26] Despite these rival groups, however, Monmoth County Investigator George Corbiscello stated that most Five Percenter violence in New Jersey was aimed at other Five Percenters.[27] The community tried to maintain peace by banishing any Five Percenter who acted violently against another God or Earth. Universal Shaamgaudd refers to the episode in which Dumar ("Goomar") Complete attacked Allah Live and his family. After allegedly making a taped confession that threatened the First Born, Dumar Complete "fled into prison for security." It was agreed within the Five Percent Nation that Dumar would be "exiled for the rest of his natural life as long as that shall be!"[28]

> Being a Five Percenter was nothing more than a license to be brutal.
>
> LL Cool J

Queens native and Grammy-winning rap icon LL Cool J, who had flirted with Five Percent ideas as a teenager, concedes that his experience did not reflect the true nature of the teachings: "at its core there is strict religious doctrine, but we weren't following that. We were just using the Five Percent label as a shield to do our dirty work—fighting and eventually robbing."[29]

In 1981, community-minded Five Percenters purchased property at a city auction to establish an Allah School on 150th Street in Queens. "It was our way of cleaning up," recalls Beloved Allah. The location was strategic, responding to an ugly new monster that threatened to destroy the Poor Righteous Teachers.

> The rise of drugs is the downfall of Gods.
>
> Jamar Allah

Through the 1960s and 1970s, Five Percenters survived Muslims, Ansars, gangs, cops, feds and assassins. In the 1980s, the enemy was a new method of using cocaine. Rather than neutralizing the base with an acid to make a sniffable hydrochloride salt, street chemists were heating the rock crystals and smoking the vapors. When heated, the rocks made a "cracking" sound that resulted in the new style's name.

There is no question that if the Father had lived into the 1980s, he would have forbidden Five Percenters from using crack, as he had with heroin, which he called the "pig of stimulations."[30] Without the Father's guidance, however, crack ran rampant on his Suns. Monthly Parliament attendance, claimed to have averaged in the 900–1,000 range throughout the 1970s, fell below 600 in 1982.[31] By 1988, according to Five Percenter sources, the average count had dipped to 450.[32] Many Gods that lingered on at parliaments and rallies were shells of their former selves, such as First Born Uhura, who had formerly "kept himself looking right."[33] Beloved Allah says that "after the crack days, there was a big contrast in how brothers looked."[34] God Kalim's *Five Percenter* newspaper today maintains an emphatic anti-drug message. Amar Allah, who comforted and encouraged jailed Gods with penpal correspondence until his death in 1998,[35] offered a painfully honest testimonial:

> As you know I am in the hospital. I can not walk due to my CRACK SMOKING and not knowledging the wisdom born to me by the Gods who stayed in my ALLAH SAVIOR SELF. Yes! I am in a WHEELCHAIR. Been in a chair since JAN of '94. JUMPED OUT A WINDOW IN THE PROJECT AND BROKE MY SPINE. THOUGHT THEY WERE COMING TO KILL ME. I don't know if I'll be able to walk again. They had to fuse my spine back together. My Lungs broke down and I could not speak for about a month. YES! CRACK KILLS.[36]

> Some fiends scream about Supreme Team
> a Jamaica, Queens thing
>
> Nas, "Memory Lane
> (Sittin' in Da Park)"[37]

> Back in the 80s, 'Preme was the legend.
>
> Irv Gotti[38]

Kenneth "Supreme" McGriff is believed to have obtained the Knowledge of Self from the exiled Dumar Complete. Supreme (or 'Preme) came up as a member of the "Peace Gods," a group of hustling Five Percenters from Linden Boulevard. The Peace Gods, observes journalist Ethan Brown, "embraced Five Percenter ideology less as a religion and more as a rebellious pose" and provided 'Preme with backup.[39] 'Preme started his own small-time operation at Baisley Park Houses, employing Five Percenters such as God B. His initial cadre of supporters became known as the "Original Seed"[40] of a new organization, the Supreme Team. Named in part after a Five Percenter rap crew, 'Preme and company "loved the Nation," remembers Jamar Allah, "but they were hustlers." Ernesto "Puerto Rican Righteous" Piniella brought in Latino dealers and connected the Team to Colombian cocaine distribution. Supported by united legions of black and Latino street soldiers in matching red jackets with *Supreme* emblazoned across the back, 'Preme came to rule the Baisley projects. Using rooftops as surveillance towers, his watchmen encoded their walkie-talkie communication with the Supreme Alphabet and Mathematics. Following 'Preme's 1985 arrest and incarceration, leadership of the Team went to his nephew Gerald "Prince" Miller, who drove a Mercedes equipped with over $100,000 of defense options, including gun ports, oil slicks and smoke screens.[41]

One of the Team's soldiers was Shameek Allah, born Kelvin Martin in 1964. The South Bronx native found Knowledge of Self at the age of sixteen while living at Brooklyn's R.V. Ingersoll Houses. He dabbled in the science, but as his friend, hip-hop star Eric B. remembers, Shameek "would come to the mosque and want to rob somebody."[42] He had a stint at Rikers Island, where he decorated his cell with a black-and-white photocopied page of Five Percenter folk art: Allah's 1965 mugshot superimposed on a *mihrab* (the niche in a mosque indicating the direction of Mecca), framing the Father within the mihrab's rectangular arch of Islamic calligraphy. The artifact's creator had also cut strips of typewritten text and glued them on each side of the Father. Above his head, it offers a misspelled but orthodox Muslim creed: "THEIR IS NO GOD BUT ALLAH." Below him, its new meaning: "Allah is not a spirit. Allah is the Blackman of Asia." On the Father's right and left sides read the 1st degree from the 1–40: "Who is the original man? ANSWER: The original man is the Asiatic Blackman, the maker, the owner, the cream of the planet earth, father of civilization and God of the Universe."

Shameek joined the Supreme Team after his release. Eric B. remembers that the Team mentored Shameek on "the ins and outs of the streets." Rather than sell crack himself, Shameek robbed crack dealers. With his own boosting crew, he would eventually target everyone from clubgoers to storeowners to—legends say—LL Cool J, who handed over a gold rope when Shameek held him at gunpoint in a White Castle parking lot, as well as fellow Five Percenter and Eric B.'s rap comrade Rakim, who was jacked for a pendant.[43]

Kelvin Martin/Shameek Allah was better known by his street handle, "50 Cent." One story says that he earned the nickname after betting fifty cents in a dice game and winning $500. As 50 Cent he became a full-fledged folk hero, strutting through Brooklyn with a Colt .45 and .357 Magnum on his hips and making nonchalant robberies in broad daylight of every liquor store on

Myrtle Avenue. Sometimes he took aim on a parking meter and gave the coins inside to neighborhood kids, who'd toss quarters into the air for him to shoot—after twirling his pistols like a black Billy the Kid of the projects. 50 Cent moved on to extort the local hustlers, sometimes kidnapping their loved ones for ransom. He seemed invincible to both his rivals, who shot him numerous times in various failed attacks, and the NYPD, who caught him here and there for small offenses but never a serious crime that could put him away. But 50 knew his time would come. "I'm gonna die before the year is out," he told Eric B. "Either I'm gonna get killed in a police car chase, a shootout, or someone's gonna kill me. I'm telling you, I'm gonna live my life to the fullest right now."[44]

In October 1987, Julio "Wemo" Acevedo learned that one of his family members had been abducted. Against the lives of his family, the kidnappers gave Wemo an order: kill his friend 50 Cent. So Wemo went to 50's girlfriend's apartment at the Albany projects in Brooklyn, and later that night 50 was found on the seventh-floor stairwell full of holes from a shotgun and handgun. He was taken to Kings County Hospital and died after three days. The twenty-three-year-old was survived by a newborn daughter, Shamika.

Shameek's legacy was later claimed by a second 50 Cent: Curtis Jackson of Jamaica, Queens. "I took the name 50 Cent because it says everything I want it to say," explains Jackson. "I'm the same kind of person 50 Cent was. I provide for myself by any means."[45] Jackson sold crack in the Supreme Team's former turf of South Jamaica and in 1994 went to Monterey prison for nearly a year. He turned to rap music as a way out of street life, and a 1996 encounter with Run-DMC's Jam Master Jay led him to a deal with Columbia Records. He began work on an album, *Power of the Dollar*, and scored an underground hit in 2000 with its intended lead single, "How to Rob" in which he joked about sticking up various rappers. Around the same time that 50 Cent prepared for his album's release, his friend stole a chain from rapper Jeffrey "Ja Rule" Atkins. Ja Rule was the franchise star of record label Murder Inc., which in 2003 would be raided by over fifty NYPD, ATF, and IRS agents alleging that 'Preme was the "true owner of the company."[46] Ja Rule boasts of the connection in "Survival of the Illest 2 Intro:"

> you wouldn't deceive top dog Supreme Team
> how and why would you try to fuck us? On the real[47]

Murder Inc. president Irv "Gotti" Lorenzo reportedly took the matter of Ja Rule's stolen chain to 'Preme, who, according to an affidavit, "promptly secured the return of the jewelry ... using his reputation for violence to intimidate and threaten the robber."[48] As an added retaliation, 50 Cent was punched by Gotti and his brother and stabbed by Ramel "Black Child" Gill. Two months later, he was shot nine times while sitting in his car on 161st Street in Jamaica, Queens. 50 survived, but Columbia shelved *Power of the Dollar* and dropped him. He refused to name the assailant or anyone that could have ordered the attack. In November 2005, former 'Preme associate Jon Ragin would testify that after the 50 Cent shooting he met with 'Preme, God B and alleged gunman Robert "Son" Lyons in a Brooklyn garage, where he heard 'Preme boast, "I got him."[49] An affidavit regarding the federal investigation of Murder Inc. alleges that "McGriff was involved with the shooting of another rap artist, '50 Cent,' who wrote a song exposing McGriff's criminal activities."[50]

The song in question, "Ghetto Qu'ran" from the unreleased Columbia album, was a Qur'an less in the Islamic sense than the Five Percenter one, in which man "renews his history." The lyrics paid tribute to legendary figures of 50's childhood—including McGriff and his nephew:

> yo, when you hear talk of the southside
> you hear talk of the Team
> see niggas feared Prince and respected 'Preme
> for all you slow muthafuckas
> I'm a break it down iller
> see 'Preme was a business man
> and Prince was the killer[51]

"As a youth," 50 raps, "all I ever did was sell crack, I used to idolize Cat." *Cat* was Lorenzo "Fat Cat" Nichols, who in the 1980s ran the trade on 150th Street and was believed at one time to be pulling in $10 million a year.

Fat Cat had beef with Allah Supreme God dating back to 1972, when Cat belonged to the 7 Crowns gang that ran Queens for a time. Allah Supreme God had convinced his brother, Supreme Master Allah, to quit the gang. One night the 7 Crowns, led by a "Mr. Black," attempted to rob a pizza shop and got chased out by the owner. Allah Supreme God witnessed the fiasco and offered to help. "Give me the gun," he told Mr. Black, "and I'll rob the store." Mr. Black handed over his gun and Allah Supreme God managed to slip away with a free pistol. The humiliated Crowns threatened revenge, so Allah Supreme God drummed up support from Medina warriors such as Father Divine, More Divine and Universal Justice. The Five Percenters ran up on the Crowns and challenged them. The beef was squashed and the Crowns gave no further trouble, but Fat Cat remembered the God.

Through the 1980s, Allah Supreme God lived in Medina and his brother served as eyes and ears in the Desert, alerting him to the details of any big upcoming deals: who was doing it, when and where and how much. Allah Supreme God, known and feared in Queens as "Supreme from Brooklyn" could then ambush the dealers and take their money. He also became tight with a trio of crack-slinging brothers, Peter, James, and Donald Corley, who ran things in the 40 Projects (Jamaica Houses). James was a former Five Percenter and none of the Corleys got along with Fat Cat.

Allah Supreme God later did time in Sing Sing, where the Nation of Islam imam happened to be Rasul, the former Ebeka. One day Rasul gave him a message to call home, saying that it sounded "real bad." Allah Supreme God called home and learned that his brother Supreme Master Allah had tested positive for HIV. Supreme Master Allah blamed it on his longtime drug use with Fat Cat's guys, so he took to robbing them for revenge. Allah Supreme God was back on the streets when word came that Fat Cat had ordered a hit on his brother. Tit for tat, the God embarked on a plot to kidnap Cat's wife, Joanne "Mousey" Nichols.

His team consisted of King Allah, Albert "BJ" Griffin and a white kid named Richard Frejomil. They got a van, police light and plastic officers' badges and staked out the house. Their plan was to wait until Mousey drove somewhere, follow the car and then turn on their police light to make her pull over. With Mousey taped, cuffed and blindfolded in the van, Allah Supreme God made calls from a mobile phone to her mother, sister and the jailed Fat Cat himself, demanding a ransom of ten kilos. After three days of negotiations, arrangements were made for Fat Cat's men to leave $77,000 by the garbage can outside the White Castle on Atlantic Avenue. Allah Supreme God and Richard Frejomil waited in Frejomil's car. Cat's boys arrived with a big black trash bag, but messed up the drop-off—there were two garbage cans on opposite sides of the White Castle, and they went to the wrong one. God's squad knew that the place would be staked out either by the NYPD or Cat's crew waiting to shoot them, but ultimately decided to roll the dice with his life. "Ego was involved," admits Allah Supreme God. Frejomil drove over by the money, the God ran out and scooped it up and then they spilled into traffic. Thankfully for Allah Supreme God and Frejomil, an officer inside the White Castle had given the wrong description of their car.

After stopping for gas and cigarettes, they met King Allah and BJ, split up the money and went their separate ways. Allah Supreme God went to his mother's house in Flatbush. The next day he sent his niece Yakeema to the store for cigarettes, orange juice and a newspaper. She came home with a front-page headline announcing that Fat Cat's wife had been kidnapped and accompanying photo of Frejomil in police custody. Allah Supreme God met up with King Allah at King's mother's house and they promptly bailed for D.C. After a few days at the Harrington Hotel on F Avenue, Allah Supreme God went back to New York to appear in court for an unrelated gun charge. He managed to handle his business and get out of there before anyone knew better, and soon he was back in Washington. He later returned north to pick up his brother Curtis, his sister-in-law and their son before heading down to Atlanta. They spent about a week in College Park on the outskirts of town before King called; back in New York, members of Fat Cat's organization had attempted to kidnap Supreme Master Allah. Allah Supreme God made one more trip to Queens and "did a lot of work" to make sure that his family was safe. The two brothers then drove King Allah's black Mercedes-Benz 280 SCL down to Maryland.

They were having dinner at King's place when the cops busted in. At first the Cee Cipher Powers arrested Supreme Master Allah, mistaking him for his brother.

Allah Supreme God has been incarcerated on the kidnapping conviction since 1988 and now sits in Auburn, where one of Malcolm's killers once refereed inmates' basketball games. When I see Allah Supreme God he runs me through the twenty-five thousand years of his personal Koran, starting back when he was a little Muslim kid in Harlem. Hanging out at both Mosque No.7 and Karate Bob's dojo, he knew Allah and Justice before the two knew each other.

We talk about the 7 Crowns, and he tells me that in jail he intervened on Mr. Black's behalf and saved him from the Tomahawks. Out in Medina he went down Bushwick and ran into Imam Isa al-Mahdi, who told him that he was only the Mahdi inside the mosque; on his way to the studio, he was Dwight York. Allah Supreme God goes on about various characters from the time, like Tasheem who left the Five Percent Nation for the Dar ul-Islam, and God Kalim, who allegedly started a false rumor that Allah Supreme God had pulled a gun on him.

He remembers a Five Percenter named Dihoo shooting two Gods because they were selling weed and not giving money to the school like they said they would. Dihoo's running partners Rahiem and Minister Allah were somehow held responsible and exiled from the Nation. Allah Supreme God went to parliament at the Harriet Tubman and closed the auditorium doors to let everyone tell their sides and settle it. "That prevented a Mecca-Medina war," he says.

Well-traveled as a guest of the State of New York, many of his tales over the last thirty years come through the criminal justice system. While in court for shooting a dog, he bumped into Jahad and Ra'jab, the Five Percent's "Supreme

Investigator." Because Ra'jab was older than the average Five Percenter convert, many believed that he was one of the Muslims who left the mosque with the Father. In the courtroom that day, Jahad reached for Allah Supreme God's 120 pin but Allah Supreme God blocked him. At Rikers Island, Allah Supreme God met Old Man Sha Sha, sometimes known as 24-Hour Sha Sha, who had alleged given up a chance at evading police to get behind the wheel of a cop car and drive a wounded officer to the hospital. At Elmira Reception Center, Allah Supreme God studied karate under two Five Percenters from the famous Black Panther 21, a group that included the parents of Tupac Shakur. Great Meadows had as many as five hundred Gods at any given time in the mid-1970s, including Born Allah, Knowledge Allah, Merciful Allah (Walter Thomas/Jahad from the Harlem Six) and Eminent Allah (from Robert Walker's First Born Muslims). At Napanoch he met Akbar (Robert Barnes), who showed him a thirty-five-page affidavit recanting his testimony against the Harlem Six. Akbar asked Allah Supreme God to put him in touch with William Kunstler.

The original 50 Cent's old fence-man, One Arm Monk, remarked that "in the '80s, Five Percenters were like the Bloods and Crips is now."[52] Gods from the street academy generation, such as Um Allah and Dumar Wa'de Allah, did what they could to promote the Father's original message of education and positive community involvement. However, efforts to reclaim the movement from gangs were impeded by fear of the "Ten Percenter" elitism that could come with anyone assuming a leadership position. "What is now called organization was then called separation," remembers Elamjad Born Allah. "The idea that any group of Gods and Earths would build as a collective was contrary to the disarray of the whole and was viewed by some as a threat to the nation."[53]

Five Percenters such as Beloved Allah, who obtained his GED while in the Navy, studied engineering at Columbia, and became partner in a major firm, represented a changing climate in the community. The former catch-phrase, "we ain't no organization"[54] was replaced by talk of "nation building." The 1985 Show and Prove witnessed what Elamjad Born Allah calls the first "mass marketing" of Five Percenter regalia and merchandise; to generate revenue, once derided as "Ten Percentin'," was now "economic development."[55] In 1987 Beloved began publishing a newsprint journal, the WORD, which featured articles on topics such as science, mathematics, nutrition, women's health, current events in the black community and issues specific to the Five Percent. The front page of the first issue showed a small child holding a framed portrait of the Father with the quote, "If I die, who is going to teach the babies?"[56] The WORD affirmed Five Percenters as healthy, productive, nonviolent, and family-oriented, and aspired to reach all corners of the movement.

Beloved frequently published articles, letters, and poetry from incarcerated Five Percenters, as well as elementary school children:

> I promise I will sit in the classroom and
> listen to what the teacher says,
> I will not waste time or let anyone get
> in my way.
> I can be anything I want to be,
> Watch me grow and you will see,
> My parents, my teacher and my
> principal will be proud of me.
> I will always be kind to older people,
> I will always have respect for God,
> humanity, and my self.
> Get wise and get smart,
> Time to read and write and make a new start.
> As for me, I'll get high on education and
> dignity,
> Because lying idle and wasting time is
> definitely not for me!
>
>   Born Allah, 4th Grade, P.S. 45,
>   Queens, NY[57]

Dumar Wa'de Allah declared through the *WORD* that every Five Percenter must be either employed, in school, learning a trade, self-employed, or a homemaker, and invited all men and women without a "positive direction and true understanding" to "leave from our midst in one form."[58] In 1989, as Five Percenters celebrated the twenty-fifth anniversary of their movement, the front page of the *WORD* gave a "vision for the future:" a drawing of a new Allah School that occupied an entire block, including its own public school, laboratory and domed observatory, all graced with the Universal Flag.[59]

The top of every front page declared the *WORD* to be the "national newspaper of the Nation of Gods and Earths." Up to that point the community had known a series of names: most notably the Five Percenters and Five Percent Nation, but also the Nation Builders, Allah's Nation, Allah's Nation of the Five Percent, Five Percent Nation of Islam and Universal Nation of Allah. Universal Shaamgaudd Allah had launched an initiative to "restruct our Nation" under the banner of "Allah's Nation of Islam." In a February 1987 article for the *WORD*, Prince A Cuba dismisses use of the term "nation" for Five Percenters as "inexact, and incorrect, and in fact divisionist and reactionary."[60] Citing street gangs such as the "Blackstone P Nation," he maintains that "creating a sect, and calling it a nation, is stepping back from going forward and being truly Universal."[61]

Though allowing for Cuba's dissent, the prominence of the *WORD* helped to establish "Nation of Gods and Earths" as the community's accepted title.[62] For Beloved Allah, the change countered negative media portrayals and was "subconscious or not ... an attempt to redefine ourselves."[63] The *WORD* bolstered the new name with an apocryphal quote from Allah, claiming that in 1968 he announced, "after this year there won't be any Five Percenters anymore. You'll be the Nation of Gods and Earths, not the Nation of Islam."[64] Cuba considers the quote to be a fabrication of Shabazz Adew Allah, who he blames for promoting "ideological confusion."[65] Despite issues of authenticity, the Allah quote reflects two crucial and very real transitions made within the movement. A final break was made from the legacy of the NOI, allowing Five Percenters to develop their own identity; and in the Father's absence, his army of adolescent boys had grown into men (Gods).

F. Scott Fitzgerald called youth a "chemical madness," and the Gods and Earths that survived theirs hoped to rebuild. In 1992 Gykee suggested a "total reconstruction of our nation, beginning with the newly recruited. They are not to be allowed to use drugs or alcohol in any form, shape, or fashion."[66] I have seen a slight difference in the way that young Gods and old Gods speak at parliaments. Young Gods, having just discovered the lessons, often aspire to be High Scientists—masterfully juggling the relationships between concepts in Allah's Math and the inner workings of the 120. While keeping the lessons as their foundation, middle-aged and older Gods tend to speak less from the text than the heart—*these were my victories and defeats, but all I want now is to save the babies and steer you right*—

Young men are young men in every culture; impressed by the show of militancy and eager to prove their new strength, they sometimes get tough and territorial. Elders have built through it. This was only Supreme Mathematics manifesting in front of me: Knowledge comes before Wisdom, and after Wisdom comes Understanding. One Five Percenter essay states that "you really don't begin to see or understand until you reach the understanding degrees (30s) ... It also takes seven years for the swine to be removed from within your system."[67] The Five Percenters evolved, says Allah Supreme God, as "we got older and started understanding our lessons ... at the beginning, we didn't understand what we were saying ourselves."

12

Belly of the Beast

Here is a black man, caged behind bars, probably for years, put there by the white man. Usually the convict comes from among those bottom-of-the-pile Negroes, the Negroes who through their entire lives have been kicked about, treated like children—Negroes who never have met one white man who didn't either take something from them or do something to them. You let this caged-up black man start thinking, the same way I did when I first heard Elijah Muhammad's teachings: let him start thinking how, with better breaks when he was young and ambitious, he might have been a lawyer, a doctor, a scientist, anything. You let this caged-up black man start realizing, as I did, how from the first landing of the first slave ship, the millions of black men in America have been like sheep in a den of wolves. That's why black prisoners become Muslims so fast when Elijah Muhammad's teachings filter into their cages by way of other Muslim convicts. "The white man is the devil" is a perfect echo of that black man's lifelong experience.

Malcolm X

If the Nation of Islam is a religion that finds converts in prison, Five Percenters find their converts under the prison. That's how street it is.

Russell Simmons

In 1957 Walter B. Martin, warden at Attica State Prison, wrote to Commissioner Paul McGinnis with concern after four of his inmates had adopted a peculiar ideology:

> This "fad" for Qu'ran has been developing over recent months. I have been trying to puzzle out just what the "gimmick" is in this matter but haven't solved it yet. Because I haven't immediately granted permission ... to buy "Qu'rans," they are now writing you protesting that I am interfering with the freedom of religion and their constitutional right to pursue any line of religious observance that they may choose. If a sufficient number of them join this movement, we probably will be in receipt of requests for the visitation of a Muslim priest.[1]

The commissioner offered his full support. A grateful Martin replied, "I shall do what I can to prevent it from spreading at Attica."[2] McGinnis requested that every prison in the state provide him the names of inmates that identified their religion as Muslim; he also asked to include prisoners that listed "no religion" or associated with Muslim groups; the list would ultimately include Christians that associated with inmates who *might* practice Islam:

> ——was received from Greenhaven Prison. He claimed his religion to be Protestant but the record card shows a keeplock for taking part in a large aggressive gathering in the yard suspected to be Muslims.[3]

In addition, McGinnis wanted disciplinary reports involving Muslims and the future addresses and phone numbers of Muslim inmates awaiting release. Attica's Muslims were observed throughout February 1961 to "ascertain the disposition they made of the pork served to them at the regular meals." Inmates were recorded as displaying one of the following behaviors: "brings ration to cell," "gave ration away," or "refuses ration." Reading materials were censored; in the later 1960s, some facilities would ban the *Autobiography of Malcolm X*. Inmates secretly read typed copies, which they protected "like gold."[4]

A good deal of Five Percenters' early propagation transpired in New York city jails, from there spreading to the state prisons. Though many Gods at Rikers ditched their lessons after the Father's death, U-Allah and Wabu "taught strong" in B Block.[5] Later sent upstate to Elmira, U-Allah and Shara taught Gods with righteous names such as I-Freedom-Born, Asiatic, Know-Allah and Mitek. The Five Percenters' post-1970 revival and explosive growth is often credited to Gods in prison, who continued to teach even though some believed that the group no longer existed on the outside.[6] At first they had small numbers—only seventeen counted at Sing Sing[7]—but their reputation spread fast. Few guards seemed to understand what distinguished Five Percenters from the NOI or even Sunnis, but still the group was "generally considered to be more militant and violent than followers of Elijah Muhammad."[8] Like their fabled forebears, the Blood Brothers, it remained unclear to corrections officers whether Five Percenters were even real[9] or just a story that white guards told to scare each other.

The social upheaval taking place across America had found its way into the prison. Growing tension, according to the 1970 Annual Report from Attica, was "directly attributable to the increased number of young militants in our population."[10] Hundreds of workers at Attica's metal shop (nicknamed the "slave shop" for its daily pay of six to twenty-nine cents) went on strike for higher wages, forcing negotiations with McGinnis. Though the demonstration had been nonviolent, the state grew concerned as increasing numbers of inmates "demanded the right to gather and form associations for religious and political purposes."[11] The Five Percent Nation evolved alongside the Black Panthers and Young Lords, with all three groups targeted by prison administrators just as they had been by police on the outside.[12] Inmates considered to be "troublemakers" or have "leadership abilities" were constantly transferred from one prison to another to keep them from developing organizations.[13]

New York City jails were overflowing, especially due to the 1967 Penal Law that cut in half the time that prisoners could earn off their sentences for good behavior. A 1970 study found that the Bronx House of Detention held 911 prisoners in a facility designed for 476; the Queens House of Detention had 1,011 prisoners despite a maximum capacity of 520; the Brooklyn House of Detention, early teaching ground for the First Born, held 1,480 prisoners in cells for 841.[14]

In March, 1,500 inmates at Rikers went on a hunger strike. At the Manhattan House of Detention, prisoners working in the kitchen showed their support by delaying breakfast for several hours. The Tombs, which once hosted Allah and then his suspected killer Aubrey Cline, were intended for a maximum of 932 prisoners but held 1,815.[15] "What!" wrote Charles Dickens after visiting the original Tombs in 1842. "Do you thrust your common offenders against the police discipline of the town in such holes as these?"[16] 10 of the 1,815 were members of the famous Black Panther 21. An eleventh member sat in the Manhattan Women's House of Detention: Afeni Shakur, mother of rapper 2Pac. On April 4, some 5,000 protesters marched on the Panthers' behalf from Manhattan to Queens.

The rest of the year saw protests and minor uprisings in jails throughout the city:

August 8, Manhattan House of Detention: 2 white inmates taken hostage by 30 black inmates.

August 10, Manhattan House of Detention: 5 guards held hostage for 8 hours.

August 12, Brooklyn House of Detention: 180 inmates refused to return to cells for 45 minutes and presented a set of grievances to the warden.

August 17, Manhattan House of Detention: 94 inmates refused to leave cells.

August 25, Bronx House of Detention: inmates created disturbances and set small fires.

October 1, Queens House of Detention (Long Island branch): inmates took 7 hostages and demanded dialogue with city officials on live television.

October 2, Manhattan House of Detention: inmates seized control of an entire floor and took 18 hostages.

October 2, Queens House of Detention at Kew Gardens: 900 inmates took over a floor, smashed windows and set fires.

October 3, Brooklyn House of Detention: hundreds of inmates took over most of the facility and held 3 hostages before guards counter-attacked.

"What you've got now," McGinnis told reporters, "are prisoners who are much more conscious of their civil rights than they ever were before. Some of them, and I'm talking about groups like the Black Panthers, the Young Lords and the Five Percenters, have a consciousness of themselves as victims or political prisoners. They preach this and through coercion or force they pick up a following."[17] McGinnis then waxed nostalgic for a day when guards and inmates lived by supposedly agreed-upon ground rules.

At Auburn, authorities' refusal to allow Black Solidarity Day speeches led to inmates taking control of the yard, holding guards hostage for an eight-hour standoff. The group's Muslim leaders ensured that the guards would not be harmed.[18] After securing the Deputy Commissioner's word that there would be no reprisals, the inmates released the guards and returned to their cells. Despite the promise and the day's peaceful end, inmates involved in the confrontation were either transferred to Attica or segregated from the general prison population. Of the "Auburn Six" hit with additional charges of assault and robbery, two—Robert Clarke (Kareem C'Allah) and Michael Lewis (Sharean)—were identified as Five Percenters. On the day of his arraignment, cuffed-and-shackled Kareem C'Allah was led straight from the courtroom into a small corridor where guards kicked him, stomped him and ripped his legal papers. When C'Allah and co-defendant Charles Hill were taken to a room to make phone calls, C'Allah was told, "Hill called two lawyers, so you don't call none."[19]

On January 1, 1971, Russell G. Oswald replaced McGinnis as Commissioner. At an earlier budget meeting with Governor Rockefeller's staff, Oswald had heard McGinnis warn of an imminent "bloodbath" if spending was not increased to improve prisons. The only question was which facility would explode. It should have been obvious: Auburn and other prisons were transferring busloads of their most rebellious and "militant" inmates to Attica, where seventy-five to eighty-five percent of the prisoners were black or Puerto Rican, while all 383 guards were white and referred to their billy clubs as "nigger sticks."

Working in the state's favor was division among the inmates. The Nation of Islam faction objected to the Black Panthers' emphasis on violence; Panthers objected to the Muslims' emphasis on religion. Somewhere between them stood the Five Percenters, who appeared vaguely Islamic and, according to the state commission on Attica, "eschewed any notion of ever reaching satisfactory living conditions by peaceful requests of an unwilling administration."[20] In Attica the Black Panthers were first to seek unity, but the Muslims' leader prohibited the two groups from mingling in the yard. Inmate informants told officers that the Muslims' leader would soon be killed, causing him to get transferred out. Soon after his departure, according to the commission report, guards watched a ceremony in the exercise yard that "seemed to confirm their worst fears. Standing in a line along one side of the yard, arms folded across their chests, was a group of inmates recognized as Muslims. Facing them was another group, similarly stationed, and recognized as Panthers."[21] Leaders from the two groups met at a table between them, occupied by Young Lords, and agreed to a truce.

Confrontations between guards and inmates blew up on September 9, when inmates broke through a malfunctioning gate, took forty-three hostages and assembled in the D yard. The NOI group formed a protective circle around the hostages. Though there remains no evidence that the uprising was planned, the inmates quickly organized and chose spokesmen to represent them in negotiations with the state. The inmates issued a list of thirty-three demands, twenty-eight of which were accepted. Neither side would budge on the issue of amnesty.

In one of the yards, two tables were covered in sheets bearing the painted words, "Five Percenters."[22] The Five Percent Nation was seen by numerous inmates as one of the "major powers" behind the rebellion, but members chose to remain "behind the scenes."[23] According to inmates, the Gods led a small force inside B and D blocks and rarely went out to the yard. "It was reported that this group held the real power," read the state report on Attica, "and that many of the 'spokesmen' were under their control."[24] Five Percenter oral history places First Born Prince as a leader among the Attica Gods. Bernard Lewis, believed to have been the first inmate killed in Governor Rockefeller's bloody recapture of the yard, was a Five Percenter with the righteous name I-Jamel Lateek.[25]

Despite the unity shown at Attica, doctrinal disputes and bitter shared history kept Sunni Muslims, the Nation of Islam, and Five Percenters divided. On February 15, 1973, at Clinton Correctional Facility, a group of NOI Muslims on their way to the mess hall pushed against a Sunni and told him to get out of the way, resulting in a battle that left several inmates hospitalized. On May 21, 1976, a fight between Five Percenters and Sunnis at Great Meadows led to a full-scale riot and prisoners overtaking a wing of the prison. The trouble began earlier that day when Divine Justice was beaten with pipes by three Sunni Muslims in E Block. The Sunnis expected retaliation; as the Gods planned their attack, both sides prepared with bats, sticks, bricks, chairs, garbage cans, and shards of broken glass. Later that evening in the Big Yard, roughly one hundred Five Percenters made their move on a group of fifty Sunnis. Officer James L. Roberts fired a gas projectile at the mêlée, to which the inmates propped up tables as shields. Roberts then fired a shotgun shell and they scattered. One group fled into E Block, where they overpowered the guards, took the keys, and briefly assumed control.

The prison's superintendent, Paul Metz, described the Sunnis as running a tight organization: "they exercise very hard discipline among themselves." He considered the Five Percenters to be "younger and more violent."[26] Gods have since become popularly associated with prison violence directed both at guards and fellow inmates. The reemergence of the Latin Kings as a 1980s prison gang is attributed to Five Percenter assaults on Hispanic inmates at Collins Correctional Facility in Collins, New York.

The question of "gang or religion" was not unique to the Five Percenters. Following release from prison in 1976, the Blackstone Rangers' Jeff Fort achieved a complete takeover of his gang and swerved it toward a Moorish Science vision of Islam. Members wore red fezzes and added "El" to their surnames; Fort changed his name to Malik and renamed the group the El Rukn Moorish Science Temple of America. In 1979 a lawsuit was filed on behalf of roughly one hundred El Rukn members in Illinois prisons to seek recognition as a religion. By the time trial began in November 1985, the gang had abandoned Moorish Science for Sunni Islam. "If El Rukn is a religious group," said Cook County prosecutor Richard M. Daley, "its sacraments are narcotics trafficking, intimidation, terror and human sacrifice." Illinois Corrections Director Michael R. Lane believed that granting El Rukn the freedom to hold religious services would enable them to plot crimes, while such endorsement by the prison would give El Rukn the power to intimidate other inmates. "What this case is about is keeping the control in the hands of the prison system," he said. "We're not going to willingly give it up."

"We never took the position that our members don't do anything wrong," said El Rukn's Amir Salim Khaadim. "We say that some of us are guided rightly and some of us are guided wrongly."[27] The words of all three men would be echoed years later in a legal battle between the Nation of Gods and Earths and New York's Department of Correctional Services.

The 1990s saw a criminal-justice crackdown on Five Percenters. In 1995 the South Carolina Department of Corrections declared the Gods and Earths a "security threat group" and placed upwards of eighty Gods in solitary confinement, returning them to the general prison population only if they renounced their beliefs. Inmates won a 1997 lawsuit and a Court of Appeals upheld the decision, but similar programs were launched in North Carolina, Ohio, Massachusetts and New Jersey.

> The Five Percenters are a gang, a gang responsible for violence at every prison in New York.
>
> Richard Harcrow, president, New York State Correction Officers
> and Police Benevolent Association

Gang expert Robert Walker has given a ninety-minute presentation on the Five Percenters to law enforcement personnel in North Carolina, South Carolina, and Ohio, three states with histories of persecuting Gods in prison. Walker's presentation includes a video statement by none other than Warith Deen Mohammed, "current national leader of the Muslim Community," who "conveys how dangerous the Five Percenters are."[28] With prisons a fertile ground for missionaries of all brands, Mohammed has a clear stake in suppressing his competition. While stereotyping Gods in prison, however, Walker concedes that the perception of Five Percenters as a gang may not be entirely fair: "As with any group of citizens, let's assume that the majority of the followers are honest, law-abiding people who have deep beliefs in the teachings of the culture. Much of the problem with the group lies with the incarcerated members of the group whose propensity towards violence is well documented, particularly in the eastern region of the United States."[29]

Working against the NGE's image was not only criminal activity among its own members, but numerous precedents of violent gangs that repackaged themselves as political, cultural, or religious groups. In *An Introduction to Gangs*, George W. Knox calls it a "univesal phenomenon" that when a gang falls subject to "close criminal justice scrutiny ... the gang denies it is a gang and claims to be something else entirely—indeed, it makes a claim of being a positive force in society, a prosocial organization."[30] He provides examples in the constitutions and texts of gangs such as the Spanish Gangsters Disciple Nation that seemingly mirror the texts of Five Percenters:

> Through our nations decades we've enjoyed providing security, a sure safety and domestic tranquility among the lives of our people ... We, brother's of the S.G.D.N. must ordain and abide by the nations constitution, to eliminate poverty and inequality among our people, to provide a structure of potential developments for the individual of our nation, to maintain a liberty for our children and a more gratifying style of social living.[31]

The Almighty Latin King Nation offered a mission statement similar to that found in NGE publications:

> The name of this association shall be the ALMIGHTY LATIN KING NATION. An organization of international brotherhood which exists for the purpose of:
> 1. Promoting prosperity and freedom through love and understanding to all

oppressed people of the world, 2. To train our People to become aware of our social and political problems and of the conditions we are subjected to live under as a Third World People, 3. To provide the aid and way in our search for peace and unity, 4. To promote and encourage education and vocational learning in order to train our People in the art of survival.[32]

Members of the Gangster Disciples often interpret their group's initials as standing for Growth and Development. The Gangster Disciples established a political front group, "21st Century V.O.T.E." which reached such a level of credibility that in January 1994 its leader, Wallace "Gator" Bradley had a personal meeting with President Bill Clinton at the Oval Office.[33]

In 1996, New York prisons enacted a complete ban on all Five Percenter literature and symbols. When Lord Natural Self Allah appeared in Buffalo's Federal District Court to contest the ban, Judge Carol Heckman told him that the safety of inmates and prison staff outweighed his constitutional freedom. The NYDOCS employed a strategy of nonrecognition with the Nation of Gods and Earths, hoping to cut down Five Percenters by "refusing to legitimize their existence." Three decades before, the same mentality had New York's City Hall opposed to Five Percenters wearing pins of their Universal Flag. Prisons considered written copies of the Supreme Alphabets and Mathematics to be contraband, and Five Percenters could not even read the Supreme Wisdom Lessons, which were allowed to members of the Nation of Islam; the same document that was legally protected as religious material in a Muslim's hands became a call to gang warfare when held by a God. Five Percenters were not even permitted to postpone their meals until sundown on days that they fasted—a privilege granted to Muslims.

Panic-stricken prison administrators may have feared nothing more than the Five Percenter parliament—circles of black men, usually young, speaking in coded language, telling each other that they were the supreme masters of all things in the universe. A Five Percenter inmate was not allowed to meet with more than four fellow Gods at one time, and never on a regular basis. Some Gods got around the ban by affiliating with legally protected religious groups such as the Nation of Islam, whose incarcerated members reclaimed their own rights in the mid-1990s. At Great Meadows, King Allah worked out a deal with members of the legally recognized Moorish Science Temple: Five Percenters would display the Moorish flag and pictures of Noble Drew Ali for the right to assemble, but privately maintain their own teachings. The idea spread to Elmira and Auburn, where Allah Supreme God became the Moors' Assistant Grand Sheik.

The God that would finally take on the Beast and win was Brooklyn-born Rashaad Marria, who was arrested in 1994 after a high-speed chase and shoot-out with the NYPD. He was subsequently indicted for gunning down eighteen-year-old Paris Little, who had testified against him in the murder of a fifteen-year-old. Awaiting trial at Rikers, home of anywhere from eighty to one hundred Gods at any given time, Marria, eighteen, discovered the Knowledge of Self and changed his name to Intelligent Tarref Allah.

Empowered by his new understanding, Intelligent earned his GED while serving nineteen to life, participated in various prison classes and programs, served on the Inmate Liaison Committee and turned himself around:

> When I look at that first degree in the student enrollment and I see the black man is the God of the universe, it's endowed me with the power to know the sky's the limit. I manifested, I make changes in my life. I don't do things I did before. I became a vegan, stopped eating animals. I enhanced my discipline level. My mother's, she's amazed I've been locked up so long and haven't even had a fight. I learn to conduct myself in matters where people respect me for who I am. I don't have to be bothered no more because people respect intelligence, and once they see you living what you say, they respect that. And I learn to conduct myself in a manner which I don't put myself in predicaments that would lead to altercations and things of that nature.[34]

Newspapers sent to inmates were subjected to the Media Review Committee, which was required to issue a decision on their appropriateness within ten days. When new issues of *The Five Percenter* arrived for Intelligent, the committee wasn't sure if it pertained to the Nation of Islam or the Nation of Gods and Earths, so they sent the papers to a Sunni Muslim chaplain in Albany, who apparently lost them. After the review period came and went, Intelligent wrote to Dr. Raymond Broaddus, Deputy Commissioner of Programs, who replied that all publications relating to Five Percenters were sent to the Coordinator for Islamic Affairs, without holding him to the ten-day limit. Intelligent then wrote to the Coordinator, who replied:

> There are no directives or rules and regulations regarding Five Percenters. The reason for this is because the courts have ruled that Five Percenters are not a legitimate religious group. The New York State Department of Correctional Services does not acknowledge the claims of inmates who designate themselves as Five Percenters. You may want to explore some of the teaching of the Muslims and the Nation of Islam in your facility.
>
> Your brother in Islam,
>
> Warith Deen Umar[35]

Contrary to the imam's assurance, there had been no court ruling on the subject of Five Percenters' legitimacy as a religion. Three years later, Warith Deen

Umar would be banned from the Albany prison where he once served as imam after making statements in support of the 9/11 attacks.

Intelligent Tarref Allah recruited prestigious Manhattan law firm Sullivan & Cromwell, which accepted the case *pro bono* and took them all to court— Broaddus, Umar, G. Blaetz (chair of the prison's Media Review Committee) and Glenn Goord, Commissioner of New York State's Department of Correctional Services. The case included testimony from NGE elders such as God Kalim and Born Justice Allah, as well as Barry Gottehrer and Ted Swedenburg, Professor of Anthropology and Middle East Studies at the University of Arkansas-Fayetteville, whose affidavit placed the NGE within an academic definition of religion. Sibato Khahaifa, Deputy Superintendent for Security Services at Collins Correctional Facility, testified that as a Sunni Muslim growing up in Brooklyn, he recognized the Five Percenters to be a religious group.[36]

The DOCS defendants countered with a succession of unprepared and uninformed witnesses. Ron Holvey, a New Jersey corrections official regarded as an expert on gangs, testified that the New Jersey system considered Five Percenters its number-one threat to prison security. Admitting that he had never spoken with a Five Percenter or stepped foot in a New York prison, Holvey stated that Five Percenters do not practice a religion because "they don't have temples or mosques or churches ... there is nothing formal about their organization. They don't have priests. They don't have rabbis. They don't have imams. They don't—they worship—they consider themselves to be God."[37] DOCS official Richard Roy testified that he did not believe Five Percenters to be connected to an "outside organization" called the Nation of Gods and Earths. With the recollections of Shawangunk Superintendent Joseph Smith, who encountered Five Percenters while working as a probation officer in the 1970s, DOCS put forth an argument that because "Five Percenters outside of prison have engaged in criminal activity," the group constituted a gang and not a religion. The argument ignored the Nation of Gods and Earths' youth programs at the Allah School, as well as the chance that a Catholic, Jew or Hindu may also engage in criminal activity.

DOCS also offered the testimony of George Camp, whose report estimated that roughly 980 (1.4%) of New York's 70,000 inmates were Five Percenters, based on prison populations in Connecticut, Massachusetts and New Jersey— neither considering how those states arrived at their numbers, nor demographic differences that they may have with New York. Camp's research consisted of an email survey that he sent to prison commissioners, asking presumptive questions such as, "What sorts of problems have Five-Percenters caused you?" He arrived at the expected conclusion that "inmates whose primary identity within the prison is that of a Five-Percenter have been a disruptive force that has caused harm to other inmates and staff in a significant number of prison systems." At his deposition, Camp was asked how many prison systems constituted a "significant number."

"One," he replied.

The defense claimed that Allah's Supreme Alphabets and Mathematics may be used as a secret code by which Five Percenters could plan "assaults, intimidation, extortion and drug dealing" without the comprehension of those around them, as in the case of the Supreme Team. In a recorded 1986 phone conversation between Gerald "Prince" Miller and Chauncey "God B" Milliner, Prince alludes to recently murdered rival Fat Pete as "Power Equality Truth Equality," spelling his name in the Alphabets.[38] According to DOCS, to teach these codes to prison staff would require an inordinate devotion of resources. The argument was promptly rejected by Toni Blair, professor of criminal justice, former warden at a Virginia "supermax" and former assistant commissioner of New York City's DOCS:

> It's published. The code is published. It is on the Internet. It is in the newspapers. It's everywhere. In order for a code to be effective and used, you know, covertly to be subversive or create problems in the institution, the code must be unbreakable and must not be, you know, common knowledge ... to ban the Mathematics and Alphabets because it is a code, you know, would be ludicrous. If we do that, why don't we ban Spanish, for example, because I would dare say that there is not a tremendous number of correctional officers in DOCS that are bilingual and yet we allow Spanish not only to be spoken but documents inside institutions that are Spanish ... and they are much more difficult to translate than this code would be.[39]

Judge Noami Reice Buchwald refused the admission of prison incident reports that identified the Five Percenters as a gang, as Blair said that such reports were often obtained from "snitches" who hoped to get themselves out of trouble and would rather rat out a group than individuals.[40] DOCS had no answer to the testimony of Five Percenters that Gods and Earths in their ranks included police officers, doctors, lawyers and other professionals, or the Allah School's special tax status and favorable lease with New York City. Judge Buchwald cited their weak defense in her twenty-two-page ruling:

> DOCS proposes to treat exclusively as a gang a group that has had a law-abiding existence outside prison for the better part of 40 years, that is an offshoot of another group that DOCS considers a religion, and that has practices that largely resemble those of recognized religious groups, with the consequence that DOCS has banned literature which it concedes is facially innocuous as well as any other expression of religious identity associated with the

group. In order for such a ban to be upheld, there ought to be some sense that DOCS is substantially correct in its decision to treat the group exclusively as a gang and not a religion ... the evidence DOCS presented at trial, however, failed to justify such treatment.[41]

The defendants did try to prove that Intelligent was not a "sincere practitioner," noting that he had 1) falsely told a corrections officer that he had received legal pads from the prison commissary; 2) failed to obey a guard's order to leave while observing, as a representative of the Inmate Liaison Committee, a fellow inmate's grievance meeting in the Sergeant's office; 3) turned a toothbrush into a makeshift screwdriver, using the sliding metal piece from a pair of headphones, which constituted a possible weapon; 4) stated that Five Percenters abstain from eating pork, while another Five Percenter said that Gods and Earths additionally avoided "scavengers" such as shrimp and tuna; 5) allowed his subscription to *The Five Percenter* to lapse for a brief period in 1996; 6) adopted designation as a member of the Nation of Islam. Ignoring the more ridiculous items on the list, the judge accepted Intelligent's argument that his screwdriver was only a screwdriver, noted that Intelligent was vegan and therefore did not eat shrimp or tuna, and allowed that he let his subscription lapse because the newspaper was then looked upon as prison contraband. Addressing his designation as a NOI Muslim, Intelligent stated that he had been attending a variety of other groups' services to "get an understanding of ... why people think the way they think," but the NOI was the only group for which he was required to sign a religious designation form. DOCS claimed that Intelligent could receive his 120 lessons from the Nation of Islam, which was not true; the NOI only gave lessons to registered Muslims with affiliations to mosques outside the prison.[42]

The DOCS trump card was an issue of *The Five Percenter* with the cover page boldly proclaiming, "WE ARE NOT A RELIGION." In one deposition, Intelligent stated that his beliefs did not constitute a religion but a "way of life," only to later claim that Five Percenters fell under the *legal* definition of religion. Judge Buchwald understood that the Five Percenters' paradoxical and politically disadvantageous denial of the term "religion" reflects a major theme in their teachings. To the Gods, religion ("rely on a jinn") is strictly defined as belief in the unseen, dependant on imaginary spooks, ghosts, phantoms and mystery gods that have been used as a means of oppressing, exploiting, and ultimately pacifying African-Americans. "The law of the Free Exercise Clause," the judge stated in her ruling, "does not turn on mere semantic distinctions." Intelligent's beliefs were considered as central to his daily life as those of Christians and Muslims to theirs, and protected under the Religious

Land Use and Institutionalized Persons Act. As practitioners of a religion, they were entitled to receive their newspaper, hold monthly parliaments, observe special meal times and honor holidays such as Allah's birthday.

A *New York Post* editorial of August 25, 2003, on Intelligent's case, "The 5% Fraud," calls the Nation of Gods and Earths a "gang of violent criminals who, among other things, advocate killing police officers." "Convict 'Gods' get sweet deal," cried a *Daily News* headline. Buchwald's verdict was discussed on an episode of Fox News' *Hannity & Colmes*, in which hosts Sean Hannity and Alan Colmes tag-teamed on criminal defense attorney Steve Donziger.

"They don't want to lose their religious freedoms, then don't commit crimes," said Hannity, who called the Gods and Earths an "obviously extreme form of Islam." Donziger countered that prisons were also rife with white supremacist Christians.

"Do you really believe this garbage?" asked Hannity.

"Look, I'm repulsed by black supremacy, don't misunderstand me."

"It's an outrage."

"But I believe in the First Amendment right to protect people in prison."

"Do you support the right of prisoners to have conjugal visits?" From that moment on, Hannity harped on conjugal visits, an issue that was never mentioned in the Intelligent Tarref Allah case. "Who's going to pay for the raising of those children," he asked, "when they impregnate these women?"

"Here's why they get conjugal visits," interjected Colmes, "they call it a religion. We'll be back on the other side of the break."

After the break, Hannity jumped right back on it: "So let's say it's part of somebody's sincere religious belief that they want to have conjugal visits with many women, would you support that?" He then asked Donziger whether he'd support an inmate having sex with seven women each week.

"Don't put me in that corner," replied the attorney.

"You're already there," Hannity told him, "because you support this nonsense."

"The issue is the First Amendment. We wouldn't need a First Amendment if every religion was not offensive. The First Amendment is to protect offensive, unpopular beliefs. We wouldn't need a First Amendment if this religion didn't offend."

"You commit crimes, you lose some of your rights. Do you understand that?"

"But the Constitution still applies."

"You understand the losing some of your rights?" asked Hannity.

"The Constitution applies to—"

"It doesn't apply for the right of people in prison to have special rights to be racist or to teach a racist religion. It doesn't apply for men to have sex with women and have to produce children that they'll never provide for." They went back and forth until Colmes chimed in to suggest that all sorts of new groups would make up their own religions and get legal protection. "The idea they just concocted this a few weeks ago is ridiculous," answered Donziger. "It came out of the Nation of Islam decades ago." "They still concocted it," said Colmes.

Then the issue made Fox News' *Dayside*, where Mike Jerrick smirked, "She [Buchwald] considers this, I guess, a religion." The onscreen text answered its own loaded questions: "Do prisoners have right to practice black supremacy?" "Is black supremacy protected under freedom of religion?" When African-American civil rights attorney Leo Terell yelled and hollered, under his name it read: "supports prisoners practicing black supremacy as a religion." The whole segment was a joke and a sham, doomed from the start. Positioned against Terell they had Steven Rogers from Americop, who'd somehow relate the issue to Al-Qaeda: "the floodgates have been opened for terrorists who want to destroy this country!" Mike Jerrick asked whether a convict whose religion was "pickup trucks" could then be entitled to have a pickup truck in his cell. Then the host went to his studio audience, where a white woman said that hate and religion don't go together, and a white prison chaplain said that he doesn't believe in the right to preach "killing." Besides Born Justice Allah on the stage and a young God named Power Allah in the audience, I couldn't help but suspect that not a single person in the studio—not the chaplain or Christian soccer mom, not the Americop, not loudmouthed Leo Terell and certainly not Mike Jerrick, who wielded all the journalistic authority of a Pat Sajak—had any clue of what Five Percenters actually taught.

Born Justice gave the usual catechism about being neither pro-black nor anti-white. When he plainly stated, "it's not a religion," Jerrick jumped right in with "oh, so you don't think this guy should practice in prison then?" Born Justice tried explaining that Five Percenters practiced a "natural way of life," not a religion, but Jerrick had all he needed to shoot down *religious* freedom.

They are radical, racist revolutionaries who feel that they do not have to pay for their crimes, because there is no retribution in their belief system.

George Corbiscello, Senior Investigator, Sheriff's Office, Monmoth County, NJ[43]

We are neither murderers of police nor anyone else. I am a father and husband and I work for a living.

Messiah Lateek, 44, manager of facility for AIDS patients, New York, NY[44]

> I was born a nation member and for all of my twenty-four years my parents
> have worked hard to teach me decent values and morals. I don't see the media,
> the police or the courts categorizing millions of Catholics as pedophiles or
> rapists because some members of their faith are; and those are their leaders.
> Still, we don't vilify all Catholics because of those priests and bishops.
>
> Caliph Allah, 24, student, U-MASS Dartmouth[45]

More than two years after the Intelligent Tarref Allah case, Ted Swedenburg
regularly gets mail from incarcerated Gods in similar situations. He has
recently offered his support to the case of Jahborn Infinite Wise, a convicted
cop-killer in Massachusetts, where Five Percenters are still considered a Security Threat Group among the likes of the Mexican Mafia, Aryan Brotherhood,
Bloods, Crips and Jamaican Posse.

The crimes of convicted Five Percenters have been overwhelmingly crimes
of poverty—robbery, burglary, assault, drug possession, gun possession—the
same crimes of poor Christians and Muslims. They're not a hate group looking
for white boys to drag from trucks. Still, detectives won't hesitate to inform
reporters of a suspect's Five Percenter affiliation, regardless of whether or not
NGE beliefs were considered a factor in the crime. No matter the circum-
stances surrounding Jahborn Infinite Wise's incarceration, his murder of a
police officer will be portrayed as ideologically motivated. In a 1994 carjacking
case, when a thirty-four-year-old witness revealed that as a teenager he associated with Five Percenters, attorney Pamela D. Hayes described the group to the
court as "racist killers" who vowed to murder Caucasians. In 2002 Darryl
Barnes, who had been awarded $8.9 million after getting shot in the back and
paralyzed by an off-duty officer, saw the verdict overturned after it was
revealed that he associated with a "group that advocates killing cops."[46] The
judge's ruling stated, "Evidence of the plaintiff's membership in the Five Percenters was relevant to show that he had a specific motive to resist any police
officer's attempt to arrest him."[47]

In January 1967, eighteen-year-old Leroy Davis and seventeen-year-old
Eldridge Womeck were arrested for the shooting of a welfare worker in the
Bronx. In 1976, three Coney Island men, arrested for murdering an eighty-
two-year-old widow and robbing her of eight dollars, were named as Antonio
"Born" Bultron, Anthony "Scientific" Vinniane and Sylvester "Barseem"
Dukes. In 1979, a nineteen-year-old Brooklyn youth named Carl Miller was
arrested for murdering an elderly Hasidic rabbi on the edge of the Crown
Heights neighborhood. *New York Times* stories on all three incidents referred
to the suspects as Five Percenters. Offering inaccurate definitions of the term,
the articles ignored the "Five Percent" concept's true meaning as a statement

on organized religion to paint the men instead as radicals. In the case of the Bronx welfare worker: "85 percent of Negroes are cattle, 10 per cent are Uncle Toms and we are the 5 percent who knows what belongs to us." In a piece on the robbed and murdered Coney Island widow: "a group of teen-age Harlem militants who believed that 5 percent of black people were capable of freeing the rest from economic and racial discrimination." And on the Brooklyn rabbi killing: "95 percent of black people do not actively resist exploitation by whites and that members of the group are among the 5 percent who do."

> Someone like Allah didn't kill people, in no dealings with me was he ever anti-white.
>
> Barry Gottehrer

"No one in his or her right mind," remarked Najee Allah when asked about the September 11, 2001 attacks on the World Trade Center and Pentagon, "would feel good about the taking of any life."[48] In an issue of *The Five Percenter* immediately following 9/11, Kalim urges Gods to enlist:

> HOW MANY OF YOU WANT TO FIGHT FOR AMERICA? HOW MANY OF YOU WILL SERVE IF AMERICA GOES TO WAR? The decision is yours. Don't be foolish like the brother who was happy about the attack until he heard that his relative was in the building. Allah fought in the Korean War and was awarded a Medal of Honor. This is NOT like the Viet Nam War, we were attacked. If we are attacked and there are no repercussions, we will soon be attacked again and again, until we are destroyed.[49]

Regardless, uninformed reporting continues to sensationalize Five Percenters as Al-Qaeda supporters, race-jihad gangsters, and the Hell's Angels of black America. The Anti-Defamation League still includes the Universal Flag in its pamphlet, "Hate on Display: a Virtual Database of Extremist Symbols, Logos and Tattoos."[50] Ironically, the Five Percenters—who, as opposed to the Nation of Islam, reject "anti-white" and "pro-black" positions and even allow white members—are frequently demonized as a more militant version of the NOI:

> periodically members of the NOI who found it insufficiently genocidal, have broken off from it, and founded their own racial sects, most notably the Five Percenters and New Black Panther party.
>
> Nicholas Stix, "Pro-Al Qaeda Rapper KRS-One: Treasonous Roots, Poisonous Fruits," *Men's News Daily*, October 24, 2004

Allah was a right-wing conservative in matters of foreign policy, and Five Percenters that join the armed forces are following his own example. Brooklyn's Infinite Al'Jaa'Maar-U-Allah enlisted with the Marines in 1972. During his thirteen months stationed in Japan, a "yellow brother" made him a flag bearing the words, "a man is respected by others when he respects himself" to bring back to Mecca as a gift. The flag hung in the Allah School until 1988, when a fire destroyed the building.

For a system such as the New York State Department of Correctional Services that requires the black man to see himself as deserving of torture and degradation, rhetoric of self-respect remains, to borrow words from rapper Chuck D, "louder than a bomb." In 1972 it was revealed to a Senate subcommittee on juvenile delinquency that "some children in the institutions, particularly a group known as the 'Five Percenters,' had access to literature which could be considered objectionable."[51] Read it as violent or nonviolent, but Five Percenter texts like "Allah's World Manifest" still scare the shit out of wardens: "the black man of America has enough power lying dormant at least within the recesses of his brain that if it was ever activated, he could destroy all forces opposing righteousness overnight. This knowledge must be taught in prison first, because this is where the destroyers of the old world and their wicked ways really are."[52]

Plate 1. Allah "building" at first Universal Parliament. Mount Morris Park, April 30, 1967. From left to right: far left, holding folded jacket under left arm: Ar-Rahiem, who was nicknamed "Ezekiel" for his interest in Ezekiel 3:18. In all black, with black hat: Karriem/Black Messiah. To his left, in jacket with hands folded in front of him: Ebeka. Left of Ebeka: Sha Sha. In white jacket and white shirt, hand on hip: Gykee's younger brother Sincere. Behind Sincere in distance, wearing black hat, buttoned black sweater and collared shirt: Universal Shaamgaudd.

Plate 2. Allah with Five Percenters on Seventh Avenue. The youths in matching "crowns" are Barkim, one of the earliest white Five Percenters, and Sha Sha. In front of Barkim are his sister Mecca and younger brother Dihoo. Behind Barkim is Kiheem. Between Sha Sha and Allah, with his back to the camera stands Ra'jab, Allah's "Supreme Investigator."

Plate 3. Front row: Al-Jabbar/Prince, Justice, Uhura, Obey. Back row: Bahar, Yamuse.

Plate 4. Justice, Allah and "Young Akbar" at Mount Morris Park.

Plate 5. Allah in front row at parliament. To his left sit Mecca and Guvasia from the First Born Earths. The child in the center is Harmeen, son of Hasheem. Standing with their backs to the camera are Uhura and Karriem/Black Messiah.

Plate 6. Allah and Barry Gottehrer outside the Glamour Inn.

Plate 7. Allah, Makeba, Barry Gottehrer with Abu Shahid's son "Little Shahid," Omala, unknown.

Plate 8. Allah in NOI: young Muslim with *Muhammad Speaks* newspaper, Harlem, early 1960s. Behind him stands Clarence 13X.

Plate 9. Medina Gods at the street academy: Gykee, Hasheem, Akim and Waleak/Knowledge God, 1967.

Plate 10. Uhura, Allah and Karriem/Black Messiah.

Plate 11. Mayor John V. Lindsay and Allah on the
cover of *New York*, April 22, 1968.

Plate 12. Earths in the 1960s.

Plate 15. Five Percenter folk art, ca. 1980, incorporating Allah's 1965 mugshot, the 1st degree from the Supreme Wisdom Lessons' Student Enrollment (1–10) and traditional Islamic art.

Plate 16. Children performing at the first Show and Prove, 1971.

Plate 13. Justice and Allah with a young Earth at the street academy.

Plate 14. Allah, "the Father."

Plate 17. Allah School in Mecca, 1980s.

Plate 18. Young God, 1980s. Photo by Jamel Shabazz.

Plate 19. The Universal Flag.

13

Song of the Gods

The Father used to say, "wherever you go, if you want to know the mindstate of the people, listen to their music."

Azreal

In a lot of ways, hip-hop is the Five Percent.

the RZA

The first year of hip-hop was 1967, when thirteen-year-old Clive Campbell arrived in the West Bronx from his native Jamaica. As a party DJ in the early 1970s, Campbell—better known as DJ Kool Herc—introduced the Jamaican style of reciting rhymes over his records. Rapping during the instrumental breaks in popular songs, he'd give shout-outs to people that he knew at the party. Once he learned to stretch the instrumental sections by using an audio mixer and two identical records, the raps could grow into their own songs. Herc encountered Gods who would watch out for him at DJ gigs:

> So even the gang members loved us because they didn't want to mess with what was happening. You know? They come in, keep to themselves. Not only that, a lot of Five-Percenters (a splinter group of the Nation of Islam) used to come to my party ... you might call them "peace guards," and they used to hold me down: "Yo Herc, don't worry about it." So we was just havin' a good time.[1]

Years before hip-hop's emergence, the Five Percenters had secured a cemented place in New York's collective black psyche. Allah's First Born had become grown men and fathers; the city would be home to teenaged Five Percenters that had been raised with the Mathematics from birth. In 1965, teachers suspended students who insisted on using their "Muslim names;" a decade later, elementary school children had Allah for their legal name.

JDL (Jerry Dee Lewis) of primeval rap crew the Legendary Cold Crush Brothers, was born in 1961 in a fourteenth-floor apartment in the St. Nicholas projects. Later in the decade his father, Rondu Allah, would take him across the street to Allah's street academy, where he was called "Lil' Rondu." While Lil' Rondu played, his father built on the Mathematics with Allah and Justice. Young Jerry also participated in city programs offered to Five Percenters and their children, such as free admission to the Apollo where he saw James Brown and the Jackson 5. On one occasion he was given a Five Percenter pin, which later earned disapproval from his mother. She even whipped him and forbade him from seeing his father after learning that they had attended Universal Parliaments at Mount Morris Park.

For the generation that would produce hip-hop's "Golden Age"—artists like Rakim and Big Daddy Kane, both born in 1968, Year Four of the NGE's calendar—the Five Percenters were an established orthodoxy, their traditions a vital part of the surrounding cultural scene. The classic 1980s "b-boy" stance is said to have derived from the posture of Gods "standing on their square" at parties. The language of Five Percenters became the language of early rap: expressions like "peace" and "dropping science" come straight from the Gods and Earths. Even the affirmation, "word!" had its start with Five Percenters, as an abbreviation of the phrase "word is bond" from the 120. To praise an emcee's rhyme as "the bomb" came from the teaching battles in which Five Percenters "bombed" each other with memorized lessons. And to call someone "G," which is now read as "gangsta," represented *God* in the Supreme Alphabets, as Rakim brings to light in "No Competition:"

> I'm God
> G is the seventh letter made[2]

Malcolm McLaren's pioneering group, the World's Famous Supreme Team, had its own late-night radio on New Jersey's WHBI with artists such as Just Allah the Superstar and See Divine the Master Mind. The group hails Five Percenters in their 1984 hit, "Hey D.J."

> rockin' the house with the greatest of ease
> for the Gods, Earths, men, women and babies[3]

When God Kalim called and told them of the Father's dream of hearing "The Enlightener" on the radio, the Supreme Team began singing it on every show.[4]

The 1980s saw both hip-hop and the Five Percenters spread far beyond New York. Rappers such as LL Cool J and Run-DMC enjoyed MTV exposure and a nationwide audience, while Five Percenter lessons reached Chicago in 1985 and California by the end of the decade. Through the Gods and Earths' video archivist, Rasheen Universal Allah, I obtained an episode of *Yo! MTV Raps* from 1992—the old-school show with the cartoon word-balloon *Yo!* and the intro sequence of people like Heavy D, Salt N Pepa, KRS-One and Flavor Flav. This episode featured host Fab 5 Freddy with group Brand Nubian in front of the Allah School, which had been recently rebuilt; in 1990, two days after a Brand Nubian video shoot at the school, the building burned down for the second time.

As a youth hanging out at the mall, Brand Nubian's Lord Jamar met a security guard named Barkim Allah who would pull him aside and ask questions such as, "do you know that the black man is God?" Barkim, remembers Lord Jamar, had just returned from a stint in prison, during which he had sharpened himself physically and mentally. Receiving the knowledge from Barkim connected the youth to a lineage of teachers going back to First Born Bisme Allah. Along with Grand Puba, who had been raised in the Five Percent from birth, Jamar in turn shared the knowledge with bandmate Sadat X. As Brand Nubian, the trio would serve as a virtual missionary wing for the Nation of Gods and Earths. "We were just talking about how we lived," says Sadat X.[5] Lord Jamar, however, had been inspired by the World's Famous Supreme Team to fuse Brand Nubian's lyrics and performances with the message. The group's video "Allah U Akbar" showed elder Born Justice Allah as he lectured a 120 class, and Brand Nubian even recorded its own version of NGE anthem "The Enlightener," titled "Allah and Justice."

Addressing the departure of Grand Puba from the group, Sadat X told Fab 5 Freddy that "we can never fall off 'cus this is God right here." Brand Nubian and Fab 5 then entered the Allah School and sat in classroom-style chairs to receive a lesson from Born Justice. Freddy and the group listed various Five Percenters in rap music, including Supreme Team, Rakim, Poor Righteous Teachers, King Sun, Lakim Shabazz and Big Daddy Kane, each of them hailing from New York or the surrounding area.

> Five Percent taught me to understand the significance of my responsibility as a black man and my nature being God-like; so I started to strive to live that way, and believe and feel that there's nothing that I can't do, there's nothing that I'm not capable of becoming or being or doing.
>
> Busta Rhymes[6]

In both of her books, Asma Gull Hasan naively identifies Busta Rhymes as Muslim because he replied to her "as-salamu alaikum" with "wa alaikum as-salam."[7] A Brooklyn seed, Busta Rhymes found the Five Percent as a teenager. The Islamic motifs present in Five Percenter rap encourage the misconception that Gods and Earths view themselves as a Muslim sect. Brand Nubian sampled the *adhan* (Islamic call to prayer) in a song, which may be misconstrued as binding them to *al-Islam*. In a translingual breaking-down, however, the Arabic *Allahu Akbar* (God is the Greatest) finds a new meaning as "Allah U Akbar."[8] Some Muslim youths were confused by Nas' seeming contradiction of including an excerpt of the Qur'an (*suratul-Nas*) in a CD insert while referring to himself as "the God" or "God's Son." A product of New York's Queensbridge Houses and the son of a Sunni Muslim, Nas encountered Five Percent teachings at the age of twelve. The Gods often find peripheral references in Nas lyrics, such as his tribute to the critically revered Rakim, "U.B.R. (Unauthorized Biography of Rakim):"

> William changed his name at sixteen to Rakim Allah
> 'cause Clarence 13X had New York on lock
> Gods on every block, jams in every park[9]

Lord Jamar had hoped to be the first emcee to explicitly promote the Five Percent, but was beaten to it by Rakim.[10] "The Mystery (Who is God)" remains a masterpiece of both hip-hop artistry and NGE metaphysics, in which Rakim asks the question and then leads us to the answer. He begins by challenging the listener to properly decipher his words:

> if you can, see if you can solve the mystery
> the answer revolves around your history
> so carefully, I drop this degree
> scientifically, and realistically,
> who is God?[11]

He then takes us to an "eternal darkness" and the primordial intellect that wills the universe to exist:

> no beginning or ending, the seven dimensions
> enough space for more than a million words and inventions
> to travel through time within enough room to be the womb
> of the most high's great mind which he will soon make shine
> with intelligent elements in sight that he will gather
> in the realms of relativity electricity struck matter
> energies explode he below to keep releasin'
> atoms by the millions, til the numbers increasin'
> til it was burnin' he kept returnin' itself to the source
> the hotter his thoughts it gave the center more force
> he gave birth to the sun which would follow his laws
> all caused by his mental intercourse, who is God?[12]

While Rakim proceeds to unravel God's mathematics, to the attentive listener he is revealing his own intentions for upcoming verses.

> he began to explain his craft, the master in the attic
> he dealt with measurements
> his language was mathematics
> his theoretical wisdom of the numerical system
> the complete number nine which means born or existed[13]

Rakim then uses Supreme Mathematics to frame his lyrics, arranging hidden mathematical attributes in their proper order. For those that know their sacred algebra and recognize that Earth is the black woman, Rakim has given a glimpse of his conclusion.

from unconsciousness, to consciousness
by knowledging [1] his wisdom [2] his response is this
an understanding [3], which is the best part
he picked the third planet where new forms of life would start
he pursued show and prove every move in order
back to the source he let off his resources in the water
climb his climax, where the climate is at, high degrees
see he start to breathe deep in the darkest seas
and the plan is, to lay in the clays to form land
and expand, using the same clays to born man
in his own image our origin begins in the east
culture [4] rise to breed, with the powers [5] of peace
deal in equality [6] nature's policy is to be God [7]
build or destroy [8] positively born [9] life like Allah
And each one was given everlasting perfection
if each one keep living in the same direction
and life was life, and love was love
we went according by the laws of the world above
they showed us physically, we could reach infinity
but mentally, through the century we lost our identity
life start and ending, we got trife and started sinning
lost touch with the beginning now ciphers (0) stop spinnin'[14]

Rakim now brings his gnosis to the surface:

check Revelations and Genesis, St. Luke and John
it even tells us we are Gods in the Holy Quran
wisdom, strength and beauty, one of the meanings of God
G.O.D. you and me Gumar Oz Dabar
Knowledge, Wisdom, Understanding, Sun, Moon, and Star
man, woman and child, and so is Allah[15]

Finally, it is time to unveil the Divine Face:

the universe was man, and man was the universe
and the universe was always existing and existence was life
and life is Allah and Allah had no beginning
because he is, what always was Rakim Allah,
peace now who is God?[16]

Sun Ruler Allah, who was first introduced to the NGE through Rakim, Big Daddy Kane, Lakim Shabazz, Poor Righteous Teachers, Brand Nubian, and others states that in the early- to mid-1990s, "a lot of Gods were not taking these lessons seriously" and Five Percenters were "more like a rap-era hype."[17] To discourage the poseur element, according to Sun Ruler, many Gods in Philadelphia "would beat your ass down if you didn't come right and exact with your degrees."[18] He mentions one neophyte who learned the 120 while his teacher kept a gun on the table, pointed directly at him.[19]

The nine-emcee collective Wu-Tang Clan has been praised for giving a high profile to the culture; in 1994, during a group appearance on the *Arsenio Hall Show*, Ol' Dirty Bastard declared, "the Black Man is God!" However, the Clan also draws controversy within the NGE for promoting an image that associates Five Percenters with drugs, alcohol, crime and the objectification of women. "There are many pictures to paint in hip-hop," the Wu-Tang's Raekwon told me, and the Wu paints them all.[20] At a show in New York, Wu-Tang founder/producer/emcee, the RZA, told the audience that in the streets one would find pimps and drugs, but also "wise words spoken." The Wu-Tang Clan offered wisdom on each of its albums, he contended, beneath the group's surface-level hedonism.

"How do you answer what you do?" asked the RZA when I inquired about the Wu-Tang Clan's message and legacy. "You just *do*. I'm just being me. If it affects others in a positive way, all praise is due. If it affects others in a negative way, I'm sorry. I apologize out of respect."[21]

Wu-Tang lyrics have turned Five Percenter patois and lessons into slang for suburban white kids in "Wu-Wear" hoodies. References to the 120 in the RZA's "The Birth" would be lost on those unfamiliar with the text:

> Little Boy Peep, has lost his sheep
> but I found 'em, in a deep long sleep
> nine thousand miles away from home
> livin' the life of a modern-day Flintstone[22]

The 120 states that Africans who had been kidnapped and taken to North America "wanted to go to their own country, but they could not swim nine thousand miles." And after Yacub created white devils, they were exiled to the *caves* of Europe; thus, a black man who is forced to conform to White America and its culture lives like a "modern-day Flintstone."

> this whole plan was a perfect scam
> see that's why they called it the Six Million Dollar Man
> six is the limitation of the devil
> in the million square miles of land that he settles[23]

According to the Supreme Wisdom, a white man's brain weighed six ounces (compared to the black man's seven and a half). It took six hundred years to create the devil, after which he was given six thousand years to rule the earth.

they use you as a tool to deceive your own people
and fill up my children's heads with pins and needles[24]

In Yacub's eugenics law, nurses were ordered to kill black babies by sticking needles in their brains. The phrase "pins and needles" occurs frequently in Five Percenter discourse, referring to negative mental states brought on by the harmful messages in American culture.

In the final lines of his poignant, mournful monologue, the RZA answers that he is God—author of the Bible, Qur'an and Egyptian texts, but nonetheless bewildered by the plight of his people—

rewrite the script of Egypt,
who made the Holy Bible or Quran, how long ago,
who made the Holy Title? of I Self Lord and Master,
who control the vital parts of your heart,
who wrote the wise recitals? Ruler Zig Zag Zig Allah,
Arm Leg Leg Arm Head still puzzled like the jigsaw[25]

In these final lines, the RZA not only uses Five Percenter breakdowns of Allah (Arm Leg Leg Arm Head), Islam (I Self Lord and Master) and his own name (Ruler Zig Zag Zig Allah); his question of who wrote the Bible or Qur'an is taken from the first question of Lost-Found Muslim Lesson No.2.

In "All That I Need," Wu-Tang star Method Man's duet with R&B star Mary J. Blige, he vows, "I can be your sun, you can be my earth/resurrect the God through birth." Method Man, who elsewhere raps,

I fear for the 85 that don't got a clue
how could he know what the fuck he never knew?
God Cipher Divine come to show and come to prove
a mystery god, that's the work of Yacub
the holy ghost got you scared to death kid, boo![26]

has since become the star of feature films and his own Fox sitcom. The RZA has gone on to star in movies and provide musical scores for Quentin Tarantino's *Kill Bill* films. The Wu-Tang's *W* logo, designed by DJ Allah Mathematics, remains as recognizable a graphic as any in rap.

The RZA (Robert F. Diggs) had been born less than a month after the Father's assassination. He grew up on classic kung-fu films, attending triple features as early as 1978, and was inspired by *The Thirty-Sixth Chamber* to roam Chinatown in search of books on Eastern philosophy. By this time in Five Percenter history, every aspect of the Father's life had turned legendary, including his tour of duty in Korea. Stories had Allah learning judo while overseas and then training the FOI in Harlem. The Far East had added to the Father's mystique, rendering him a sort of Motherplane.

Robert was eleven years old when he first received the knowledge from his thirteen-year-old cousin, Gary Grice, who had once rescued him from a crew of eight guys by putting on his tassled skullcap and announcing, "I'm Allah Justice, boy! From Brooklyn!" According to Robert, "you didn't want problems with the gods back then."[27] Robert became Prince Rakeem and began studying the lessons in 1981; by 1982 he had mastered all 120 degrees and taught them to his cousin Russell Jones, who took the righteous name Unique Ason Allah. In 1983, the year that his family moved to Staten Island, Prince Rakeem made his first visit to the Gods in Harlem. In those "old days," he remembers, "you could walk to the corner and there'd be two brothers there who knew it [the 120], too, and they'd feel it was their duty to test you."[28]

Allah Justice also enlightened his cousins to the blossoming art of rap, and the three formed a group called All In Together Now. Prince Rakeem rapped with his righteous name, but was also known as "Rza Rza Rakeem" for his graffiti signature, "Razor." Allah Justice instructed him to stop using the letter S, since "we're completing ourselves with a Z." Prince Rakeem considered the Z in *Rza;* in the Supreme Alphabets, Z stood for "Zig Zag Zig," which symbolized a Z drawn in the air—always upwards, reflecting the elevation that comes with Knowledge, Wisdom and Understanding. Z was the "final step of consciousness." Robert Diggs/Prince Rakeem became the RZA: Ruler *Knowledge-Wisdom-and-Understanding* Allah. Gary Grice/Allah Justice would call himself GZA. Russell Jones/Unique Ason Allah rapped as Ol' Dirty Bastard.

When the three cousins of All In Together Now formed a new rap group with six fellow Five Percenters, RZA named it the Wu-Tang Clan after the kung-fu film *Shaolin and the Wu-Tang.* His breakdowns of *Wu-Tang* included "Wisdom of the Universe and the Truth of Allah for the Nation of the Gods." While Five Percenters typically rename cities and boroughs using an Arab-Islamic motif or the Supreme Alphabets, the RZA reclaimed his home of Staten Island as "Shaolin." In contrast to Gods that treated their culture as quasi-Islam, the RZA's worldview syncretized Five Percenter philosophy with his Buddhist leanings:

> sight beyond sight we stand up as divine warriors
> who smite with the mighty right hand of God
> yield the holy sword, swings the holy rod
> then bathe in the pond of Nirvana,
> escape the realm of Karma
> allow the true grace of God
> to shine through my persona[29]

As members focused on solo endeavors, the Wu-Tang Clan functioned more as a crew of allies than an actual group, with all nine emcees rarely appearing on the same stage. Around the Clan swarmed an ever-expanding network of proteges and side projects, the "Wu-Fam," including groups such as Sunz of Man, GraveDiggaz, and Killarmy, which featured the RZA's younger brother, 9th Prince.

Killarmy had a brief turn as media scapegoat in the fall of 2002, when a series of sniper-rifle killings in and around Washington, D.C., Baltimore, Maryland, and along Virginia's I-95 resulted in the arrest of John Allen Muhammad, who had fed the police anonymous notes with phrases like "I am God" and "word is bond." Police found a Killarmy tape in Muhammad's car, leading to speculation that the sniper had picked up his beliefs from rap. On an episode of *Meet the Press,* comically ignorant Tim Russert noted that the phrase "word is bond" could be found in both the sniper's latest letter and Killarmy's album, *Silent Weapons for Quiet Wars.* On top of that, Russert informed us, a tarot card left by the sniper bore the inscription, "Dear Policemen, I am God" while *Silent Weapons* contained the quote, "My name is Born God Allah, King of North America." In a *USA Today* piece entitled "Hip-Hop's Grim Undertones," Mark Goldblatt imagined a link between John Allen Muhammad and the NGE, which was apparently responsible for rap music's "apocalyptic visions of race war" that were assumed to inspire the killings. Goldblatt seems to have forgotten that the "D.C. Sniper" also shot African-Americans.

Goldblatt clearly wrote without any effort to research the Five Percenters. As John Allen Muhammad drew five stars on one of his letters, Goldblatt claimed that five stars were a symbol of the Gods and Earths. Goldblatt even took stock in Muhammad's quote, "word is bond," as specifically tied to the NGE. While originating in W. D. Fard's 120, today the phrase is widespread enough to be ideologically meaningless; I once heard a generic rapper say "word is bond" in an ad for the new Dodge Charger. Goldblatt's work was thoroughly ripped to shreds in a piece by Dasun Allah for *The Village Voice,* and John Allen Muhammad was finally identified not as a Five Percenter but a former member of the Nation of Islam. While experts tried to construct a read on the sniper by his religion and the music he listened to, it rarely came up that he also had a background in the United States military.

In response to critical readings of his article by Five Percenters, Goldblatt wrote, "You are inspiring the most hateful, misguided, delusional art ever to emerge from black culture, and thus you are indirectly undermining the confidence of young black people that America is their nation as much as anyone's—a confidence which they need in order to succeed."[30]

There is more informed coverage than Goldblatt's. Ted Swedenburg provided what may be the first academic recognition of Five Percenters in the genre in his paper for a 1997 Anthropology Colloquium, "Islam in the Mix: Lessons of the Five Percent." The paper continues to be read online and is received favorably within the NGE community. Felicia M. Miyakawa, Assistant Professor of Musicology at the Robert W. McLean School of Music (Middle Tennessee State University) wrote an entire book dedicated to the manifestations of Five Percent culture in rap music, 2004's *Five Percenter Rap: God Hop's Music, Message, and Black Muslim Mission.*

Despite increased awareness of the role played by Allah's nation in shaping modern hip-hop, Five Percenters have not been a force in the industry for years. Where the Poor Righteous Teachers once boasted, "the Gods are ruling up in hip-hop," Chace Infinite of Self-Scientific now laments, "it ain't cool to represent knowledge of self no more."[31] The Five Percenters' declining influence can be attributed to the rise of "gangsta" rap, centered on crime and violence, and "shine" rap devoted to outlandish boasts of wealth and material possessions. Another factor has been rap's growing geographic diversity. In the 1990s, New York rappers lost their dominance to the west coast, and in the years since have had to share the genre with artists from Detroit, Chicago, Atlanta, St. Louis, and Houston, where the Gods were not nearly as ingrained in local culture. Five Percenter artists to find mainstream success after the "God-hop" boom include Outkast's Andre 3000, an Atlanta native who was introduced to the teachings by singer Erykah Badu (the two have a son, Seven Sirius) and Common, who has performed at NGE Show and Prove events in Harlem. Dasun Allah went from his *Village Voice* internship to briefly become editor-in-chief of rap magazine *The Source.* In October 2005 he was accused of vandalizing a Jehovah's Witness hall in Harlem and related the incident to his "personal history with organized religion and the Jehovah's Witnesses in particular."[32]

Lord Jamar has since taken to acting and portrayed the first recurring Five Percenter character on American television, as "Supreme Allah" in the HBO prison drama *Oz.* He also landed a part on *The Sopranos* and continued his music career with a solo album titled *The 5%,* featuring appearances by the Wu-Tang Clan's RZA, GZA, Raekwon, Papa Wu, and former Brand Nubian comrades Grand Puba and Sadat X. The RZA, widely recognized as the Five Percent's ambassador to pop culture, unveiled a new group called the Harlem 6. The RZA's a deep God; I know that he sees the history being renewed. The reference may escape a general audience—it's not Ol' Dirty Bastard shouting that the black man is God on national television—but for those already versed in the knowledge, the group's name is a knowing nod. Between rap's worldwide popularity and the Five Percenters' insider language and folklore, outright proselytism like Brand Nubian's "Ain't No Mystery" and the esotericism of Rakim's "The Mystery," a God emcee can have it both ways. He can use the medium to teach the world, but while millions listen, he can also engage his Five Percenter family in a private conversation.

14

The Builders Build

Prejudice against new religious movements causes some to view the beliefs and practices of groups such as the Five Percenters as bizarre or even humorous in comparison to time-honored "world religions." But the builders continue to build, and with each passing decade the Five Percent Nation grows into its own intellectual tradition. Five Percenters that have spent years with the Mathematics can spin your head around; the layers of meaning that they pull from these numbers and their attributes show the NGE science to be as deep and "real" as more orthodox belief systems. The Supreme Wisdom has also been treated with a wealth of interpretation, ranging from literalism to allegory to politically progressive readings. Allah's original Suns were largely drop-outs and delinquents who taught the 120 on the corner, but today's NGE includes graduate and undergrad students who complement Five Percenter thought with their mainstream educations in history, philosophy, religious studies, anthropology, sociology, and science. For many, the truth of 120 does not rely on a blind faith in Master Fard and Elijah Muhammad. Divine IZ Earth writes that Five Percenters "don't teach this because someone said this is true," but because they have done the knowledge and can prove it: "no one can tell you that the black man is not the original man. Period."[1] "As we continue to grow and develop," promises I Majestic Allah, "you will continue to see the many manifestations of our Culture."[2] The Gods and Earths won't need 1400 years to produce their own Imam Ghazali, Ibn al-Arabi and Ibn Rushd.

At the time of Allah's assassination, the Five Percenters were nearly all teenagers. Members that stayed with the movement and continued to teach on the streets or in prison, having walked with the Father in person, functioned as heirs to his authority. Today, stories of Allah's actions and sayings are shared much in the fashion that early Muslims told *hadiths* of the Prophet. A Five Percenter can bolster his statement by tracing a narrative's transmission to the First Born or another of Allah's companions. However, memories do not always agree, and elders' personal experiences with the Father may lead them to differing interpretations. Not all elders hold the same weight. Allah B is respected as a leader in the community with an especially close relationship to the Father. First Born ABG's essays are trusted as historical sources. Many

Gods and Earths follow God Kalim's perspectives, though he has alienated others. The writings of Universal Shaamgaudd Allah are alternately treated as sacred or held suspect for his tendency to mythologize. Controversial elders like Abu Shahid and First Born Prince Allah are often revered but not accepted uncritically. Rather than a single definitive vision, there are as many histories as there are Five Percenters; each time an elder shares his recollections with a young God, he in fact creates a new history.

Through these loosely bound oral traditions, Five Percenters have been faced with the tasks of determining authentic narratives, establishing uniform versions of texts and their applications and promoting a proper symbology to be accepted by all members of the community. There is occasional but usually minor doctrinal discord: Five Percenters still discuss whether a man could use *Allah* for his first name or only his surname, and whether "7" in the Math was originally *God* or *Allah-God*.[3] There have also been evolving responses to the questions of how Gods relate to women, white people and the religion of Islam.

> Is it a branch of Muslim? They are Muslims who do something else?
>
> Alan Colmes

In his article "Is the Nation of Gods and Earths a Muslim Community?" I Majestic Allah argues that the Five Percenters cannot be understood within limitations of Islam, and "to place the NGE in an Islamic scope does a disservice to both groups."[4] While Gods and Earths today teach that Allah uttered the words, "my Five Percenters are not Muslims, and they will never be Muslims," there are numerous interpretations of the Five Percenters' connection to Islam. Sincere Merciful Allah God's essay "Why We are Not Muslims" reduces the link to mere language:

> Allah and Islam are "Arabic" words and not "Muslim" words. Islam means peace. The word "Islam" is not "owned" by the "religion" of Islam ... We utilize "Arabic" for it underscores our utilizations of Mathematics as the Foundation for our Science. Numerals are represented as "Arabic" numerals in Mathematics. Therefore we utilized various "Arabic" words to show this connection.[5]

Five Percenters often find their way around the Muslim/non-Muslim issue by claiming, as C. M. Bey had in the 1940s, to live Islam as a "science" or "culture" rather than a religion. I have also heard it said echoing Elijah Muhammad, that a black man has no need for religion because Islam is his nature.

Others would draw a thin line between the two. First Born Prince Allah, who had found Islam with the Blood Brothers and originally called himself Al-Jabbar, would in the 1990s attend Sunni *jum'aa* prayers at Masjid Malcolm

Shabazz and receive derision from Abu Shahid for wearing that "Yassir Arafat rag around his head."[6] Prince's recorded reading of the 120 ends with a recitation of *al-Fatiha* and other short *suras* from the Qur'an, entirely in Arabic. In the November 1997 essay "One With God," Kalim refers to Prince's explanations of Islamic concepts *shirk* and *ihsan*.[7] According to Prince, the Father invited Five Percenters to follow any path they chose, as long as they understood that God was the black man. Universal Shaamgaudd Allah, who became such a piece of Five Percenter history that Brooklyn parliaments are called "Universal Shaamgaudd Parliaments," mentions that the Father advised Five Percenters interested in Islam to study the Qur'an as translated by A. Yusuf Ali, in part for its detailed commentary.[8] Though Shaamgaudd rejects identification as a Muslim, he implores Five Percenters to show tolerance towards *al-Islam*:

> I even heard brothers and sisters speak against True Moslems here in America without trying to see past their Knowledge and Wisdom and show them your Understanding, you must always remember that Moslems are lovers of their religion, their QUR'AN, their Prophet Muhammad, their Truth and Allah and because of their Knowledge and Wisdom of The Holy Qur'an they will refuse to understand you.[9]

Shaamgaudd adds that while Five Percenter names may appear blasphemous, asking the "True Moslem" to read them from right to left will show the names to instead be praising Allah's glory.[10]

Prince drew up his own plus-lesson: "Lost-Found Muslim Lesson No.3, The Third Prophecy," which he sold at the Allah School for two dollars a copy. This collection of eighty-five questions and answers appears to be an effort to harmonize the Five Percenters with "religious" Islam. Defining *Muslim* as "a person who accepts the Islamic way of life and acts upon it," Prince creates a setting in which man is simultaneously Allah and a submitter to Allah's will.

1. What is Islam?

Answer. Islam is mathematics. It is a complete way of life. It is the guidance provided by Allah through His Messenger for the human families of the planet Earth.

2. What does Islam teach us?

Answer. Islam teaches us the purpose of our creation, our final destiny and our place in the universe. It also teaches us the best way to conduct all our worldly affairs in society.

3. Tell us why does Islam mean Peace?

Answer. Submission and obedience to Allah's will brings about peace. Submission is acceptance of Allah's command. Obedience means "putting Allah's commands into full practice."

4. What is the meaning of I-S-L-A-M?

Answer. Islam. Islam is an arabic word which means "submission and obedience to Allah," the proper name of God. It also means "I Self Lord and Master."[11]

For Five Percenters, the Islam in question is not so much traditional Sunnism as the Nation of Islam, due to their shared scripture and historic figures. While acknowledging the orthodox belief that Muhammad was the final prophet, Prince writes that the "seal of prophethood" had been broken by W. D. Fard, and the final "messenger" was Elijah Muhammad. Kalim defends Five Percenters' use of NOI lessons as following the path that led the Father to realize that he was God, adding that if the Nation of Islam was in error, so was the Nation of Gods and Earths.[12]

The reverence that Five Percenters hold for the NOI tradition does not always extend to the NOI as an organization. One text of unknown origin, "Teaching for the Civilized Lost Found Tribe" announced that "the rule of 10% in the Nation of Islam has come to a head" and had "produced its own destruction." Five Percenters are then portrayed as bringers of justice upon "so-called righteous Muslims" that have failed to teach what Fard had given them. The lesson promises an imminent explosion of "mental and physical fighting" between the Nation of Islam and Five Percenters, particularly in the West, which will become the "fountain of dripping blood and insanity, murder, rape, 100% violence."[13]

Some opposition to Islamic conformity has been at least partly in response to an Atlanta-based group called the "Allah Team" that published articles with hopes of building bridges between the NGE and NOI. According to Allah Team members such as Wakeel Allah, who had studied under Prince at the Allah School, all Gods were Muslims and belonged to the NOI. The Allah Team's article, "Is Allah a Righteous Muslim?" warranted a 167-page, 42,000-word refutation from Supreme Scientist Allah, one of Milwaukee's First Born. In *Out of Doors*, Supreme Scientist argues that Allah's Supreme Mathematics, not the NOI's 120, provides Five Percenters with their ideological basis:

True Islam: "Unfortunately, we don't have the words of the Father to settle the argument one way or the other. We do, however, have the next best thing: the source from which he drew his understanding ... The Lessons ..."

The above assertion, and many of its kind, only continue to reveal that the Allah Team is extremely far removed from understanding the fundamental principles in which Our Nation is founded. The "source" from which Allah, the Father "drew his Understanding" was not the collection of questions, answers and statements the Allah Team refers to as the "lessons." The "lessons (Supreme Wisdom) which are utilized by the Muslim Community of the Nation of Islam, ARE NOT THE FOUNDATION! Having a thorough and great Understanding of the principles of the Supreme Mathematics is the foundation. That is the BEST THING!"[14]

Supreme Scientist Allah then deconstructs the 120 and Elijah Muhammad's teachings as allegory:

For instance, in the story of the making of the devil, who is the chief character? Yacub. Is it at all possible for this character to be the creation of man's imagination, as opposed to having been a physically living person? ... we can better understand the writings of Elijah Muhammad and the Muslim Community by familiarizing ourselves with the historical, social, cultural, and literary context in which they were formed. Figurative language paints a mental picture. It introduces Us to a person, place, or thing to our brains that may have been alien to our actual observations in life. However, it should be worth the redundancy to state that confusion emerges whenever we mistake a mental reality for a physical reality ... while these stories are informative and inspiration, they are not very reliable.[15]

Supreme Scientist Allah proceeds to pick apart the NOI's theology, identifying contradictions and going so far as to remark that "Elijah Muhammad quite literally doesn't know what he is talking about."[16] He reminds his reader that despite the Allah Team's assertion that the Father had developed in the "womb" of Mosque No.7, Allah did in fact dissent from the Nation of Islam with a serious grievance:

Elijah Muhammad only understood himself to be a servant of Allah, not Allah ... the Supreme understanding of the Nation of Gods and Earths represents a growth in perspective. No longer did Allah, the Father see his person as the Arabic name "Abdullah," which was a name given to him by Elijah Muhammad and meant "servant of God." Instead, the so-called "Allah" of the Muslim Community had proven himself to be a mystery god.[17]

For Five Percenters coming from Christian backgrounds, Shaamgaudd's work incorporates more familiar material. The figure of Jesus looms heavily over his narratives of conversations with Allah. Similar to Elijah Muhammad's use of the Bible, Shaamgaudd reframes an Islamocentric message within his own

Christocentric experience. In one episode Allah explained to him that "Jesus had to speak in parables because he knew his knowledge would be used by the devils to try to deceive his own people."[18] Allah is also said to have taught that Jesus never asked, "Father, why hast Thou forsaken me?" because "Jesus knew in advance what type of death he would suffer and could have avoided it if he chose to."[19] Shaamgaudd maintains that if Jesus had lived and continued to teach without interference from devils, Adolf Hitler would have been born as a "prophet of peace" named Abdula Muhammad, since "the very symbol of the swastika is the bent cross or the broken cross."[20] Shaamgaudd even treats the issue of Allah's relationship to the Nation of Islam with Christian imagery. Echoing Noble Drew Ali's portrayal of Marcus Garvey as his herald, Shaamgaudd describes Elijah Muhammad as a "John the Baptist" who baptized Allah with his wisdom.[21]

Unlike Elijah Muhammad, Allah left behind no book or barely any record of his teachings, apart from whatever Gods you could find at Mount Morris Park or the street academy. In the presence of the Father, Five Percenters had no need for a written statement of principles—Allah was the living statement in flesh and blood. With Allah's death came a lack of formalized tenets beyond the NOI lessons and his numerology. A new Five Percenter in the early 1970s learned no more about Allah's life or message than the often second- and third-hand anecdotes he'd pick up from his mentor. Details of Allah's life and teachings would become even more diluted during the Gods and Earths' nationwide expansion.

As the "miles of history" added on, Five Percenters encountered a growing need to maintain cohesion. In or around 1977, Justice-U-Allah approached Infinite Al'Jaa'Maar-U-Allah and Understanding God Allah with the idea to create a newspaper. Justice-U-Allah was unsure of how Gods would react. Infinite replied that the Five Percenters would accept a paper if it was free; but if he charged money, some would call him a Ten Percenter who "sold the knowledge." The group agreed to charge only ten cents per copy to support printing costs. Infinite named their paper the *Black Family News*. The top right corner featured the Universal Flag, and the left had an image of a man, woman and child forming the shapes of a seven, crescent and star. This logo, designed by Infinite, still appears frequently in Five Percenter media. The *Black Family News* lasted nearly ten years, discontinued only after Justice-U-Allah went to prison.

In 1982 Universal Shaamgaudd Allah started his newsletter *Sun of Man*, which included editorials, stories about the Father and an occasional "Universal View" of astronomical trivia:

SPACE VOIDS A/K/A BLACK HOLES

Space voids are formed by the destruction of a sun to its very core, the term black hole describes its appearance, they range in mass from 7 to 50 times that of our sun. When the sun destructs it creates such a powerful gravitational pull that it literally sucks in everything in its immediate solar system, from planets, gases to light itself. Thus the term space void, while each space void has a companion sun, it only acts to show the limit and range of the space void's gravitational pull. Scientists have only discovered one black hole (there are others!). It is over a thousand light years away. They call it CYGNUS X-1. I call it JESUS!!! Space voids are caused by the unnatural deaths of a Supreme or Divine Being!!![22]

Shaamgaudd announced plans for an additional zine, the *New Moon*, which would be written by the daughters of First Borns. It is unknown whether the project materialized. In 1986, Gods and Earths assembled a coalition with plans to produce a national Five Percenter newspaper. Disagreements over content caused the group to splinter and create two publications, Elamjad Born Allah's *Five Percenter* and Beloved Allah's the *WORD*.[23] In 1995 Elamjad handed control of his paper to God Kalim, who has since faced criticism for poor presentation, "dictatorial rule" and his use of the forum to attack rivals within the community.[24] Dissatisfaction with the *Five Percenter* under Kalim led Elamjad to start a short-lived alternative paper, the *NGE Power*. Many confused one paper for the other, and now Kalim's *Five Percenter* is commonly referred to as the "Power Paper."

The *WORD* was intended to synergize diverse Five Percenter media within one unified voice, inviting contributions from other publications such as the *Sun of Man*. The *WORD*'s 1987–89 run has permanently impacted the Five Percenters, through popularizing the name "Nation of Gods and Earths" and also by producing seminal texts that have outlived the paper itself. Beloved Allah and his core contributors, Allah Mind and Allah Supreme, drafted the NGE's first formal mission statement, "What We Teach, What We Will Achieve," which appeared regularly on the paper's back page. The text was imitative of the NOI's bulleted "Muslim Program," which consisted of two lists: "What the Muslims Want" and "What the Muslims Believe."[25] A similarly formatted ten-point program appeared in Black Panther newspapers. "What We Teach, What We Will Achieve" continues to appear on NGE websites and is read as a standard Five Percenter manifesto:

What We Teach

1. That black people are the original people of the planet earth.
2. That black people are the fathers and mothers of civilization.

3. That the science of Supreme Mathematics is the key to understanding man's relationship to the universe.
4. Islam is a natural way of life, not a religion.
5. That education should be fashioned to enable us to be self sufficient as a people.
6. That each one should teach one according to their knowledge.
7. That the blackman is god and his proper name is ALLAH. Arm, Leg, Leg, Arm, Head.
8. That our children are our link to the future and they must be nurtured, respected, loved, protected and educated.
9. That the unified black family is the vital building block of the nation.

What We Will Achieve

1. National Consciousness: National Consciousness is the consciousness of our origin in the world, which is divine. As a nation of people we are the first in existence and all other peoples derived from us. National Consciousness is the awareness of the unique history and culture of Black people and the unequaled contributions we have made to world civilization, by being the fathers and mothers of civilization. National Consciousness is the awareness that we are all one people regardless to our geographical origins and that we must work and struggle as one if we are to liberate ourselves from the domination of outside forces and bring into existence a Universal Government of Love, Peace and Happiness for all the people of the planet.

2. Community Control: Community Control of the educational, economic, political, media and health institutions in our community. Our demand for Community Control flows naturally out of our science of life, which teaches that we are the Supreme Being in person and the sole controllers of our own destiny; thus we must have some control on the collective level that we strive to attain on the individual level. It is prerequisite to our survival that we take control of the life sustaining goods and services that every community needs in order to maintain and advance itself and advance civilization. Only when we have achieved complete Community Control will we be able to prove to the world the greatness and majesty of our Divine Culture, which is Freedom.

3. Peace: Peace is the absence of confusion (chaos) and the absence of confusion is Order. Law and Order is the very foundation upon which our Science of Life rests. Supreme Mathematics is the Law and Order of the Universe, this is the Science of Islam, which is Peace. Peace is Supreme Understanding between people for the benefit of the whole. We will achieve Peace, in ourselves, in our communities, in our nation and in the world. This is our ultimate goal. PEACE[26]

The RZA prints the entirety of "What We Teach" in his *Wu-Tang Manual* as "Nine Basic Tenets of the Nation of Gods and Earths."[27]

Another surviving legacy of the *WORD* is the first attempt at a biography of the Father: Beloved Allah's "The Bomb: the Greatest Story Never Told," which was serialized in four parts in 1987. The work was a milestone, indicant of the Five Percenters' developing self-awareness as a culture with its own tradition and historical figures. The complete text now floats on the Internet, copied and pasted onto various homepages and online message boards. Lord Jamar uses "The Bomb" as a blueprint for his song, "The Greatest Story Never Told," hip-hop's most detailed treatment of the Father.[28]

Allah told young Gods to "keep it simple," but forty years of analysis, articulation and elaboration have made the message more complicated than it ever was in his lifetime. Five Percenter literature now offers some knotty metaphysics:

> Until we can rise above 6 into the 7th plane of energy, we as a Black nation have been putting our wisdom before our knowledge following this misunderstanding of the 21 ciphers for the last 444 years ... The religion of Islam say jinns mean hidden evil spirits. The jinns are the gentile for short, plus gentile means heathens. See they are the heathens that kept it hidden from the people about their evil spirit seeking to destroy all life including their own. Because if by chance they could destroy this the Black man's whole universe would go back to gases from which we created it from because we are the magnet (or bond and bond is life) that's holding it all together. Allah, the Black Man, means all in all. All mind and all matter all together. The atom of life which is the atomic Black man (Allah).[29]

The same text offers an arcane breakdown of why whites play golf:

> Golf spelled backward spells flog which means to beat or whip something. So pain was their Father's (founder) Dr. Yacub or Jacob number one weapon ... Listen a 12 stage program had to be set up which was a check up, once a month 12 times a year. The 12 stage program is also symbolic to the 12 tribes of Jacob or Yacub, the Father of the white race. It took 600 years to make Black people into white people. 12 X 600 = 7,200 check up in a 600 year period. The 7,200 check ups represent the amount of strokes it takes to make par 72 strokes. Par meaning the number of strokes considered necessary to be an expert golf player. Most golf courses par is 72 in 18 holes of golf. Also their biggest tournament, they play 72 rounds of golf. 4 x 18 = 72. The grafting process or changing process that Dr. Yacub set up lasted for 600 years. Each generation took 33-1/3 years in 18 different time periods in three 200 year cycles. The 18 holes of golf represent the 18 generations it took to make the devil ... when you break down his golf course, it has 9 holes on the front side and 9 holes on the back side. See 9 is the number of completion. 9 also means to reveal the light of the white race history ... Tiger Woods, a young Black man (I don't care what nobody says he is

Black) won the masters which is the devil's biggest golf tournament. The youngest man ever to win the masters. This represent how our young Blacks are learning to master his small white ball ... At least one golf hole on a golf course is on a little island surrounded by water called by golfers, the water hole. See water is symbolic to wisdom. What they are saying is this is the place where they got wise ... The holes on the golf courses are surrounded by greens which is a symbol of their love for money ... The golf greens are surrounded by traps with sand in them which is symbolic to the hot burning sands of the desert that we ran them across which they stayed trapped in for 2,000 years. Okay, the fairways are symbolic to the highway or road that we ran them on, also the highways of defense that they drive on everyday. As a matter fact the golf sticks they tee off with is called a driver by golfers. The golf sticks they use are called clubs which represent fraternity clubs also the meeting place on the golf course is called a club house. The fairways are boarded by high grass that they call roughs, which represent the rough and rugged road that they traveled when we drove them from among us for telling lies and stealing and trying to master the original man and being filthy in all his affairs because he knows he cannot find happiness worshiping a mystery God. So see what I am saying is that the white race golf game is nothing but symbols and signs for them to remember their history and make money (their God). So this is really why the devils love to play golf, a game that reminds them of how they were made by us.[30]

In his previous work, *The Secret Society of Freemasons Revealed*, Almighty God Dawud Allah explains that nine out of every ten Caucasian babies are born with tails. While this secret has been hidden by doctors (who are all Masons), Dawud names it as the reason for a preponderance of the word "tail" in white speech ("heads or tails," "boy I will beat your tail," "tailgate party," etc.).[31] It would be a mistake to consider Almighty God Dawud Allah's work as representing the Five Percenters' intellectual high point. First Born Bisme Allah's essay, "The Five Percent," matures the NGE worldview, expanding the definition of "Five Percenter" to include anyone engaged in the timeless struggle for freedom, justice and equality:

> Whenever there were masses of people who were being oppressed or used, abused and exploited by those who held the power (10%) the Five Percent (5%) emerged to bring the masses out of their world of suffering.[32]

Bisme goes on to salute figures such as Toussaint L'Ouverture, Nat Turner, Frederick Douglass, Marcus Garvey, Sojourner Truth, and Harriet Tubman as fellow Five Percenters.[33] This broader perspective is shared by the RZA, who told me that one could find Five Percenters, "titled and untitled," all over the world: "if you put one hundred niggas in a room, five of them will be real, eighty-five of them will be 'whatever,' and ten of them will be on some bullshit."[34]

The NGE's emphasis on all black men being their own Gods, which prevents a "Ten Percent" ruling class from taking form within the community, also prevents the development of an organization that could govern Five Percenter media. Um Allah did incorporate Allah School in Mecca as a not-for-profit group, but distinction is made between the street academy and the Nation of Gods and Earths. Shaamgaudd suggested that Five Percenter literature be screened for approval by First Borns or elders prior to publication,[35] but his Universal Flag was never copyrighted and can be used by anyone to grace a book cover, newspaper or CD, regardless of content. The obvious difficulty with this democratic spirit is that Five Percenters have no control over what is presented as "Five Percenter" material. In 1997 a zine appeared at parliaments, titled "the Relief," mocking Abu Shahid as a devil.[36] That summer a pamphlet surfaced on 125th Street, purporting to be the long-lost transcript of a 1933 debate between Wallace Fard Muhammad and Albert Einstein at a Detroit radio station. "Mr. Muhammad, do you speak Arabic?" asks Einstein in the text. "Would you know how to say my name in Arabic Mr. Muhammad?" Fard answers, "Yes, in Arabic you would say *Yacub!*" The document, which has since been presented online by an NOI branch as authentic, was an edited version of a short story written by college student Aleek Allah for his creative writing class in the early 1980s.[37]

For years the closest thing to a book on the Nation of Gods and Earths has been Prince A Cuba's 1994 work, *Our Mecca is Harlem: Clarence 13X (Allah) and the Five Percent*. The book runs fifty-seven pages and consists mainly of newspaper articles from the 1960s. Nearly a third of the text is reprinted material from Barry Gottehrer's *The Mayor's Man*, which has gone out of print and become notoriously hard to find; Prince A Cuba attributes this to the book being "stolen from most public libraries, only to be hidden by the priests (10%)."[38] A major obstacle to academic study of the NGE has been the near inaccessibility of homemade and micropress publications such as *Sun of Man*. Cuba may have been the first Five Percent writer to reach for an audience outside the community, through his 1992 article "Black Gods of the Inner City" in alternative spirituality magazine Gnosis.[39] The full article has been disseminated throughout the Internet.

Today the most sophisticated Five Percenter discourse takes place in the online blogosphere, an initiative pioneered by Gods such as I Majestic Allah and C'BS ALife Allah to reflect the NGE in a positive light. "We are often painted as being a one-dimensional group of convicts and rappers that use funny words that no one understands," explains I Majestic, "and that happens when you don't have any influence on how people perceive you."[40]

A "5% Network" website has existed since 1999, providing articles, links to other NGE-related sites and contact information for ciphers throughout the country. The NGE's first online publication was *Black 7*, started in 2003 by Five Percenters in England. The e-zine featured interviews with prominent Five Percenters and members of the hip-hop community, poetry, articles, and open letters from Dumar Wa'de Allah, who has been regarded as a spokesman for the NGE.

Not everyone recognizes Dumar's authority to give "national statements." The Five Percenters' evolution into the Nation of Gods and Earths was met with opposition by Prince A Cuba, whose outspoken essays won a growing reputation as "poisonous," "divisive," and "destructive."[41] Among Cuba's thought-crimes is the argument that Allah's disavowal of racism was simply a political move to woo City Hall: "Only a fool would expect Allah to flatly tell Gottehrer that the white man was a devil. His job was not to reform Gottehrer, but to teach the young. God is not bound to tell the devil the truth."[42] It remains a disturbing suggestion to Five Percenters who place value in Allah's friendship with Gottehrer as well as Allah's personal integrity. "Is Prince A Cuba saying that God can lie?" asks Lord Absolute Pacific God Allah in a letter to the *Five Percenter*.[43]

To Cuba, Five Percenters today have no sense of Allah's real history, but instead deal in fables that have been passed around so long that they are now assumed true. He rejects tales of confrontations between Allah and Captain Joseph in the mosque, Allah shouting edicts from a Bellevue window, or the stifling of FOI at the first Universal Parliament. Cuba puts much of the blame for these stories on a cultish reverence of the First Born, comparing Allah's early disciples to those that corrupted Christianity:

> Jesus' "Apostles," like Allah's "First Born" went on to produce a mythology surrounding his person, while essentially developing their own privileged priesthood, with their own status highlighted by the sanctity attached to the absent deity, and their association with him ... As Jesus' own "first-born to knowledge" had him walking on water and changing water to wine, we have had our own "apostles" claiming miracles on 125th Street.[44]

"Miracle on 125th Street" is the title of Universal Shaamgaudd's account in which Allah displays his control over the weather and teaches a nonracial view of devilishment. Cuba rejects the "fable" for both its supernatural element and outright contradiction of the 120, which plainly states that the devil is the white man.[45]

As "Supreme Editor" of Salaam Allah's *Universal Truth* zine, Cuba opposes the "clique" that apparently took control of the Allah School in Mecca and thus the Gods' popular history:

> Whereas there are differences in opinion concerning the "succession" of these individuals claiming that Allah put them in charge, there is no evidence to

support their claims in photographs or printed documentation. In fact, these "pretenders" went out of their way to discredit anyone outside of their homeboy clique. Excluded were so-called Power Rules (Puerto Ricans) who "walked with the 'Father,' " and those from the outlying boroughs. Consider the case of Sha-Sha from Medina. The old-timers who have much earlier left the general corrupt cipher can fill you in on that.[46]

The concept of "First Born" has developed over the years, and seems to carry different meanings among elders. I have heard Azreal use the term to describe any Five Percenter who knew Allah, and in writings Abu Shahid has referred to himself as "the First Born."[47] According to Cuba, the definition of First Born as a specific list of individuals originated in the mid-1970s and at that time included Brooklyn Five Percenters such as Sha Sha, but was later revised to become "Harlem-centric."[48] The *Sun of Man* published a tree-like chart showing the First Born as Karriem/Black Messiah, Al-Salam, Al-Jabbar/Prince, Niheem/Bismi Allah, Akbar, Kiheem, Bilal/ABG, Uhuru and Al-Jamel, and dared anyone to argue:

> This is the original and proper order of the first born. Anything or anyone else is totally contrae or a down-out lie and I accept any and all challenges from anyone to prove me different ... I say correct and amend your ways, and as we use to say, stop claim-jumping, find yourself back to the original teacher and trace your rightful heritage to the proper order of your teachings.[49]

In "The Bomb," the First Born are named as Karriem/Black Messiah, Niheem/Bisme Allah, Uhuru, Al-Java, Dihoo, Ar-Rahiem, Sha Sha, Ubeka and Salaam.[50] Beloved Allah's history would acquiesce to Universal Shaamgaudd Allah's, which became standard, and versions of "The Bomb" that circulate online have been edited to conform.[51] There are slight variations in the spelling (i.e., Uhuru/Uhura, Bisme/Bismi) and order of names. The current roster favors Shaamgaudd and his friends at the *Sun of Man*: Black Messiah, who for a time was involved with publishing duties, remains at the top of the list as Allah's very first student. ABG, who along with Gykee maintained the newsletter after Shaamgaudd's death, has kept his Mathematically special place as the seventh youth to follow Allah. He frequently signs articles "ABG#7." ABG is also recognized on the *Sun of Man* tree as the earliest God to teach in Brooklyn, with his students Shaamgaudd and Gykee named the very first of Medina's own First Born.

To Cuba, these charts become the "priestly pretenders'" instrument of exclusion:

> If you are not on that map, then you are a "renegade." But who made that map but those who want to be our "leaders?" And the only ones they recognize are

those who accept them as leaders. I have met youth who have more intelligence and a deeper comprehension of their studies than that clique of Harlem dope fiends who think their claims of "walking with the 'Father' " mean anything to *the real 5%*. If they walked with Allah, then how come they don't have his lessons? Why are they typing up these bogus sets?[52]

In Cuba's view, the "Nation of Gods and Earths" was itself an offshoot of the Five Percenters, founded in the 1980s, that somehow took over the movement. "We don't recognize them as our leaders or authorities," he declares. "We didn't select or elect them. We have been tired of their claims of 'The Father said' and all the stuff they *make up*."[53]

Cuba blames this NGE "clique" for altering the Universal Flag. For decades, the flag showed the top of the crescent moon rising above the 7. After Shaamgaudd's death in 1987, the WORD promoted a new interpretation depicting the 7 as taller than the moon. Gods qualified the reform as having taken place during Shaamgaudd's lifetime and true to his actual design,[54] while Cuba accused imposters of forging posthumous Shaamgaudd plus-lessons.[55] Cuba sparked major controversy when he published a photo of Gykee, Hasheem, Akim, and Waleak standing in front of Allah's street academy, circa 1967, with a moon-dominant flag painted on the front window.[56]

"Priests," writes Cuba, "without intelligence or moral values have changed not only lessons, made up stupid stories, put words in Allah's mouth he never said, but have also changed the Universal Flag ... Really, ask yourself the question: 'Who put them in charge?' "[57]

In the most seeming contradiction of Allah's message, these "priests" went so far as to craft *prayers*. While in prison, Born Allah and Kihiem U Allah co-authored "A Prayer of Reality" which at first glance positions the Father as a mystery god:

SURELY, WE, THE 5% NATION OF GOD'S AND EARTH'S, HAVE TURNED TO THEE, ALLAH, STRIVING TO BE STEADFAST AND RIGHTEOUS IN THY TEACHINGS ...

SURELY, OUR PRAYER, OUR SACRIFICE, OUR LIFE AND OUR DEATH ARE ALL FOR THEE, FATHER, WE ARE THEY SEED ...

NO ASSOCIATES HAVE THEE, ALL, OF THIS WE ARE COMMANDED. WE ARE OF THOSE WHO LIVE AND BREATHE THEY TEACHINGS OF UNIVERSAL KNOWLEDGE, DIVINE WISDOM AND SUPREME UNDERSTANDING ...

ORIGINALMAN, ALLAH, THOU ART KING, THERE IS NO GOD SAVE THEE, THOU ART OUR LORD, AND WE THYSELF ...

WE, ORIGINAL PEOPLE, HAVE BEEN UNJUST TO SELF AND WE CON-
FESS AND ASK FORGIVENESS FOR ACQUIRED FAULTS, GRANT US
PROTECTION FROM IGNORANCE AND EVIL, FOR THROUGH EXPERI-
ENCE WE HAVE LEARNT THAT NONE CAN GRANT PROTECTION
FROM ERROR, SAVE THEE, FATHER ...

TURN US FROM FAILURE, INDECENT MORALS, SWINE EATING, BIRTH
CONTROL, AND WHATEVER TRICK OR TRAP DEVISED BY THINE
ENEMY KEEP US IN SLAVERY. WE, THEY SEED HAVE TRIED NUMER-
OUS SO-CALLED SOLUTIONS TO THESE ILLS AND HAVE DISCOVERED
THE ONLY CURE IS THEE, THE GREAT BLACK GOD OF TRUTH AND
RIGHTEOUSNESS, WHO'S PROPER AND ETERNAME IS ALLAH ...

OUR FATHER, ALLAH, THE ORIGINALMAN, GUARD AND GUIDE THEY
SEED, MAKE US SUCCESSFUL IN ALL OUR OVERTAKINGS, FOR
SURELY, ALLAH, THOU ART PRAISES AND MAGNIFIED ...

O! ALLAH, BLESS THEY RIGHTEOUS SEED, HERE IN NORTH AMERICA
AND ALL OVER THE EARTH, BLESS US FATHER SO WE MAY LIFT
THIS YOKE OF OPPRESSION WE HAVE BEEN FORCED TO ENDURE
FOR 431 YEARS. BLESS THEY SEED ALLAH WITH HINDSIGHT, INSIGHT
AND FORESIGHT, PREPARE US FATHER FOR THE BATTLE TO COME ...

FOR SURELY, ALLAH, THOU ART PRAISED AND MAGNIFIED ...

AMIN (ALLAH GREAT BLACK MIND).[58]

The prayer was published in the December 1986 issue of Five Percenter zine
The Enlightener. "Why would anyone teach or advocate a prayer?" scoffs Cuba.
The prayer does support more than one interpretation, as Allah is every black
man (or black men collectively) and First Born Prince taught that "if you pray,
you pray to yourself."[59]

In his 1995 letter to God Kalim, Lord Absolute Pacific God Allah complains
of growing disharmony among Five Percenters:

> In the plantation [prison] on which I reside we have Gods who are branched
> into different teachings. Some teach that the Black woman had 6 1/2 oz. of
> brain, and others teach 7 1/2 oz. We have some brothers who are not at peace
> with U-Gods at Mecca, but who follow the teachings of other Gods. We even
> have some Gods who teach that Master Fard Muhammad was a devil. The
> question I ask, is why are we so divided God?[60]

"Especially in these caves," he continues, "the teachings become so diluted
and PLUS LESSONS are written by those who can barely add on to the day's
mathematics and this is what forms these branches of the 5%."[61] One

plus-lesson from the 1970s, titled the "Great Understanding," argued that "Yacub was not a man but Yacub was man himself." A lesson attributed to Elijah Muhammad named the twenty-three holy scientists that elected Allah. In the 1980s, Siheem referred to plus-lessons as "Pac-Math" and Universal Shaamgaudd called them "Space Invader Lessons."[62] Shaamgaudd mentions one plus-degree erroneously naming Allah's birthplace as Georgia and a Five Percenter even calling himself General Monk Monk Allah after a Robert Walker lesson. "The FATHER taught us that our Lessons are the 120 original degrees," writes Shaamgaudd, adding that Allah had ordered the burning of Walker's lessons. Plus-lessons today are viewed as often worthwhile but potentially dangerous territory, and many Gods will remind you that Allah said to keep it simple.

Another factor in the development of Five Percenter thought has been influence from the Ansaru Allah teachings of Dwight "Malachi" York/Imam Isa al-Mahdi. Though most Gods and Earths would abandon a concept found to have roots in York's "scrolls," his massive amount of literature has smuggled ideas and motifs into the NGE. Many of York's linguistic breakdowns resonate with Five Percenters (i.e., "gospel" as "ghost spell"[63]). Shahid M. Allah's 1989 work, *Thy Kingdom Come* promotes York's presentation of the word "God" as *Gomar Oz Dubar*,[64] supposedly a Greek acronym of Hebrew words meaning Strength, Wisdom and Beauty (thus a description of God with manlike qualities). Further explanation by a "Freemason" is offered by a dead link on the "5% Network" website, and Rakim incorporates *Gomar Oz Dubar* into his Five Percenter opus, "The Mystery."

York included the Universal Flag among religious and Masonic symbols in his "Pyramid of Truth," and in 1991 published a *Book of the Five Percenters* with Allah's portrait on the cover. The text praises "Messenger Clarence 13X" and his Nation, but also contrasts Five Percenters' "Distorted Lessons" with the original NOI version and then abrogates both with York's "Real Meaning by the Reformer."[65] York's admitted goal was to merge the Gods and Ansars under his leadership:

> We are establishing the greatest black nation on the planet Earth, a nation that is divinely guided by ALLAH Himself under His teachings by way of me ... Let's work together. United we are an undefeatable force. You'll find out the differences came about due to the opinions of men.[66]

The Mahdi and his sect (now known as the United Nuwaubian Nation of Moors) have both undergone a series of aesthetic and doctrinal makeovers and continue to influence the Five Percenters. York's manipulations of Islamic studies, Egyptology, Freemasonry, etymology and racialized science-fiction have obvious appeal for Gods and Earths, and his *Book of the Five Percenters* provided many with their first exposure to the NGE. Each community borrows from the other, and today it often blends together: Allah and the Mahdi, degrees and scrolls, right and exact, pins and needles, original, grafted. York even used Supreme Mathematics as a basis for his three pillars of Right Knowledge, Right Wisdom, and Right *Over*standing. In turn some Five Percenters replace "understand" with York's "overstand" (itself grafted from Rastafari) in regular conversation, and the Five Percenter "Prayer of Reality" asks for help in all "overtakings."[67]

The Five Percent has also seen the sprouting of numerous short-lived subsects within its own culture. Troubled by the presence of "drunks, dopeheads, dealers and the like," in the 1990s a group of Five Percenters in Atlanta declared themselves a separate entity from the Nation of Gods and Earths.[68] Word also spread of a "Five Percenter Foundation" coming out of North Carolina, reportedly training a "Warriors of Islam" (WOI) wing. The group's newsletter included "Foundation Laws" and NOI-styled talk of Captains and rules of conduct. The "Nineteenth Law" conjures images of Captain Joseph's Doom Squad:

> The call to Wisdom Allahs Rule [war] shall only be made by the Minister of Defense; No Other is Allowed or Authorized to do so. Before any physical acts can be projected at anyone inside or outside the foundation that may effect this cipher, it must be approved or disapproved by the Minister of Defense, who will personally over see the mission.[69]

Kalim exposed the group in his newspaper, called its members "Five Pretenders" and issued what reads as a Five Percenter *fatwa*: "THESE SO AND SOS, WHO ARE USING OUR NAME TO SHIELD THEIR DESIRE TO TEN PERCENT, AS WELL AS MIXING, DILUTING AND TAMPERING WITH OUR UNIVERSAL FLAG SHOULD BE FOUND AND VISITED."[70]

In this chaos of multiple voices, many Five Percenters stress adherence to the original source. Attempts have been made to codify the 120, which is known to have been corrupted since the early days of oral transmission. The copy that Allah submitted to Lindsay for the "Book of Life" had been retyped by a college-educated Earth who saw fit to edit the text for spelling and grammar, resulting in usually negligible differences between the Nation of Islam and Five Percenter texts.[71] Allah is said to have caught the changes later and deemed them minor enough; but for a culture that viewed perfect command of every last punctuation mark as crucial to proper understanding, any kind of alteration kept a God's science from being "right and exact." The mutation of lessons worsened as years went by. While imprisoned at Comstock, First Born Prince complained that inmates' handwritten copies contained sloppy mistakes. "I can't rely on brothers who claim they can type," he wrote in 1991. "I intend on going to an agency and paying to have it done." The Father himself made deliberate changes in the text, even affecting the meanings of degrees. First Born ABG attests that it was Allah who removed the word "skunk" from the 2nd degree in the 1–10, which described the Caucasian as "Skunk of the Planet Earth;"[72] on an audio recording of the 120 narrated by Prince, "skunk" is replaced simply by "white man."[73] The Father also altered the 39th degree in the 1–40, in which Muslims are instructed to "fast and pray, Allah, in the name of His Prophet, W. D. Fard." The mention of Fard was removed, according to Prince, because prayers offered in the name of a prophet, "somebody outside yourself," were akin to worshiping a mystery god.[74] Not all Five Percenters accepted that Allah would change lessons. A "National Proposal" issued in the 1980s, advocating a standard and original 120, blames alterations on "several mysterious men" who tampered with degrees while Allah was in Matteawan.[75]

One version of the Supreme Wisdom became public knowledge on the Internet in 1999, courtesy of Melchisedek Shabazz-Allah, who wears a fez and describes himself as the "Universal High Priest of the Nation of Islam on earth and in the universe having no mother, no father, no descent, no beginnings of days and no end of life." Many disapprove of the High Priest and his website. The lessons, though both Five Percenters and many state prisons disagree, comprise an artifact of *religion.*

Making information widely accessible should not be a bad thing; but as Muslims often complain that reading the Qur'an in a language other than the original Arabic will sacrifice its meaning, the 120 gives up its heart when translated to hypertext. Shared on a playground or prison yard, the degrees become living things. I received my 120 on a hallway floor in the St. Nicholas houses. The lighting was dim, the walls tagged with graffiti, my teacher stoned but still holding a lineage to his own teacher, who went back to *his* teacher and *his* teacher and so on through the unbroken trees of transmission drawn in the *Sun of Man* to the First Born, to the Father, to Malcolm and the mosque and the Muslims on back to Elijah Muhammad himself on February 20, 1934, answering questions as they were given to him by Master Fard. The lines of teachers and students all begin at that same original source and are cousins to one another. On the project floor with a document soft in the way that paper gets when it's old, the creases becoming tears, stained with coffee and scented with the same oils that Muslims put on their Qur'ans, I became a link in one chain. In contrast, a computer screen offers only dead words, an experience about as real as sitting on your couch to watch Muharram self-flagellations from Teheran on the Discovery Channel.

Where we came from, we had to find it in the streets. Know what I mean? We had to go dead to the source and go to the Gods on the corner. Back in the day, they wasn't giving out no lessons. Nothing! Until you showed and proved that you wanted light.

Rakim[76]

Though Allah is credited with "liberating" the lessons from the mosque, he also guarded them in his own way. Five Percenters practiced an intimate teacher–student experience, as described by Infinite Al'Jaa'Maar-U-Allah:

Wise Allah ... told me that I had to go on a three-day fast before he would give me my first lesson. After the 3-day fast, he told me to bring a notebook and pencil to his home ... Wise Allah had me write down my Supreme Mathematics and Alphabets and also the first 5 degrees of the Student Enrollment (1–10). After I had mastered every lesson that I wrote down, he gave me the last 5 degrees of the Student Enrollments and that is when he chose a name for me, in which I had to break down and take it through the Supreme Mathematics and Alphabets and then I had to build on my name and show and prove what my name meant. Wise Allah was my brown-seed and I was his black-seed even though I was his student, meaning when you saw one, you saw the other, because in those days brothers always travelled in two's or pairs.[77]

Some in the culture had mixed feelings about the RZA including the Supreme Alphabet and Mathematics in his book, the *Wu-Tang Manual*. Others resigned themselves to the fact that both codes had become public knowledge long before; many even applaud the RZA's effort to educate a mainstream audience about the Nation of God and Earths.

"Allah (the Father) taught me never to write the Supreme Mathematics or Supreme Alphabets on paper, that this language should be taught by word of mouth," wrote First Born Prince in the 1990s. "However, he also taught us that 'as time change you must what? Change, or you are gonna die.' " Prince contributed a touchstone version of the codes to Kalim's *Five Percenter*, professing that it was needed to "rectify the crisis we are faced with."[78]

The crisis was a widespread confusion of the proper Math and Alphabets. Like the 120, Allah's systems had become subject to differing versions. Debate centered on the validity of "Culture or Freedom" for 4 and "Power or Refinement" at 5. It is often held that the original Supreme Mathematics contained only Culture as 4 and Power at 5; the question remains whether the additions were made by Allah or later interpreters. The Father has been quoted as telling Gods, "you have culture, but no freedom" and "you have power, but not refinement." The change has root in the Supreme Wisdom: the 17th degree in Lost-Found Muslim Lesson No.2 defines civilization as "having

knowledge, wisdom, understanding, culture, refinement and is not savage."
Placing Freedom at 4 has its root in Abu Shahid's "Living Mathematics."
The Father is said to have added Refinement to Power after his release from
Matteawan, as a means of steering his Suns' energies in a more positive direction. Allah Supreme God believes that at one point, 5 was "Power, *Justice
or Refinement*." 5 had represented Justice in Living Mathematics. I have
also heard Justice used for 10, but more in regular conversation than as a tool
of exegesis.

In the 1980s, Black Messiah and Universal Shaamgaudd Allah spearheaded
an effort to standardize the Mathematics as created by the Father and Old Man
Justice. The Messiah/Shaamgaudd codex, known as the Original Manuscript,
was printed in the February 1986 *Sun of Man* and presented at the June parliament.[79] The Original Manuscript opposed dualities: Freedom could be used as
4 only in 40 or a greater number, and Refinement was outright condemned.
Shaamgaudd claimed to have noticed Refinement entering the Math only after
Allah's assassination, and "watched and corrected my fruit when they started
going with the flow." Shaamgaudd compared Refinement to a trick of the
ancient Romans: "when they refine your power they cultivate your seed ... by
refining the seed of power they created homo-sexuals."[80] He also stated that 7
was not God but rather Allah-God, since the devil was a god "over everything
caught up in six ... his number 666 should be self explanatory to those with
understanding."[81]

Kalim insists that Allah taught him to use both Power and Refinement on
the street academy's chalkboard. As the WORD had for Beloved Allah in the
1980s, Kalim's control over the *Five Percenter* allows him to present his views
to the community at large as "official" dictums. Kalim promotes Culture or
Freedom, Power or Refinement and puts only God at 7, but there is still dispute
from advocates of the Original Manuscript tradition.

Meanwhile, Abu Shahid continues to practice and teach his own system;
"why should I change it if it works for me?"[82] He also tells Gods to "develop
your own and make it work for you."[83] The Mathematics have been comple-
mented with an additional system, the "Twelve Jewels of Islam," based on the
"Twelve Jewels of Life" found in a Nation of Islam newspaper from 1972:

1. Knowledge
2. Wisdom
3. Understanding
4. Freedom
5. Justice
6. Equality

7. Food
8. Clothing
9. Shelter
10. Love
11. Peace
12. Happiness

The Twelve Jewels are treated with varying degrees of importance; at times they seem an essential third component of Five Percenter text behind the Math and Alphabets. The degree also inspired "Feasts of the 12 Jewels," charity dinners organized and hosted by the Wu-Tang Clan. A 12 Jewels event in Chicago fed over one thousand people.

Both Black Messiah and Universal Shaamgaudd passed away before they could standardize the Alphabets, but the allowing of certain letters to have more than one attribute (such as *S* representing Savior or Self) may demonstrate a reconciliation of multiple versions. Other meanings may have been discarded or forgotten. Prince A Cuba claims that *F* originally meant "Freedom" but had been changed to "Father" to reflect a growing emphasis on patriarchy.[84] According to Yusuf Nuruddin, in 1966 *Z* stood for "Zelda Zee," representing a weak, wicked woman, and by the 1970s had become "Zig Zag Zig."[85] First Born Prince Allah's reading of the Alphabets is rejected by many Five Percenters for his inclusion of "Evil" alongside Equality as the attribute for *E*. Dumar Wa'de Allah, Beloved Allah and Um Allah came together to set up a Committee of Elders that would reestablish the original Supreme Alphabets and 120 as taught by Allah. Elders with equal sanction, however, continued to transmit the lessons as they knew them, and old copies still travel through the prison system. Today there are at least five readings of the 120, which is fine; there are more variations on the Holy Qur'an. Each man being his own God, he can follow his personal tree of teachers and work with the sources that he considers "right and exact."

15

Mothers of Civilization

Sometimes Allah took me aback. I couldn't get used to the young Five Percenters, the girls who had several children while they themselves were still children of thirteen or fourteen. I didn't know what to make of that.

Barry Gottehrer

The only way you find God is to keep on reproducing.

Allah

In March 2005 I visited the Allah School and purchased a burned CD with the handwritten title, "Born Lessons" for ten dollars from Cee Allah, who attained knowledge of self while in prison with William Craig of the Harlem Six. Cee Allah told me that these Born Lessons were the Father's earliest teachings to his First Born, expressed in a question/answer format similar to the Supreme Wisdom Lessons. This particular recording was narrated by First Born Prince, allegedly from memory.

The Born Lessons turned out to be actually more plus-lessons attributed to Robert Walker, who had reportedly told the Medina Gods that the degrees came from Allah. "Robert Walker is the amorphous one," Prince A Cuba told me; "any deviation from the norm was ascribed to Walker."[1] For all I know, they could have come from First Born Prince himself. One Born Lesson, "Allah's World Manifest" refers to Clarence Smith not only as Allah but Christ and describes 1969 as the year that he showed forth the birth of his nation. The lesson, apparently written in 1969, after Allah's assassination, prophesies that in 1970 "the wicked will have become his footstool" and in the last days of 1984, Five Percenters will take over the world. "Allah 360 Degrees" promises that if Gods cultivate the powers of hypnotism, by 1987 they would have babies speaking at seven months old and cure all genetic defects.

The Born Lesson "Sex Control" aims to regulate sexual relationships. The author taught that the missionary position caused an unfair exertion on men, resulting in a lower life expectancy than that of females. Proper intercourse was achieved by man and woman both lying on their sides, the man's legs between those of the woman. It was also required that a woman have sex at least once in twenty-eight days; otherwise, she'd become "high-strung" because she could not "release" like a man.[2] The lesson also blames this inability to release as the cause of female homosexuality.

In 1975, Infinite Al'Jaa'Maar-U-Allah was holding a Civilization Class at 1629 Park Place in Brooklyn and built on the question, "Does woman have a mind?" When Infinite taught that she did, a handful of Gods rose to challenge him, asserting that woman "didn't have a mind, but she had access to the mind." Sha Sha and Hasheem from the Medina First Born stepped up and affirmed that woman did in fact have a mind.[3] Infinite's challengers were supposedly influenced by Robert Walker lessons, but the question was considered a legitimate issue to be discussed. The Nation of Gods and Earths remains a *Gods'* club; the adult male-female ratio at your average Mecca parliament easily runs ten to one. What did a movement aimed at empowering adolescent males have to say about females?

Allah's own concepts of gender roles grew simultaneously from Nation of Islam teachings and the natural patriarchy of life on hard streets, where physical might made right and Barry Gottehrer observed prostitution as a mere footnote to survival. Allah's brown seed was a known pimp; the night they met, Justice offered Gottehrer "all kinds of women" for one hundred dollars. By definition the Father was a patriarch, and as with orthodox Islam, the NGE narrative since its founder's passing has been all but owned by men. While male elders make speeches on their time with the Father and young Gods name-drop the First Born like celebrities, there remains very little information on women in the Five Percent. In an early issue of her zine *Earth's Equality*, Queen Sha-Asia Mecca cites a great deal of Brooklyn Gods' contributions—ABG making the knowledge born, Universal Shaamgaudd designing the flag and founding the *Sun of Man*, Medina Gods spreading the culture to New Jersey, Connecticut, Maryland and Georgia—before asking, "Knowing our history is of the utmost importance. Sisters, what about us?"[4] "There were no women in the beginning," writes ABG; "the only sister recognized was sister Carmen," Abu Shahid's girlfriend.[5] Almighty God Dawud Allah writes that eventually "brothers started bringing their girl-friends around so we started calling them Nurses."[6] As with young Gods wearing the designation of "Minister," the title of Nurse came from the 28th degree in the 1–40, which described the principal characters who carried out Yacub's eugenic laws. It was the minister's job to marry only those couples that were qualified by Yacub's doctors, while the nurses were instructed to inject needles into the brains of black babies and feed them to wild beasts. Five Percenters used these titles with the sense that they were undoing Yacub's process.

For Allah's early Five Percent brotherhood, it seems that young women functioned as a girlfriends' auxiliary. In 1967 he renamed the Nurses "Earths," with twelve women later recognized as First Born Earths: Sister Carmen, El-Latisha, Makeba, Armina, Omina, Demina, Asia, Mecca, Tamisha, Guvasia (Mecca's sister), Kenya, and Ebony. Guvasia came into the fold through her then-boyfriend, Otis "B-Allah" Jowers. Allah had reportedly warned his son, "she's only using you to meet me" but B-Allah wouldn't hear it.[7] Forty-year-old father and seventeen-year-old son were briefly estranged over the girl. She later became pregnant with the senior Allah's baby—another boy, who he named "Little Allah."

At the May 1967 parliament, Barry Gottehrer observed "a great many young girls, most with small babies pulling at their skirts or held in their arms." Allah maintained that Five Percenters could take over the world if they produced more children than other nations. Sun-Africa, the young woman profiled in Anne Campbell's 1984 study of female gang members, *The Girls in the Gang*, moved to the Bronx to live with a God, his first Earth and their children. At sixteen years old she was seven months pregnant.[8] Five Percenters problematically follow Elijah Muhammad's ban on birth control while ignoring his ban on premarital sex. When Allah-U-Akbar, founder of the "Allah School in Medina" youth center passed away on January 1, 1999, he was survived by twenty-one daughters and twelve sons.[9] In the *Five Percenter* newspaper, Kalim stresses that a baby be made at every available opportunity:

> Young brothers are talking about women swallowing their babies? Emphatically Now Cipher [no]! That may feel good (real good) b-u-t babies come from the womb, not the esophagus. Plant those seeds in the womb ... Old Man Justice used to tell us, "y'all better be careful with those things—you only get one to a customer" meaning our life rod.[10]

In the May 2000 issue dedicated to Old Earths (mothers), Kalim praises the four women that have borne him children—Adiybah, Shebest, Lazel, and Eluna—while condemning contraception and abortion as the work of a modern Yacub:

> don't believe the picture that this devil has painted saying it is better for you to become childless FREAKS, WHORES, AND HOOKERS ... when one grows old and have no Fruit from their loins, they come to know the meaning of BARREN and WASTELAND. Without children, Black woman, you will be wasted land with no fertile fruit and (more importantly) no FUTURE. Your lifeline will end with you, by not having children to carry on your legacy.[11]

C. M. Bey wrote in the 1940s that God was the Asiatic woman, but Allah taught that "man is the creator of woman, whether she likes it or not."[12] The womb receives God's seed and nurtures life, but is not treated as a creative force itself. "I didn't come from a woman," proclaims Almighty God Dawud Allah; "I came through one, her duty is to hold the power of God, not be the power."[13] Earths seem to endorse this view; in the *Five Percenter*, Queen Be'Natural concedes that men make babies, and women "just carry them."[14]

Since a boy came only from his father, Allah held faith in a simple paternity test: "If he don't look like you, boy, he ain't you. That's somebody else messin' around with your Earth."[15] His theory would nearly provoke a Mecca-Medina beef. When El-Latisha's Brooklyn boyfriend Rayheem went to prison, she hooked up with Dumar from Harlem and became pregnant. The baby allegedly looked like Rayheem but El-Latisha insisted that the father was Dumar.[16]

A man aspires, in the words of Method Man, to "resurrect the God through birth," the God being himself. Announcing the birth of Lord Shyheim Justice Allah's son, the *Five Percenter* declares that the God had successfully "manifested himself."[17] To have a daughter would not quite mean the same, as Allah explained in his 1967 Otisville interview:

> If a man can't go produce him a boy, he's not blessed, 'cus the woman has cultivated his seed into a girl. And he shows you right there that he is not blessed. The woman is what? Blessed.[18]

Allah excused his own daughters, since he also gave Dora sons ("I let her cultivate the seed a little bit ... but I'm blessing her"[19]) and reportedly mocked Malcolm X as a "weak seed" ("he went into that woman five times and couldn't make a son"[20]). The womb was a battlefield in which woman directly opposed the will of her man:

> She'll bring destruction to you, you know that? The woman's a cultivator. She'll turn you into a girl every time. If you don't—the man don't become strong, the woman's gonna cultivate every one of his child into a what? Into a girl. And you don't have no girls in you.[21]

Allah's science of reproduction led him to a disturbing place: "What is a mother? A man don't have a mother."[22] Likewise, if a boy was the manifestation of his father, "who is my daughter if she ain't my wife, and I can give her away if I want to?"[23] Rather than allow someone to "contaminate" his Earth, the Father would choose her mate. "I feel exactly the way the Queen do in England," said Allah.[24] As with royalty, his daughter's body was capital, an award that could be used to fortify political bonds.

Though Barry Gottehrer has donated the copyright to his memoir, *The Mayor's Man* to the NGE to raise money for the school, the Gods have not yet reprinted the book due to objections from Allah's sister Bernice to one passage:

> Once Allah asked me to take his teen-age daughter home with me for the night. He looked as if he thought it was a special favor—he was bestowing a gift upon me. I turned him down and he later apologized, but I wasn't sure we completely understood one another.[25]

The issue is sensitive, not only for the gravity of the accusation but the fact that it comes from a dear friend of Allah and the community. I have seen three primary responses to Gottehrer's claim from Five Percenters: 1) Gottehrer is a devil and made it up; 2) Allah offered his daughter as a means of "testing" Gottehrer; 3) the story may or may not be true, but the divinity of the black man is not dependent on Clarence Smith. It is also a critical NGE value, drawn from Lost-Found Muslim Lesson No. 2, to never accept stories on face value.

According to the anonymously authored *Earth Degrees*, it is unnatural for a woman to be simultaneously involved with more than one man, since the Earth orbits only one Sun;[26] however, the reverse is not true. The scandal of Elijah Muhammad having extramarital affairs with his secretaries, while devastating to Malcolm X's perception of the Apostle, offered no challenge to the Father. Like Noble Drew Ali, Allah in his later years went from the home of one common-law wife to the next. He appears to have been deeply hurt by the collapse of his marriage, and would not settle down again:

> Whoever love me, that's who I'm gonna love. I'm not lovin' no more. They gotta love what? Me. I found that out through my wife. She didn't write me a letter, nor come to see me out of twenty-three months [at Matteawan].[27]

When it came to women, the Father taught his Suns, "if one act crazy, get another one."[28] As the Nation of Islam's strict moral code and enforced monogamy turned away potential Muslims, Allah's take on sex won male converts in the city's high schools. In 1980, Father Bushawn had six women to his name and admits that Gods came to Truth City classes just looking for Earths.[29] Allah's advocation of polygamy has been intellectualized as part of a Darwinian struggle for racial survival:

> in the ages of 20–24, there are about 49 employed Blackmen for every 100 Blackwomen and in the same ages of and between 24–34, there are about 59 Blackmen to every 100 Blackwomen ... 47 percent of all Black households are headed by Blackwomen, and 55 percent of all Black babies are born to single mothers ... the Euro-American social system of Monogamy, becomes workable

in a society that has an equal balance in numerical ratio between men and women ... The practice of having more than one wife is rooted in our ancestral (CULTURAL) customs, until they fell victim to the rule of the grafted seeds of Yakub, as it was predicted ... the Father (ALLAH) taught against marriage under this government of monogamy, which is plain as black and white an imperfect system that can only lead to genocide for us as a people.[30]

Allah did not offer a statement on marriage "under the government" until later in the movement. In 1966, while the Father was at Matteawan, First Born Uhura married Makeba of the First Born Earths. Five Percenters attended their wedding reception at the home of Uhura's mother on 127th Street. Though Gods at the time were said to be making regular trips to visit Allah, the issue was not approached. "We never asked," states Allah B, "and he never told us." The Father later clarified his opposition to marriage. Again, the root is found in Elijah Muhammad's story of Yacub:

> [Yacub] called the doctor first and said: Doctor, let all the people come to you who want to marry; and if there come to you two real black ones, take a needle and get a little of their blood and go into your room and pretend to be examining it, to see whether their blood will mix. Then, come and tell them that they will each have to find another mate, because their blood does not mix ... Give them a certificate to take to the minister, warning the minister against marrying the couple because their blood does not mix. When there comes to you two browner ones, take a pretended blood test of them; but, give them a certificate to say that they are eligible to marry ... The doctors of today hold the same position over the people. You go to them to get a blood test to see if you are fit to be married. Today, they say it is done to see if there are any contagious germs in the blood.[31]

When Radu married Nisa in the summer of 1967, Five Percenters were invited to the reception at Radu's mother's apartment in the St. Nicholas projects. Allah B states that before the wedding, he and two other Gods verbally "bombed the mess out of Radu" for betraying their way of life. The Father, however, was upset to hear that the Gods had come down so hard on their brother. He told them that although Five Percenters did not marry under the government, marriage was not prohibited in the same sense as pork, heroin and white women.

"If Radu wanted to give his word," the Father told the Five Percenters, "Radu was and is our brother and he didn't sell his birthright." He added, "the Gods is married to me through the mind and the sister is married to the brother through the mind." The black woman belonged to the black man and was not a slave "to be bought or sold by the, what?"

"The devil," replied the young Gods. Allah then asked them if they viewed Radu as God. Yes, they answered. The Father told them to "accept Radu's decision to give his woman the power under the government but over the devil," while warning that if Radu "messed up," Nisa could now get the police on her side and "put his ass in jail." If Radu fell victim to Nisa, said the Father, or failed to keep his word to her, then he'd be a "sorry motherfucker under the government." Allah once remarked that he always taught Five Percenters the biblical tale of Samson and Delilah.[32]

"Radu caught pure hell after that," recalls Allah B, "because he hadn't mastered Nisa nor did he keep his word to her." However, Allah B reminds us that the Father did not "disparage or disown" Gods and Earths that married. Allah never reprimanded Green Eye Zumar for marrying, and Allah B allows that marriage "under the government" could have benefits for Gods and Earths in the penal system.[33]

Allah's own relationships nearly split Five Percenters down the middle in early 1997, when plans to sponsor a fundraising dance for Dora were contested on the grounds that she had abandoned the Father during his time at Matteawan. The anti-Dora Gods formed a rival camp in support of Willieen. On February 22—the Father's birthday—Five Percenters hosted two competing fundraisers, each attended by its respective beneficiary. "Dora's Dance," held at the Allah School in Medina, raised $2,100. At an event in Asbury Park, $400 was raised for Willieen. "This thing ain't about Dora or Willieen," remarked Knowledge Divine at Dora's Dance, insisting that Five Percenters "opposed this for other reasons."[34] Dora's Dance had also been touted as a "Mecca-Medina Bond Dance," and the schism may have been related to some Harlem Gods' rejection of Allah School in Medina.

Prince A Cuba believes that since Allah's murder, the Five Percenters have grown consumed by a "preoccupation with male supremacy"[35] manifesting in all aspects of the culture. Gods altered their Universal Flag to make the 7 dominate the crescent moon, he argues, to assuage their "inferiority complexes about the Black woman."[36] In Cuba's reading of the original flag, the 7 appeared within the crescent to "show man entering the womb or Equality of the Woman."[37] For Cuba, the movement's adopted name, "Nation of Gods and Earths" also reflects inequality when compared to other options such as "Gods and Goddesses" or "Suns and Earths."[38]

Gods today often profess a respect for women within their male dominance: females are precious items to be *taken care of* and *protected*. "What kind of man would desecrate the pricelessness of our women?" asks "The Earth is the Home to Islam," an NGE editorial against domestic violence. The piece goes on to compare a man's role in his house to that of a king, "the coordinator of divine intelligence, the sovereign ruler who maintains peace in his kingdom at all times and is the righteous personification of living law."[39] First Born ABG quotes Abu Shahid as saying, "home is where the *ho* and *me* are."[40] The Five Percenter family is a benevolent dictatorship in which the man rules until violating his social contract. "He lays out the culture to be lived out by her within his kingdom," writes Sha-King Allah in his online blog. "There is nothing chauvinistic about this. Patriarchal, yes. The majority of the world's population is patriarchal."[41] Sadly, some Gods advocate their subjugation of women with the same defense (that such roles are natural, traditional and widely accepted) that was once used to justify racial oppression and colonialism.

Though Gods hail mothers as the teachers of children, it is understood that a woman cannot be the enlightener for a man. There is also debate over whether a woman can teach another woman. An episode of Five Percenter comic strip *Akee, Wise & Essence* depicts a female character asking if she will ever have to "born the knowledge" to anyone. The male character tells her that as she is the Earth, it is not her responsibility, and "if you do the job of the Sun, who will do the job of the Earth?" The young woman then recognizes that her duty is to "reflect the fields of Home Economics, Culture & Refinement onto the young" and with a smile declares, "that's why the Blackwoman is the Mother of Civilization."[42] These attitudes regarding women have been cemented in the culture through decades of plus-lessons and interpretive literature. The cover of *The Blackwoman and Islam* bears a large "17," which in the Supreme Mathematics means Knowledge God, i.e. to know God, to recognize the Black Man as the true and living God on this earth.

While black men do not practice the religion of *Islam* (submission) since "God can't submit to God," Earths are often considered to be Muslim because they *do* submit to Allah—in the form of the black man. Like both NOI and traditional Muslims, Five Percenters enjoin modest dress for women. Because three quarters of the earth is covered by water, Earths today are taught to keep three fourths of their bodies covered at all times and often cover their hair with a brightly colored headwrap. Adherence to this concept is often referred to as wearing "Refinement," which has been interpreted as the feminine balance to "Power" in the Supreme Mathematics. Though Allah welcomed Afrocentric styles, photographs from 1960s parliaments do not suggest that he maintained a dress code or disapproved of contemporary fashion. The only noted instance of Allah enjoining modest clothing came before the Five Percenters' first bus ride to Long Island State Park, when girls asked if they could wear bathing suits. After Allah gave permission, the excited young Earths began discussing what they would wear and the boys began discussing who they wanted to see in bikinis. Hearing boys talk about each others' girlfriends, Allah changed his mind and prohibited swimsuits, "because the brothers were not ready."[43]

In a culture with the bulk of its membership consisting of males under twenty-five, female sexuality is regarded as a blessing that could turn treacherous if ungoverned. *The Blackwoman and Islam* defines and explains "negative sex powers" used by women to "keep the Blackman weak, if he has not mastered them," including "Separation:"

> The Blackwoman keeps herself separated from her Blackman through many ways, if she has income coming into her home, then her money is hers, and his money is hers, this subconsciously tells the Blackman, that he does not own his Blackwoman. Many Blackwomen are more educated than their Blackman, so they feel they are more intelligent and won't take his orders seriously, this subconsciously tells the Blackman that he has no control over his woman. The Blackwoman can have every degree existing but until she gains True knowledge of Self & God, can she mentally be elevated, and this can only be done through the Asiatic Black Man.[44]

"It is crucial that the Blackman master the Blackwoman," reads the "Trickknowledge" section, "and all of her sex powers before bringing her into his cipher. Though your Queens are beautiful, they can be your physical and mental downfall, if not controlled and taught how to be a Righteous Woman and submit to God."[45]

Hip-hop remains the public face of the Five Percent. Many Gods and Earths see it as problematic that musicians are embraced by youth as doctrinal rhetors, particularly given the genre's common treatment of black women. In the song "Wildflower" from his solo album *Ironman*, the Wu-Tang Clan's Ghostface Killah expresses a paradoxical view toward Earths: in his role as God, he takes responsibility to civilize woman, but also rebukes her with sexually degrading language:

> You gained crazy points baby just bein' with God
> I taught you how to eat the right foods, fast and don't eat lard
> I gave you Earth Lessons, I came to you as a blessin'
> You didn't do the knowledge what the God was manifestin'
> You sneaky fuck bitch, your ways and actions told it all
> I fucked you while you was bleedin', held you down in malls

Elsewhere in the song he asks, "remember when I long-dicked you and broke your ovary?" but also acknowledges fellow Five Percenters for preventing domestic violence: "I shoulda slapped you but the Gods said chill." "Wildflower" ends with Ghostface telling the female character, "I'm God Cipher

Divine [G.O.D. in the Supreme Alphabets], love my pussy real fine/that means clean the FDS smell with a shine/respect that, ho."[46]

A rejection of the attitudes in "Wildflower" can be found elsewhere in the Wu-Tang's body of work. "Wu Revolution" begins with Ol' Dirty Bastard decrying misogyny as part of the "mental death" from which the NGE offers resurrection:

> I'm callin' my black woman a bitch
> I'm callin' my people all kinds of things they are not
> I'm lost brother, can you help me?
> Can you help me brother, please?

Within the song, Papa Wu answers, "If you fake-ass niggas thinkin' you're gonna survive out here without your black woman, you're wrong."[47] Brand Nubian also offers atonement to the Earths, in "Sincerely" from the album *Foundation*:

> Now I'm the sun and I know
> you're my reflection
> let me give you love
> and my protection
> proper education
> Allah's correction
> eternalized within your eyes
> I hope you realize
> that I apologise for all the lies
> I never meant to make you cry
> all the mistakes that I may have made
> and games that I've played
> been put to an end
> black woman[48]

Earths are making their own expressions of the culture, in varying degrees of obeisance to the Gods' vox populi. Kalim has published letters from Earths complaining about their experiences in the NGE, such as Queen Be'Natural, whose God was "living out nothing that the Father put out there for him." An anonymous letter to the *Five Percenter* tells the Gods,

> The way you treat the Earths young and old has to improve. We are the mothers of your nation and the destruction of us will eventually lead to the destruction of yourselves.[49]

In March 2004, *Black 7* introduced *Black 17*, a special section of the magazine devoted completely to Earths. Like many traditional Muslim women living in western countries, *Black 17* writer Serenity Refine views the Earths' "three-fourths" dress code as a protection from unhealthy messages within the mainstream culture: "In this society we live in we are constantly bombarded with images of half naked females who leave nothing to the imagination but just endeavor to create the feeling of lust in their male counterparts." Serenity Refine complements her Refinement (5) with Knowledge (1) and Wisdom (2) to *born* Build or Destroy (8). "Build" means to add positivity; to "Destroy" is to rid the self of negative things, in this case "separating yourself from the 10% ideal of what true beauty is, having enough confidence in self and rebuild and construct a new positive representation of the Black Woman."[50] Supported by her self-image as the Earth, Serenity Refine condemns the negative treatment of women in songs like "Wildflower:" "I lost count of the amount of Original men that stepped to the mic talking about how they treat their B$%&hes and Hoes, degrading our Original women and smiling about it, with full respect from their peers!"[51] An alternative voice is found in Erykah Badu, whose ballad "Orange Moon" is laden with NGE imagery:

> his light was too bright
> so they turned away
> and he stood alone
> every night and every day
> then he turned to me
> he saw his reflection in me
> and he smiled at me
> I'm an orange moon
> I'm brighter than before
> brighter than ever before
> I'm an orange moon
> and I shine so bright
> 'cus I reflect the light
> of my sun[52]

While signing her *Earth's Equality* articles "In the Name of Born Everlasting Allah his reflection" and endorsing full NGE orthodoxy, Queen Sha-Asia Mecca's work lashes out against Five Percenter chauvinism. One issue mentions the inside joke, "too many wisdoms bring about a bad culture." Referring to the common portrayal of woman as Wisdom (2) to her man's Knowledge (1), it's a play on words and Supreme Mathematics—too (2) many wisdoms (2) bring about a bad culture (4). Queen Sha-Asia's response: "My culture is I SINCERELY LOVE ALLAH'S MATHEMATICS [I.S.L.A.M.]

and I don't see anything bad about that." In *Black 17*, Serenity Refine pleads that the oppression of black women began with the devil, but continues with God:

> Our women have been subject to both physical and mental abuse for CEN-TURIES by the Coloured man. Raped, Beaten and Disrespected, treated like a cheap belonging and still have to put up with and accept these twisted mental-ities now adopted, enforced and continued by Original men. These chains of deception need to be broken through your respect and love for her.[53]

Women are often spoken of as "Queens," a title that appeared in Five Percenter history sometime between "Nurses" and "Earths." A movement to call women "Goddesses" has taken root; some women even use the surname "Allat" in ref-erence to the fertility goddess of pre-Islamic Arabia. An online plus-lesson by Just I C Equality Allah argued that God was the black man, but because *man* could be defined as "a member of the species Homo Sapien, or all the members of the species collectively without regard to sex," black women were also Gods:

> How can woman not be God as well as man? First of all, we are the Arm Leg Leg Arm Head (Allah). There is no gender type, we all have the components that make the physical. Allah is the all in all. How can we be the all in all if "all" isn't included?[54]

Kalim published the article in the *Five Percenter*, with commentary: "This arti-cle is bullsh-t ... Adam was thrown out of the Garden of Eden for listening to his woman (Eve) instead of God." He then implicates the work's author among those who had been "sent" by unnamed enemies to "mix dilute and tamper with the teachings of Almighty God Allah. Their job is to get you to change your lessons & rob you of your blessings."[55]

Gods often attribute the Goddess idea to Dwight York's influence, break down the word condescendingly as "God in a Dress"[56] and insist that a woman who claims to be God has simply been brainwashed by the devil's culture. "It's natural in hell for the Black woman to want to be God," explains Almighty God Dawud Allah, "because hell is heaven turned upside down."[57] In the *Five Per-center*, Truth Shateek Allah compares the "Earth/Queen" to the "Goddess/So-Called 'Independent Woman:' " an Earth/Queen strives for balance and achieves "love, peace and happiness for her righteous endeavors" while a God-dess values her career over her children, complains about her problems and breaks up the black family through "tactics of division."[58]

There were self-labeled Goddesses in Allah's lifetime. The earliest Five Per-center to call herself "Goddess" may have been a Medina First Born's girlfriend who used the term as her righteous name. Added historical precedent is found with Tawanna, who at one point defected to Robert Walker's First Born Muslims and was renamed Allah's Most Precious Jewel.[59] Tawanna and C-Asia, the sixteen-year-old mother of three-year-old Vaconia, were placed in psych wards for telling police officers that they were God. Following her release in early 1969, male Five Percenters tried "bombing" Tawanna with the 120, but she maintained her position. They took her to see the Father, doubtful that she'd claim to be God in his presence. When Tawanna stood firm, Justice exclaimed, "she's more God than some of the men!" Allah answered, "she ain't God, she's a Goddess." Tawanna is believed to still be in the NGE, now using the righteous name Empress. C-Asia eventually gave up her own claim to be God. In 1970 she gave birth to a boy and named him Sun, and in 1971 or 1972 was beaten to death by her boyfriend.[60]

Goddess Earth Equality's "A Letter with Love to Allah," published in the Cuba-edited *Universal Truth*, reads as a Five Percenter call for gender justice. Introducing herself in the opening lines, the author demonstrates how knowledge of self uplifts her just as crucially as a man: "My westernized title is woman, female, girl, bitch and ho. My Original, Asiatic, Righteous name is Earth, Mother of Civilization, Queen, Allat..........Goddess!"[61]

Her letter then becomes a loving critique, firm in its resolve but gentle in its words. Goddess Earth Equality makes it clear that she treasures her identity as a Five Percenter, and holds equality as a core tenet of the culture. Bitterness between Gods and Goddesses stems from their centuries together under the devil's rule, but they now need to heal those wounds and come together as "one unit, one accord, one love:"

> I know this uncivilization has caused you to forget my greatness, my ability to lead Nations and love my BlackMan willingly and compliantly. We have battled and degraded each other for so many hundreds of years that our division has blurred us ... Now, we are of the 5% and our third eye is open. Just as you have mentally elevated, so have I ... Open your third eye and see me for who I truly am.

> You do not have to fear me, I am here to assist you in maintaining y(our) reign in our U-N-I-verse. I need you so desperately Allah. Please don't put limitations on me or feed them to my mental. I think I have proven myself worthy of running a cipher alone (without you) long enough. Of course it was not ran to perfection. The physical foundation was not present (you) but your Goddesses and seeds maintained. Thank you for returning to us.

> While standing back and admiring your Black beauty, I unfortunately heard you say mentally damaging things about me. They have confused me and hurt me deeply. I need to share them with you hoping we can come to a proper understanding ...

When I became a 5%er ... I thought finally, a place of security for me and our seeds, I had found my true family, my village to help raise our seeds and Asiatic Nation. You finally loved yourself enough to love me and our seeds equally; a place that was mine, no longer a second class citizen; a place where I could finally use my mind, my physical energy and emotional power, my intellectual strength to better our Original Nation together, side by side with my God—

Instead, I was smacked with some of the most chauvinistic, degrading statements ever thrown at me ... I never let anyone condition me in believing I was secondary for any reason or for anybody ... You are the highest masculine form of physical energy ... Why can't you see me, the highest feminine form of physical energy just as high? We are equal Allah. There has never been you without me ...

Our most powerful source of survival is My womb which I have decided to give to us. I choose with my mind to endure the physical burden and sacrifices it takes to bring our Gods & Goddesses into our U-N-I-verse. Once you have blessed me with the water of life, it is only by my choice to bless that seed with existence into our world. We used to rule countries together—why limit me to just bearing our fruit?[62]

After opening Gods' eyes to a crisis that has stagnated the culture, Equality promises, "If we are able to correct this problem, I can guarantee many Goddesses will come forth to the 5% and stand by your side." She concludes with a breakdown of *peace* as "Please Elevate Allah's Cherished Earths."[63] But the problem has not been corrected, and the Goddesses are not there. Parliaments in Harlem will always host a core of Earths and scattered girlfriends, but the culture's unapologetic phallocentrism alienates many women. "These folks have issues with females," states Prince A Cuba, "which is okay, personally, but they've institutionalized their bias."[64] Beloved Allah admits that not all Gods have the most enlightened view of women, as "everyone is limited by their own knowledge or lack of knowledge."[65] He agrees that the "Original Man" includes both male and female, while dismissing the question of "Goddesses vs. Earths" as semantics.[66]

"Can a house without a father have peace?" asked Divine Prince at a 2006 parliament in Harlem. After a tense pause he answered, "Yes, it can have peace." Divine Prince then stated that "Earth is God in the female form" because the letters in *Earth* break down mathematically to a numerical value of 7. When challenged by a God in the audience, Divine Prince replied that "if you're not there, she is truly qualified to do your job ... in a lot of respects, Earth is standing up and doing the job the man is supposed to do."[67] Earth-friendly attitudes can also be found in a 1993 issue of the *Sun of Man*:

ALLAH gave not only the Sun the freedom to choose. He also gave the freedom of choice to the sisters. At that day and time the very same brothers who profess to be so civilized could not handle that freedom of choice ... the sisters have the right to choose their life styles, and the attire that they wear. They should not be dictated to for the choice is up to them solely. If you the GOD'S are secure in yourself then the EARTH'S share that same security.[68]

Five Percenters' emphasis on reproduction and adherence to "natural" gender roles leads to a predictable condemnation of homosexuality. In his online blog, Sha-King Cehum Allah expresses the Gods' standard position: "Homosexuality is devilishment and all that is produced is, not children, not growth and development, but DEVIL." To Sha-King, gays and lesbians are the "dissatisfied" members of society, who decide to cut themselves off from the mainstream (much as the rebels who followed Yacub into exile). As a result of their isolation at Pelan, he warns, "the Devil was made and then travelled back to civilization to destroy it."[69] The Father taught that "homosexuality brings destruction to a what? A nation!"[70] In the October/November 1987 issue of the WORD, Salhudeen A. Raheem, an inmate at Green Haven, suggested segregation of homosexual and drug-using prisoners to prevent the spread of AIDS. Raheem also saw a need to "redefine homosexuality in prison to let the ignorant know that both the giver and the receiver, the rider and the rode are BOTH HOMOSEXUAL."[71] In 2005 Louis Farrakhan held a historic meeting with gay and lesbian leaders. While asking, "what happened to the old quote, 'there are no punks and faggots in the Nation of Islam?' " Kalim also considers that divisiveness on the issue could get in the way of black unity and concedes that there were most likely gay men at the first Million Man March.[72] Ted Swedenburg remarks that homophobic lyrics appear in Five Percenter rap on a scale comparable to the genre as a whole, but also mentions that members of the Wu-Tang Clan have appeared at numerous AIDS benefits, some sponsored by gay organizations.[73] Brand Nubian courted controversy for homophobic content, but Lord Jamar has stated that while the NGE emphatically disapproves of homosexuality, Gods and Earths treat everyone in a respectful manner.[74]

Five Percenters were confronted with the issue in their own cipher during the summer of 2004, when a youth discovered two Gods kissing in the restroom during a Brooklyn parliament. In a letter to the Five Percenter, Justice Born Allah calls for the guilty parties to be exiled and suggests that the Father would be rolling over in his grave.[75] To Justice Born, the presence of gay men was comparable to various conspiracies designed to weaken the Nation of Gods and Earths:

I READ HOW THEY SENT WISDOMS [women] WITH AIDS IN THE GOD CIPHER. I READ HOW THEY SENT INFORMANTS IN THE GOD CIPHER.

I READ HOW THEY SENT CRAZY DRUGS IN THE GOD CIPHER, SPIES
AND SO ON AND THE GODS RAN ALL OF THAT POISON FROM
AMONG THE RIGHTEOUS. BUT YOU (WE) ARE HAVING PROBLEMS
WITH FAGGOTS?[76]

Kalim believes that "the powers that be purposely put homosexuals in our
parliament space," as part of a plan to create "dynamic static" within the
community.[77]

In 1970, Huey Newton wrote in the Black Panthers' newspaper that African-
Americans should view the oppression of gays and lesbians as parallel to their
own, suggesting that "maybe a homosexual could be the most revolutionary."
He rejects the notion that modern homosexuality stems from "the decadence
of capitalism ... I rather doubt it."[78] To Newton, threads of homophobia and
misogyny run through black nationalism as a result of America's psychological castration of African-American males:

> Sometimes our first instinct is to want to hit a homosexual in the mouth and want
> a woman to be quiet. We want to hit the homosexual ... because we're afraid we
> might be homosexual; and we want to hit the woman or shut her up because
> we're afraid she might ... take the nuts that we might not have to start with.[79]

The deification of manhood provides healing for some, validation for others.
Almighty God Dawud Allah equates an Earth's refusal to submit to her God
with her "looking down on the Black man."[80]

It doesn't help that so much of NGE culture evolved among men in prison, a
society completely devoid of women. It's in prison, as Malcolm X's grandson told
me, that boys are beaten into men and men are beaten into boys. A young black
man emasculated by racist cops, judges and jail might find his nuts by becoming
God, but it can be a defensive position. Five Percenter manhood remains a prison
manhood, in which masculinity must be established and reinforced at every turn.
It is not enough to call yourself King or Supreme; you must show and prove.

The central and most prized belief of the Five Percenters—that the Original
Asiatic Black Man is creator and sustainer of the universe—makes it easy to
assume that Gods are preoccupied only with race, and define themselves
through opposition to Yacub's grafted devil. However, the white man receives
nothing near the barrage of spiteful plus-lessons directed at the Gods' true
Other, the black woman. The Born Lesson "Allah 360 Degrees" describes Caucasians and the black woman as allied against the Gods;[81] "Allah's World Manifest" calls the black woman "only a trick used against us while Lost and
Found."[82] Plus-degrees from the 1980s describe the female anatomy as an
"open sore" and advise that a man should not have sex with the same woman

more than once every twenty-eight days;[83] one text names Hatred, Envy, Lust, and Greed as the "4 Devilish Mindstates of the Black Woman." I have even heard of some Gods teaching that woman herself is devil, which may not seem so different from the uglier strains of major world religions.

As the Nation of Gods and Earths adapts to its growing diversity, some lessons will be discarded and others will find new meanings. Within *al-Islam*, self-empowered women have been the major impetus to a "Progressive Muslim" movement, reading feminism into the same Qur'an used by traditional scholars in Saudi madrassas. In the United States, female imams have already led mixed congregations of men and women—a drastic innovation to most Muslims. The movement finds historical support in the case of a woman named Um Waraqa, who had been authorized by Muhammad to lead her entire household, including men outside her family, in prayer.

Western feminism has been criticized for ignoring the concerns of women of color. The right to work outside the home was a rallying cause for white women in middle-class marriages; black women had already been supporting their families for decades of unemployment, underemployment, broken homes, and imprisoned black men. An NGE alternative to feminism may be offered in Afrocentric "womanism," which could empower women without breaking the God-Earth solidarity needed to overcome the devil's rule. Womanism already has advocates in the Five Percent, and according to Patricia Hill Collins offers a "way for black women to address gender-oppression without attacking black men."[84] This approach can be found in Erykah Badu's lyrics for "One," her duet with Busta Rhymes:

> ask my son right, he bears witness to you
> being the foundation you can come home
> and watch the babies too
> the one way we agree on how to follow tradition
> this one family coming first
> play your position
> you make the sacrifices, I make the same too
> the mother struggle
> that I see, that's why my love is for you
> you always hold it down for me, so I'm a hold it for you
> and watch the babies while you secure the food that comes through
> now don't let my ambition make you feel like competition
> we should both play a role in our whole living condition
> true indeed
> I know you symbolise the strength inside the family
> then show me you can handle womanly responsibilities[85]

Busta Rhymes' line, "one understanding amongst me and my woman so that we can't fall," carries a possible double meaning. There is the literal understanding shared by a man and woman, but also the added responsibility of family when one reads it with Mathematics:

1 Knowledge (the black man)
2 Wisdom (the black woman)
3 Understanding (the black child)

"And keep moving forward based on Actual Facts," he adds. "Yes y'all my beautiful Mother Earth, respect her to the max."[86]

Even Progressive Muslim feminists in the United States are perceived as failing to include African-Americans, who comprise the largest segment of America's Muslim population. Interestingly, the first woman to head a mosque in North America was not a self-termed "Progressive" but Sister Minister Ava Muhammad, national spokesperson for the Honorable Minister Louis Farrakhan. The Sister Minister's womanist readings of 120 are embraced by both NOI and NGE circles. In Judeo-Christian tradition, she reminds us, the first woman was created from the first man's rib; but in NOI/NGE tradition, woman springs forth from man's brain.[87]

Debate over the nature and proper status of the black woman will not end anytime soon. The NGE's lack of leadership allows its teachings to remain fluid, capable of change between individual speakers at a parliament. The validity of a builder's interpretation is essentially up to the audience, and every generation has the power to shape its values. There is still time for women to have a hand in the NGE's development and claim the best parts of their tradition while leaving the worst parts behind.

16

The Azreal Question

The white race knows God. But they can't represent God as you and me.

Elijah Muhammad

Very few Whites, if any, ever give Elijah Muhammad credit for providing them with a psychoanalysis of themselves.

Dorothy Blake Fardan

Being Azreal is a lonely thing.

Azreal

Kendu Islam, the latin God who pulled the lever to cremate the Father, was said to have journeyed to Puerto Rico to teach Allah's Mathematics and a Spanish version of the Supreme Alphabets. Puerto Rican Gods are often called "Power Rules." One of the earliest Power Rules, Sha Sha was assigned the task of teaching North America's "2 million Indians." In a *Five Percenter* piece entitled, "The Incomplete Misunderstanding of the Understanding Seed," Sunez Allah writes of the difficulty faced by Latinos in coming to the knowledge: "I needed to understand that I was the Asiatic Blackman, in all its infinite reality, to even fathom that the Blackman is God." He credits First Born Prince's constant referral to him as "Blackman" as helping him grasp his true identity.[1] Prince spoke from his own experience as a light-skinned God, encountering challenges of "who's more original." Some Five Percenters in the early days mocked him, calling him the closest thing to a devil; in one incident he was pushed down a flight of stairs.[2]

The Fard history holds that Yacub's grafting process resulted in brown and yellow races, but did not create a devil until its final stage. Therefore, anyone but the fourth human family (the "Culture Seed"), i.e. the Caucasian, can be considered Original. Bengali-American Sujan Kumar Dass came to the knowledge at the age of fifteen in Jersey City and changed his name to Supreme Understanding Allah.[3] I have also heard of Chinese, Filipino and Arab Five Percenters, all recognized as Original people, Gods and Earths.

Felicia Miyakawa, the Caucasian author of *Five Percenter Rap*, conducted her research without any substantial interaction with the Gods and Earths. She excuses her lack of field experience with the assumption that a Five Percenter's attitude on race is completely identical to that of a NOI Muslim: "the Nation of Islam and the Five Percent Nation both essentially exclude whites from participating."[4] The truth is far more complicated. For many in the NGE, the white man is not a big Devil as Elijah Muhammad had made him, but rather a little devil, more like God's errant child. Allah B says that while Five Percenters accept the white man's history as taught in the 120, "we don't hold that against him."

Even before the Father claimed to be "neither pro-black, nor anti-white," remembers Allah B, "he demonstrated it."[5] Contrary to Miyakawa's assumption, whites are welcome to the cipher; I have even been greeted at parliaments with "peace, blackman." At one Harlem parliament, a latin God approached me and asked if I believed that a white Five Percenter could "perform the same tasks" as a black God. I wasn't sure what he meant. "You and I are about the same complexion," he said; "what's the difference?"

It was through Intelligent Tarref Allah that I first learned of John "Azreal" Kennedy, the Father's white student from Matteawan State Hospital for the Criminally Insane. Ron Casanova writes in *Each One Teach One*, "the officers who were killing people in Matteawan were all white,"[6] and Azreal believes that most guards were members of the American Nazi Party and Ku Klux Klan. In 1970, only 14 of Matteawan's 335 guards were African-American or Latino;[7] it seems unlikely that there would have been more black guards five years earlier. Barry Gottehrer describes Matteawan as "pure hell."[8] Allah would have been justified to leave the asylum with a raging hatred of Caucasians; but trapped in this brutal, state-sanctioned racism and the meanest snakepit offered by New York State, he took the time to reform one of Yacub's seeds. In a departure from Elijah Muhammad, who wrote that white Muslims "know righteousness, but they cannot be righteous,"[9] Allah greeted a young John Kennedy with the words, "you are a righteous man."

As the Father's "death-angel," Azreal enjoys a legendary status. Beloved Allah first heard of Azreal in 1975 while visiting Allah B in prison. Looking through the window at the visiting room, Beloved noticed a white man running back and forth with a group of smiling children. Allah B told Beloved that the man was named Robert Kennedy, and had a brother named John to whom the Father had taught the "science of how to become President of the United States by age 42."[10] Beloved Allah met John four years later. On December 1, 1979, Beloved was knocking on the front door of the Allah School when out came Azreal to introduce himself with a rambling but rehearsed summary of his time with the Father and special role among the Gods. I have heard the same ramble, or at least a version of it; someone like Azreal has to explain himself often.

There were other white Five Percenters in the early days. In 1967 Allah B gave the lessons to a white friend in the Bronx, who then took the righteous name Barkim and taught his younger siblings. "I taught him that he was the Original Man," says Allah B, who concedes that the Father may have "refined and crystallized" that understanding. Allah B remembers Barkim as "a strong young man ... who withstood all prejudices that may have come to him in his position."[11] The Father treated Barkim with "love and admiration." To ensure that Barkim would receive the same from Five Percenters, the Father sent his "Supreme Investigator" Ra'jab to discuss the issue at a parliament in the Bronx.[12]

In the 1960s, jazz became a bridge for Noble Drew Ali's Moorish Science doctrines to reach white hipsters at NYU and Columbia, who then formed their own "Moorish Orthodox Church." In the 1990s, rap music enabled Five Percenters to reach, in the words of the 120, "all human families." Thomas Cowles, a white youth whose parents had him committed to Hampton Behavioral Hospital in the early 1990s at age thirteen, was placed in the same unit as a Five Percenter named Dwight. When he heard Dwight and another God discussing Brand Nubian, Thomas chimed in that the group was better before Grand Puba left. Impressed, Dwight began teaching Thomas literal mathematics, such as "tricks for multiplying and dividing huge numbers and fractions"[13] and later gave him the Supreme Wisdom Lessons. Cowles learned his 120 and began calling himself "Tommy Mathematics." As a young devil who found God in a mental institution, his life mirrors that of Azreal.

According to Intelligent Tarref Allah, Azreal and other whites with the knowledge (commonly referred to as "Muslim Sons and Daughters") were not Five Percenters per se, but did have the Five Percenters' respect. Njeri Earth, a D-Mecca (Detroit) emcee who wore a headwrap and NGE pin during her appearance in the film 8 Mile, told me that Azreal was in fact a Five Percenter because "he believes in it and really lives for it, and no one can deny him." And of course, the Father himself said that anyone could be a Five Percenter if he or she was civilized. Regardless, Intelligent Tarref Allah made it clear during our correspondence; white people were devils, and that included me. So I had to ask him: was there anything that I could gain from this knowledge? What if a devil understood the truth of his or her nature, and hoped for redemption?

In 1975, Wallace D. Muhammad's newly integrated Nation of Islam managed to attract one white convert, Dorothy Dorsey at Harlem's Mosque No.7. Dorsey had first encountered NOI teachings at the start of the decade and soon after found her own "knowledge of self:"

MESSAGE TO THE BLACKMAN IN AMERICA (by the Honorable Elijah Muhammad) was a message to me, a Caucasian woman. It opened up the long lost tunnel of origins that I had failed to penetrate in all my efforts to see the past. It confirmed my estrangement from America, and it sketched out a future in which I could hope to carve out some place within, despite my less than noble white legacy. That others thought my attachment to these teachings a bit abnormal if not insane, didn't really bother me, because I felt that nearness of truth in them, and for once in my then thirty years sojourn on this earth, I felt someone had reached into some absolute bottom that lay beneath the facade and fantasy of the white world I was struggling to get out of.[14]

Understanding that Elijah Muhammad's Nation did not permit white members, she had visited a Sunni mosque but was turned off by their "signs of westernization"[15] and disrespectful attitude toward the NOI. When Wallace D. Muhammad opened the Nation's door to all races, she quickly joined, but was soon disappointed by this reborn community and its new teachings. Wallace not only turned the flock toward orthodox Islam but also watered down the political implications of his father's message, such as the association of the American flag with "Slavery, Suffering and Death." The changing message only alienated Dorothy:

> when the Nation of Islam was later transformed to the American Muslim Mission, its direction seemed to be more ameliorative towards the United States. The American flag appeared in the mosque and on the paper (which had undergone numerous name changes). I grew uncomfortable in an atmosphere I considered to be more collaborative than revolutionary, and withdrew from active participation.[16]

As Dorothy Blake Fardan, she authored *Yakub and the Origins of White Supremacy: Message to the Whiteman & Woman in America*. Interpreting Elijah Muhammad's religious history through a very real history of race in America, she presents the Nation of Islam's doctrine as a means for whites to undo their own racial baggage. "Not every Caucasian male," she writes, "need be a 'white man.'"[17]

I first met Azreal at the Allah School on the weekend of 2004's Show and Prove. He agreed to teach me, provided I pay for some *equality*, so I gave him ten dollars and we walked to Malcolm X Boulevard. After he got it, I followed him to a bench outside the St. Nicholas projects. While rolling his paper Azreal told me that Allah had taught him how to smoke. We quickly developed a bond; he seemed excited to find another white guy that was interested in the lessons. He told me that my first name was his middle name and called me his "Caucasian angel." While I built with various Gods at the Show and Prove,

Azreal would dart back and forth between circles, building with everyone. Sometimes he'd find me to ask for a dollar for beer, call me his Caucasian angel again and then disappear into the crowd. Everyone there knew Azreal; even outside New York, it's hard to come across a Five Percenter that hasn't heard of him. Gods and Earths that have built with him personally often smile at his mention. They give Azreal a certain tenderness, knowing that the Father had loved him and in fact saved his life. Gods and Earths often help Azreal with food, clothing and shelter.

Azreal has a unique place in the Nation (a "special responsibility," remarked I Majestic Allah, "that many of us don't have"). The Father had given him the keys to heaven and hell; Azreal could come and go as he pleased, perhaps moving in and out of whiteness. For teaching that the black man is God, Azreal has alienated himself from family members and even experienced physical aggression from whites.

Other Muslim Sons included a blond-haired child whose father ("a light-skinned man of understanding") had named him W. D. Fard. C'BS ALife Allah told me of Robert, whose parents were anthropologists and had raised him in Africa. Shortly after coming to America, Robert was named a Muslim Son by one of Farrakhan's sons. C'BS ALife also knew a white man and black woman in Savannah, GA who married and had a son before they both arrived at the knowledge and joined the NGE. A Muslim Son named Kevan changed his name to Justice, acknowledged that humankind originated in Africa and maintained a Geocities webpage to "civilize the uncivilized." "The UNIverse is out of order," he wrote; "we see this but don't know what is wrong." His guestbook included words of encouragement from various Gods and Earths, as well as a white female who hoped to find knowledge of self.

Jason Jarmacz, a white Five Percenter incarcerated in Norfolk, Massachusetts, understood himself to be a devil by nature, but righteous by intention:

> I, self, am the devil, but in the same I refuse to allow my fate to become that of my people. I know and understand that the devils were grafted by Yukub from the Original Asiatic Blackman. So I also know and understand that it is my ability and my destiny to elevate towards righteousness. Knowing that the word Caucasian derives from Caucasoid (Yakub's people, banished to the Caucasus mountains 6000 years ago) and Asian, or Asiatic (the yellow seed) I see a place for myself in this glorious nation. I can trace my lineage back to Africa, along with all blackmen. Though the nature of my race is devilishment, I choose a different path.[18]

The *Black7* e-zine published an interview with a white youth named Justin, whose father had once written Elijah Muhammad with hopes of joining the Nation of Islam. Elijah denied the man but provided instructions for how he could behave among his own people. At twenty-six Justin began studying with the Gods, receiving his Math and 120 from C'BS ALife Allah. Justin took the righteous name Gadreel, which represented the serpent that led Eve astray and literally meant "God is my helper." While also viewing himself as a helper to God, Gadreel "knew the ledge" and understood his limitations:

> as a Colored man, my place in the Universe is not to Civilize God. I can lead him to another God with Knowledge of Self who can enlighten him, but I am in no place to Civilize God.[19]

In 2002 an anonymous internet persona known only as "Yacuwb" attempted to lead "Caucasian Muslim Sons" as an organized movement. Lord Adeeb Shabazz Allah attributed the rise of Muslim Sons to a growing white interest in hip-hop culture and stated that while Gods and Earths will welcome anyone to their knowledge, the Nation has never advocated separate cliques or racially divided factions.[20]

During the 2004 Show and Prove, I asked Azreal the obligatory question of whether he actually believed that he was the devil. His reply would not only challenge my understanding of the Five Percent, but shake many Five Percenters' understanding of Azreal: "you know, I can say that I'm Allah because I wasn't taught by a man or prophet or anything. I'm First Born; the Father was right there in front of me. We can all be angels, you know, but I believe we can be more."

After my article on Azreal ran at *MuslimWakeUp*, an online magazine, and was later reprinted in the *Five Percenter* newspaper, I received several comments from Five Percenters requesting specific confirmation of Azreal's claim to be God. I was even accused of either mishearing the quotes or completely manufacturing them. Apparently, the piece contradicted Azreal's previous explanations of his status in the Nation, even to white Five Percenters such as Gadreel. When asked whether he was Allah, Azreal was known to have replied, "I *met* God, how can I *be* God?"

"Fuck Azreal!" Abu Shahid snapped at me before a parliament in Power Born (Pittsburgh). "The white man can't be God! He's not no one to get any recognition for nothin! The white man is the devil, fuck him! The Father named him Azreal after the angel of death—that punk ain't kill nothin' but time! Check his history out!"

"He was with the Father in Matteawan," I answered.

"They pulled him buck-naked out of a tree across from the school, did he tell you that?"

I later watched a VHS tape of Abu Shahid addressing the matter at a Universal Parliament in Harlem. It was October 2004, the fortieth anniversary of Allah making his Knowledge Born, and the various older Gods were standing in front of the Harriet Tubman Center's stage to tell their stories and answer questions. Despite being the only Five Percenter qualified to speak on the Father's time in Matteawan, Azreal was not included. Azreal, according to Prince A Cuba, "has been largely pushed aside because he has a more authentic history with Allah than most of the pretenders."[21]

"You got agents provocateur running around up in here," declared Abu Shahid. "They come amongst us ... but they are not of us ... THE WHITE MAN IS NOT GOD!"[22] As Shahid made his announcement, the cameraman showed Azreal sitting in the audience, wearing a black and gold skullcap, lone devil in a sea of Gods. In a later issue of the *Five Percenter*, God Kalim salutes Shahid "for clearing up that white man is God bullshit."[23] This may appear to betray the statement of being neither pro-black nor anti-white, but Kalim nonetheless discourages prejudice against individual members of any race:

> It is not the skin color that makes a person good or bad! Have you ever seen a good whiteman or a bad blackman? Have you ever seen a good devil or a bad God? To say that all whites are bad and all blacks are good (on this planet) is bullshit! Because when you find one good white or one bad black, the premise that all whites are bad and all blacks are good = invalid.[24]

Heresy-friendly Muslims (myself included) have attempted to categorize the Nation of Gods and Earths as some sort of indigenous African-American Sufism. It is easy to imagine parallels with medieval saints such as Ibn al-Arabi, who saw man as reflecting the divine, or al-Hallaj, who famously called himself by one of Allah's 99 Names (*al-Haqq*, "the Truth"). While not always off the mark, it's a naïve assumption that Five Percenters approach "God" with mysticism. Sufi themes of divine union or Manifesting God's Attributes represent a closeness to the *mystery god* whose existence is denied in the 120. Though building on a unique cosmology and legendary characters, Allah positioned himself as anti-religion. Known as a "High Scientist" during his time in the mosque, he later discouraged high science in favor of "city science." Many Gods take a practical look at their divinity; the word *God* to both Fard and the Father, in I Majestic's interpretation, "has no religious context here, it's not about claiming to be an astral being."[25] The Five Percenters would respond to anarchism's ethos of "no gods, no masters" with *I God, I Master*. For a black man to call himself God means that he will take responsibility, as the Father of Civilization, to lift himself up in the here and now—as opposed to waiting for a *mystery* to solve his problems or reward him in the afterlife. The black man is God of the universe, but an episode of NGE comic strip *Akee, Wise & Essence* explains that "a God's universe is his family."[26] Some allow that Azreal could be God in his own universe, but cannot approach the African-American community as God in that specific sense of the term.

For those that view man's divine nature with a Sufi sensibility, however, the death-angel's claim to be God set an important precedent. "I'm glad that Azreal said that," said Malaki, a white rapper in Detroit; "Clarence 13X said a lot of things about us all being God." Malaki had a background with both Five Percenter and Nuwaubian texts. He believed in there being only one source of energy and consciousness in the universe, with that singular source uniting the whole of humanity. And even if he was grafted from the Original Man, he insisted that he was at least made in the Originals' image. Malaki understood the paradox and predicament of being a white Five Percenter, having stumbled into knowledge that was not meant for him. "I wasn't supposed to be given anything," he said. He likened his catch-22 to that faced by Satan in the Qur'an, when Allah told the angels to bow to Adam: does he revere something other than Allah, or disobey Allah's command? For Malaki, whiteness was a cultural construct that could be undone by proper living: "I can't change my lineage, but I can change my actions. Once you're accepted as an Asiatic person, you're not what you were before."

In his early theological gymnastics, Warith Deen Mohammed preached of *devilishment* as the condition of having a "grafted mind," the inherited mentality of white privilege. He gleaned his perspective largely from Malcolm X, who found brotherhood with Caucasians in Mecca because Islam "removed the 'white' from their *minds*, the 'white' from their *behavior*, and the 'white' from their *attitude*."[27] Louis Farrakhan has offered a similar perspective while still adhering to the Supreme Wisdom Lessons. "It is not the color of the white man that is the problem," Farrakhan stated in a lecture; "it is the mind of the white man that is the problem. The mind of white supremacy has to be destroyed."[28] By 1974 the white man's inescapable wickedness had become a complicated matter even for the Honorable Elijah Muhammad, who seemed to echo the Father during his final Savior's Day address:

> Chicago white people are to be thanked for making it possible for us to obtain the Country Club and to get us to such a position where we can prove ourselves worthy. You do not disrespect people that are trying to respect you. Honor and respect the white man while his flag still flies over America ... It's time for us to stop calling white folks the devil because there's some black devils too ... Give justice to him when it is due.[29]

A C-Medina (Chicago) God named Jura Shaheed Allah told me that he'd never call a white man the devil, as that potential existed in all of humanity. In "Koto

Chotan" the RZA states that "every devil ain't pale;"[30] the concept is also articulated by KRS-One, who is not a Five Percenter, in "Build and Destroy:"

> let's build
> it ain't enough to study Clarence 13X
> the white man ain't the devil I promise
> you want to see the devil, take a look at Clarence Thomas
> now you're saying, who? like you a owl
> throw in the towel, the devil is Colin Powell[31]

For many Five Percenters, the Original (black) Man could be the devil or God,
while the Colored (white) Man could be the devil or *righteous*. The only thing
that kept the white man from being God, according to Jura Shaheed, was that
he did not create the black man; the black man had created him. Prince A Cuba
criticizes what he calls the "Baby Yacub Devil Worship Cult" of Five Percenters
"dedicated to making the Black Man a devil, and to absolve and protect the
so-called white man from his devil status."[32] Some Caucasians come to the
Nation of Gods and Earths with an interest in the philosophy, but leave when
they're unable to find a role for themselves. C'BS ALife informed me that
Gadreel has since parted ways with the NGE on terms of mutual respect.

John Walker Lindh, the famous "American Taliban" who was captured by
U.S. forces in Afghanistan in late 2001, discovered the Five Percenters as a
teenager through his interests in hip-hop and Malcolm X. An aspiring rapper,
young Lindh would post his lyrics online, at one point condemning Masta Ace
for writing "simple rhymes ... crafted to make money for the grafted."[33] One of
Lindh's posts received encouragement from Jahzid Allah, webmaster of the
"5% Network" website: "You bad, You bad! Go 'head, Go 'head!"[34] Lindh
briefly corresponded with Gods online[35] and even pretended to be black in
Usenet newsgroups, lecturing African-Americans on use of the word "nigger"
("It has, for hundreds of years been a label put on us by Caucasians") and
announcing, "I abolish the stereotypes they've brought upon us ... word is
bond." He later resolved his white-boy angst through Sunni Islam and sold off
his massive collection of CDs. His final post at rec.music.hip-hop came in
response to Earth Divine Wisdom, who wrote that "Nas acknowledges himself
as a true and living God, the only God there is, and doesn't fall prey to
spookisms." Lindh offered a standard Sunni objection:

> Dear Ma'am,
>
> Is Nas indeed a "god"? If this is so, then why is he susceptable to sin and wrong-
> doing? Why does he smoke blunts, drink moet, fornicate, and make dukey
> music? Why is it if he is a "god" that one day he will die? That's a rather pathetic
> "god" if you ask me.

If something by your logic does not exist unless you can see it, why do you, the members of the 5% Nation, live a life of "pursuing happiness"? I have never seen happiness myself. Perhaps you can enlighten me as to what it looks like and where I can go to sneek a peek at it.

Air cannot be looked upon by the human eye. Neither can God. Yet without either of these things humans could not exist. Perhaps one day the members of the 5% will wake up and see who is in fact the slave and who is indeed the Master.

Salaam[36]

I Majestic Allah told me that being white and Five Percent is a hard fit: a Muslim Son either hates himself for being white and wants to repent for his ancestors' crimes, or he wants to be God himself, "and neither is accurate." Azreal, watching the news in Matteawan's Rec Room to see civil-rights protesters getting attacked with fire hoses and police dogs, turned in tears to Allah and cried, "I'm so ashamed of what my people are doing to your people, I'm so ashamed to be white." The Father reassured Azreal by saying that he could not be blamed for the skin in which he had been born.

The Five Percenters' preoccupations with race and gender intersect at the white woman, considered one of the devil's more dangerous weapons against God. Despite the Father having reportedly forbidden his Suns from pursuing white women, some "Muslim Daughters" encounter the knowledge through dating Five Percenters. A handful of Gods are even rumored to have taught their white girlfriends that the Caucasian woman was Earth, portraying this knowledge as a "secret taught in the holy city of Medina."

"Destiny," a Muslim Daughter of Sicilian heritage, decided that she had Moorish blood and was therefore "half-original" (a designation given to Genoa-born Christopher Columbus in the lessons). In December 2003, she described her struggles with identity and acceptance online via the Milwaukee Five Percenters' message board:

i feel alone in the world. trapped by reality of two possibilities. being a sicilian/italian female. society sees me as white, after doing the knowledge to the phenomenon of Italians, i see that they are of mixed blood. that might explain my features looking the way they do ... i remember just last week sitting at the parliment and listening to the gods build. and one of them talking about how "white woman" should be left alone. and i thought to myself, ok, thats peace. still be knownst to me, that alot of my peers, in this nation are not sure what i am. and the fact of the matter is i get asked alot of times, what i am. and it drives me crazy. even after i have sat in equality and builded with them. and i think to myself, what now u wont like me no more? when i tell them what my so-called heratage is ... do i sit quietly and let others think what they will of me or do i wear a sign that says. "I am Yacobs Daughter. Beware!!"?? laugh if u want. ive seen how the gods and earths treat colored men such as the famous "azreal". who i see as someone with a good heart, born you truth [but], no direction. no desire to be civilized as such. seems like he was drawn up by the father as an example of "equality". Equality being the number of the devil, the one that he/ the devil can never get passed. 600 years to make devil, 6,000 years of reign, 6 ounces of brain, water never being drawn above 6 miles from the earths surface by the sun and moon. I however want this more than anything in the world, i see this as the last house on the block for me, since psyciatry, medication, being prayed over, holy water thrown on, DID NOT worked for me. i lost faith in the 85ers mystery god a long time ago. How do I believe in something that allows cruelty? poverty? ect- ... and in my own life, pain misery and suffering. I want to be a mother to my children, i have Equality [6] seeds, Power [5] of which are from a black man. The one child that is not from a black man, has been tampered with to the point i can not help her, only she when she is of age can have the pins that were put in her brain pulled out. I have many pins myself in my brain, from mis information. I have the willing-ness which is most important. I take this very seriously. so now what? my destiny lies in 2 roads, the road paved with good intentions, and the road of freedom justice and equality which belongs to the 5 percent, the poor righteous teacher.[37]

As in the case of John Walker Lindh, Caucasians often move from the Five Percent to a Malcolm-inspired Sunni Islam, with a vision of racial brotherhood based on his pilgrimage to Mecca. Fardan, however, believes that white people have failed to take a serious look at Malcolm's letter from Jeddah: "Instead, most interpreted his words as 'vindicating' Whites from all that Elijah Muhammad had taught about them. They therefore failed to explore in any meaningful way why white people in Mecca seemed different to him, nor did it lead them to question in any deep way the psychological malaise of white supremacy."[38] Likewise, Sunni Muslim narratives tend to deemphasize Malcolm's observations on race, simplifying his *hajj* as orthodoxy's triumph over a "distorted" version of Islam.

It seems that before his assassination, Allah was creating increased space for the Azreals, Barkims and Barry Gottehrers—not through *al-Islam*, but an allowance that perhaps a white man could slay his own internal devils. Declaring that Five Percenters must "rewrite the lessons,"[39] the Father removed the word "skunk" from the 120's description of Caucasians. And it says a great deal that Allah—who disapproved of birth control because he hoped to fill the earth with black babies—would try to set up his daughter with a white Gottehrer. Allah might have seen himself as fulfilling the 120's prophecy; in the last year of his life, he told his Suns that "the so-called devil was removed from our planet, because God and the Devil walk hand in hand."[40]

17

The Road to Cream City

We will no longer allow others issues concerning the colored man's humanity to be settled on our best part. We will continue transcending all barriers; and all those who can't transcend to the Supreme perspective of understanding will continue to be in that Six (Black vs. White). It is our duty as poor righteous teachers to teach freedom, justice, and equality to all human families ... the time is now for our nation to end the separation within. All those who separate will eventually graft themselves from the root and the nation as a whole creating a real devil.

Universal Knowledge Allah[1]

Milwaukee's history with black Gods goes back almost as far as Detroit and Chicago. W. D. Fard and Elijah Muhammad visited in 1934 and established the Nation of Islam's Temple No.3. Facing power struggles after Fard's disappearance, Elijah sought refuge in Milwaukee for two weeks, leaving after the appointment of Sultan Muhammad as temple minister.

Following Elijah's death in 1975, the Milwaukee mosque was claimed by Warith Deen Mohammed and subjected to his sweeping reforms. As part of Warith Deen's nationwide movement toward Sunnism, the mosque's Minister Henry X was replaced by Mustafa Ali. In 1987, Louis Farrakhan's revived NOI established its own Muhammad Mosque #3 in Milwaukee.

The Nation of Gods and Earths first appeared in Milwaukee in the late 1980s or early 1990s. Alternate lineages name Allah Sun Truth and God King Allah as the first to bring the knowledge. Milwaukee's righteous name, Cream City, was actually a longstanding nickname due to the cream-colored bricks in the city's older buildings.

Cream City has its own Street Academy, headed by C Latiff Allah, who's not only a Brooklyn seed going back to December 1964 but also the cousin of Universal Shaamgaudd Allah. As Shaamgaudd claimed to have been taught a non-racial concept of devilishment by the Father, C Latiff has gone so far as to assert that white men could be Gods. His heresy has caused a split of the Cream City cipher into rival factions, each with its own 120 class. The Street Academy's opponents, led by Self Kingdom Allah, hold their 120 classes at a local college and offer a disclaimer on the Five Percent Network website: "we only teach that the Original man is God and that the White man is not God but he is Devil." Self Kingdom Allah, Supreme Life Allah and C-Power Allah issued statements in Kalim's paper to defend Milwaukee's reputation. "Cream City should not be confused with the individuals in the Street Academy," writes C-Power. "Instead of being discouraged by the falsehood," Supreme Life comments, he and other Gods "continued to make knowledge born the right & exact way the Father taught it." Self Kingdom calls C Latiff the "black John Kerry" because "one minute he says the white man is God then he say the white man is the devil. He's a flip flopper."[2]

Before heading out to Milwaukee, I made an unrelated call to the Allah School in Mecca and ended up on the phone with Azreal. It had been almost a year since we last spoke at the Show and Prove, and he seemed to have disappeared after the release of my article; he had given me a phone number, but it was disconnected shortly thereafter. Azreal, as I've come to appreciate, is just one of those guys that come and go and during times that he's gone, you'll never really know if he's gone for good.

He told me that he was now living in a van behind the Allah School and doing well, but felt a need to get out of the city for a while. I told him that I was going to Milwaukee and he said he'd come along. I suggested that on the way back, we drive to Fishkill Correctional and visit a God there. Azreal agreed. Fishkill stood on the former grounds of Matteawan State Hospital for the Criminally Insane.

Later that week I headed down to the Allah School and learned from the Gods that Azreal had been taken away the night before in an ambulance. The Gods believed it was a stroke but they weren't sure. I walked to Harlem Hospital but he wasn't there; after a few calls I learned that he had been discharged that day from North General. Walking back to the Allah School, I found him joking around with an Earth.

The veins bulge out of his forearms. He's got a wiry strength to him, physically fit in an Iggy Pop way, nothing but muscle and bone and he's covered with scars, most notably the long line of staples up his right calf from kicking through that window at Matteawan.

It wasn't a stroke; he had hurt his back working in the Allah School garden, but he was feeling better and still wanted to hit the road. Before we left, Azreal took me around the corner and smoked his equality—the best places to elevate, he said, were those one-way streets where you could have an easier time watching out for the Cee Cipher Powers. As he smoked I noticed that he wore a ring bearing Allah's Name in Arabic. He said that he had been given it by a Muslim who came around the Allah School sometimes, and Azreal even made *salat* with him in Masjid Malcolm Shabazz, the former Mosque No.7—"but not in the main area upstairs, we prayed in the basement where the Father was." Then he showed me a button of a very young Louis Farrakhan that he had unearthed while digging in the Allah School's garden. "You remember that show *CHIPS*?" he asked. "There was a *CHIPS* sticker over it, and I scratched it off and there he was." Azreal grabbed his garbage bag of things and we drove out of Mecca. He didn't have much in the way of clothes so I gave him some of mine, including an old Buffalo Bills shirt with Doug Flutie's name and number on the back. "Hey look," said Azreal, admiring the 7.

First we headed to Skidmore, a private college just a hair north of Albany, where Laury Silvers, Professor of Religious Studies, wanted to treat Azreal to dinner. So we met up with her and the Religion/Philosophy Club and Azreal regaled them all with his amazing tales. He demonstrated the special 360-spin-move Allah had taught for when someone pulled a gun on him and said that Allah's lessons also came in 360 degrees—120 for the Supreme Alphabets and Mathematics, 120 for W. D. Fard's Supreme Wisdom and 120 for "life lessons," of which Azreal received more than anyone because he was locked away with the Father for all of 1966 and three months of 1967. The kids ate up his stories and Laury looked at him in light of the Sufi concept *majdhub*, someone so "mad for Allah" that it made him appear clinically insane to the rest of the world. Laury and Azreal built on the meaning of his name in Islamic mythology and the death-angel seemed to get into it, and she even told him he reminded her of Khidr, the green-robed enigma that taught Moses. From there we headed back to the I-90 and continued west. I asked him about my earlier article and how his claim to be God had caused some trouble within the Nation. Kalim had seemed pissed about it, I told him, and Abu Shahid seemed mad. Let them be mad, said Azreal. Despite Azreal's self-assured statements to me, it sometimes becomes a different story when he's with the Mecca Gods. After my article ran, Five Percenters put Azreal in front of a camcorder and conducted an interview. When asked if he was God, Azreal initially replied, "I'm the first Culture God, begotten not made" but immediately caught himself and came back to the party line: "in other words, I'm not born God. I've got 6 ounces of brain, the white man can't be God. I'm Allah's world death-angel. In other words, uh, I'm Allah's death-angel." The interviewer made sure to clarify that Azreal viewed himself strictly as a righteous man.[3] Most Five Percenters that reject notions of Azreal's godhood nonetheless remain respectful and friendly to him. Some do accept him as God; First Born Al-Jamel allegedly told a parliament that Azreal only refrained from publicly declaring himself God to avoid causing trouble at the Allah School. A handful in the NGE have qualified that Azreal could call himself God, but not use the name Allah.

"Allah means Arm Leg Leg Arm Head," Azreal exclaimed in my car, "it doesn't mean black." Then he sang the Five Percenter anthem, "The Enlightener," and showed me how it said "the Culture is I-God." Azreal and I were the Culture Seeds; Universal Knowledge Allah had built on the math of it in the Milwaukee Gods' digest, *Cream City*:

> The 4th Human family deals with their culture given to them by Yacub which is devilishment, unless allowed to go under the study and be civilized.[4]

I asked Azreal about the 120's statement that the white devil could not be reformed, because Allah had tried sending prophets such as Moses to civilize him without success. "I wasn't taught by a prophet," he reminded me. "Allah was no prophet, he was Allah."

Azreal told me stories of Plattsburgh, where he crossed a creek by stepping on stones just beneath the water's surface and caught the attention of a mayoral candidate, who became convinced that he had watched Azreal walking on water. He even gave Azreal his Masonic ring, which Azreal put in the collection plate at a Catholic church. The candidate not only lost his election due to following Azreal around, but was later committed to a mental institution. Azreal wound up in the Napanoch prison with Allah's son A-Allah, but maintained a safe distance so that A-Allah could build with the Nation of Islam cipher.

In Buffalo we met up with Divine and Shatik, who both looked to be in their early to mid-20s. They got Azreal his equality and then we went out on Divine's back porch to build. Another God came through after Divine had called and told him that Azreal was in town. It always amazed me to watch Azreal build with Five Percenters. They were usually cool kids in fresh new clothes, worlds hipper than a fifty-six-year-old white man wearing someone else's old Buffalo Bills shirt, but they'd sit and listen to him with full reverence. Divine understood that he was in the presence of his Nation's living history. The Gods asked questions about Allah's time in Matteawan and what he said about Farrakhan and what he said about Elijah. Azreal looked at Farrakhan as small-time back then, just a kid trying to be the new headliner. Shatik heard that back when Allah was still Clarence 13X, Elijah told him that his beliefs were true, but he could not teach them in the temple. Elijah knew that the black man was God, but he had a practical mind and felt that Muslims weren't ready to ditch the Mystery just yet. Azreal called Elijah an "understanding seed without the understanding." The Gods said that the NOI was strong in Buffalo and Five Percenters attended its annual Savior's Day rally. Divine and Shatik did not consider themselves Muslims, but thought of Muslims as their cousins. I had heard Gods say that before. Shatik said he had become serious about the knowledge during his bid at Fishkill. Azreal built with him for a minute about all the terrors of that place and how he witnessed the guards killing a Black Muslim his first day there. Shatik said he had heard some stories. They spoke about the legendary tunnels. After reliving all of that, Azreal decided that he did not want to visit Fishkill "because the staff there would recognize me and catch wind of my plans." Azreal hung out and smoked well into the night, building with men young enough to be his sons on whatever they asked him.

Azreal went off for a minute about how they shouldn't call themselves "Asiatics" but Africans, or at least "Asiatic African Blackmen." For a moment I was concerned that Azreal had just put his own foot in his mouth, since the 120 says that the *devil* speaks of "Africans" to divide the Original people. The Gods let it pass and we moved on to the topic of Master Fard. I built on how Fard had supposedly returned in disguise as a Sunni imam, running one of Warith Deen's mosques out in California until his death in the early 1990s, and various reasons that the story could be truth or fiction. Shatik theorized that maybe Warith Deen had only meant that it was the *spirit* of Fard, not necessarily the body. I asked if Buffalo had been given a righteous name. Divine said that they called it Kemet, but imagined that there could be another cipher in town that had given it another name. Rochester had been named Egypt by the Gods there.

The young Gods wanted to know about the Prince/Kalim situation and how things were going back in Mecca. Azreal said that the Parliaments were still hurting, but he didn't blame either party. Several years ago, rumors flew around that Kalim was getting rich off the Allah School and buying homes down south, while Prince was said to be getting high and even dealing at the school and at some point became the second First Born to be exiled from the Nation. Prince, according to Sunez Allah, "was a microsm of our present day nation. With his exile ... the problems we needed to face were left unspoken and forgotten."

From his platform at the *Five Percenter*, Kalim lashed out against "minions" and "Big Time Dimes." "Many are addicted to substances," he wrote, "that 'makes him other than his ownself' and are easily led in the wrong direction. It is very easy to put an IDEA in their heads, by first giving them a DRINK, giving them a JOINT, giving them a SNIFF, and then giving them an IDEA ...' Kalim did this and Kalim did that."[5] The issue's front page showed a photo of First Borns Prince, ABG and Al-Jamel beneath the headline, "WHAT HAPPENED TO WORD IS BOND." During one confrontation, Kalim allegedly put his hands on Prince, who by then was spending much of his time in a wheelchair. Prince—the former Al-Jabbar, who the Father used to say would jab his way out of trouble—pulled out a gun and shot him.

Kalim survived, and in the September 2001 *Five Percenter* portrayed the shooting as part of a larger conspiracy against the Gods and Earths:

> Don't get it twisted the attempt on God's life is linked to them trying to get our school ... the only time God plots to kill God is when he BECOMES that ANY man who is made weak and wicked—by the abuse/overuse of alcohol and drugs. God if you want to know who made plots against the Father just look at those making plots against his Sun. They are one and the same mentality from one and the same devil.[6]

On October 15, 2001, Prince was shot and killed execution-style by unknown assailants. Though he had died in a state of exile, his funeral costs were covered by Allah's Universal Development, the Five Percenters' Albany-based national treasury.

Prince was good, Azreal assured us; he just couldn't get away from the damned *understanding* (cocaine) that kept him from sleeping, kept the wound on his leg from healing and would do in the best of us if we let it. Prince had once put a gun to Azreal's head for waking him up at the Allah School, and if the gun had not jammed Azreal would have "returned to the essence."

Azreal made it clear: he did not believe that Kalim had anything to do with the death of Prince, and refused to take sides on the matter.

"As long as we don't have unity," he told the young Gods, "we don't have what? Power."

Two of the young Gods had tattoos of the Universal on their forearms. For most of forty years, Shaamgaudd's flag has been picked apart, probed and "scienced out" as a rhetorical artifact. The "7" represents God, the Black Man; the moon, the Black Woman. The black star symbolizes the Black Child. The eight points of the sun represent the ever-expanding universe, while the circle containing the 7, moon and star comprises a twenty-five thousand-year cycle of history. Allah Supreme God recalls verbal confrontations between Five Percenters and Robert Walker's First Born Muslims, each side attempting to prove the superiority of its flag. Walker's "top captain," Eminent Allah, advocated the thirteen-pointed flag, claiming that the points stood for the thirteenth letter, *M*, meaning Master because First Born Muslims were the "Master Gods who master all sciences of life." The Five Percenters' eight-pointed flag, in Eminent's interpretation, meant that they "build, build, build but don't have the sense to add a ninth point and be Born." A God named Just Allah countered the argument by drawing a Universal Flag on the ground. "See the moon?" he asked. The moon had two points, each symbolizing 180 degrees. $180° \times 2 = 360°$. The star had five points, $72°$ each, and $72° \times 5 = 360°$. Finally, there were eight outer points, $45°$ each, $8 \times 45° = 360°$, and Just Allah had negated Robert Walker's thirteen-pointed flag by showing and proving the complete ciphers in the Universal.[7]

In the March 1997 issue of the *Five Percenter* newspaper, an analysis of the flag by Positive Energy Malachi Allah brings to mind C. M. Bey's Clock of Destiny Moors. In his "Supreme Clock of Time," Positive Energy shows stations on the Universal's outer circle to represent crucial moments in the Gods' interpretation of history. Starting at the flag's "northern" point, history progresses clockwise. Near the southern point (the Asiatic Calendar's year 12,500), we find Musa (Moses) coming to civilize the devil. En route to the western point we reach the year 15,000 (1914 C.E.), in which the devil's rule comes to an end, and 15,083 (1997). The Clock is roughly ten thousand years from its northern point, the "midnight hour" or year 25,000, in which man renews his history and a new cycle begins. "The 25,000 yrs. cycle," writes Positive Energy, "is the reality of GODS (2 + 5 = 7)."[8] The eight solar points around the circle are said to each represent part of the lessons studied by Gods and Earths: The Supreme Mathematics, Supreme Alphabets and sections of Supreme Wisdom: Student Enrollment, English Lesson, Lost-Found Lesson No.1, Lost-Found Lesson No.2, Actual Facts, and Solar Facts.

In the newspaper's December 1996 issue, Malik Allah offered a diagram in which points on the Universal reflected stars and constellations. Thuban in the Draco constellation was placed at the bottom of the 7 in the Universal, while Al-Rai in the Cepheus constellation represented the star on the flag. According to Malik, the two stars were six thousand years apart, which of course was no accident:

> The four large points of the Universal Flag also indicate 6,000 year periods along the precession circle. These 6,000 year periods were recognized in the Moorish Science Temple, where their Holy Koran bears a Seven enclosed in a circle broken by four (4) equal parts representing 6,000 year periods on the front cover.

> However, there was no star representing the time when the Black Man would come to rule on the Moorish Science Symbol. By including that star, Allah gave us the clue and the Key to show forth and prove that there is no "mystery" god.[9]

It was getting late so we bid our peace to the Gods of Kemet and said we'd hopefully see them all at the Show and Prove in a month. Before returning to the Born Cipher road, we stopped at Wegmans to pick up the latest issue of *The Source*, which featured an article by Sun-God Scientific, "All Praises Due," on the fortieth anniversary of the Gods and Earths. Inside we found another Universal Flag, as well as a big photo of Allah and Justice. The article would offend Five Percenters for naming the First Born from Beloved Allah's version, rather than the currently taught list.

Driving through the night and taking a few naps at rest-stops off the 90, we arrived in Chicago the following evening. Azreal remembers Allah predicting that the Five Percenters would really take off in Chicago. Some fifty years before Allah, Noble Drew Ali called Chicago the new Mecca.

We gave Jura Shaheed Allah a call and he couldn't believe that I had Azreal in the car. Azreal got his equality and we walked through the park, Jura doing the knowledge on all the chaos and discord among the local Gods. Chicago was given the name "C-Medina" by a punk known as Allah Jihad, who supposedly issued "warnings" and even calls for war between the Five Percenters and New Black Panthers.[10] In a *Five Percenter* column he announced that Milwaukee brothers who taught that the white man was God were "not allowed to step foot in our city."[11] His Internet boasts and threats performed a great disservice to the Nation and some Gods were coming out from Mecca (under the guise of a "120 conference") to settle things. Azreal felt a temptation to stay and help out; "we could freeze him with justice," he said, referring to the common breakdown of "justice" as "Just-Ice." It went back to Abu Shahid's Living Mathematics; Shahid saw 5 as representing not Power but Justice, as Just-Ice froze at 32 degrees and $3 + 2 = 5$.

As he had with the Gods in Buffalo, Azreal took a moment to build for Jura on the Prince/Kalim situation and absolve both parties of blame. Jura had known Prince. One night when Jura was sleeping in the Allah School, Prince handed him a shotgun and said "you'll be needing this." Jura speculated that Prince could have been mentally ill, remembering how he'd go in the back of the school and make his *salat* loud enough to bother everyone else in the building. The Gods "hated the shit out of that," he said.

We told Jura that the next stop was Milwaukee, and he warned us of the incorrect teaching going on out there: "there's brothers out there saying that the colored man is God." He said it was an older God who had influenced some younger Gods and had a white kid named James that hung around them. Azreal did not say anything.

For a time I walked behind them. Azreal had on an oversized black hooded sweatshirt and wore the hood up over his head with his hands in the front pocket, looking almost like a *shaykh* of some kind as he listened to the young Jura. It was one of those times when Azreal made a sudden transition of character, going from funny stoner to serious builder, exuding his very real authority as an elder of the Nation. When he went into builder mode, he could hold his own with any God and people listened to him with full respect.

We left Jura with peace and headed up to Cream City. It wasn't that far so we had time to pull over at a rest stop. Azreal elevated and told more stories. I felt like I was in that early stage of Islam that immediately followed Prophet

Muhammad's death, when people followed his companions around hoping for tidbits and scraps of history. To look at it in a Sufi way, everything that Azreal said put me in a direct *silsila* with the Father. I let him tell me to hold in the smoke, just so I could have that lineage—learning how to elevate from the kid who was taught by Allah himself back in 1969, the year Allah went home to the essence. Azreal pointed out that he used Zig Zag rolling papers—zig zag, *Zig Zag Zig*, 1–2–3, Knowledge Wisdom Understanding. That's how Gods and Earths read *Z* in the Supreme Alphabet now, but in the 1970s Zig Zag Zig represented a "snake who wanders to and fro, ever deviating from the right path back to the wrong path."[12] We slept at the rest stop and drove into Milwaukee early the next morning.

The Street Academy turned out to be a regular house with a Five Percenter sticker on the front door: "one word can change the world." C Latiff greeted Azreal with a big hug and brought us inside, where he fixed us eggs and bagels and we got to take showers. We met the Street Academy's other residents, Self Wise and Universal Knowledge Allah, both in their early twenties. C Latiff put in a video of their recent "Region 7" conference, in which Gods and Earths from nine midwestern states came together in the upstairs of Cream City's Street Academy. C Latiff wore a suit and bowtie, looking almost like a Nation of Islam minister, and with his bellowing old-time minister-speak he could have done well on the street corners of Harlem back in those days of stepladder preachers. He told the group that separation equaled *grafting*, and when you added fractions you needed to go to the lowest common denominator. The Street Academy of Cream City follows the spirit of the Father's original school and its work with the Lindsay administration, through a "Peer Mentors" program offering one-on-one support and field trips for Milwaukee youth.

C Latiff drove Azreal Universal Knowledge Allah and I to the lake, where we walked on the rocks and took pictures. Azreal loved telling tales. He had Universal Knowledge cracking up with the story of Allah smelling ham on a God's breath and telling him to go away for thirty days, and when the God came back he let out a ham-smelling fart and Allah kicked him in the ass. Later, riding around town, Azreal rode shotgun while I sat in the backseat with Universal Knowledge Allah, whose journey toward knowledge of self began with the Vice Lords. Branches of the Lords had followed the Blackstone Rangers' lead in embracing Moorish Science; they were still around, said Universal Knowledge, but have since dropped Moorish Science for pure hustling. He went in the opposite direction, dropping gang life for the Nation of Gods and Earths, but he still cuts hair for some of the Vice Lords in Milwaukee.

We built for a minute on the Blackstone Rangers/El Rukn, whose relationship to the gang underworld, Islamic overtones, brushes with civic approval, and backdrop of 1960s Black Power made them a sort of Chicago parallel to New York's Five Percenters. "The El Rukn," writes Mattias Gardell, "has had the double reputation of being the most ferocious, violence-prone gang in Chicago and also a black nationalist youth movement working for community improvement."[13] The group's story of million-dollar grants and Nixon inaugurals had an interesting postscript: in 1987 El Rukns were caught securing a $2.5 million contract from Libya to commit terrorist acts on American soil.

Universal Knowledge and I then found ourselves on the topic of the Allah Team and I made the mistake of asking his take on the question, "is Allah a Muslim?" which brought C Latiff out of his conversation with Azreal. "WHAT IS THAT BULLSHIT?" he shouted. "Who are you to come here and try to get psychological profiles on us?" Out of left field he had done a complete turn and lost his composure. I was stunned. Many people have reacted to my interest in the NGE as though I was risking my life by associating with a violent hate group. *But don't they think you're the devil?* they ask; *don't they want to kill you?* Gods and Earths have treated me with warmth and respect; as it stands now, the only Five Percenter to ever speak to me in a threatening manner was the leading advocate of the white-god movement. When we got back to the house I tried to find a quiet corner and remove myself for a while; but heading down to the basement, I inadvertently walked in on C Latiff as he sat around a table with the Gods, still cursing my bullshit and going off about psychological profiles. When he saw me he stormed back upstairs and I took a seat at the end of the table, almost oppositionally placed from Self Wise, Universal Knowledge and Azreal at the far side. A bag of weed and multiple bottles of liquor occupied the center of the table. Self Wise pressed me to give my own answer to the matter of whether Allah was a Muslim. I told him that I stood neither here nor there on the issue, I was only making small talk with Universal Knowledge and had no idea it'd become such a problem. Azreal was rolling the Zig Zag paper; without looking up from his task, he told me matter-of-factly that it's rude to ask a question without first providing your own opinion. I insisted that I had no opinion, that it wasn't something I troubled myself with and I was only interested in the God's perspective. Self Wise wouldn't let up; he knew that I'd fucked up with a stupid question and he had the writer by the balls.

Across the table I could read that Universal Knowledge was still cool with me, and Old Man Azreal was a calming influence. I told Self Wise that the question depended largely on what it meant to be "Muslim." If a Muslim was someone who submitted to the will of Allah, theoretically Allah could be a Muslim if he had knowledge of self and lived true to his own nature. On the other hand, I added, the word "Muslim" usually implied submission to an unseen mystery and many would resist the label for that reason. Self Wise wanted to know what brought me to the Five Percenters. I had been asked that enough times and told him what I told everyone else: that I had once been contained within a rigid perspective of Islam, which shut me off from the wisdom of other points of view. I now built with everyone—Sunnis, Shi'as, Sufis, Gods—and felt that the Five Percenters had their own truth.

"What is that truth?" he asked.

"That to wait for the Mystery to bring you food, clothing and shelter will only result in hard times and things of that nature." From there it was peace. I later went upstairs and exchanged apologies with C Latiff, who by then had returned to his old self. I understood C Latiff to be a nice enough man, though slightly shady and a loose cannon if rubbed the wrong way.

The parliament was held upstairs in a room that I recognized from the video. The day's Mathematics read as Build or Destroy. Build meant to add on, Destroy meant to take away. Gods took turns doing the knowledge on adding good and destroying evil and building on the day's degree in the 1–14:

Why does the Devil keep our people apart from his social equality?

Because he does not want us to know how filthy he is in all his affairs. He is afraid because when we learn about him, we will run him from among us. "Social" means to advocate a society of men or groups of men for one common cause. "Equality" means to be equal in everything.

We were joined by Born Logic Allah, the God responsible for bringing Knowledge of Self north to Green Bay. Reclaiming the city from the devil, he had renamed it the Promise Land. Supreme Solar Allah was there, son of Gwen Moore, Wisconsin's first African-American member of Congress. During the 2004 elections he was part of a group charged with slashing tires on vans that had been rented by the GOP. When Azreal stepped into the cipher, he didn't build so much on the Math or 120 but just shared whatever was on his mind, telling stories about the Father and so on. C Latiff invited me to speak and all I could do was thank him for the opportunity to build. Then we sang the "Enlightener." The song seems to change every time I hear it. Supreme Solar slipped in a *bismillah* ("in the Name of Allah") between lines of the chorus.

After the parliament we were sitting on the front porch, building on W. D. Fard, who he could have been and where he might have gone. Azreal left with a God to get equality. James, the white kid that Jura Shaheed Allah had warned us about back in C-Medina, showed up with his hair in cornrows, Egyptian-themed tattoos on his arms and a t-shirt reading, "blackalicious." He told me that he had received the knowledge from Self Wise and that he knew five or six other white Gods in town. Supreme Solar Allah educated me on the six human families: the black, brown, yellow, white, half-original, and red. The half-Original was black mixed with white, and the red was half-original mixed with brown. If half-original men like Master Fard could come as Allah, asked Supreme, and they came from the Culture Seed, why couldn't Culture Seeds be God?

Azreal came back with the equality and we exchanged peace with the Gods. C Latiff told us that we'd be welcome back anytime. "Travel in harmony," said Supreme Solar Allah as we made our way back to the car.

Heading back down the 94, Azreal wanted to pull over in Chicago and build. We found a place to park near Lake Michigan and walked to the beach. Azreal lit his equality. I asked him why weed was called "equality;" he didn't know, but back in his day they called it "earth." *Earth* and *Equality* still appear nearly interchangeable. Five Percenters often refer to a woman's "equality," which turns out to be a statement of inequality, since (like the white man) she cannot pass her Equality (6) to become God (7). The connection between Earth and Equality may come in part from Universal Shaamgaudd, who in 1983 described an "ostrich syndrome" in which some

> bury their Minds or Heads in the Earth. By Earth, I mean 6. Equality (Drugs, Alcohol, Money, Food, women, Cars, Crime, etc.) All seems well while the Head is in Equality. However, if the Equality doesn't do permanent damage to the Head or Mind, when one finally pulls his Head out of 6 (the EARTH) he finds that not only is the problem or danger still there, it usually has increased in size or in its threat, this is what happened to most of us after the Father left us.[14]

Azreal did not like the way that many Gods reduced females to "baby-makers." When it came to the Nation, he found himself in the same boat as women. "They don't get equal say," he told me, "and they should have a lot to say. Their reality is your reality. It's all about the baby so in that family they're your 180, and they got 360 so why aren't they Goddesses and Queens when you had a child with them?" He again broke down *Allah* as Arm Leg Leg Arm Head, shrugged and asked, "where's it say 'Penis?' "

I asked him to tell me about First Born Prince. "He knew the most about our Nation, and about Islam and Arabic. He could say prayers in Arabic, he could speak Arabic. And he taught it to himself. He had a lot of people that he brought all the way to 360; that's why it was such a split. Kalim had a lot of students too."

"With all of Prince's reasonable oddities and unfortunate degeneration," wrote Sunez Allah in Kalim's newspaper, "I had prized his knowledge and understanding." Azreal viewed our road trip as a special mission at a time of crisis, when Gods everywhere needed to hear the truth about the conflict.

Azreal remembered that Prince loved pigeons and kept some coops on the roof of the Allah School. "When Prince came home the last time from whatever belly of the beast and whatever reason he went there—I don't know, it don't matter—he came home and the pigeon coops were full of inches of piled-up pigeon shit, no one cleaned it up because no one went up there." One pigeon coop had an entrance that was only a square foot, and Azreal was the sole Five Percenter who could enter it; he had learned how from the Father Allah and Allah the Sun back in Matteawan. Prince was at Matteawan too, admitted under his old name Al-Jabbar, but Azreal wasn't sure if they were there at the same time.

In his later years Prince took on the role of First Born with an anthropologist's command of what it meant. He was a village elder, a sacred storyteller, a persona from the Old Testament desert. He had a gifted eye for the motifs at work. Watch him in films of old parliaments, the way he lets that Arab headdress hang off him and move when he moves, the way he leans on his cane and darts his index finger at young Gods while he imparts the oral tradition. Follow his cadence when he recites the 120. That's *recite*, not read. He might have been the NGE's first real theologian. And Sunez was right; the demons of Prince were the demons of Gods. He had drug issues, maybe mental health issues. He killed a God and many believe that he was killed by Gods. Some speak of his murder as an assassination.

I had seen a video of Prince's funeral service, starting with the crowds of Gods lingering outside Griffin-Peters Funeral Home on Seventh Avenue, all the ones I recognized like Gykee and Ja'mella, the mainstay Gods you'd spot at any Mecca parliament. Inside the parlor, the cameraman lingered on the funeral's program, the cover bearing a photograph of Prince in tinted sunglasses with his face outlined by a black-and-white kifaya.

Knowledge Allah, co-writer of the "Enlightener," led the group in a soft, sorrowful rendition, turning the joyous national anthem into a funeral dirge. I imagined that it sounded like those boys singing on the ballfield after the Father went home in 1969. Prince's Earth read a letter he had written from prison in 1985. Between the tape's sound quality and her tears, I could only make out scattered words—oxygen, carbon dioxide, *sun* of man, compounding molecules and the phrase, "I am living energy." First Born Al-Jamel used his turn at the podium to sing al-Fatiha, opening passage of the Qur'an in Arabic; and he did not recite in the traditional Muslim way, he *sang*.

Then came Ebeka, who as Eugene 32X was with the Father back in Mosque No.7. Ebeka, now Rasul, was a sturdy, stocky knowledge-seed in a kufi. He told the gathering that he studied the Qur'an and "a whole lot of us are imams" as the Father had never restricted anyone from going in the paths that they wanted. Ebeka recited from the Qur'an in Arabic first, then English, and said that the first time he ever made *salat* was with Justice for the Father's sake in Harlem Hospital. They say that Ebeka/Rasul is now an imam at one of Warith Deen's mosques in New Jersey, or maybe still a prison imam somewhere in New York. He had the brothers come to the front and stand shoulder-to-shoulder for Prince Allah's *salat ul-janazza*, acknowledging that most of the people in the room had never prayed like this before.

The tape also included footage from a December 1999 parliament in Mecca, during which Prince and Kalim stood together by the Harriet Tubman's stage and defended each other against the assorted rumor mills and backbiters. It was good to see, and good to know that Rasheen still has that moment in his archives.

Back to Lake Michigan. Azreal told me about his favorite student, a kid named Ariel who had ended up his roommate at Bergen Pines, a psychiatric hospital in Paramus, New Jersey. Ariel came from a rich family that owned the whole top floor of an office building in Fort Lee and ran a telemarketing business. With his family's money he had gotten into selling coke and partying with members of the Wu-Tang Clan. First thing he asked Azreal was, "have you heard of the Five Percenters?" Azreal answered that he had been waiting for that question ever since he was taught.

Ariel's family came from Uruguay, and Azreal helped him find the Knowledge of Self. "I was the one who made him do his own history," he told me. "He was Original. He was Indian, not Spanish, and what a difference—there's a guy who doesn't know his uncle's language."

They remained friends after leaving Bergen Pines. Ariel met up with a God named Complete and decided that he'd get telemarketing jobs for all the Five Percenters. He once took Complete and Azreal to the office after hours. They looked out the windows across the George Washington Bridge and couldn't hold in their joy—*oh man, it's gonna happen, the Nation's gonna make money.* They were Poor Righteous Teachers about to get rid of the *poor* part. That night they celebrated with equality and mushrooms. While they were all elevated, Complete began flashing "Muslim signs" that Ariel took the wrong way. Ariel stormed out, and within an hour crashed his car and went back to the essence.

Azreal had a story about getting high outside the street academy with Allah and Old Man Justice, who was still calling himself Jesus at the time. He told me that Allah was twisting up the equality, and "he was so serious when we smoked a joint that I used to always like to get him to laugh and I could always do it, find a way." So Azreal asked Allah and Jesus, "if you're the Father, and you're the Son, what am I? The Holy Ghost?" The trinity laughed so hard that it had the academy students running outside. That got us to talking about Old Man

Justice. Azreal said that Justice, the only Elder without a real background in the mosque, was more into "life lessons" than the lessons. A tribute in the *Five Percenter* describes him as "that older family member who you could hangout with or get high with when you were young ... the one who 'hipped' you to 'Streetlife.' "[15] Gods remember him as keeping things together in that first decade without Allah. "Keeping things together?" asks Prince A Cuba, who describes Old Man Justice as "someone you could buy wine for and talk to."[16]

Allah bless the ones who returned to the essence.

Shabu

In July 1974, Allah's first-born son Clarence "A-Allah" Jowers, twenty-five, and Monroe Whitaker, thirty-six, brought a .38 revolver and .32 pistol into Cannon's Bar and Grill on 145 Dyckman Street. An off-duty officer stopped the robbery and took a shot in the leg. Jowers and Whitaker escaped and headed straight to the Vinegar Hill Bar and Grill on 215th and 10th. With Jowers stationed at the door, Whitaker went in, jumped over the bar and wrestled with its fifty-year-old co-owner, Arthur Guy. Whitaker shot Guy in the neck and was then jumped by the bar patrons, who shot and killed Whitaker with his own gun and seconds later shot Jowers. The shot left A-Allah paralyzed. He was identified by detectives as a member of the Five Percenters, a "militant Harlem gang of youthful terrorists" and did five years in prison. "The Father used to tell him, 'put down that gun or it'll kill you,' " I heard from Allah Supreme God. Like First Born Prince, A-Allah's leg became swollen with gangrene and he refused to do anything about it. When the doctor told him that he either get it amputated or die, A-Allah said he'd die.

In 1987 A-Allah returned to the essence and Azreal didn't even want to know the cause. "It could have been something as simple as a blood-clot," he told me, but he couldn't deal with any more loss. A-Allah was survived by two children, Allah Clarence Jowers and Shakira Jowers. Shakira named her own son A-Allah and remains active in the Five Percenter community. Allah Clarence is a born-again Christian.

Too many Gods from the old days went out as tragic figures. Bahar, Raheem and Lubar were all done in by alcohol or drugs. Big Hasheem, who once came to Sihiem's rescue on the lower East side and battled with a paralyzed arm against an entire housing development, was shot in 1977 by a dust-user named Born God. Bishme from Brownsville was killed in front of a liquor store. Shamel from Kusa Heights was shot in Flatbush. I remembered the *Sun of Man* where Shaamgaudd wrote about black holes in space being caused by the unnatural deaths of divine or supreme beings.

Not all Gods leave footprints—some of those kids from the First Born and their generation just walked off the pages and disappeared, their fates unknown or at least respectfully forgotten. Akbar and Al-Salaam are only names on a list. According to Abu Shahid, addiction made a "snaggle-toothed rattlesnake" of Uhura, who in time lost his wife, shot his friend and overdosed back to the essence. In Attica Kiheem was scared into submission by Norman Butler, who was doing time for the killing of Malcolm X (the conviction was later overturned). Butler reportedly told Kiheem, "you keep teaching that, I'll kill you."[17]

"I left my robe in the crackhouse," laments God Kalim. Drugs put him in the Franklin Avenue shelter where Muslim Shaheed worked. Muslim Shaheed asked Kalim how he let himself get so bad. "How do you know you are God," Kalim replied, "if you ain't been through nothing?"[18]

In 1986 Shaamgaudd presented the concept of a "tri-master," which consisted of the last six months of an Equality year and the entire God year that followed. "During these periods," he theorized, "those who are caught up in six seem to fall back to earth harder each year."[19] And there always seemed to be a new "drug flood" to help. In 1966 it was heroin, '76 had dust and in '86 it was crack. In the summer of 1987 Kiheem showed up at the Allah School and introduced himself to Prince with "some long ass Muslim name." Prince described Kiheem then as "cracked out and back to his normal thing, stealing anything that wasn't nailed down."[20]

> For many, with character defects galore, their only saving grace was their association with Allah in the 1960s, when they, themselves, *were children.* As to their adding on ... We have seen the level of their progress in over 20 years. That level of progress can be measured in comparison with the body of mythological literature created during the same period.
>
> Prince A Cuba, 1994

The "mythological literature" is the work of schizotypy: not clinical schizophrenia by any stretch, and not even deliberate fabrication, but lives navigated with magical thinking. You can find it in tales of the Father having his own office, throne, and private phone line at Matteawan, appointing Hasheem his ambassador to the United Nations, changing the weather five times in four minutes and telepathically bringing his friend Pop back from the dead. I saw it in Azreal, who told stories in the same manner that Gottehrer describes Allah:

> blending hucksterism, whimsy, and preaching with enough incomplete thoughts and *non sequiturs* to convince me he was half crazy, only to slip in an insight or an argument that changed my mind ... most stories emerged with

many variations and some events were left shrouded in mystery. Much of what he told me he made up on the spot.[21]

First Born Prince blended actual facts with imaginary ones in his telling of the 1965 murder of Cedric Avery, the Five Percenters' first martyr. For Prince the youth was not fifteen but thirteen, and his righteous name was not Kaseim but Allah Hamdu, one of those names that won't offend a Muslim if you read it from right to left. Gods were drinking behind the building that would become the street academy, Allah Hamdu finished off the bottle and threw it over a fence. Then a man came over, saying that the bottle had crashed at his feet and he wanted to know who threw it. Allah Hamdu confessed and they fought. At first it looked like the man was punching Allah Hamdu, but the Five Percenters soon realized that the man had a hook for a hand and was stabbing him. The Gods then went after the man, but he escaped into the St. Nicholas projects. After hearing what had happened, Prince scolded the Five Percenters, since one of them should have remained with Allah Hamdu to stand over him and chant, "Allah is God, Allah never dies."[22]

Universal Shaamgaudd Allah was only a teenager when he made the Universal Flag, and in doing so took on a psychological weight beyond what he could bear. Gods wrote letters to Shaamgaudd asking for the hidden meanings, drew up intricate diagrams of their own interpretations and had the Universal tattooed on their arms. As the years and emotional energy piled on, poor Shaamgaudd himself became part of the power. The flag was no longer a kid's artwork but now a revelatory manifestation of Allah's Supreme Mathematics, the principles that bind the universe. Shaamgaudd took on a prophetic authority, which he would use to turn Five Percenter history into Bibles and comic books: Allah was targeted for assassination after refusing an offer of ten million dollars to leave Harlem and abandon the Five Percent, and in 1964 Carlos shot Allah with an elephant gun.[23] The night that authorities "snuck" Allah out of Bellevue to take him to Matteawan, New York City suffered a major power failure; "the light was leaving New York City," claims Shaamgaudd. "That's why we had the blackout."[24] Allah then reportedly told officials that he would "burn them with the sun," causing a city-wide water shortage.[25]

Shaamgaudd lost himself in Christian fantasies. "When they were first trying to form the original Black Panther Party," he writes in a Sun of Man, "they came to some of the First Borns and took us up on the Mountain by offering us homes, cars and unlimited expense accounts if we would accept the leadership positions and teach and train their troops. I'm glad to be able to say that none of us accepted."[26]

Boasting that "my complete understanding would have to cover every minute math term and angle from Solomon's child to the compass square to the Galaxy M83,"[27] he demonstrated his esoteric knowledge by claiming to reveal one of the forgotten "rules and regulations" of Yacub's government on Patmos:

WARNING REPEAT WARNING!!!!!!!!

USE EXTREME CAUTION IN DEALING WITH THE BLACK AND BROWN BABIES FOR THEY ARE THE SEEDS OF ALMIGHTY GOD ALLAH, WHAT EVER YOU DO TO THEM OR TAKE FROM THEM AND THERES WILL COME BACK ON YOU AND YOURS 6,000,000 or 7,000,000 FOLD!

FOR THIS IS THE SCIENCE OF DO UNTO OTHERS AS YOU WOULD HAVE DONE UNTO YOU!!! or WHAT GOES AROUND COMES AROUND!!![28]

Shaamgaudd even divulged the Father's secret prophecy that 1984 would be the "year of Supreme Understanding" in which "we as a Nation should be ready to rise again because we would be the solution for what is presently destroying Society as we know it today."[29] He attempted to supplant his own 8-pointed flag with a 16-pointed version, similar to the compass rose on the seal of the Central Intelligence Agency, insisting that the Father had told him not to reveal it until the Five Percenters were ready.[30] The new flag was rejected and Shaamgaudd died of heart-related causes in 1987. He was perhaps forty years old. The 8-pointed version survived without him, as hip-hop emcees conquered the world and planted the flag wherever they landed. The cover of Rakim's album *Follow the Leader* shows a gold and black Universal on the back of his bootleg-Gucci jacket. The Poor Righteous Teachers put the flag inside a Star of David on the cover for *Black Business*. King Sun has a track titled "Universal Flag" on his album *Righteous but Ruthless*. The RZA, who raps, "Y'all might just catch me in the park playin' chess, studyin' math/shining seven and a sun"[31] made appearances on *Chappelle's Show* with a platinum-and-diamond Universal hanging from his neck.

The Born Lesson "Allah's World Manifest" had also promised that near the end of 1984, the Five Percenters would take over the world. 1984 would have made it God Cipher years since the devil's time expired, as good a time as any for the wicked to become the Gods' footstool. The Born Lessons' assumed author, Robert Walker is still alive, but barely; since 1983 he has been locked up in Florida on a life sentence for murder. His mugshot looks terrible and his current name is Allahzar God Allah. The man that Prince called a "sick son of a bitch" still claims that the Father had named him ruler of the Five Percent Nation.[32]

In 2005 Gods were trying to raise money to exhume Black Messiah's remains and give him a proper cremation. The story that I heard had him returning to the essence in a parking lot in 1987, fallen to heroin. Now he rests at Potters Field on Hart Island, where 750,000 of the unbefriended dead lie buried in pine coffins placed in ordered columns and rows in mass plots. Each plot holds 150 adults or 1,000 infants. The work is done by convicts bused in from Rikers and ferried in from City Island for a wage of 25 or 35 cents an hour. In 1948, the year that Black Messiah was born, the inmates offered to build a monument on the island and the warden allowed it, so they made one thirty feet high with a cross on one side and, on the other, just the word "PEACE." Chances are strong that Black Messiah was put in the ground by Five Percenters. And they would not have known.

One must say PEACE to: all the YOUNGER GODS that held the house together when some elders fell apart.

God Kalim[33]

The Nation of Gods and Earths is in a time of transition, with members representing a far wider range of economic and educational backgrounds than during Allah's lifetime. In 2004 Gykee's nephew Siheem Allah Roseborough became licensed to practice law in the State of New York. "I am so damn proud of him," writes Gykee in the *Sun of Man*; "Allah continue to bless you and yours and congratulations on the birth of the baby son."[34] The earliest Five Percenters were often fatherless, but today young Gods are lawyers' sons. Now there are Five Percenter children in the suburbs who make high honor roll and have their action figures greet each other with "peace, God." They memorize the names of the First Born, sing songs in tribute, make arts and crafts like any Sunday School kids and it's all for the doomed ancients, the tried and tribulated, Prince going home with coke and bullets, Kiheem disappearing with crack and Islam—the kids don't need to know. Allah wanted them as far from that world as he could get them.

Childrens' versions of the Bible leave a great deal out.

Even when Allah stood up at the Universal Parliament and said, "DOPE [heroin] IS FORBIDDEN TO THE 5%," many brothers who were addicted to it STILL used it. While some brothers who did not USE DOPE chose to SELL DOPE instead. You Cee, certain substances are put amongst us to retard/stop/prevent/impede/and cease the growth our Nation. Back then HEROIN was the culprit. We thought that COCAINE/ALCOHOL/REEFER and the other stuff was okay, AS LONG AS WE DIDN'T USE DOPE! HOW

WRONG WE WERE ... is seen today in EVERY ALWAYS DRUNK GOD;
EVERY CRACK SMOKING GOD; EVERY ALWAYS PUFFING HERB GOD.

God Kalim[35]

The Father taught that it was okay to use drugs and elevate, said Azreal, but not
to let *them* use *you*, "where you need them three days in a row, and you've got
a runny nose." Black Messiah and Knowledge Allah once scolded Azreal for
bringing dope to the street academy, as the Father wouldn't be happy about
it.[36] Allah used to tell Gykee, "I'm trying to make you my 'KEE,' you just keep
fucking up, son" and predicted that one day the Five Percent would have to
stop "drinking and drugging."[37] At a Harlem parliament, ABG told me that the
Father had tried leading Gods away from drugs. "You see what it does," he said.
"You see what it did to brother Unique?" Unique Ason Allah, known to his
mom as Russell Jones and to the hip-hop world as Ol' Dirty Bastard, was a
Brooklyn seed who said that his rhymes were "rugged like burnt buildings in
Harlem." Azreal had built with him a few times without ever knowing that he
was a rap star. Unique gave time and money to the Nation, but never introduced himself at parliaments as "ODB of the Wu-Tang Clan;" Azreal only
learned who he was after the God went *home*.

Azreal then revealed the secret of his missing big toe. To escape his addic-
tions, he took a bus from New York to Virginia and got a job mowing lawns.
One day he walked into the lawnmower, lost his toe and then went back to
Mecca. At the street academy he kicked up his bare feet on a desk and Allah saw
what had happened. The Father grew heated, demanding to know where
Azreal had been and what kind of trouble he'd found. Azreal cried that he had
only left the city to get away from his disease, and had chosen the place of
Allah's birth. Unable to stay angry, Allah gave his troubled death-angel a hug.
Azreal also told me that he saw Allah the night before his assassination, in a bar
on Seventh Avenue. Allah ordered gin with water on the side and the same for
Azreal. They played songs on the jukebox: Allah played "Stay in My Corner" by
the Dells, and Azreal played "Color Him Father" by the Winstons. Azreal said
that he had a Muslim back in the city making him a tape of both songs and
could get me a copy.

After Allah's assassination, Lindsay came to the Allah School and Azreal saw
the goosebumps on the scared mayor's arms. Azreal was so emotional that the
Gods were forced to lock him in the bathroom. "I knew the Father was being
watched," he told me. Azreal believed that Lindsay was in on it and the order
had come from Nixon himself. He even had a theory on how they pulled it off.
Allah's brother was a cab driver, and Allah usually rode with him, but that
night it was someone else. Azreal believes that Allah was set up, that they shot

him in the head while still in the cab and then dragged him into the building. And the stories say that Allah was hit seven times, but Azreal says it was six; Allah still had a bullet in him from the shooting at the Hole nearly five years before.

Azreal capped off the build with a medley of old songs and then we began our long drive back, arriving in Mecca the following afternoon. I hung out at the Allah School's store, going through old newspapers with Cee Allah while Azreal ran over to the St. Nicholas projects.

18

Show and Prove

Just a few weeks after our trip, the news team for Milwaukee's Fox affiliate ran a segment on the Cream City Street Academy, claiming that Allah had "promised to destroy the white race."

Again I was driving around Harlem's sacred sites, while listening to the RZA and his cousin Ol' Dirty Bastard rap about snatching devils by the hair and cutting off their heads. Earlier I had been reading Amir Fatir's *Why Does Muhammad & Any Muslim Murder the Devil?*, a work solely dedicated to one question in the 120:

> 10. Why does Muhammad and any Muslim murder the devil? What is the duty of each Muslim in regards to four devils? What reward does a Muslim receive by presenting the four devils at one time?
>
> ANS. Because he is one hundred per cent wicked and will not keep and obey the laws of Islam. His ways and actions are like a snake of the grafted type. So Muhammad learned that he could not reform the devils, so they had to be murdered. All Muslims will murder the devil because they know he is a snake and also if he be allowed to live, he would sting someone else. Each Muslim is required to bring four devils, and by bringing and presenting four at one time his reward is a button to wear on the lapel of his coat, also a free transportation to the Holy City Mecca to see brother Muhammad.

For Amir Fatir, the four devils are actually the genital, heart, throat and pituitary chakras, which must be sacrificed:

> Presenting the four devils at once means to unite the energies of the four chakras ... when these devils are thus "murdered," the Muslim receives a button to wear on his coat's lapel. This is a symbol of the opening of the heart chakra ... the successful Muslim also receives "a free transportation to the Holy City Mecca to see brother Muhammad." This free transportation is the ability to soul travel beyond space and time to actually see Muhammad as Muhammad actually saw Abraham and other ancient masters. This also represents understanding Muhammad or "becoming" Muhammad in the sense of character development and enlightenment.[1]

The weekend of June 13, I went back for the Show and Prove, the Gods' and Earths' annual convention, and took part in a childrens' walking tour of Harlem. Allah B led the way while Gods such as Divine Prince Allah and Rasheen Allah protectively surrounded the maybe two dozen kids, mostly girls around ten years old. Throughout our walk it seemed to rain only on the opposite side of the street.

Divine Prince was a lanky and sharply dressed God from the Desert. Before coming to the knowledge, he called himself "Cold Blood." In 1970 he co-founded the Black Liberation Party and served as its Chief of Staff, befriending and working with the likes of Lumumba and Afeni Shakur, Angela Davis, H. Rap Brown and Pablo Guzman, Minister of Defense of the Young Lords—who'd later become a newscaster for Channel 4. Selling his group's newspaper on Jamaica Avenue, Cold Blood often heard brothers greet each other with "peace, God." Then his friend Chaddy went to prison and came back as Hakim, which he said meant "the Wise." Hakim walked Cold Blood through Bricktown and Liberty Park and up and down Liberty Avenue, revealing truths that "seemed to open up the skies." Hakim later taught him the Supreme Alphabets, Mathematics and 120, one lesson at a time. Cold Blood initially took the name God Sahiem Allah but later changed it to Divine Prince Allah. He remembers Five Percenters coming together from all the projects in Queens. There was Judgement and Allah Savior from the Baisley projects, Dahlu, Allah Islam and Justme Allah from the Jamaica Houses, and Earths like Queen I Bear Witness, Shaquana, I-Asia, and She Wisdom. In 1975 Divine Prince was part of a group that opened the first Allah School in the Desert on New York (now Guy Brewer) Boulevard between 169th and 170th Streets in South Jamaica.[2]

Rasheen Allah's history went back to the early 1980s. Today he can be found with his brother Rasheem videotaping every Mecca parliament. As the Nation's video archivist he holds footage of Abu Shahid's public-access talk shows, Prince's funeral service, the Allah-U-Akbar memorial, Earth conferences, NGE education summits, Wise Jamel giving the history tour, and Allah B's release after serving twenty-seven years in prison.

Allah B had first met Allah in November 1964. The sixteen-year-old Ralph Taylor, known then as "Colty" for often carrying a Colt .45, had stolen a hat from a store on 125th. Running up Seventh Avenue with a cop behind him, Ralph saw Allah's silhouette in the window of the Wellworth Bar on 126th. Allah came outside and jumped in front of the cop, telling him that he couldn't run on the sidewalk, slowing him down enough for Ralph to run through the St. Nicholas projects and escape. The next evening Ralph came back to thank Allah and found him surrounded by a circle of youths, preaching on the lessons. Ralph stood in the back and watched. Allah paused his build to give Ralph a smile and wink. Ralph nodded. He'd first take the righteous name Hakeim, but when Allah instructed Five Percenters to shed their Muslim names he became Born Allah, and would later change it to Allah B.

Near the end of 1971, Allah B was arrested for the murder of thirty-nine-year-old Robert Davis, Jr. The story went that Davis saw Allah B riding his son's stolen motorbike and took it back by threatening Allah B with a .22 revolver. A witness claimed that there were upwards of twenty-five kids on the street. Allah B allegedly yelled, "come on, let's get him" while Davis shouted back, "tell your boys, 'don't come toward me' " and fired two shots in the air. At 10:30 p.m. at Fordham Hospital, a stabbed and beaten Davis was pronounced dead on arrival. Bronx District Attorney Burt Roberts identified the suspects in custody as Born Allah, Messiah Allah, Knowledge Allah, and Lado. Born Allah/Allah B gave his address as 2122 Seventh Avenue—Allah's Street Academy. During the nearly three decades that followed, behind bars Allah B became an award winning writer, obtained two college degrees and completed training programs to qualify him as a plumber, air conditioner repairman, photographer, and conflict resolution mediator. He also became a certified teacher's aid and obtained counselor's certification.

In "The Bomb" Beloved Allah described Allah B as a political prisoner, convicted of "teaching black youth to be sovereign over themselves and community."[3] I don't know what happened back in 1971, but you can't find a killer in the God's eyes today as he leads Five Percenter kids on walking tours of Harlem, showing them the Father's old apartment building, Masjid Malcolm Shabazz and the Apollo Theatre. Allah B told the children how everyone used to say that the Father was the greatest, but the Father would correct them and say no, the babies were the greatest. "He used to tell me that I was going to be greater than him," Allah B said in a magazine interview. "At that time I couldn't see it. But I see it now. That the next generation would have what he had and more." Allah B is now involved with arranging trips to Asia for community children. His Five Percenter vision remains one of tolerance and compassion, a manifestation of the last three Jewels of Islam: love, peace and happiness. If an idea is only as true as its advocate standing before you, the Father's message as offered by Allah B sounds as mature and universal as that of Jesus or Muhammad.

A culture or religion is what you make it, and I wondered what these kids would do with their Nation. The character of the movement seems to change every decade, influenced in turn by Elijah/Malcom's Islam-as-racial-resistance, Brooklyn turf gangs, Queens drug empires, conscious hip-hop, prison culture, and finally its own self-identity. Barry Gottehrer has observed a revolving-door effect at the Allah School, with steady flows of youth coming in and out of the community. He marvels at the fact that they keep the school going, since it seems that every few years a new group of Gods is in charge (along with a few mainstays such as Um Allah and God Kalim). Periodically the Gods and Earths graze mainstream consciousness; at other times it looks as though the movement will die out soon after its present generation of elders. The 1980s saw parliaments decimated under the strain of crack, but a Five Percenter renaissance blossomed in the early '90s due to Spike Lee's *Malcolm X* and rap acts like the Wu-Tang Clan and Brand Nubian. After a few years, the parliaments emptied out again. Ciphers in New York have been deeply wounded by the shootings of Kalim and Prince, and many (including Kalim) have stopped attending parliaments altogether. Of course you can no longer judge the entire Five Percent Nation by what happens in Mecca. Throughout the wilderness of North America and beyond, parliaments are thriving. A "First Born" in Haiti is translating the lessons into Creole. Gods and Earths in the United Kingdom appear to be as organized as any cipher in the US. Supreme Understanding Allah brought the knowledge to Ghana. I often hear rumors of Gods and Earths in China and Japan.

The tour of Mecca brought us to Mount Morris Park, now called Marcus Garvey Park, where Allah B told the kids to stay in school and reach their full potential. Then we all sang the "Enlightener," with an emphatic *peace!* at the end.

"Remember, the Gods love you," Allah B told the seeds.

"And the Earths love you," another God added.

"Thank you," said one of the kids' moms.

The concept of "the black man is God" is most true when you see it applied to young boys. At one Harlem parliament a man pointed at a toddler and told me, "he's God." How can you argue with that?

If the Gods and Earths worship anything, it's their children. Hear the reactions when a young seed stands to give his or her first build at a parliament. Even if the child is too quiet and nervous to be heard past the front row, even if it's only a recitation of one line from a degree, the audience gives a thunderous PEACE! that can shake the walls. There are also special "Children's Day" parliaments and back-to-school rallies. The Allah School in Medina holds a costume party at which kids dress like black historical figures and give presentations on them, with awards given to the best young God and Earth. The Allah School in Mecca offers after-school tutoring and even provides children with their own computers. Born Justice Allah most recently started a new initiative, "Positive Seeds in Pelan, Inc.," to provide mentoring, counseling, and "scared straight" programs in which at-risk youths visit inmates to learn about life in prison.

Children are the most honest reflections of their parents' values. A small child does not know how or when to diplomatically downplay the less popular elements of a belief system. If the Gods and Earths were genuinely racist, you'd see it in their Stars, their seeds. But these babies weren't taught to be hateful or scared of white people; they never even looked at me like it was odd for whites to be walking alongside them through the Father's history.

Back in front of the Allah School I overheard an elder telling teenagers about the late Zumar who could "jump up and kick the limbs off a tree." Then I saw the oldest of the old Gods, Allah's original brown seed walking around by himself.

"Peace, Abu Shahid."

"What are you doing here?" he asked.

"I'm getting the story straight."

"Haven't you gotten it straight already?"

Shahid puts on a gruff exterior for this devil at parliaments and Show and Proves, but when I call him he helps me out, politely answering most questions that don't deal with specific dates ("I'm not the calendar boy," he says).

Dates don't matter anymore; the Five Percenters have little need to record actual history. The movement's chronology comes in bits and scraps through tall tales that often stress the importance of the God telling them. It's hard to find the truth, and many will complain of claim-jumpers. Go to a Harlem parliament and hear how many elders tell stories about "busloads" of youths going to see Allah at Matteawan, when there's not one record of a visit in the institution's logs. Tellings of the first attempt on Allah's life erase any mention of a twenty-dollar bar debt; Allah was shot for saving the babies, for being Allah, for coming to liberate the Original Man and end the devil's civilization. Al-Jamel has stated that all nine of the First Born were present at the Hole when Allah was shot,[4] but ABG writes that he first met Allah while Allah was recovering in the hospital. Gods also say that Malcolm X was about to join the Five Percenters before his assassination, Lindsay offered Allah ten million dollars to stop teaching, the Pope came to see Allah at Matteawan and China was planning to recognize the Gods and Earths as a sovereign nation. It's only myth now—what rank Allah had in the Fruit of Islam, the special title he received from Elijah, why and when he left the mosque, what happened at his arrest on Memorial Day and who orchestrated his death—the real lives are gone. Universal Shaamgaudd tells the story of guards at Rikers and Atlantic Avenue House of Detention cutting off the lights on the night of December 31, 1964 and letting Five Percenters out of their cells. The Gods, believing that the devil lost his respite in 1964 and would be off the planet come New Year's, began to celebrate until ambushed by a waiting riot squad.[5] Take the narratives for what they are, but they don't have to be true to be valid.

Myth is the twilight speech of an old man to a boy ... Myth is the facts of the
mind made manifest in a fiction of matter ... The speech of an elder in the twilight of his life is not his history but a legacy; he speaks not to describe matter
but to demonstrate meaning.[6]

Abu Shahid has his own stories but will tear down any God who tries to say that
Allah pointed at a star and made it move: it was a shooting star that Allah
pointed at, he says, or the lights of a plane, and "if it sounds like a fairy tale, it
is." To John 37X Brooks, Clarence 13X Smith was thoroughly human; and
when I listen to Shahid describe the old days, I can't get the sense that Allah was
trying to build some fully articulated new value system or *movement* or *culture*
or *Nation* that would go this far. They were just two Muslim outcasts in a basement, John a number-running heroin addict and Clarence a master gambler
with two years of high school and two years of Korea under his belt. Clarence
wasn't trying to become a mystery; he discouraged High Science for city-
science and at times favored life lessons over the 120. Elijah Muhammad had
worked out a sophisticated eschatology involving the Motherplane, the massive Ezekiel Wheel spacecraft with all of its smaller ships inside loaded with
bombs, but Clarence brought it back to earth and broke it down: "the Mothership is the mother's hip." He used to shine shoes and work a fruit stand, he
liked to drink gin with water on the side, he smoked weed, did coke, shot craps
and enjoyed women. But during John's six months in prison on gun possession, Clarence became bigger than any man called Puddin or 13X, and whatever they had in the Hole had taken on a greater life.

I thought of Allah and the Desert Fathers that came before him: Father
Divine, Noble Drew Ali, the Honorable Elijah Muhammad. They were all born
in the south and came north as young men in search of a better tomorrow, but
found the American Dream to be a mystery god: an empty promise that took
blind faith and gave only hard times.

Father Divine attempted to uplift his people by presenting himself as
God, Noble Drew Ali was a divine prophet, and Elijah Muhammad was the
Most Honorable Messenger. Clarence said that he was Allah, but informed
the teens that followed him that they were Allah too. And that could be the
difference.

After Father Divine's death, Mother Divine held a vigil for his certain return.
At Peace Mission banquets, followers continued to fix him a plate and speak of
him as though he were present. In the wake of Noble Drew Ali's martyrdom,
his Moorish Science Temple was all but destroyed by schisms among his various reincarnations. When Elijah passed, son Wallace took over and detonated
the Nation of Islam. The communities were each dependent on a cult of

personality, ultimately falling apart with the loss of the figurehead. The Peace Mission is gone, the scattered remnants of Moors oppose each other and Farrakhan's resurrected NOI is a sad shell of Elijah's version. Allah, however, had given his crown to his entire nation; there was nothing that a Messenger of Allah or Allah Reincarnated or Allah in the Wisdom Body could do for them that they couldn't do themselves. He once took some Gods into the back of the school and, according to U-Allah, "manifested to us that He was no longer our 'Father,' but He was our 'Big Brother.' " Of Father Divine, Noble Drew Ali, Elijah Muhammad and Allah, only Allah's nation would reach its peak without him. The Five Percent is not stagnated by the limitations of a leader, nor is it a personal money-machine for one man and his inner circle; and for this, the Nation of Gods and Earths will probably outlive the Nation of Islam.

Is it a religion? Of course, but I do understand what *religion* means to the Gods and Earths, and why the word doesn't sit well in this cipher:

"Mas'r will find out that I'm one that whipping won't tame. My day will come yet, if he don't look out."

"What are you going to do? O, George, don't do anything wicked; if you only trust in God, and try to do right, he'll deliver you."

"I an't a Christian like you, Eliza; my heart's full of bitterness; I can't trust in God. Why does he let things be so?"

"O, George, we must have faith. Mistress says that when all things go wrong to us, we must believe that God is doing the very best."

Harriet Beecher Stowe, Uncle Tom's Cabin, 1852

11. Will you sit at home and wait for that mystery God to bring you food?

ANS. Emphatically No!

12. Tell us why the Devil does not teach that?

ANS. Because he desires to make slaves out of all he can so that he can rob them and live in luxury.

The Supreme Wisdom Lessons

There really is a devil, and like the Lost-Found Muslim Lesson No.1 says, he does keep you from his social equality. The bloodsucking Ten Percenters, peddlers of the Mystery God, rule the Eighty-Five Percent with priests, imams, ministers, mullahs and theologians, trained experts in phantoms, selling what cannot be seen. An old man who has only been an MTA bus driver all his life cannot stand up in a mosque and give *khutbah* on what he learned while struggling in the city and supporting a family. It's not enough; he has to go to Al-Azar, perfect his *Arabiyya*, master *tajwid*, eat up medieval scholars, fill his head with *fiqh* and learn all the schools of thought. But in the new Mecca of Harlem, he can come to the front of the Harriet Tubman's auditorium in his MTA work jacket and he's God as is.

Sitting with Azreal in a hallway at the St. Nicholas projects, listening to him build as he smoked, I looked at that fifty-six-year-old and tried to see him at seventeen, a scared kid in a mental institution fighting off guards and missing his mom. For a moment I could see the elders as boys: young Allah B chased by the cops; Kalim thrown out of his mother's house; Karriem at sixteen already a veteran among pimps and pushers at the Hole; Al-Jabbar a Muslim that the mosque never wanted. They were throw-away kids but the Father showed them love. Allah said that they were the cream that would rise to the top; he made them feel like they ruled the galaxies and turned Black Mack into Black Messiah. Allah, Clarence 13X, Clarence Edward Smith, Clarence Smith Jowers/Clarence Jowers Smith as he was called sometimes, properly the Father—a genuine father, the *only* father for a lot of them; Allah with his Virginia twang told the throw-away kids that they were older than America, older than Christ and Buddha, older than Time with no birth record, possessors of the same Black Mind that spawned the sun, moon and stars. When spotting one of his Suns with a black eye, Allah asked him if he had gotten in a fight. Yes, Allah, replied the young God. Allah asked him again and got the same answer. He asked a third time and again the kid said yes, so Allah gave him a hug and took him out for a soda.

For insisting that the black man was God, white men in positions of real power called him psychotic and threw him down into the deep pit of Matteawan State Hospital. During this research I ran into a long line of men and women of color that were found mentally ill for claiming godliness, starting with Father Divine in 1914. In 1933, W. D. Fard told Detroit police that he was the Supreme Being and they put him in a straitjacket. In 1965, the Harlem Six were transferred from Elmira to Dannemora for telling guards that they were Gods. "What could be more natural," asks Prince A Cuba, "than a bunch of devils calling a Black man crazy because he said he was god?"[7] A similar pattern is found with white Five Percenters. Azreal found the truth in Matteawan's horror house and his student Ariel at Bergen Pines, while Tommy Mathematics and that James kid in Milwaukee had both been committed by their parents before discovering the Five Percent. Black Gods are thrown into psych wards for coming to the knowledge, and white Muslim Sons find it after already getting labeled as insane. That's what it means to be a Poor Righteous Teacher in the devil's kingdom.

> If I'm not Allah, who is?
>
> Allah

Was Allah crazy? Minister Akbar Muhammad, international representative of Louis Farrakhan, calls the Father "confused."[8] Amir Fatir calls him an "intelligent but confused nutcase."[9] Sid Davidoff remembers him as "a little bit snake-oil salesman and a little bit crazy, but no more unstable than anyone else preaching a gospel on the street corner" and less insane than Abbie Hoffman.[10] "Of course he wasn't crazy," says Barry Gottehrer. Allah was "as smart on the streets as anybody," adds Davidoff; however, a few of the Father's statements seem to have been made without awareness of their implications. With his rising fame in the late 1960s and the scene what it was—with surging Black Power and student protests across the country—if Allah had played his cards differently, he could be painted today as a counterculture icon. He might have been Malcolm or Che, the immortal face on t-shirts and posters with a blockbuster biopic. He could have had it all if he wanted it; but standing before a crowd of black Marxists and Amiri Baraka, he discussed the height of Mount Everest. In the age of feminism he told boys that they were gods and girls that they were soil. In his only surviving recorded interview, he endorsed capital punishment and the right of police to shoot without provocation. He accused anti-war demonstrators of being Communist agents, and when an interview turned to Vietnam he said to bomb the uncivilized. In the post-9/11 "War on Terror," Allah would be standing at the right side of George W. Bush. And now Beloved Allah calls him "a man history has yet to remember."

Davidoff has no trouble with Allah's place as an ideological island: "I don't think Allah ever gave a shit what anyone ever thought of him. That's why he said some of the things he said."[11] If Allah had lived to see the Five Percenters spread worldwide, how might he have worked with his changing position? The street academy helped some youths into college, but eventually functioned as a hangout. Allah did not display the political sharpness of Malcolm, nor were his Five Percenters organized empire-builders like Elijah's Muslims. "I don't want that kind of power," said Allah.[12]

> I've been in jail with 'em and having conversations with brothers; "I'm God, I'm God." You God, open the gate for me. You know how far the sun is and how far the moon is, how the hell do I pop this fuckin' gate? And get me free and up outta here. Then I'll be a Five Percenter for life.
>
> Tupac Shakur[13]

When a kid on the wrong side of that razor-wire fence can come up with a name for himself like I-Freedom Born, it's clear that Allah gave him something that he needed; but it won't always pop the gate. Had he lived into the 1970s, the man that John Lindsay later called "the Al Sharpton of his day"[14] might have found himself on a stage for which he was not prepared. Expected to deliver a serious idea for social change, Allah could revert to magical alphanumerics or what caused rain, hail, snow and earthquakes. Despite Black Messiah's statement that the only valid plus-degree was a GED or job training, High Scientists have pumped out decades of mysticism. Gods and Earths, writes Prince A Cuba, "may come to the construction site every month and discuss the contents of the blueprints, but never pick up a hammer. They are not 'building.' They build nothing. They only exhale carbon dioxide, warmed by their lungs, and call their words 'wisdom.' "[15] The wisdom is often fantasy, and perhaps a bit of hustle:

> those of you who can, open up a checking account and a savings account at a commercial bank because in the very near future I'm going to teach you something I call the Universal Money Game! It is a system that will dramatically increase one's financial worth. And if just a small number of you master this science, some of you younger brothers and sisters should be able to retire at 30 years of age and in 10 years time not only will we be able to hold our rallies at Madison Square Garden, we should have the ability and the capital to buy that corporation out from under them and rename it the Garden of Allah!
>
> Universal Shaamgaudd Allah, 1984[16]

The Talmud tells the story of Moses ascending to heaven to find God adding crownlets to various letters of the Torah. When Moses asks their purpose, God replies, "One man is destined to interpret mountains of laws on their basis." God then shows Moses a vision of Rabbi Akiba teaching a class. Moses is distraught to learn that he is unable to follow the lesson, though Rabbi Akiba tells his disciples, "This is a law given to Moses on Mt. Sinai." Likewise, Allah was not an answer to all questions, but a foundation on which others could build; and they have. Allah was right when he said that the babies would be greater, that Suns would surpass their Father, and he would beam with pride at seeds like Supreme Understanding Allah submitting their doctoral dissertations. An intellectualization of the culture is gradually replacing the fables of Shaamgaudd's generation.

Like other prophetic figures whose biographies must be adjusted for changing times, the rough spots in Allah's years are explained away, contextualized and sometimes avoided. His drug use and gambling are understood as a means for him to have reached the youth. "The Father waddled in the mud with the lot of us," says Gykee. "Had he not utilized that means of facilitation, there might have possibly been no 'Five Percent Nation.' "[17] The First Born receive their own apologia, such as the claim that they put themselves in jail intentionally for the purpose of teaching troubled kids. Maybe they did, but Prince also shot and killed Black Messiah's brother. The heirs to any culture imagine their own values to coincide perfectly with those of the original community, and they often cling to notions of an early Golden Age that did not exist.

When we were on the road, Azreal gave me a righteous name: Azreal Wisdom. In Supreme Mathematics, it means "Azreal 2." It's a big responsibility, he said, but I'd still have an easier time than the original Azreal, who had earned his name for waking from a Matteawan coma. "*You* won't have to die to get it," he said with a wink. He added that someday he'd drop his own name and take a new one, something really crazy that would make people step back, maybe "Albino Unicorn Allah" or "John Michael Puddinhead Smith." Whether Azreal can be God remains a touchy subject. One can see why he is and also why he is not, and why the answer depends on who asks the question; there's more than one truth to consider. While the Five Percent's orthodoxy does have its firm defenders, some Gods and Earths accept the idea of relative truth. When Azreal told me that he was God, one Five Percenter seemed more opposed to my publishing the quote than he was to Azreal actually saying it. "That might have been just meant for you," said the God, "and *your* understanding." Azreal can say that he's God, and Abu Shahid can say that Azreal's the devil, and they both possess untouchable authority as custodians of distinct chapters in Allah's life: Shahid was with him in the mosque, Azreal the asylum. According to ABG, any Five Percenter's breakdown was valid "because it demonstrated that person's level of understanding ... each brother has his own story, and can speak of his own journey, his life's experience. Only he can identify the crucial periods in his life."[18] Allah, while basing his ideas on the 120, felt free to change degrees to his liking and even mocked W. D. Fard as a mystery god. In the tradition that Allah engaged, the Nation of Islam, he employed religious imagination against Elijah Muhammad's religious authority. He adhered to the inner heart of the tradition while openly rebelling against both its founder and its designated protector; and in allowing the Suns to use his name, Allah shared that power.

Going into the Harriet Tubman I had to pass an inspection of my backpack and body pat-down by members of the Gods' security team. Originally called the FOA (Fruit of Allah), the unit was first established in 1989 under the guidance of Born Justice Allah, who worked as a bodyguard to the lyrical god Rakim. The auditorium was packed with Gods and Earths who came to see their babies on the same stage as rap stars such as Lord Jamar and the RZA, who brought his new group, the Harlem 6. In the back of the room I let Lost-Found degrees run through my head: *Have you not heard that your word shall be bond*

*regardless of whom or what? Yes, my word is my bond and my bond is my life and
I will give my life before my word shall fail.*
Allah told his Suns that their bond expired the Qur'an.
His friend John Vliet Lindsay died on December 19, 2000 of complications
from pneumonia and Parkinson's. A memorial service was held at New York's
Cathedral of St. John the Divine. In his piece for BBC News Online, Paul
Reynolds noted the attendance of one fifty-year-old Gykee Allah. It was purely
an accident; the reporter, who thought he had picked a random citizen, a mid-
dle-aged black slice of New York life, remained clueless as to just how qualified
Gykee was to speak on Lindsay's years.

Reynolds quoted Gykee as saying that he had come to Lindsay's service to
"give back that which he gave to us." Gykee was only eighteen, Reynolds wrote,
when he and his father marched with Lindsay in Harlem. The whole thing flew
over Reynolds' head—who Gykee was, who Gykee's *father* was, who he meant
by "us" and what Lindsay had given him that he came to give back. We can
assume that Paul Reynolds had never heard of Gykee's old comrade Universal
Shaamgaudd Allah or knew what it meant to be the First Born of Medina. And
Reynolds had no idea that just a few years before Gykee walked with the mayor,
he had been caught on a Harlem rooftop supposedly ready to burn the
city down.

The early Five Percenters wrote Odysseys, Bhagavad-Gitas and Epics of Gil-
gamesh with their own lives. They performed *hajj* to a new Mecca, carried out
hijras to Medina, found the devil at Pelan and chased him across the Desert.
They made sacred sites of the St. Nicholas projects and the Tompkins projects
and countless street corners and playgrounds and basketball courts. Gykee
tells the story of fifteen-year-old Sihiem coming back from a meeting with the
Father to bring a special message; Gykee was too drunk to hear it, so Sihiem
drew up all the alcohol out of him, leaving Gykee "no longer drunk, just hung
over bearing witness to the power of Allah." When Universal Shaamgaudd
took his 120 degrees to school and had them confiscated by the principal, Born
Justice stole them back, right out of the principal's desk; and that's the same
Born Justice you'd see forty years later in a suit and tie on Fox News. "Don't
look to the sky," he said on one of my parliament tapes; "look within."

Back in 1968 Hasheem would rent a U-Haul for moving jobs, and before
returning it he'd furnish the back with sofas and couches and drive crews of
Gods all over Medina, each U-Haul or Ryder van a rolling pantheon of skinny
teen heroes with tassled skullcaps and names like Mentality Allah, Minister
Allah, Righteous Mathematics, Doctor God Latik, Universal Zig Zag Zig, Black
Prince, Prince Saladine, Prince Love, Prince Allah, King Allah, Born Allah, He
Allah, See Allah, U-Allah, Allah Foundation, Allah Education, Bushwick Allah,

270 THE FIVE PERCENTERS

Allah Seed, Allah Mind, Allah Real, Allah Forever, Allah Wonders, Allah the Original Man, Freedom, Knowledge, Sincere, Divine, Eminent, Barkim, Kasheem, Rasheem, Karate Rasheem, Positive Zubar, Green Eye Zumar, Big Melsun, Little Melsun, Koran, Ratuk, Shaliek, Shabu, Lamik, Ladu, Shyheim, Monik, Armel, Akmier, Young God, Wise Allah, Lord Serious, Amar the Great Mind from the East—

As Old Man Justice said, "Allah took young boys and made Gods out of them." Allah told the kids to never make a statue of him; they were his living monuments. Some are still around and you can find them at parliaments, Five Percenter grandfathers ... maybe they'll share their stories, maybe they won't. Others have left their places in the pantheon but might still be in the city somewhere with less provocative names, or turning old in the belly upstate, and the rest are just gone, that's it; returned home, returned to the essence of life, no need for a heaven, immortal only through the babies. Better to live like a God in the world and let that be all, than live in the grave to drink milk and honey.

There's no fruit in the sky, announced a raspy-voiced old Five Percenter in front of the Harriet Tubman—no fruit in the sky, no God in the sky; *you're* the fruit, you're the God.

Appendix of Names

Some historically significant figures in the Nation of Gods and Earths (Five Percenters) have been known by more than one name. For accuracy's sake, I refer to an individual by the name that he or she used during a certain time period; for example, when discussing Allah after 1964, it is generally inappropriate to refer to him as Clarence 13X.

ALLAH AND THE ELDERS

Five Percenters use the term "elder" in a general sense for anyone that has been in the movement for many years. The specific title of "Elder," however, is reserved for Abu Shahid, Justice and Ebeka, who, as adult Five Percenters, carried special respect among the teenagers that followed Allah.

1. Allah (Clarence 13X Smith, the Father)
2. Abu Shahid (John 37X Brooks)
3. Justice (Brother Jimmy, Jesus, Old Man Justice)
4. Ebeka (Eugene 32X White, Rasul)

FIRST BORN

The Five Percenters today recognize nine youth from Mecca (Harlem) as the First Born, the first teenagers to follow Allah. In addition to the original First Born, other lists of "First Born" have been compiled to honor Five Percenter history in particular boroughs or cities. Some of the First Born changed their names after Allah instructed them to stop using "Muslim names."

1. Karriem (Black Messiah)
2. Al-Salaam
3. Al-Jabbar (Prince Allah)
4. Niheem (Bisme Allah)
5. Akbar
6. Kiheem
7. Bilal (ABG)
8. Uhura
9. Al-Jamel

Medina (Brooklyn) First Born

1. Gykee Mathematics Allah
2. Universal Shaamgaudd Allah
3. Gamal (God Def)
4. Bali
5. Ahmad
6. Lakee (Uhoso)
7. Akim
8. Siheem
9. Ali
10. Raleak
11. Waleak (Knowledge God)
12. Sha Sha
13. Byheem
14. Hasheem

Pelan (the Bronx) First Born

1. Wadu
2. Jahard
3. Ladu
4. Barkim
5. Dihoo
6. Shameik (U-Allah)
7. Rubar
8. Hakiem (Born Allah, Allah B)
9. Harmin
10. Kassiem

The Desert (Queens) First Born

1. Prince-I-Allah
2. God B Uhuru
3. Prince Allah
4. Allah Education
5. Born Allah
6. Sincere
7. Raheem
8. Judgement
9. Just Allah

THE HARLEM SIX

The Harlem Six were a group of teenagers falsely charged with the murder of a Hungarian-American woman in the summer of 1964. Aligned with the semi-mythical "Blood Brothers," they were part of a renegade Nation of Islam scene that predated Allah's movement. The Harlem Six are credited with teaching early Five Percenters, and William Craig was the cousin of First Born Al-Jabbar/Prince Allah.

1. Wallace Baker (Walik)
2. William Craig (Amin, Eye God)
3. Robert Rice (Malik)
4. Ronald Felder (Al-Rahim)
5. Walter Thomas (Jahad, Merciful Allah)
6. Daniel Hamm (Latik)

Notes

Chapter one

1. Jacoby, Tamar, *Someone Else's House: America's Unfinished Struggle for Integration*, p. 108.

Chapter two

1. Austin, Allan D., *African Muslims in Antebellum America*, p. 12.
2. *Ibid*, p. 6–17.
3. *Ibid*, p. 40.
4. Leaming, Hugo P., "The Ben Ishmael Tribe: A Fugitive 'Nation' of the Old Northwest," *Gone to Croatan*, ed. Ron Sakolsky and James Koehnline, p. 20.
5. *Ibid.*
6. *Ibid*, p. 50–51.
7. *Ibid*, p. 27.
8. Bey, Hakim, *TAZ*, p. 119.
9. Leaming, Hugo P., "The Ben Ishmael Tribe: A Fugitive 'Nation' of the Old Northwest," *Gone to Croatan*, ed. Ron Sakolsky and James Koehnline, p. 45.
10. *Ibid.*, p. 47.
11. Watts, Jill, God, *Harlem U.S.A.: the Father Divine Story*, p. 26.
12. *Ibid.*
13. *Ibid*, p. 28.
14. *Ibid.*
15. *Ibid*, p. 30.
16. *Ibid*, p. 36.
17. *Ibid*, p. 38.
18. *Ibid*, p. 41.
19. *Ibid*, p. 34–36.
20. *Ibid*, p. 67.
21. *Ibid.*
22. *Ibid*, p. 43.
23. *Ibid*, p. 65.
24. *Ibid*, p. 90.
25. *Ibid* d, p. 88.
26. *Ibid*, p. 89.
27. Gomez, Michael A., *Black Crescent*, p. 210–211.
28. Cronon, E. David, *Marcus Garvey*, p. 163.

29. *Ibid*, p. 176.
30. Saadi El, Chief Minister Ra, *The Moorish Science Temple of America & the Nation of Islam.*
31. Saadi El, Chief Minister Ra, *I am Your Prophet.*
32. Wilson, Peter Lamborn, *Sacred Drift: Essays on the Margins of Islam*, p. 29.
33. Cronon, E. David, *Marcus Garvey*, p. 181.
34. *Ibid*, p. 181–182.
35. *Ibid*, p. 179.
36. *Ibid*, p. 180.
37. Nance, Susan, "Respectability and Representation: the Moorish Science Temple, Morocco, and Black Public Culture in 1920s Chicago," *American Quarterly*, Vol. 54, No.4, p. 630.
38. Leaming, Hugo P., "The Ben Ishmael Tribe: A Fugitive 'Nation' of the Old Northwest," *Gone to Croatan*, ed. Ron Sakolsky and James Koehnlein, p. 49.
39. Nance, Susan, "Respectability and Representation: the Moorish Science Temple, Morocco, and Black Public Culture in 1920s Chicago," *American Quarterly*, Vol. 54, No.4, p. 636.
40. *Ibid*, p. 631.
41. Leaming, Hugo P., "The Ben Ishmael Tribe: A Fugitive 'Nation' of the Old Northwest," *Gone to Croatan*, ed. Ron Sakolsky and James Koehnline,
42. Saadi El, Chief Minister Ra, *I am Your Prophet.*
43. Koran Questions for Moorish Americans.
44. Nance, Susan, "Respectability and Representation: the Moorish Science Temple, Morocco, and Black Public Culture in 1920s Chicago," *American Quarterly*, Vol. 54, No.4, p. 643–644.
45. *Ibid.*
46. Saadi El, Chief Minister Ra, *I am Your Prophet.*
47. *Ibid.*
48. Saadi El, Chief Minister Ra, *The Controversial Years of the Moorish Science Temple of America*, Book 2.
49. Clegg, Claude Andrew, *An Original Man: the Life and Times of Elijah Muhammad*, p. 17–18.
50. *The Watchtower*, April 1, 2004, p. 5.
51. *Detroit News*, November 23, 1934.
52. Supreme Wisdom Lessons.
53. Beynon, E.D., "The Voodoo Cult Among Negro Migrants in Detroit," *The American Journal of Sociology*, Vol. 43, No.6 (May, 1938), p. 901.
54. *Ibid*, p. 902.
55. *Ibid.*
56. Muhammad, Wallace Deen, *As the Light Shineth from the East*, p. 210.
57. *Detroit News*, November 22, 1932.
58. *Detroit News*, November 23, 1932.
59. Evanzz, Karl, *The Messenger*, p. 96–100.
60. *Ibid.*
61. Supreme Wisdom Lessons.

62. *Bilalian News*, March 19, 1976, 23–26.
63. *Ibid.*
64. Supreme Wisdom Lessons.
65. Gardell, Mattias, *In the Name of Elijah Muhammad: Louis Farrakhan and the Nation of Islam*, p. 144.
66. Allen, Ernest, "Satokata Takahashi and the Flowering of Black Messianic Nationalism," *The Black Scholar*, Volume 24, No.1, p. 29.
67. Moorish Science Temple of America, FBI file.
68. Allen, Ernest, "Satokata Takahashi and the Flowering of Black Messianic Nationalism," *The Black Scholar*, Volume 24, No.1, p. 37.
69. *Ibid*, p. 32.
70. *Ibid*, p. 37.
71. Wolcott, Victoria W., *Remaking Respectability: African American Women in Interwar Detroit*, p. 168.
72. *The People's Voice*, February 28, 1942, p. 2.
73. Moorish Science Temple of America, FBI file.
74. Dannin, Robert, *Black Pilgrimage to Islam*, p. 32.
75. Bey, C.M., *Clock of Destiny*, p. 41.
76. *Ibid.*
77. Bey, C.M., *Clock of Destiny Volume II*, p. 5.
78. *Ibid*, p. 21.
79. *Ibid*, p. 17.
80. *Ibid*, p. 42.
81. Bey, C.M., *Clock of Destiny Volume II*, p. 5.
82. Bey, C.M., *Clock of Destiny*, p. 42.
83. *Ibid.*
84. Interview with Muhammed al-Ahari El.
85. Saadi El, Chief Minister Ra, *The Controversial Years of the Moorish Science Temple of America, Book 2.*
86. York, Malachi, *Shaikh Daoud vs. W.D. Fard*, p. 88.
87. *Sun of Man*, Issue #4, p. 3.

Chapter three

1. "Jim Crow Laws: Virginia," jimcrowhistory.org.
2. *The WORD*, Vol.1, No.2 (July 1987), p. 3.
3. *The Autobiography of Malcolm X*, p. 222.
4. *Ibid*, p. 224.
5. Clarence 13X, FBI file.
6. Fatir, Amir, *Why Does Muhammad & Any Muslim Murder the Devil?*, p. 16.
7. *Ibid.*
8. Allah, Supreme Scientist, *Out of Doors.*
9. Clarence 13X, FBI file.
10. Shahid, Abu, "Let's Straighten it!" black7.org.
11. Allah, Um, "Nation History, Part 2," audio recording, black7.org.

12. "History of the Father," VHS recording.
13. Allah, Um, "Nation History, Part 2," audio recording, black7.org.
14. Cuba, Prince, *Our Mecca is Harlem: Clarence 13X (Allah) and the Five Percent*, p. 6–7.
15. Allah, Beautiful Life, *History of the First Born of Allah: Black Messiah*, p. 3.
16. Supreme Wisdom Lessons.
17. *New York Amsterdam News*, June 21, 1969.
18. correspondence with Allah Supreme God, November 24, 2005.
19. http://www.mosque7.org/livewebcam/liveatthemosque.htm.
20. Dodd and Pearson, "Black Gods in Red Bank: the Five Percent Nation in Central New Jersey," *Journal of Gang Research*, Volume 10, Issue 1, p. 68.
21. interview with Allah Supreme God, June 2005.
22. interview with Willieen Jowers, August 23, 2005.
23. interview with Abu Shahid.
24. interview with Abu Shahid, February 2005.
25. "Abu Shahid," VHS recording.
26. conversation with Akbar Muhammad, September 2005.
27. Dodd and Pearson, "Black Gods in Red Bank: the Five Percent Nation in Central New Jersey," *Journal of Gang Research*, Volume 10, Issue 1, p. 68.
28. interview with Allah Supreme God, June 2005.
29. interview with Abu Shahid.
30. *Learn and Know Your History, Part 3*, p. 3.
31. *The Autobiography of Malcolm X*, p. 313.
32. Allen, Ernest, "Religious Heterodoxy and Nationalist Tradition: The Continuing Evolution of the Nation of Islam," *The Black Scholar*, Vol. 26, No.3–4, p. 14.

Chapter four

1. Nelson, Truman, *The Torture of Mothers*, p. 9–11.
2. *The Black Power Revolt: a Collection of Essays*, Floyd B. Barbour, ed, p. 240–242.
3. interview with Abu Shahid, February 2005.
4. *New York Times*, May 29, 1964.
5. *New York Times*, May 7, 1964.
6. *New York Times*, May 10, 1964.
7. *Malcolm X Speaks*, George Breitman, ed, p. 67.
8. *New York Times*, February 22, 1969.
9. Baldwin, James, *Price of the Ticket*, p. 424.
10. "History of the Father," VHS recording.
11. Malakiy#17, "The Love that Hate Couldn't Destroy," *FEDS*, Vol. 4, Issue 1, p. 66.

Chapter five

1. interview with Allah Supreme God.
2. The Supreme Wisdom Lessons.
3. *Learn and Know Your History, Part 2*, p. 10.

4. *Ibid.*
5. *The Problem Book.*
6. interview with Abu Shahid, June 2005.
7. *Learn and Know Your History, Part 2*, p. 10.
8. *Ibid.*
9. *Ibid.*
10. *Learn and Know Your History, Part 2*, p. 12.
11. Bey, C.M., *Clock of Destiny*, p. 18.
12. Muhammad, Elijah, *Theology of Time*, p. 290.
13. *Learn and Know Your History, Part 2*, p. 12.
14. interview with Abu Shahid.
15. *Learn and Know Your History*, Part 2. p. 12.
16. "Abu Shahid," VHS recording.
17. Eye God, October 2004 Universal Parliament, video recording.
18. *Ibid.*
19. "Nation History, Part 1," audio recording, black7.org.
20. *The Five Percenter*, September 1995.
21. "Abu Shahid," VHS recording.
22. Bey, C.M., *Clock of Destiny*, p. 41.
23. interview with Allah Supreme God.
24. *Ibid.*
25. interview with Abu Shahid, August 12, 2005.
26. interview with Supreme Understanding Allah, April 22, 2006.
27. *Learn and Know Your History, Part 2*, p. 18.
28. *Learn and Know Your History, Part 2*, p. 17.
29. Simmons, Russell, *Life and Def.*
30. *The Five Percenter*, July 1996, p. 5.
31. Allah, Beautiful Life, *History of the First Born of Allah: Black Messiah.*
32. *Ibid.*
33. interview with Supreme Understanding Allah, April 22, 2006.
34. interview with Ja'mella God Allah.
35. "Wisdom of Allah the Father," audio recording.
36. *Learn and Know Your History*, p. 7.
37. interview with Allah Supreme God.
38. interview with ABG Allah, December 19, 2004.
39. interview with Jamar Allah, June 2005.
40. *Sun of Man*, January 2006.
41. Lefever, Harry G., "Leaving the United States: The Black Nationalist Themes of Orisha-Vodu," *Journal of Black Studies*, Vol.31, No.2 (November 2000), p. 178–179.
42. *Ibid*, p. 180.
43. *The Five Percenter*, September 1995.
44. interview with Abu Shahid.
45. *Learn and Know Your History, Part 2*, p. 41.
46. Malakiy#17, "The Love that Hate Couldn't Destroy," *FEDS*, Vol. 4, Issue 17, p. 69.
47. interview with Willieen Jowers, August 23, 2005.

48. interview with Allah Supreme God.
49. interview with Jamar Allah, June 2005.
50. Al'Jaa'maar-U-Allah, Infinite, *A Peek into the Five Percent Nation*, p. 16–17.
51. interview with Allah Supreme God, June 2005.
52. interview with Al-Jamel, May 2005.
53. *Learn and Know Your History, Part 2*, p. 20.
54. Dannin, Robert, *Black Pilgrimage to Islam*, p. 170.
55. *Learn and Know Your History, Part 3*, p. 3.
56. *Learn and Know Your History, Part 2*, p. 20.
57. interview with ABG Allah, December 2004.
58. *Sun of Man, Issue #4.*
59. *Ibid.*
60. *Learn and Know Your History*, p. 54.
61. Universal Parliament, October 2004, DVD recording.
62. interview with Abu Shahid.
63. conversation with Freedom Allah.
64. Universal Parliament, October 2004, DVD recording.
65. Dannin, Robert, *Black Pilgrimage to Islam*, p. 151.
66. *The Autobiography of Malcolm X*, p. 225.
67. *Learn and Know Your History, Part 2*, p. 21.

Chapter six

1. interview with First Born Al-Jamel.
2. *Blood Bath: The True Teaching of Malcolm X*, p. 14.
3. *Ibid*, p. 15–16.
4. *Ibid.*
5. Evanzz, Karl, *The Judas Factor: The Plot to Kill Malcolm X*, p. 303.
6. *Ibid*, 19–51.
7. interview with Supreme Understanding Allah, April 22, 2006.
8. Clarence 13X Smith, FBI file.
9. interview with Allah Supreme God.
10. Allah, Beautiful Life, *History of the First Born of Allah: Black Messiah*, p. 7.
11. interview with Al-Jamel, May 2005.
12. *New York Times*, June 2, 1965.
13. *Ibid.*
14. Five Percenters, FBI file.
15. *Learn and Know Your History, Part 3*, p. 24.
16. interview with Gykee Mathematics Allah.
17. *New York Times*, June 20, 1965.
18. Five Percenters, FBI file.
19. *Ibid.*
20. *Ibid.*
21. Watts, Jill, *God, Harlem U.S.A.: The Father Divine Story*, p. 93.
22. Allah, Beautiful Life, *History of the First Born of Allah: Black Messiah*, p. 9.

Chapter seven

1. interview with Allah Supreme God.
2. Five Percenters, FBI file.
3. *New York Times*, October 20, 1965.
4. Five Percenters, FBI file.
5. *New York Times*, October 20, 1965.
6. Five Percenters, FBI file.
7. *New York Times*, October 22, 1965.
8. *New Pittsburgh Courier*, October 16, 1965.
9. *New York Times*, October 16, 1965.
10. *New York Amsterdam News*, October 16, 1965.
11. *New York Times*, October 19, 1965.
12. *New York Times*, October 16, 1965.
13. *New Pittsburgh Courier*, October 16, 1965.
14. Five Percenters, FBI file.
15. *Ibid.*
16. *Ibid.*
17. Clarence 13X, FBI file.
18. "Wisdom of Allah the Father," audio recording.
19. Casanova, Ron, *Each One Teach One*, p. 48.
20. *Ibid*, p. 47.
21. American Civil Liberties Union archives, Mental Health Issues, box 1061, folder 23. Seeley G. Mudd Manuscript Library, Princeton University.
22. *New York Times*, May 21, 1968.
23. American Civil Liberties Union archives, Mental Health Issues, box 1063, folder 19. Seeley G. Mudd Manuscript Library, Princeton University.
24. New York State Archives, folder A1516.
25. *Ibid.*
26. Gottehrer, Barry, *The Mayor's Man*, p. 100.
27. "Wisdom of Allah the Father," audio recording.
28. *Ibid.*
29. *The WORD*, Vol.1, No.1 (June 1987), p. 8.
30. "History of the Father," VHS recording, June 13, 1997.
31. New York State Archives, folder A1507.
32. *Learn and Know Your History, Part 2*, p. 22.
33. interview with Allah B conducted by Paul Greenhouse, DVD recording, August 19, 2005.
34. *Learn and Know Your History, Part 3*, p. 18.
35. *Learn and Know Your History*, p. 24.
36. *Ibid.*
37. interview with Um Allah, May 2005.
38. Sackett, Russell, "Plotting a War on Whitey," *Life*, June 10, 1966, p. 106–109.
39. *Ibid.*
40. *Ibid.*
41. *Ibid.*

42. *Ibid.*
43. *New York Amsterdam News,* June 21, 1969.
44. "interview with the Father," black7.org.
45. *The Five Percenter,* May 1996, p. 3.
46. conversation with I Majestic Allah.
47. interview with Azreal, May 2005.
48. interview with Azreal, June 2004.
49. Wilmore, Gayraud S., *Black Religion and Black Radicalism,* p. 201.
50. Five Percenters, FBI file.
51. *Learn and Know Your History, Part 3,* p. 17.
52. *Ibid,* p. 4.
53. interview with Azreal.
54. Gottehrer, Barry, *The Mayor's Man,* p. 100.
55. *Ibid.*
56. Clarence 13X, FBI file.
57. *Ibid,* p. 92.
58. *The WORD,* Vol.1, No.3, August/September 1987, p. 7.
59. *Ibid.*
60. *New York Herald Tribune,* October 15, 1965.
61. *Learn and Know Your History,* Part 3, p. 29.
62. interview with Um Allah.
63. *The Five Percenter,* November 1997, p. 11.
64. Allah, Almighty God Dawud, "Rebuttal to the Article Entitled, 'An Appeal to the Nation of Gods and Earths.' "
65. *The WORD,* Vol. 1, No.1 (June 1987), p. 8.
66. Supreme Wisdom Lessons.
67. *Sun of Man,* March 2006, p. 8.
68. *Learn and Know Your History, Part 3,* p. 18.
69. *The History and Designing of Our Universal Flag,* p. 2.
70. *Sun of Man,* March 2006, p. 3.
71. *Ibid,* p. 7.
72. "Wisdom of Allah the Father," audio recording.
73. Universal Parliament, October 2000, VHS recording.

Chapter eight

1. Dawley, David, *A Nation of Lords: the Autobiography of the Vice Lords,* p. 9.
2. *Ibid,* p. 65.
3. *Ibid,* p. 143.
4. Ciccone, F. Richard, *Daley: Power and Presidential Politics,* p. 202.
5. Dawley, David, *A Nation of Lords: the Autobiography of the Vice Lords,* p. 130.
6. Fry, John, *Fire and Blackstone,* p. 102.
7. Adam Cohen and Elizabeth Taylor, *American Pharaoh: Mayor Richard J. Daley: His Battle for Chicago and the Nation,* p. 441.
8. interview with Sid Davidoff, August 2005.

9. Gottehrer, Barry, *The Mayor's Man*, p. 67.

10. *Ibid*, p. 67.

11. *Ibid*, p. 92.

12. interview with Sid Davidoff, August 16, 2005.

13. *Ibid*.

14. Gottehrer, Barry, *The Mayor's Man*, p. 92.

15. *Ibid*, 93–94.

16. Featherstone, Joseph, *Schools Where Children Learn*, p. 116.

17. *Ibid*, p. 117.

18. *Ibid*, p. 119.

19. *Ibid*, p. 120.

20. *Ibid*, p. 120–121.

21. Gottehrer, Barry, *The Mayor's Man*, p. 95.

22. *The New York Times*, September 22, 1968.

23. Gottehrer, Barry, *The Mayor's Man*, p. 66.

24. *The New York Times*, August 6, 1967.

25. interview with Sid Davidoff, August 16, 2005.

26. *Ibid*.

27. Gottehrer, Barry, *The Mayor's Man*, p. 100.

28. Featherstone, Joseph, *Schools Where Children Learn*, p. 121–122.

29. *Ibid*.

30. *Ibid*, p. 133.

31. "Wisdom of Allah the Father," audio recording.

32. Featherstone, Joseph, *Schools Where Children Learn*, p. 133.

33. *Ibid*.

34. *New York Times*, October 2, 1967.

35. Featherstone, Joseph, *Schools Where Children Learn*, p. 117.

36. *Ibid*, p. 132.

37. Gottehrer, Barry, *The Mayor's Man*, p. 101.

38. "Wisdom of Allah the Father," audio recording.

39. *New York Times*, October 2, 1967.

40. *The NGE Power*, October 2002, p. 16.

41. letter from First Born Prince Allah to Knowledge Born Azee Allah, August 16, 1991.

42. Featherstone, Joseph, *Schools Where Children Learn*, p. 133.

43. *New York Times*, August 22, 1967.

44. *New York Times*, May 8, 1968.

45. B, Allah, *The Father's Educational Show and Prove*, p. 4.

46. interview with Allah Supreme God.

47. Gottehrer, Barry, *The Mayor's Man*, p. 102.

48. interview with Knowledge Allah.

49. King James Bible.

50. Koran Questions for Moorish Americans.

51. *Sun of Man*, June 2005, p. 10.

52. *Learn and Know Your History*, p. 19–21.

53. Bey, C. Kirkman, *The Mysteries of the Silent Brotherhood of the East*, p. 37–43.
54. conversation with Paul Greenhouse.
55. Ansaru Allah Community, FBI file.
56. interview with Infinite Al'Jaa'Maar-U-Allah, April 30, 2006.
57. *Learn and Know Your History*, Part 3, p. 29.
58. *Learn and Know Your History*, Part 2, p. 25.
59. *Learn and Know Your History*, p. 34.
60. *Ibid*, p. 35.
61. *Learn and Know Your History*, Part 2, p. 25.
62. interview with Infinite Al'Jaa'Maar-U-Allah, April 30, 2006.
63. *Ibid.*
64. *The Five Percenter*, January 2005.
65. "History of Allah the Father," video recording, June 13, 1997.
66. Gottehrer, Barry, *The Mayor's Man*, p. 102.
67. *Ibid*, p. 238.
68. Cannato, Vincent J., *The Ungovernable City: John Lindsay and His Struggle to Save New York*, p. 131.
69. interview with Omar Abdul-Malik, April 12, 2005.
70. *Ibid.*
71. Supreme Wisdom Lessons.
72. interview with Omar Abdul-Malik, April 12, 2005.
73. Cannato, Vincent J., *The Ungovernable City: John Lindsay and His Struggle to Save New York*, p. 219–220.
74. *Learn and Know Your History*, p. 25.
75. *Ibid.*
76. U.S. Senate. Committee on Appropriations. Hearings, 28 February 1968, p. 69.
77. *Ibid.*
78. interview with Sid Davidoff, August 16, 2005.
79. Gottehrer, Barry, *The Mayor's Man*, p. 210–211.
80. Cannato, Vincent J., *The Ungovernable City: John Lindsay and His Struggle to Save New York*, p. 211.
81. Lindsay, John, *The City*, p. 98–99.
82. Adam Cohen and Elizabeth Taylor, *American Pharaoh: Mayor Richard Daley: His Battle for Chicago and the Nation*, p. 454–455.
83. *Ibid*, p. 454.
84. *Ibid*, p. 455.
85. *Washington Post*, April 12, 1968.
86. *New York*, April 22, 1968, p. 32C.
87. interview with Sid Davidoff, August 16, 2005.
88. *New York*, April 22, 1968, p. 32H.
89. *Ibid.*
90. *Learn and Know Your History*, Part 3, p. 20.
91. *Time*, November 1, 1968, p. 20.
92. interview with Allah Supreme God.
93. interview with Willieen Jowers, August 23, 2005.

94. "Wisdom of Allah the Father," audio recording.
95. interview with Sid Davidoff, August 16, 2005.
96. *Ibid.*
97. "Wisdom of Allah the Father," audio recording.
98. *New York*, April 22, 1968, p. 32F.
99. Clegg, Claude Andrew, *An Original Man: The Life and Times of Elijah Muhammad*, p. 240–241.
100. Cannato, Vincent J., *The Ungovernable City: John Lindsay and His Struggle to Save New York*, p. 213.
101. "Wisdom of Allah the Father," audio recording.
102. *New York*, April 22, 1968, p. 32F.
103. *Ibid.*
104. *Ibid.*
105. *New York Times*, February 28, 1966.
106. "Wisdom of Allah the Father," audio recording.
107. *Ibid.*
108. *New York Times*, September 22, 1968.
109. *Learn and Know Your History*, p. 20.
110. *Ibid*, p. 26.
111. *The Five Percenter*, September 1995.

Chapter nine

1. interview with Allah Supreme God.
2. *F.E.D.S.*, Vol.4, Issue 17, p. 70.
3. *The Five Percenter*, November 1997, p. 11.
4. *The Five Percenter*, May 1996, p. 2–3.
5. *The Five Percenter*, June 1996, p. 13.
6. *Ibid.*
7. Gottehrer, Barry, *The Mayor's Man*, p. 234.
8. Gottehrer, Barry, *The Mayor's Man*, p. 239.
9. *Ibid.*
10. *Ibid.*
11. interview with Sid Davidoff, August 16, 2005.
12. *Learn and Know Your History, Part 3*, p. 20.
13. *Learn and Know Your History*, p. 26.
14. *Ibid*, p. 26.
15. October 2004 Universal Parliament, VHS recording.
16. *Learn and Know Your History*, p. 26.
17. *New York Times*, June 24, 1969.
18. Gottehrer, Barry, *The Mayor's Man*, p. 240.
19. *Sun of Man*, August 2005, p. 8.
20. *New York Amsterdam News*, August 16, 1969.
21. *Ibid*, p. 245.
22. interview with Abu Shahid.

23. *The WORD*, Vol.1, No.4 (October/November 1987), p. 7.
24. interview with Willieen Jowers.
25. interview with Allah Supreme God.
26. Gottehrer, Barry, *The Mayor's Man*, p. 245.
27. interview with Barry Gottehrer, May 2005.
28. interview with Abu Shahid.
29. *Learn and Know Your History, Part 2*, p. 13.
30. interview with Allah Supreme God.
31. Gottehrer, Barry, *The Mayor's Man*, p. 246.
32. *Learn and Know Your History, Part 2*, p. 23.
33. *New York Times*, October 21, 1969.
34. Gottehrer, Barry, *The Mayor's Man*, p. 257.
35. *New York Times*, March 4, 1970.
36. *Learn and Know Your History, Part 3*, p. 21.

Chapter ten

1. correspondence with Amir Fatir, August 27, 2005.
2. Hobbs, Sterling, *Black Angels*.
3. *The Five Percenter*, August 2002, p. 2.
4. *The WORD*, Vol.1, No.4 (October/November 1987), p. 7.
5. interview with Beloved Allah, January 29, 2006.
6. Labov, William, *Language in the Inner City*, p. 210.
7. *Learn and Know Your History*, p. 26.
8. Allen, Ernest, "Making the Strong Survive: the Contours and Contradictions of Message Rap," p. 188.
9. *The Five Percenter*, February 1998, p. 10.
10. *The Five Percenter*, June 2003, p. 2.
11. interview with Omar Abdul-Malik, April 12, 2005.
12. *Wattstax*.
13. Hobbs, Sterling, *Black Angels*, p. 56–58.
14. Cannato, Vincent J., *The Ungovernable City: John Lindsay and His Struggle to Save New York*, p. 484–487.
15. Clegg, Claude Andrew III, *An Original Man: The Life and Times of Elijah Muhammad*, p. 277.
16. Gardell, Mattias, *In the Name of Elijah Muhammad: Louis Farrakhan and the Nation of Islam*, p. 155, 179, 225.
17. Allah, Wakeel, "Did the Most Honorable Elijah Muhammad Recognize the Five Percenters?", http://www.allahteam.com/5percentprops.htm.
18. *Ibid*.
19. http://www.muhammadspeaks.com/TheLastSermon.html.

Chapter eleven

1. Dannin, Robert, *Black Pilgrimage to Islam*, p. 67.
2. *Learn and Know Your History*, p. 47.

3. interview with Allah Supreme God, August 2005.
4. Campbell, Anne, *Girls in the Gang*. p. 232.
5. *Learn and Know Your History, Part 3*, p. 45.
6. *Ibid.*
7. *The Five Percenter*, September 1995.
8. Campbell, Anne, *The Girls in the Gang*, p. 177.
9. *Learn and Know Your History, Part 3*, p. 47.
10. *Learn and Know Your History, Part 2*, p. 27.
11. *Ibid.*
12. *Ibid*, p. 55.
13. interview with Allah Supreme God.
14. *The Five Percenter*, October 1995, p. 16.
15. *Ibid.*
16. People v. Allah (1988), Court of Appeals of New York.
17. People v. Allah (1987), Court of Appeals of New York.
18. People v. Allah (1988), Court of Appeals of New York.
19. Campbell, Anne, *The Girls in the Gang*.
20. *Learn and Know Your History, Part 3*, p. 47–49.
21. *The Five Percenter*, November 1997, p. 5.
22. interview with Beloved Allah, January 29, 2006.
23. *Learn and Know Your History*, p. 55.
24. *Sun of Man*, August 2005, p. 14.
25. *New York Times*, February 16, 1982.
26. Dodd and Pearson, "Black Gods in Red Bank: the Five Percent Nation in Central New Jersey," *Journal of Gang Research*, Volume 10, Issue 1, p. 71.
27. Corbiscello, George, "A Nation of Gods: the Five Percent Nation of Islam," *Journal of Gang Research*, Volume 5, Issue 2, p. 65.
28. *Sun of Man*, August 2005, p. 9.
29. LL Cool J, *I Make My Own Rules*, p. 52.
30. *Learn and Know Your History*, p. 15.
31. *The Five Percenter*, January 2006, p. 11.
32. *Ibid.*
33. interview with Beloved Allah, January 29, 2006.
34. *Ibid.*
35. *The Five Percenter*, February 1998, p. 11.
36. *The Five Percenter*, October 1995, p. 16.
37. Nas, "Memory Lane (Sittin' in Da Park)," *Illmatic*.
38. Brown, Ethan, *Queens Reigns Supreme*, p. xx.
39. *Ibid*, p. 8.
40. *Ibid*, p. 9.
41. *Ibid*, p. 37.
42. Boots, Tone, "Get Rich or Die Trying," *Stuff*, September 2005, p. 114.
43. *Ibid.*
44. *Ibid*, p. 116.
45. *Ibid.*

46. Brown, Ethan, "Rap Attack." *New York Magazine*, December 1, 2003.
47. Ja Rule, "Survival of the Illest 2 Intro,"
48. Brown, Ethan, "Rap Attack." *New York Magazine*, December 1, 2003.
49. New York Daily News, November 22, 2005.
50. Brown, Ethan, "Rap Attack." *New York Magazine*, December 1, 2003.
51. 50 Cent, "Ghetto Qu'ran," *Power of the Dollar.*
52. Boots, Tone, "Get Rich or Die Trying," *Stuff*, September 2005, p. 112.
53. *The NGE Power*, October 2002, p. 2.
54. *Ibid.*
55. *Ibid*, p. 13.
56. *The WORD*, Vol.1, No.1 (June 1987), p. 1.
57. *The WORD*, Vol.1, No.3 (August/September 1987), p. 2.
58. *The WORD*, Vol.1, No.5 (December/January 1988), p. 5.
59. *The WORD*, Vol.1, No.9 (August 1989), p. 1.
60. *The WORD*, Vol.1, No.6, (February 1987), p. 2
61. *Ibid*, p. 15.
62. interview with Beloved Allah, January 29, 2006.
63. *Ibid.*
64. *The WORD*, Vol.1, No.4 (October/November 1987), p. 6.
65. correspondence with Prince A Cuba.
66. *Sun of Man*
67. *Learn and Know Your History, Part 2*, p. 23.

Chapter twelve

1. *Attica: the Official Report of the New York State Special Commission on Attica*, p. 122–123.
2. *Ibid.*
3. *Ibid.*
4. Herman Badillo and Milton Hayes, *A Bill of No Rights: Attica and the American Prison System*, p. 11.
5. *Learn and Know Your History*, p. 26.
6. U.S. House. Committee on Internal Security. Revolutionary Activities Directed Toward the Administration of Penal or Correctional Systems, hearings, March 29 and May 1, 1973, p. 317.
7. *Ibid*, p. 316.
8. *Ibid*, p. 308.
9. *Attica: the Official Report of the New York State Special Commission on Attica*, p. 129.
10. *Ibid.*
11. *Ibid*, p. 120.
12. *Ibid*, p. 121.
13. *Ibid*, p. 121.
14. *New York Times*, August 16, 1970.
15. *Ibid.*

16. *Ibid.*
17. *New York Times,* November 15, 1970.
18. *Attica: the Official Report of the New York State Special Commission on Attica,* p. 129.
19. *New York Times,* March 12, 1971.
20. *Attica: the Official Report of the New York State Special Commission on Attica,* p. 138.
21. *Ibid,* p. 139.
22. U.S. House. Committee on Internal Security. Revolutionary Activities Directed Toward the Administration of Penal or Correctional Systems, hearings, March 29 and May 1, 1973, p. 317.
23. *Ibid.*
24. *Ibid,* p. 308.
25. interview with Allah Supreme God.
26. *New York Times,* May 24, 1976,
27. *New York Times,* December 27, 1985.
28. http://www.gangsorus.com.
29. *Ibid.*
30. Knox, George W, *An Introduction to Gangs,* p. 147.
31. *Ibid,* p. 215.
32. *Ibid.*
33. *Ibid,* p. 507.
34. *Maaria v. Broaddus* (2003), 21.
35. *Ibid,* 28.
36. *Ibid,* p. 43.
37. *Ibid,* p. 44.
38. Brown, Ethan, *Queens Reigns Supreme,* p. 25–26.
39. *Maaria v. Broaddus* (2003), p. 57–58.
40. *Ibid,* p. 45–46.
41. *Ibid,* p. 40.
42. *Ibid,* p. 25–27.
43. Corbiscello, George, "A Nation of Gods: the Five Percent Nation of Islam," *Journal of Gang Research,* Volume 5, Issue 2, p. 69.
44. *Ibid.*
45. *Ibid.*
46. *New York Post,* March 3, 2002, p. 21.
47. *New York Post,* July 12, 2002, p. 14.
48. *Ibid,* p. 9.
49. *The Five Percenter,* October 2001, p. 2.
50. http://www.adl.org/hate_symbols/Five_Percenters.asp.
51. U.S. Senate. Committee on the Judiciary. Subcommittee to Investigate Juvenile Delinquency. Juvenile Confinement Institutions and Correctional Systems, hearings, 1972, p. 677.
52. "Born Lessons," audio recording.

Chapter thirteen

1. *Yes, Yes, Y'all: The Experience Music Project Oral History of Hip-Hop's First Decade.*
2. Eric B. & Rakim, "No Competition," *Follow the Leader.*
3. World Famous Supreme Team, "Hey D.J."
4. *The Five Percenter,* January 2002, p. 10.
5. interview with Sadat X, August 18, 2006.
6. audio recording, black7.org.
7. Gull Hasan, Asma, *American Muslims,* p. 5; *Why I am a Muslim,* p. 12.
8. Brand Nubian, "Allah U Akbar," *In God We Trust.*
9. Nas, "U.B.R. (Unauthorized Biography of Rakim)," *Street's Disciple.*
10. interview with Lord Jamar, August 18, 2006.
11. Rakim, "The Mystery (Who is God)," *The 18th Letter.*
12. *Ibid.*
13. *Ibid.*
14. *Ibid.*
15. *Ibid.*
16. *Ibid.*
17. *Black Seven,* January 2003, p. 23.
18. *Ibid.*
19. *Ibid.*
20. interview with Raekwon, August 17, 2006.
21. interview with the RZA, August 17, 2006.
22. The RZA, "The Birth," *Birth of a Prince.*
23. *Ibid.*
24. *Ibid.*
25. *Ibid.*
26. Ol' Dirty Bastard, "Rawhide," *Return to the 36 Chambers: the Dirty Version.*
27. The RZA, *The Wu-Tang Manual,* p. 8.
28. *Ibid,* p. 43.
29. RZA, "The Birth," *Birth of a Prince.*
30. Allah, Dasun, "Civilized People," *Village Voice,* November 13–19, 2002.
31. *The Source,* June 2005, p. 16.
32. *Village Voice,* November 23–29, 2005, p. 28.

Chapter fourteen

1. http://www.divineizearth.blogspot.com.
2. http://www.imajestic.blogspot.com.
3. *Sun of Man, Issue #4.*
4. Allah, I Majestic, "Is the Nation of Gods and Earths a Muslim Community?"
5. http://www.metalab.unc.edu/nge/notmuslims.html.
6. "Abu Shahid," VHS recording.
7. *The Five Percenter,* November 1997, p. 11.

8. *Sun of Man*, p. 2.
9. *Ibid.*
10. *Ibid.*
11. Allah, Prince, "Lost-Found Muslim Lesson #3, The Third Prophecy."
12. *The Five Percenter*, August 1998, p. 2.
13. "Teaching for the Civilized Lost Found Tribe."
14. Allah, Supreme Scientist, *Out of Doors.*
15. *Ibid.*
16. *Ibid.*
17. *Ibid.*
18. *Sun of Man*, July 1983, p. 2.
19. *Ibid.*
20. *Ibid.*
21. *Sun of Man*, October 1984, p. 2.
22. *Sun of Man*, August 2005, p. 21.
23. *NGE Power*, October 2002, p. 7.
24. *Ibid.*
25. Noor, Abdul, *The Supreme Understanding: the Teachings of Islam in North America*, p. 157–161.
26. *The WORD*, Vol.1, No.7 (May 1988).
27. The RZA, *The Wu-Tang Manual*, p. 44.
28. Lord Jamar, *The 5% Album.*
29. Allah, Almighty God Dawud, *The Black Babies are the Greatest*, p. 41.
30. *Ibid*, p. 25–33.
31. Allah, Almighty God Dawud, *The Secrets of Freemasonry Revealed*, p. 33.
32. *The Five Percent Concepts: Allah World Manifest.*
33. *Ibid.*
34. interview with the RZA, August 17, 2006.
35. *Sun of Man*, Issue #4.
36. *The Five Percenter*, February 1998, p. 5.
37. *The Universal Truth*, Vol.2, No.6, p. 17.
38. Cuba, Prince, *Our Mecca is Harlem: Clarence 13X (Allah) and the Five Percent*, p. 5.
39. *Gnosis*, Fall 1992, p. 56–63.
40. http://www.imajestic.blogspot.com.
41. *The Five Percenter*, October 1995, p. 16.
42. *Ibid*, p. 56.
43. *The Five Percenter*, November 1995, p. 11.
44. Cuba, Prince, *Our Mecca is Harlem: Clarence 13X (Allah) and the Five Percent*, p. 6.
45. *The Universal Truth*, Vol.2, No.4, p. 12–14.
46. *Ibid*, p. 5.
47. *Learn and Know Your History, Part 2*, p. 9.
48. correspondence with Prince A Cuba, August 25, 2005.
49. *Sun of Man*, Issue #7, p. 3.
50. *The WORD*, Vol.1, No.3 (August/September 1987), p. 6.
51. http://metalab.unc.edu/nge/thebomb.html.

52. *Ibid*, p. 5–6.
53. *Ibid*, p. 7.
54. http://www.metalab.unc.edu/nge/graftedflag.
55. correspondence with Prince A Cuba.
56. Cuba, Prince, *Our Mecca is Harlem: Clarence 13X (Allah) and the Five Percent*, p. 52.
57. *The Universal Truth*, Vol.2, No.5, p. 8.
58. *The Enlightener*, December 1986, p. 22.
59. October 2000 Universal Parliament, VHS recording.
60. *The Five Percenter*, November 1995, p. 11.
61. *Ibid.*
62. *Sun of Man*, August 2005, p. 14.
63. York, Malachi Z., *Bible Interpretations and Explanations, Booklet 2*, p. 23.
64. *The Universal Truth*, Vol.2, No.3, p. 29.
65. Al Mahdi, As Sayyid Issa Al Haadi, *Book of the Five Percenters*, 516–564.
66. *Ibid*, p. 625.
67. *The Enlightener*, December 1986, p. 22.
68. *The Five Percenter*, January 1999, p. 2.
69. *The Five Percenter*, November 1995, p. 5.
70. *Ibid*, p. 4.
71. interview with Allah Supreme God.
72. *Learn and Know Your History, Part 2*, p. 21.
73. First Born Prince Allah, *120 Lessons*, audio recording.
74. First Born Prince Allah, October 2000 Universal Parliament, VHS recording.
75. *Learn and Know Your History, Part 2*, p. 38.
76. http://www.allahteam.com/rakim.htm.
77. *Learn and Know Your History*, p. 33.
78. letter from First Born Prince Allah.
79. *Learn and Know Your History, Part 2*, p. 37.
80. *Sun of Man, Issue #4*.
81. *Ibid.*
82. interview with Abu Shahid, August 2005.
83. *Learn and Know Your History*, p. 11.
84. correspondence with Prince A Cuba, August 25, 2005.
85. Nuruddin, Yusuf, "The Five Percenters: a Teenage Nation of Gods and Earths," *Muslim Communities in North America*, Yvonne Yazbeck Haddad and Jane Ideleman Smith, ed, p. 127.

Chapter fifteen

1. correspondence with Prince A Cuba, August 25, 2005.
2. "First Born Lessons," audio recording.
3. *Learn and Know Your History, Part 2*, p. 31.
4. *The Earth's Equality*, vol.1, issue 2.
5. *Learn and Know Your History*, p. 49.

6. Allah, Almighty God Dawud, *The Black Babies are the Greatest*, p. 63.
7. *Ibid.*
8. Campbell, Anne, *The Girls in the Gang*,
9. *The Five Percenter*, February 1999, p. 3.
10. *The Five Percenter*, December 2004, p. 2.
11. *The Five Percenter*, May 2000, p. 2.
12. "Wisdom of Allah the Father," audio recording.
13. Allah, Almighty God Dawud, *The Black Babies are the Greatest*, p. 61.
14. *The Five Percenter*, January 2006, p. 4.
15. "Wisdom of Allah the Father," audio recording.
16. interview with Allah Supreme God, June 2005.
17. *The Five Percenter*, December 1998, p. 5.
18. "Wisdom of Allah the Father," audio recording.
19. *Ibid.*
20. interview with Allah Supreme God.
21. "Wisdom of Allah the Father," audio recording.
22. *Ibid.*
23. *Ibid.*
24. *Ibid.*
25. Gottehrer, Barry, *The Mayor's Man*, p. 105.
26. the Earth Degrees.
27. "Wisdom of Allah the Father," audio recording.
28. "History of the Father," VHS recording, June 13, 1997.
29. *Learn and Know Your History, Part 3*, p. 47.
30. *The Blackwoman and Islam*.
31. Muhammad, Elijah, *Message to the Black Man in America*, p. 117.
32. "Wisdom of Allah the Father," audio recording.
33. Allah, Born, "Marriage," http://trueschool.com/lok/marriage.html.
34. *The Five Percenter*, March 1997, p. 5.
35. correspondence with Prince A Cuba.
36. *The Universal Truth*, Vol.2, No.5, p. 8.
37. *The Universal Truth*, Vol.2, No.4, p. 27.
38. correspondence with Prince A Cuba, August 25, 2005.
39. Silence, Unknown, "The Earth is the Home to Islam," *The Best of Black 7 Vol.III*, p. 17.
40. *Sun of Man*, August 2005, p. 10.
41. http://www.yellowseed.blogspot.com.
42. *The Five Percenter*, March 2006, p. 12.
43. *Learn and Know Your History*, p. 38.
44. *The Blackwoman and Islam*, p. 4
45. *Ibid.*
46. Ghostface Killah, "Wildflower," *Ironman*.
47. Wu-Tang Clan, "Wu Revolution," *Wu-Tang Forever*.
48. Brand Nubian, "Sincerely," *Foundation*.
49. *The Five Percenter*, April 2006, p. 11.

50. *Black 7*, March 2004, p. 53–54.
51. *Ibid*, p. 58.
52. Erykah Badu, "Orange Moon," *Mama's Gun*.
53. *Black 7*, March 2004, p. 60.
54. *The Five Percenter*, November 1997, p. 5.
55. *Ibid*.
56. interview with Allah Supreme God, August 21, 2005.
57. Allah, Almighty God Dawud, *The Black Babies are the Greatest*, p. 60.
58. *The Five Percenter*, September 2001, p. 8.
59. interview with Allah Supreme God, August 21, 2005.
60. *The Five Percenter*, December 2004, p. 2.
61. *The Universal Truth*, Vol.2, No.6, p. 27–29.
62. *Ibid*.
63. *Ibid*.
64. correspondence with Prince A Cuba, August 25, 2005.
65. interview with Beloved Allah.
66. *Ibid*.
67. Universal Parliament, March 2006.
68. *The Sun of Man*, Issue 8.
69. yellowseed.blogspot.com.
70. "Wisdom of Allah the Father," audio recording.
71. *The WORD*, Vol.1, No.4 (October/November 1987), p. 11.
72. *The Five Percenter*, September 2005, p,2, 11.
73. Swedenburg, Ted, "Islam in the Mix: Lessons of the Five Percent."
74. DVD recording, Paul Greenhouse.
75. *The Five Percenter*, October 2005, p. 5.
76. *Ibid*.
77. *The Five Percenter*, August 2005, p. 2.
78. *We are Everywhere: a Historical Sourcebook of Gay and Lesbian Politics*, Mark Blasius and Shane Phelm, ed, p. 404–406.
79. *Ibid*.
80. Allah, Almighty God Dawud, *The Black Babies are the Greatest*, p. 60.
81. "Born Lessons," audio recording.
82. *Ibid*.
83. email correspondence from Allah Jihad, March 16, 2006.
84. Collins, Patricia Hill, "Womanism, Black Feminism and Beyond," *Black Scholar*, Vol.26, No.1 (Winter/Spring 1996), p. 11.
85. Busta Rhymes, "One," *When Disaster Strikes*.
86. *Ibid*.
87. http://www.divineizearth.blogspot.com.

Chapter sixteen

1. *The Five Percenter*, December 2001, p. 10.
2. interview with Supreme Understanding Allah, April 22, 2006.

3. *Ibid.*
4. Miyakawa, Felicia, *Five Percenter Rap: God Hop's Music, Message and Black Muslim Mission*, p. 6.
5. interview with Allah B, March 8, 2006.
6. Casanova, Ron, *Each One Teach One*, p. 54.
7. Badillo, Herman, and Haynes, Milton, *A Bill of No Rights: Attica and the American Prison System*, p. 10.
8. interview with Barry Gottehrer.
9. Muhammad, Elijah, *Our Saviour Has Arrived*, p. 90.
10. interview with Beloved Allah, January 29, 2006.
11. interview with Allah B, March 8, 2006.
12. *Ibid.*
13. email correspondence with Thomas Cowles.
14. Fardan, Dorothy, *Yakub and the Origin of White Supremacy: Message to the Whiteman & Woman in America*, p. 12.
15. *Ibid*, p. 142.
16. *Ibid.*
17. *Ibid*, p. 57.
18. *The Five Percenter*, May 2005, p. 10.
19. "Interview with a White Five Percenter," black7.org.
20. *The NGE Power*, October 2002, p. 15.
21. correspondence with Prince A Cuba, August 25, 2005.
22. Universal Parliament, October 2004, video recording.
23. *The Five Percenter*, December 2004, p. 2.
24. *The Five Percenter*, June 2005, p. 2.
25. conversation with I Majestic Allah, February 2005.
26. *The Five Percenter*, April 2006, p. 12.
27. *The Autobiography of Malcolm X*, p. 347.
28. Gardell, Mattias, "The Sun of Islam Will Rise in the West: Minister Farrakhan and the Nation of Islam in the Latter Days," *Muslim Communities in North America*, Yvonne Yazbeck Haddad and Jane Idleman Smith, p. 30.
29. Evanzz, Karl, *The Messenger*, p. 419.
30. The RZA, "Koto Chotan," *Birth of a Prince*.
31. Boogie Down Productions, "Build and Destroy," *Sex and Violence*.
32. *The Universal Truth*, Vol.2, No.5, p. 13.
33. Best, James, "Black Like Me: John Walker Lindh's Hip-Hop Daze," *East Bay Express*, September 3, 2003.
34. *Ibid.*
35. conversation with I Majestic Allah, February 2005.
36. rec.music.hip-hop, May 20, 1997.
37. groups.yahoo.com/CreamCity/messages, December 26, 2003.
38. Blake Fardan, Dorothy, *Yakub and the Origins of White Supremacy: Message to the Blackman & Woman in America*, p. 125.
39. *Learn and Know Your History, Part 3.* p. 20.
40. *Ibid.*

Chapter seventeen

1. *Cream City*, Issue 6, Volume 3.
2. *The Five Percenter*, August 2005, p. 4.
3. NGE video archives.
4. *Cream City*, Issue 1, Volume 2, p. 3.
5. *The Five Percenter*, July 2000, p. 2.
6. *The Five Percenter*, September 2001, p. 2.
7. interview with Allah Supreme God, June 2005.
8. *The Five Percenter*, March 1997.
9. *The Five Percenter*, December 1996, p. 4.
10. http://groups.yahoo.com/group/CreamCity/message1195.
11. *The NGE Power*, October 2002, p. 8.
12. Nuruddin, Yusuf, "The Five Percenters: a Teenage Nation of Gods and Earths," *Muslim Communities in North America*, Yvonne Yazbeck Haddad and Jane Idleman Smith, ed, p. 127–128.
13. Gardell, Mattias, *In the Name of Elijah Muhammad: Louis Farrakhan and the Nation of Islam*, p. 210.
14. *Sun of Man*, August 2005, p. 16.
15. *The Five Percenter*, September 1995.
16. correspondence with Prince A Cuba, September 29, 2005.
17. interview with Allah Supreme God, June 2005.
18. *The Five Percenter*, January 2005, p. 2.
19. *Sun of Man*, p. 12.
20. letter from First Born Prince Allah to Knowledge Born Azee Allah, August 16, 1991.
21. Gottehrer, Barry, *The Mayor's Man*, p. 94–99.
22. interview with Supreme Understanding Allah, April 22, 2006.
23. *Learn and Know Your History*, p. 20.
24. *Sun of Man*, August 2005, p. 10.
25. *Learn and Know Your History*, part 3, p. 29.
26. *Sun of Man*, August 2005, p. 15.
27. *The History and Design of Our Universal Flag*, p. 3.
28. *Sun of Man*, August 2005, p. 6.
29. *Ibid*, p. 15.
30. Cuba, Prince, *Our Mecca is Harlem: Clarence 13X (Allah) and the Five Percent*, p. 56.
31. the RZA (as Bobby Digital), "Protect Ya Neck (the Jump-Off)," *the W*.
32. correspondence with Allahzar G Allah.
33. *Sun of Man*, Issue #4.
34. *Sun of Man*, August 2005, p. 2.
35. *The Five Percenter*, May 1996, p. 3.
36. interview with Jamar Allah.
37. *Learn and Know Your History*, Part 3, p. 19.

Chapter eighteen

1. Fatir, Amir, *Why Does Muhammad & Any Muslim Murder the Devil?*, p. 39–49.
2. *Learn and Know Your History*, p. 60–61.
3. *The WORD*, Vol.1, No.4 (October/November 1987), p. 7.
4. *Learn and Know Your History, Part 2*, p. 18.
5. *Sun of Man*, Issue #4, p. 3.
6. Deren, Maya, *Divine Horsemen: the Living Gods of Haiti*, p. 21.
7. *The Universal Truth*, Vol.2, No.4, p. 11.
8. conversation with Akbar Muhammad, September 2005.
9. correspondence with Amir Fatir.
10. interview with Sid Davidoff, August 16, 2005.
11. *Ibid.*
12. "Wisdom of Allah the Father," audio recording.
13. *The Outlaw Bible of American Literature*, p. 147.
14. Jacoby, Tamar, *Someone Else's House: America's Unfinished Struggle for Integration*, p. 108.
15. *The Universal Truth*, Vol.2, No.5, p. 22.
16. *Sun of Man*, August 2005, p. 20.
17. *Learn and Know Your History, Part 3*, p. 19.
18. *Learn and Know Your History, Part 2*, p. 20.

Index

Note: Personal names beginning with prefix Al- are indexed under Al-. Page references in *italics* indicate photographs that appear in the plate section in the center of this book.